Essential Windows Phone 8

Essential Windows Phone 8

■ **Shawn Wildermuth**

✦✦Addison-Wesley

Upper Saddle River, NJ • Boston • Indianapolis • San Francisco
New York • Toronto • Montreal • London • Munich • Paris • Madrid
Capetown • Sydney • Tokyo • Singapore • Mexico City

The publisher offers excellent discounts on this book when ordered in quantity for bulk purchases or special sales, which may include electronic versions and/or custom covers and content particular to your business, training goals, marketing focus, and branding interests. For more information, please contact:

U.S. Corporate and Government Sales
(800) 382-3419
corpsales@pearsontechgroup.com

For sales outside the United States, please contact:

International Sales
international@pearson.com

Visit us on the Web: informit.com/aw

The Library of Congress cataloging-in-publication data is on file.

ISBN-13: 978-0-321-90494-2
ISBN-10: 0-321-90494-X

Text printed in the United States on recycled paper at Edwards Brothers in Ann Arbor, Michigan.
First printing May 2013

To Resa Shwarts—for her patience and education on the passive voice.

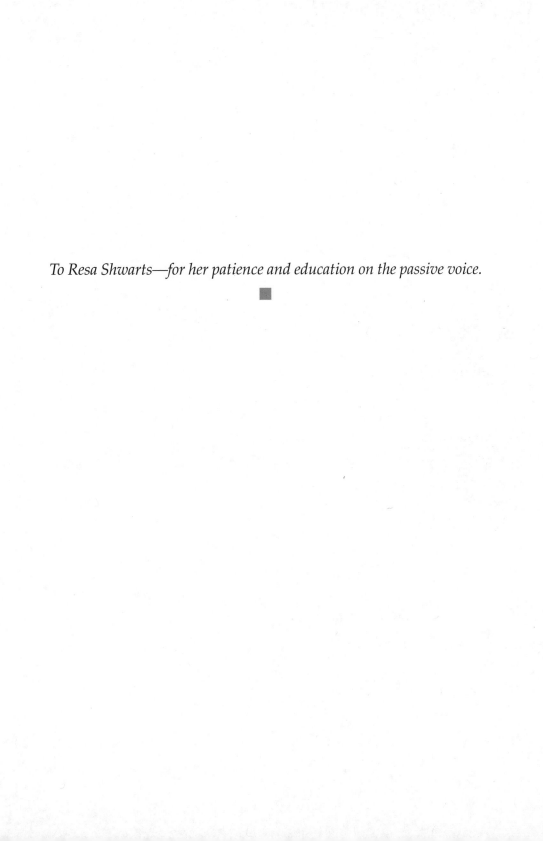

Contents at a Glance

Contents

Preface

I never owned a Palm Pilot. But I did have Palm tops and smartphones. I dived into writing software for a plethora of devices but never got very far. My problem was that the story of getting software onto the phones was chaotic and I didn't see how the marketing of software for phones would lead to a successful product. In the intervening years, I got distracted by Silverlight and web development. I didn't pay attention as the smartphone revolution happened. I was happily neck deep in data binding, business application development, and teaching XAML.

The smart revolution clearly started with the iPhone. What I find interesting is that the iPhone is really about the App Store, not the phone. It's a great device, but the App Store is what changed everything. A simple way to publish, market, and monetize applications for these handheld powerhouses that people all wanted. Of course, Apple didn't mean to do it. When the original iPhone shipped, Apple clearly said that Safari (its web browser) was the development environment. With the pressure of its OSX developer community, Apple relented and somewhat accidently created the app revolution.

When it was clear that I had missed something, I dove headlong into looking at development for phones again. I had an Android phone at the time, so that is where I started. Getting up to speed with Eclipse and Java wasn't too hard, but developing for the phone was still a bit of a chore. The development tools just didn't seem to be as easy as the development I was used to with Visual Studio and Blend. In this same timeframe, I grabbed a Mac and tried my hand at Objective-C and Xcode to write something simple for the iPhone. That experience left me bandaged and bloody. I wanted to write apps, but because it was a side effort, the friction of the toolsets for Android and iPhone left me wanting and I put them aside.

Soon after my experience with the iPhone and Android, Microsoft took the cover off its new phone platform: the Windows Phone. For me, the real excitement was the development experience. At that point, I'd been teaching and writing about Silverlight since it was called WPF/E, so the ability to take my interest in mobile development and marry it to my Silverlight knowledge seemed like a perfect match.

I've enjoyed taking the desktop/web Silverlight experience I have and applying the same concepts to the phone. By using Visual Studio and Blend to craft beautiful user interface designs and quickly go from prototype to finished application, the workflow of using these tools and XAML makes the path of building my own applications much easier than on other platforms.

After my experience writing the first edition of this book, I was excited about the newest version of the Windows Phone that Microsoft unveiled: Windows Phone 8. It was more than just a few added features—it was a real change to the underlying operating system. This was a big change, but how did it affect Windows Phone 7 and 7.5 developers? Microsoft could have really affected those developers by just shuttering the entire back catalog and changing the APIs in the new edition. I am happy to tell you that Microsoft walked the razor-thin line between change and backward compatibility. But how would that change the book I wrote?

Coming back to a book for a second edition is a challenge for any author. At the face of it, I could have just done a quick search-and-replace to change Windows Phone 7.5 to Windows Phone 8 and moved on, but I felt like I could really highlight and improve the first edition. My goal was to make the book approachable for both developers new to the Windows Phone, as well as show the new features. I hope I've been able to accomplish this.

While the changes are peppered all over this edition, for me the most striking change comes in the very last chapter: enterprise development.

Microsoft allows you to build your own applications for the phone that can be delivered to your own employees without certification or validation. Microsoft is finally opening the door to the power of using the Windows Phone as a platform for your employees.

Acknowledgments

This is the second edition of this book, and that changes the way you write a book. Writing is hard…editing is even more difficult. It is easy to simply miss the obvious changes that should be caught. To that end, three people have been pivotal in getting this book correct (or perhaps will shoulder the blame for any errata that got missed ;):

I want to thank Joan Murray at Addison-Wesley for maintaining her incredible patience. When I am writing, I tend to vacillate between an excited pixie and an angry imp. She handles that swinging pendulum better than most.

In addition, I want to again thank Christopher Cleveland for the job of developmental editor. He's been great at keeping the little things in mind and making sure the *i*'s are dotted and the *t*s are crossed.

I'd also like to specially thank Jeff Wilcox (of 4th and Mayor fame) for doing an exemplary job at tech reviewing the chapters. He's been critical at getting the phone story right. He's been in the thick of building a large Windows Phone application that has weathered the storms of a high number of users, and his experience shows in every chapter.

To the litany of people on the Windows Phone Advisor's Mailing Lists, I would like to thank you for your patience as I pestered the lists with endless questions and hyperbolic rants.

Like the first edition, my blog's readers and my followers on Facebook and Twitter have helped immeasurably with their passion, wit, and knowledge.

For anyone else I forgot, I apologize.

Shawn Wildermuth

May 2013

http://wildermuth.com

@shawnwildermuth

About the Author

During his 27 years in software development, **Shawn Wildermuth** has experienced a litany of shifts in software development, shaping how he understands technology. Shawn is a 10-time Microsoft MVP, a member of the INETA Speaker's Bureau, and an author of several books on .NET. He has spoken at a variety of international conferences, including TechEd, MIX, VSLive, OreDev, SDC, WinDev, MIX, DevTeach, DevConnections, and DevReach. Shawn has written dozens of articles for a variety of magazines and websites, including *MSDN*, *DevSource*, *InformIT*, *CoDe Magazine*, *ServerSide.NET*, and *MSDN Online*. He is currently helping companies with coaching and training through his company Wilder Minds LLC (http://wilderminds.com).

■1

Introducing Windows Phone

To some, the cell phone is an annoying necessity; to others, it's a critical need. Being able to use a phone to make calls everywhere has really changed the way people communicate. In the past few years, these phones have taken another leap forward. With the introduction of iPhone and Android devices, the consumer market for an always-connected device that can interact with the Internet, run applications, and make phone calls has changed people's relationship with their phone. It has also raised the bar for consumer-level devices. Consumers now expect their phones to also function as GPSs, gaming devices, and Internet tablets. For some consumers, their phones are now their primary connections to the Internet, replacing the desktop/laptop computer for the first time. As developers, our challenge is to find the best way to create the experiences the user needs. Windows Phone provides the platform, and XAML (eXtensible Application Markup Language) is the engine to power those experiences.

A Different Kind of Phone

When Microsoft originally unveiled Windows Phone, many skeptics expected the phone would simply try to play catch-up with Apple's and Google's offerings. Microsoft had other plans, though. The new operating system for the phone was a departure from existing offerings from the other mobile operating system vendors (primarily Apple, Research in Motion, and Google). Instead of just mimicking the icon pattern screens that iPhone and Android seemed to love, Microsoft thought in a different way. Application and operating system design is defined in a new design language.[1] This design language defines a set of guidelines[2] and styles for creating Windows Phone applications. The design of the Start screen laid out by this design language is similar to other smartphone designs in that it is a list of icons. Instead of separating the icons into pages, Windows Phone lets users scroll through the icons. Windows Phone is also differentiated from other smartphones in that each icon can include information about the application. These icons are called **Live Tiles,** as shown in Figure 1.1.

FIGURE 1.1   Windows Phone Start screen

---

1   Formerly called the "Metro" design language.

2   UI Design Guide for Windows Phone: http://shawnw.me/winpphoneuxguide

Windows Phone 8 ups the ante to include features for the next generation of phones including support for multicore processors, Near Field Communications (NFC), support for high-resolution screens, built-in support for Skype, and development of native game applications using the same APIs that are used on the Xbox (for example, DirectX). Windows Phone 8 is apt to be the turning point in the maturation of the platform that will bring broad adoption of the phones.

Probably the biggest change in Windows Phone 8 is not obvious at first glance. The underpinnings of the operating system are now the same as Windows 8. That means the operating system that runs the Windows RT tablets powers the new phones. A single platform will allow for better scalability and performance than previous incarnations of the phone.

■ What Is a Design Language?

Developers think about a language as a set of textual expressions that describe some machine operation(s). For designers, it is a set of rules for defining the look and feel of a set of applications (or an entire operating system in this case). Wikipedia.org defines it more generally as "...*an overarching scheme or style that guides the design of a complement of products or architectural settings.*"

The Start screen should be a place where users can quickly review the status of the phone. The Live Tiles will provide user information such as the number of missed phone calls and the number of email or text messages waiting, or even information from other apps on the phone such as the current weather. When you develop your own applications, you can either create a simple icon for the Start screen or build a Live Tile for your users.

For applications, the Windows Phone screen is divided into three areas in which the user can interact with the phone: the system tray, the logical client, and the application bar (see Figure 1.2).

FIGURE 1.2　Phone screen real estate

The system tray area is managed by the phone's operating system. This is where the time, signal strength, and alerts will appear to the user. Most applications will leave this area of the screen visible to the user. Some applications (for example, games) may hide this area, but you should only do so when critical to the success of your application.

The logical client area is where your application will exist. This area shows your user interface and any data and points of interaction.

The application bar shows options for your application. Although using the application bar is not a requirement, it is a common practice because it gives users access to your application's options and menus. For example, Figure 1.3 shows a simple note-taking application that uses the application bar to allow users to create new notes or show the menu (note that the ellipsis can be clicked to open the list of menu items).

FIGURE 1.3 The application bar in action

One big distinction that users will see in many of the applications built in to Windows Phone is the use of **hubs.** The central idea of a hub is to provide a starting point to get the user to use natural curiosity to learn what is available in the application. Usually these hubs take the form of applications that are larger than the phone screen. Instead of the typical page-based applications that are fairly commonplace on smartphones, the UX design language introduces something called a **panorama application.** For panorama applications, the phone is used as a window that looks into a larger application surface. You'll notice in Figure 1.4 that the content of the screen takes up most of the horizontal real estate, but the next section of the panorama application shows up on the right side of the screen to help the user understand that there is more content.

FIGURE 1.4   **Panorama application**

As the user navigates through the panorama application, the virtual space is moved within the window. For example, in Figure 1.5 you can see how, after sliding the application to the left, the rightmost part of the panorama becomes visible.

FIGURE 1.5   **Last pane of a panorama application**

The use of the panorama application results in a simple but powerful user interface design that users should find very intuitive.

By following the guidelines specified by UX design language, you can create applications that should be consistent with the rest of the phone, while giving you the freedom to create applications of any kind. In this way, the UX design language helps by defining basic ideas of how a Windows Phone application should look so that the user can see complete consistency. At the same time, the UX design language says you can simply take over the entire user interface and not use the basic ideas of the phone chrome, leaving you the flexibility to create either custom experiences or applications that look like they belong on the phone.

Figure 1.6 shows sample apps with and without the chrome applied.

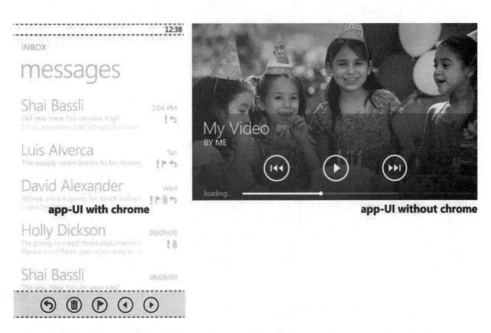

app-UI with chrome **app-UI without chrome**

FIGURE 1.6   Using Phone chrome, or not

Phone Specifications

For Windows Phone, the stakes were high in terms of Microsoft's ability to not only create the software, but also encourage its partners to build the phone. Learning a lesson from its past Windows Mobile platform, Microsoft decided to be very specific about the hardware to ensure a great user experience while giving phone designers some flexibility with feature sets so that they could compete with one another. Table 1.1 shows the hardware requirements.

TABLE 1.1   **Hardware Specifications**

Category	Requirement
Screen resolutions	480 × 800, 768 × 1280, and 720 × 1280.
Capacitive touch	At least four points of touch support.
Memory	256MB RAM, 8GB Flash.
Sensors	A-GPS, Accelerometer, Compass, Light and Proximity, Gyro.
CPU	ARM7 Scorpion/Cortex or better (typically 1GHz+). Multicore processors now supported.
GPU	DirectX 9 acceleration.
Camera	5 megapixels minimum, flash required.
Bluetooth	Bluetooth 2.1 + EDR; Bluetooth profiles provided are Hand-Free Profile (HFP), Headset Profile (HSP), Advanced Audio Distribution Profile (A2DP), and Phone Book Access Profile (PBAP).
Multimedia	Codec acceleration required; support for DivX 4, 5, and 6 as well as H.264 High Profile required (High Profile is used by Blu-ray).
Wi-Fi	802.11g radio required.
NFC	Near Field Communications for sharing of data, contacts, and payment information.
Radio	FM radio receiver required.

In addition, Windows Phone has physical requirements. The most obvious of these is that each phone must have seven standard inputs, as shown in Figure 1.7.

FIGURE 1.7   Seven points of input

Table 1.2 lists and describes these seven hardware inputs.

TABLE 1.2: Hardware Inputs

	Input	Expected Behavior
1	Power button	When powered off, a long press will power on the device. If powered on and screen is active, it will turn off screen and lock device. If screen is off, it will enable screen and present unlock UI.
2	Volume control	A rocker switch will adjust volume for current activity's sound profile, such as phone call volume while on a call. Pressing volume during a phone call will disable the ringer. Adjusting volume when no activity is presently happening will allow user to switch between sound profiles.
3	Touch screen	The capacitive touch screen will support at least four points of touch.
4	Camera button	A long press on this dedicated button will launch the camera application.
5	Back button	This button issues a "back" operation. This can take the user back in an individual application or from one application to the previous application as presented by the page API.
6	Start button	This takes the user to the Start screen of the device.
7	Search button	This launches the search experience to allow searching across the device.

Now that we have seen what the phone consists of, let's see how users will interact with the phone.

Input Patterns

You are the developer. You want users to want to use your applications. That means you must deal with the different ways the phone can accept user input. Developing for the Web or desktop means you are primarily dealing with designing for the keyboard and mouse. But when developing for the phone, you have to change the way you look at input and consider that the user is going to interact with your application in different ways. Interaction patterns for the phone include touch, keyboards (hardware and software), hardware buttons, and sensors.

Designing for Touch

The UX design language for the phone is specifically constructed to ensure the interface is treating touch as a first-class citizen and that the interface requires no training (meaning it is intuitive). By building a design language that defines the elements of a touch-based interface, Microsoft has made it easier to build such interfaces. The design language includes guidelines for which touch gestures are supported, as well as how to space and size elements for finger-size interactions. Figure 1.8 shows an example from *the User Experience Design Guide* that defines the minimum sizes for touch points and their spacing.

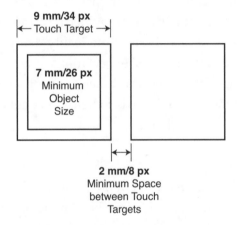

FIGURE 1.8   Windows Phone's interactive element sizes

The Windows Phone also defines the types of interactions (such as touch gestures) the device supports. Most of these interactions are well-worn gestures that have been the vocabulary of other touch devices such as the iPhone, Zune HD, and Android. These interactions include

- Single touch:
  - Tap
  - Double-Tap
  - Pan
  - Flick
  - Touch and Hold

- Multitouch:
  - Pinch/Stretch/Rotate

In addition to specifying the types of gestures, the Windows Phone specifies the use cases for each interaction. For example, the Double-Tap interaction is specifically used to zoom in and zoom out. This use case is explicitly different from what the typical desktop Windows developer might expect. But for the sake of consistency, the UX design language maps out what the user should expect with these interactions. While the design language would not be read by actual users, it would be the basis for the phone's built-in application. Interactions of your applications should match the rest of the phone, therefore adhering to the principle of least surprise for the user. This also hints at the reality that the phone design is not supposed to be based on users' expectations of how Windows works, but be more obvious than that. The touch interaction is much different from a mouse, and the overall hope is to help users get a feel for the right interaction without training them.

Hardware Buttons

Windows Phone requires that each phone has three hardware buttons on the front of the device. As described in the "Phone Specifications" section earlier in this chapter, these three buttons have discrete actions. The only one you really need to concern yourself with is the Back button. Not only should the Back button move the user from your application to the last running application (the default behavior), it should also allow the user to move from state to state in your application. As you develop applications for the phone, be aware of what the user might expect from the Back button. The Back button is part of what makes the Windows Phone different from some of the other phones in the ecosystem. Handling of the Back button is crucial to good app design, as well as being a requirement of certification for your app with the Windows Phone Store.

Keyboards

Because not all interactions will be simple gestures but must be able to support text entry, the *UI Design and Interaction Guide* stipulates that a software keyboard (or Soft Input Panel [SIP]) should be available for every text entry (as even in a keyboarded phone, users should be able to type on the screen). Keyboards are provided by the operating system by default. As users attempt to edit text (for example, the user taps on a text box), the operating system displays a software keyboard to enable touch-based keyboard entry. Figure 1.9 shows the default keyboard.

FIGURE 1.9   Default keyboard

The style guide also specifies that the keyboards should be contextually relevant depending on the type of text to be typed. For example, Figure 1.10 shows an email keyboard and a phone number keyboard.

FIGURE 1.10 **Contextual keyboards**

Although a number of layouts are available, the phone includes some standard layout for specific use cases, as shown in Table 1.3.

Table 1.3   Sample Keyboard Layouts

Keyboard	Description
Default	Standard QWERTY keyboard
Text	Includes autocorrect panel
Chat	Includes an emoticon key and autocorrect
Email address	Includes .com and @ keys
Phone number	12-key numeric layout
Web address	Includes .com key and Go key, which instructs the application that user input has completed
Maps	Includes Go key, which instructs the application that user input has completed
SMS address	Simplified layout with quick access to phone numbers

Sensors

You should consider that not all the input to the phone is typical. It is important that you, the application developer, open your mind to different types of input. Windows Phone supports a number of sensors that will allow you to take input in these different forms (see Table 1.4).

Table 1.4   Sensors

Sensor	Description
Accelerometer	Detects the position of the phone in three dimensions, as well as movement such as shaking or tilting
Compass	Determines the direction that the phone is facing in relation to the magnetic poles of the Earth
Proximity	Determines how close someone is to the face of the phone
Light	Determines the amount of ambient light around the phone
Gyro	Detects the active rotation of the phone in three dimensions
A-GPS	Determines the location of the phone on the physical face of the Earth (for example, longitude and latitude)

Application Lifecycle

The user experience is the most important feature in Windows Phone. After learning many lessons from the competition and from its own experience with Windows Mobile devices, Microsoft decided it would control process execution on the phone. The main reason for this is that on a device like this, the number of applications running can severely affect the quality of the user experience. On some platforms, full multitasking is allowed, but most users quickly learn to use a task-killer application to kill applications that no longer are required to be opened. This is an adequate solution for multitasking but does require that the memory on the device be managed by users. While power users will be comfortable with this, most users will not.

To enable developers to build rich applications that act and feel as though multitasking is enabled, Windows Phone uses an approach that allows applications to be paused, made dormant, and suspended without having to alert the user that the application is being paused. It does this by notifying the application when it is being paused; then the application is also notified when it is to resume running. In the pause and resume states, the application is given a chance to save and load data to give the user the impression that the application never stopped. Figure 1.11 shows how an application will go through the five states during its lifetime. This lifecycle is called **tombstoning.**

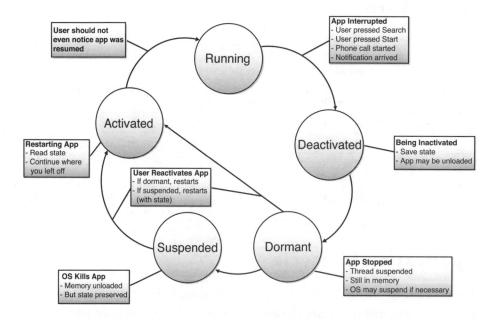

FIGURE 1.11   Application lifecycle (tombstoning)

If you ignore the pause and resume states, your application will simply return to the last state of the application by default. This lifecycle is used for the majority of applications. Microsoft allows only a small number of partners to run outside this lifecycle.

Driving Your Development with Services

Although some applications will only access data on the phone, in practice many applications will need to use the data connectivity to interact with servers and the cloud.[3] The phone is a connected device (meaning Internet connectivity is available most of the time). This means you can power your applications via traditional services such as web APIs or web services. These are typically services that are either web-enabled (like Amazon's web APIs) or custom services you write in the cloud.

To power the phone, Microsoft has also exposed a number of services to simplify phone development, as described in Table 1.5.

Table 1.5   Microsoft Phone Services

Sensor	Description
Location	Accesses information about the location of the phone. Uses GPS if available; otherwise, uses other location-based information, such as cell towers and Wi-Fi hot spots.
Notifications	Supports sending asynchronous data to the phone. Typically end up as toast notifications on the phone that can launch your application or updating of Live Tiles.
Xbox Live	Access to user's Gamerscore and other game information stored on Microsoft servers. Also allows game developers to grant Gamerscore to players.
App Deployment	Provides access to information in the Windows Phone Store and supports trial (or try-before-you-buy) purchases and update management of applications. Also includes support to tell users which rights the application is requesting.

---

3   In this book, when I say "cloud," I am referring to Internet-based services including services on your own hardware, services in cloud-based hosting (such as Windows Azure, Amazon EC2), or public web APIs (Such as Amazon's web APIs). It does not mean your services have to be hosted in a cloud-based solution.

Live Tiles

The center of the entire user interface paradigm in Windows Phone is the notion of the Start screen. The hub is the main screen that users will be presented when they boot up or turn on the phone. Unlike the interface that the two main competitors (iPhone and Android devices) present, the hub is not just a collection of application icons, but rather a set of Live Tiles. These tiles include information about the state of the information inside the application. For example, the People Tile in the Start screen will include pictures of the last few updates the people on your device have had. This is an indication that you may want to go to the People application on your phone to see the updates. Figure 1.12 shows this transition from tile to application.

FIGURE 1.12   A tile in the hub

This lets you, the application developer, control what the tile looks like. So you could decide on just a simple numbering system like the Phone or Outlook Tiles, or you could change the look and feel completely, like the People Tile.

The way that tiles get updated is powerful as well. Ordinarily you might consider that applications themselves would update the tiles, but that would assume your application would need to be launched whenever the tile needs updating. Instead, the phone uses the Notification Service to allow you to send an update to the phone through Microsoft's own service to update the tile. This works well because the update is very efficient (as the update simply includes the information about the updated tile and never needs to start your application to update the tile). In addition, this means that ordinarily cloud services (such as server-side applications) can update the tile as well in a very efficient way. Figure 1.13 illustrates a simple update to a tile.

FIGURE 1.13   Updating tiles

The home screen is not like the Desktop in Windows. It's the dashboard to the user's data, not just shortcuts to applications. Users should be able to view the hub and see the basic information they need to decide how to interact with the data. For example, if there are new email messages, voicemail messages, and Facebook updates, users should be able to see at a glance what is happening in their world and allow the phone to be a window to that world.

The Windows Phone Store

Since the release of the iPhone App Store, it's all about the apps. Unlike earlier iterations of Microsoft phone technologies (for example, Windows Mobile), all software will have to go through Microsoft to get installed on the device. This might upset long-time Windows Mobile developers, but it is something we have always needed on Microsoft phones. Users need a place to find good applications from a source that can guarantee that the software will not interfere with the device's ability to run smoothly. That's where the Windows Phone Store comes in.

Distributing Your Application Through the Windows Phone Store

As a developer, you do not have a choice of how to distribute your application; you must use the Windows Phone Store. The Windows Phone Store is a partnership between you and Microsoft. It enables you to deliver your application with very little work on your part. For Microsoft's part, the Windows Phone Store does the following:

- Handles billing via credit card or operator billing (that is, bill to provider)
- Gives you a 70% revenue share
- Allows your apps to be updated without cost, regardless of whether it is a paid, free, or ad-supported app
- Lets you deliver trial versions of applications and convert them on-the-fly to full versions
- Handles automatic updating of your application

To distribute through the Windows Phone Store, you have to join the Windows Phone App Hub so that it can validate who you are and set up revenue sharing. It costs $99 per year to join the App Hub, and membership allows you to submit 100 free apps per year (without incurring extra costs) and an unlimited number of paid apps. With App Hub membership, you can also register up to five phones as development phones. Microsoft wants App Hub membership to enable you to be successful because the more applications you sell, the more money both you and Microsoft make.

App Hub Submissions

The App Hub allows developers to submit applications to be handled through an approval process. The brunt of the approval process consists of certification testing to ensure that the application does not violate the rules of the Windows Phone Store.

The process starts with you creating your application and packaging it as a .xap[4] file. At that point, you go to the App Hub website and submit the application. Microsoft then verifies that the .xap file is valid and asks you to enter additional metadata, such as the publisher information, a short description, and so on. Next, Microsoft runs the application through a certification process to check the quality of the software (to make sure it does not destabilize the phone) and check that the application follows its Windows Phone Store policies (explained shortly). Finally, if the application passes certification, Microsoft signs the .xap file with a certificate to ensure that it has been certified[5] and posts it on the Windows Phone Store to allow it to be sold and/or downloaded.

But what does certification testing really mean? This step of the process is part quality assurance and part content filtering. The quality assurance part of the process is to ensure that your application is stable and does not affect the reliability of the phone. The quality assurance part is based on the following criteria:

- Your application must run on any Windows Phone regardless of model, keyboard hardware, and manufacturer.
- Your application must shut down gracefully even in the event of unhandled exceptions.
- Your application must not hang or become unresponsive.
- Your application must render within 5 seconds of launch and be responsive within 20 seconds.
- Your application must be able to resume after being paused without losing functionality or data.
- Your application must handle access to the Back button correctly: Back on the first page should exit the application; Back on subsequent pages should correctly move backward in the application.
- Your application must not interfere with phone calls or SMS/MMS messaging in any way.

---

4   .xap is a packaging format for Silverlight and XNA applications. It is simply a ZIP file with all the code and assets that are needed to run the application.

5   Signing of a .xap with a certificate is used to ensure that non-certified apps can't be installed on the phones, so that only apps that are safe and do not contain malware are installed on the device. The .xap files are also encrypted by the Windows Phone Store to protect them from piracy.

In addition to checking the quality of the application, the certification also checks the application for adherence to the policies of the Windows Phone Store. The two types of policies are application policies and content policies.

Application Policies

Microsoft has detailed a set of policies that every application must adhere to. These policies are meant to protect the users, Microsoft, and the phone carriers. The application requirements can be divided into basic policies that govern the size and functionality of your applications, and legal policies that stop bad people from doing things that will hurt the carriers, Microsoft, or the users. The current policies as of the writing of this book include[6]

- Basic application policies
- Legal usage policies

Basic Application Policies

A number of standard policies apply to application size, functionality, and usage:

- Your application must be fully functional when acquired from the Windows Phone Store, except if additional data is required to be downloaded as permitted (see the following).

- The size of your application cannot exceed 500MB. If you want to enable installation over-the-air (OTA), the size must not exceed 20MB. Larger applications will be available to be downloaded via Wi-Fi or a tethered connection.

- If your application requires the download of a large additional data package (for example, more than 50MB) to enable the application to run as described, the application description must disclose the approximate size of the data package and that additional charges may apply depending on connectivity used to acquire data.

---

6 Latest version can be found here: http://shawnw.me/wpcertreq

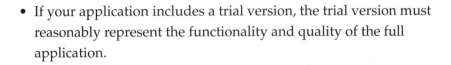

- If your application includes a trial version, the trial version must reasonably represent the functionality and quality of the full application.

Legal Usage Policies

Additionally, specific policies are related to payments, legality, and use of personal information:

- Your application may not require the user to pay outside of the Windows Phone Store to activate, unlock, upgrade, or extend usage of the application.
- Your application may not sell, link to, or otherwise promote mobile voice plans.
- Your application may not consist of, distribute, link to, or incentivize users to download or otherwise promote alternate marketplaces for applications and/or games.
- Your application must not jeopardize the security or functionality of Windows Phone devices or the Windows Phone Store.
- If your application includes or displays advertising, the advertising must comply with the Microsoft Advertising Creative Acceptance Policy Guide (http://advertising.microsoft.com/creative-specs).
- If your application enables chat, instant messaging, or other person-to-person communication and allows the user to set up or create her account or ID from the mobile device, the application must include a mechanism to verify that the user creating the account or ID is at least 13 years old.
- If your application publishes a user's personal information from the mobile device to any service or other person, the application must implement "opt-in" consent. *Personal information* means all information or data associated with an identifiable user, including but not limited to the following, whether stored on the mobile device or on a web-based server that is accessible from the mobile device:
  - Location information
  - Contacts

  – Photos

  – Phone number

  – SMS or other text communication

  – Browsing history

- To implement opt-in consent, the application must first describe how the personal information will be used or shared, obtain the user's express permission before publishing the information as described, and provide a mechanism through which the user can later opt out of having the information published.

- If your application allows users to purchase music content, it must include the Windows Phone Store (if available) as a purchase option. If the application also allows music content to be purchased from any source other than the Windows Phone Store, the application must include its own playback functionality for that music content.

- If your application uses the Microsoft Push Notification Service (PNS), the application and the use of the PNS must comply with the following requirements:

  – The application must first describe the notifications to be provided and obtain the user's express permission (opt-in) and must provide a mechanism through which the user can opt out of receiving push notifications. All notifications provided using PNS must be consistent with the description provided to the user and must comply with all applicable application policies and 3.0 content policies.

  – The application and its use of the PNS must not excessively use network capacity or bandwidth of the PNS or otherwise unduly burden a Windows Phone or other Microsoft device or service with excessive push notifications, as determined by Microsoft in its reasonable discretion, and must not harm or interfere with any Microsoft networks or servers, or any third-party servers or networks connected to the PNS.

- The PNS may not be used to send notifications that are mission-critical or otherwise could affect matters of life or death, including, without limitation, critical notifications related to a medical device or condition.

Content Policies

In addition to the basic application policies, Microsoft will also limit the types of applications based on the content of the application. This means several types of applications will not be allowed:

- Applications that promote illegal activities that are obscene or indecent as deemed under local laws.
- Applications that show or encourage harm to animals or persons in the real world.
- Applications that are defamatory, libelous, slanderous, or threatening.
- Applications that promote hate speech or are defamatory.
- Applications that could be used to sell (illegally or in excess) tobacco, drugs, weapons, or alcohol.
- Applications that allow the user to use a weapon in the real world (for example, no remote hunting programs).
- Applications containing adult content, including nudity, sex, pornography, prostitution, or sexual fetishes or content that is sexual as it relates to children or animals.
- Applications containing realistic or gratuitous violence or gore. This also includes no content that shows rape (or suggestions of rape), molestation, instructions on injuring people in the real world, or glorification of genocide or torture.
- Applications containing excessive use of profanity.

The use of these policies is to promote a safe device for all ages. Because there currently is no way to control the use of the device by people of age, some of the content limitations are fairly restrictive. Microsoft seems committed to help developers by ensuring that everyone knows the extent of the policies and, when an application fails to be certified, to be very clear about how the application failed and including suggestions on how to change the application to allow it to pass.

Where Are We?

Windows Phone represents a platform, not just a device. To application developers, Windows Phone should represent an exciting new platform and software delivery mechanism. Although developing for the phone is a very new experience, the basic tooling is not new. The fundamental underpinnings of Windows RT, XAML, and DirectX mean the platforms are mature and ready to develop for. This first chapter should excite you about the possibilities of creating great user experiences.

By combining a great device, a great platform, and the Windows Phone Store, Microsoft has enabled you to be successful even while abiding by the rules in the Windows Phone Store. For the most part, these rules are easy to live with. Are you ready to make money on the next exciting platform?

2
Writing Your First Phone Application

WHILE THE PRESS MIGHT HAVE YOU BELIEVE that becoming a phone-app millionaire is a common occurrence, it's actually pretty rare, but that doesn't mean you won't want to create applications for the phone. Hopefully the days of cheap and useless but popular phone apps are over, and we can start focusing on phone-app development as being a way to create great experiences for small and large audiences. Microsoft's vision of three screens is becoming a reality, as the phone is joining the desktop and the TV as another vehicle for you to create immersive experiences for users.

Although understanding Windows Phone capabilities and services is a good start, you are probably here to write applications. With that in mind, this chapter will walk you through setting up a machine for authoring your very first Windows Phone application.

Preparing Your Machine

Before you can start writing applications for the phone, you must install the Windows Phone Developer Tools. Go to https://dev.windowsphone.com/ to download the tools called Windows Phone SDK. This website is the starting point for downloading the tools as well as accessing the forums if you have further questions about creating applications.

To install the Windows Phone SDK, you must meet the minimum system requirements shown in Table 2.1.

TABLE 2.1 **Windows Phone Developer Tools Requirements**

Requirement	Description
Operating system	Windows 7, x86 or x64 (all but Starter Edition); or Windows Vista SP2, x86, or x64 (all but Starter Edition).
Memory	3GB RAM.
Disk space	4GB free space.
Graphics card	DirectX 10-capable card with a WDDM 1.1 driver.

Once you meet the requirements, you can run the vm_web.exe file that you downloaded from the website to install the Windows Phone SDK. The SDK installer includes Microsoft Visual Studio 2012 Express for Windows Phone, Microsoft Blend Express for Windows Phone (the Express version of Microsoft Expression Blend), and the Software Development Kit (SDK). Visual Studio Express is the coding environment for Windows Phone. Blend Express is the design tool for phone applications. And the SDK is a set of libraries for creating phone applications and an emulator for creating applications without a device.

In addition, the Windows Phone SDK's phone emulator has additional requirements. This is because the Windows Phone SDK for Windows Phone 8 includes an all-new emulator that is a Hyper-V image (instead of the old virtual machine technology). This matters because the emulator has steeper requirements than the SDK itself. These requirements are shown in Table 2.2.

TABLE 2.2 **Windows Phone Developer Tools Requirements**

Requirement	Description
Operating system	Windows 8 Professional, 64-bit version
Memory	4GB RAM
Hyper-V	Installed and running
BIOS settings	Hardware Assisted Virtualization, Secondary Level Address Translation (SLAT) and Data Execution Protection (DEP) all enabled
Group membership	Must be member of both local Administrator and Hyper-V Administrator groups

> **■ TIP**
>
> The Windows Phone emulator does not work well in a virtual machine (for example, Virtual PC, VMware, and so on) and is not officially supported. The emulator is a virtual machine of the phone, so running a virtual machine in a virtual machine tends to cause problems, especially slow performance.

Visual Studio is the primary tool for writing the code for your phone applications. Although the Windows Phone SDK installs a version of Visual Studio 2012 Express specifically for phone development, if you already have Visual Studio 2012 installed on your machine, the phone tools will also be integrated into this version of Visual Studio. The workflow for writing code in both versions of Visual Studio is the same. Although both versions offer the same features for developing applications for the phone, in my examples I will be using Visual Studio Express Edition for Windows Phone. In addition, I will be using Blend Express, not the full version of Blend (that is, Expression Blend).

Creating a New Project

To begin creating your first Windows Phone application, you will need to start in one of two tools: Visual Studio or Expression Blend. Visual Studio is where most developers start their projects, so we will begin there; however, we will also discuss how you can use both applications for different parts of the development process.

Visual Studio

As noted earlier, when you install the Windows Phone SDK you get a version of Visual Studio 2010 Express that is used to create Windows Phone applications only. When you launch Visual Studio 2012 Express, you will see the main window of the application, as shown in Figure 2.1.

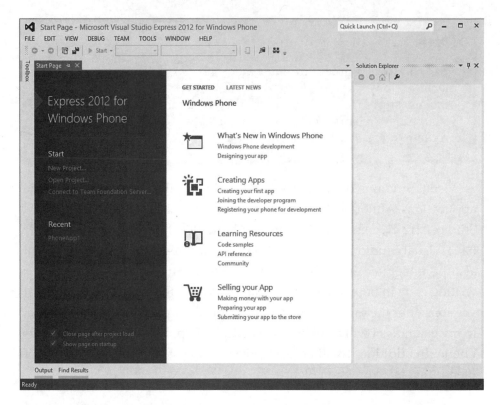

FIGURE 2.1   Microsoft Visual Studio 2012 Express for Windows Phone

Click the New Project link on the Start page; you will be prompted to start a new project. Visual Studio 2012 Express only supports creating applications for Window Phone. The New Project dialog box shows only Windows Phone and XNA projects (see Figure 2.2). For our first project we will start with a new project using the Windows Phone App template and name it HelloWorldPhone.

When you click the OK button to create the project, Visual Studio will prompt you with a dialog box where you can pick the version of the phone to target (version 7.1 or 8.0), as shown in Figure 2.3.

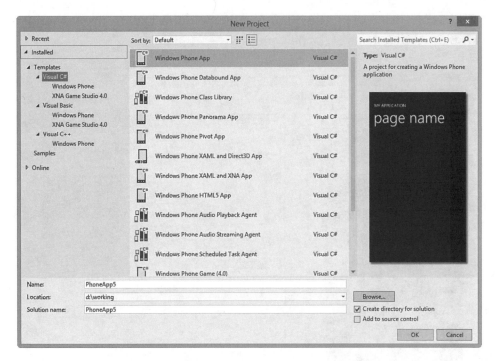

FIGURE 2.2 New Project dialog box

FIGURE 2.3 Picking the phone version to target

After Visual Studio creates the new project, you can take a quick tour of the user interface (as shown in Figure 2.4). By default, Visual Studio shows two main panes for creating your application. The first pane (labeled #1 in the figure) is the main editor surface for your application. In this pane, every edited file will appear separated with tabs as shown. By default, the MainPage.xaml file is shown when you create a new Windows Phone application; this is the main design document for your new application.

The second pane (#2 in the figure) is the Solution Explorer pane, and it displays the contents of the new project.

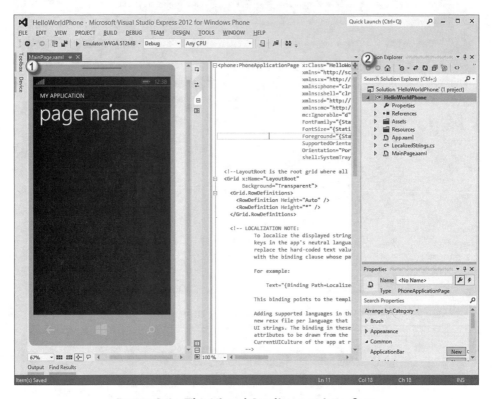

FIGURE 2.4   **The Visual Studio user interface**

Another common pane you will use is the toolbar; it is collapsed when you first use Visual Studio. On the left side of the main window is a Toolbox tab that you can click to display the Toolbox, as shown in Figure 2.5.

You also might want to click the pin icon to keep the toolbar shown at all times (as highlighted in Figure 2.5).

Before we look at how to create the application into something that is actually useful, let's see the application working in the device. You will notice that in the toolbar (not the Toolbox) of Visual Studio there is a bar for debugging. On that toolbar is a drop-down box for specifying what to do to debug your application. This drop-down should already display the words "Emulator WVGA 512MB," as that is the default when the tools are installed (as shown in Figure 2.6).

FIGURE 2.5   Enabling the toolbar

FIGURE 2.6   Using the emulator

At this point, if you press the F5 key (or click the triangular play button on the debugging toolbar), Visual Studio will build the application and start the emulator with our new application, as shown in Figure 2.7.

FIGURE 2.7   The emulator

This emulator will be the primary way you will debug your applications while developing applications for Windows Phone. Our application does not do anything, so you can go back to Visual Studio and click the square stop button on the debugging toolbar (or press Shift+F5) to end your debugging session. You should note that the emulator does not shut down. It is meant to stay running between debugging sessions.

XAML

In Silverlight, development is really split between the design and the code. The design is accomplished using a markup language called eXtensible Application Markup Language (XAML). XAML (rhymes with *camel*) is an XML-based language for representing the look and feel of your applications. Because XAML is XML-based, the design consists of a hierarchy of elements that describe the design. At its most basic level, XAML can be used to represent the objects that describe the look and feel of an application.[1] These objects are represented by XML elements, like so:

```
<Rectangle />

<!-- or -->

<TextBox />
```

You can modify these XML elements by setting attributes to change the objects:

```
<Rectangle Fill="Blue" />

<!-- or -->

<TextBox Text="Hello World" />
```

Containers in XAML use XML nesting to imply ownership (a parent-child relationship):

```
<Grid>
  <Rectangle Fill="Blue" />
  <TextBox Text="Hello World" />
</Grid>
```

Using this simple XML-based syntax, you can create complex, compelling designs for your phone applications. With this knowledge in hand, we can make subtle changes to the XAML supplied to us from the template. We could modify the XAML directly, but instead we will start by using the Visual Studio designer for the phone. In the main editor pane of Visual Studio, the MainPage.xaml file is split between the designer and the text editor for the XAML. The left pane of the MainPage.xaml file is not just a preview but a fully usable editor. For example, if you click on the area containing the words "page name" on the design surface, it will select that element in the XAML, as shown in Figure 2.8.

---

1   This is an oversimplification of what XAML is. Chapter 3, "XAML Overview," will explain the nature of XAML in more detail.

FIGURE 2.8   **Using the Visual Studio XAML design surface**

When you have that element selected in the designer, the properties for the element are shown in the Properties window (which shows up below the Solution Explorer). If the window is not visible, you can enable it in the View menu by selecting "Properties window" or by pressing the F4 key. This window is shown in Figure 2.9.

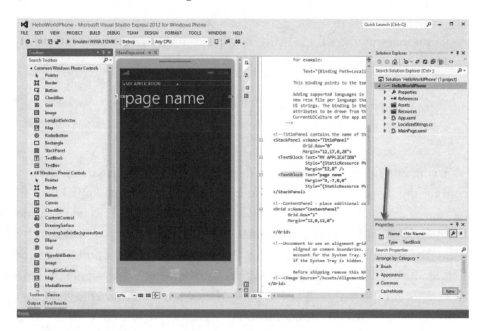

FIGURE 2.9   **Location of the Properties window**

The Properties window consists of a number of small parts containing a variety of information, as shown in Figure 2.10.

FIGURE 2.10   Contents of the Properties window

The section near the top (#1 in Figure 2.10) shows the type of object you have selected (in this example, a TextBlock) and the name of the object, if any (unspecified here so shown as <No Name>). This should help you ensure that you have selected the correct object to edit its properties. The next section down (#2) contains a Search bar where you can search for properties by name, as well as buttons for sorting and grouping the properties. The third section (#3) is a list of the properties that you can edit.

> ■ **NOTE**
>
> You can also use the Properties window to edit events, but we will cover that in Chapter 3.

From the Properties window you can change the properties of the selected item. For example, to change the text that is in the TextBlock, you can simply type in a new value for the Text property. If you enter "hello world" in the Text property and press Return, the designer will change to display the new value. Changing this property actually changes the XAML in the MainPage.xaml file. The design surface is simply reacting to the change in the XAML. If you look at the XAML, the change has been affected there as well, as shown in Figure 2.11.

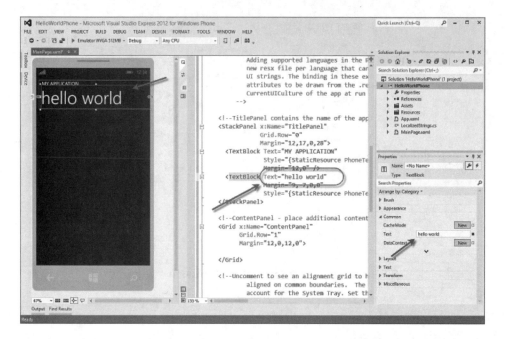

FIGURE 2.11   The changed property

You can edit the XAML directly as well if you prefer. If you click on the TextBlock above the PageTitle (the one labeled "ApplicationTitle"), you can edit the Text attribute directly. Try changing it to "MY FIRST WINDOWS PHONE APP" to see how it affects the designer and the Properties window:

```
...
<TextBlock x:Name="ApplicationTitle"
        Text="MY FIRST WINDOWS PHONE APP"
        Style="{StaticResource PhoneTextNormalStyle}" />
...
```

Depending on their comfort level, some developers find it easier to use the Properties window while others will be more at ease editing the XAML directly. There is no wrong way to do this.

Although the Visual Studio XAML designer can create interesting designs, the real powerhouse tool for designers and developers is Blend. Let's use it to edit our design into something useful for our users.

Designing with Blend

As noted earlier, in addition to offering an Express version of Visual Studio, the Windows Phone SDK includes an Express version of Expression Blend specifically for use in developing phone applications. You can launch Blend by looking for the shortcut key, or you can open it directly with Visual Studio. If you right-click the MainPage.xaml file, you will get a context menu like the one shown in Figure 2.12.

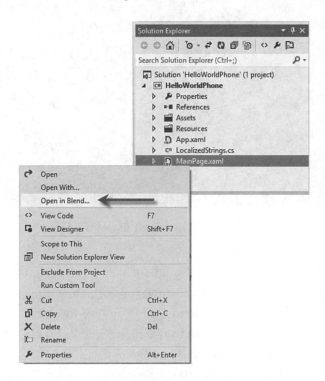

FIGURE 2.12   Opening Blend directly in Visual Studio

When you select Open in Expression Blend, Blend will open the same solution in the Expression Blend tool with the selected XAML file in the editor, as shown in Figure 2.13. You should save your project before going to Blend to make sure Blend loads any changes (Ctrl+Shift+S).

FIGURE 2.13   **The Blend user interface**

Although Expression Blend is thought of as purely a design tool, designers and developers alike can learn to become comfortable with it. And although Visual Studio and Expression Blend share some of the same features, both developers and designs will want to use Blend to build their designs. Some tasks are just simpler and faster to do in Blend. Chapter 5, "Designing for the Phone," covers which tasks are better suited to Expression Blend.

Like Visual Studio, Blend consists of a number of panes that you will need to get familiar with.

> **▪ NOTE**
>
> Blend and Visual Studio both open entire solutions, not just files. This is a significant difference from typical design tools.

The first pane (labeled #1 in Figure 2.13) contains multiple tabs that give you access to several types of functionality. By default, the first tab (and the one in the foreground) is the Projects tab (although a different tab could be showing by default). This tab displays the entire solution of projects. The format of this tab should look familiar; it's showing the same information as the Solution Explorer in Visual Studio. The next pane (#2) is the editor pane. This pane contains tabs for each opened file (only one at this point). MainPage.xaml should be the file currently shown in the editor. Note that the editor displays the page in the context of the phone so that you can better visualize the experience on the phone. On the right side of the Blend interface is another set of tabs (#3) that contain information about selected items in the design surface. The selected tab should be the Properties tab. This tab is similar to the Properties window in Visual Studio but is decidedly more designer-friendly. As you select items on the design surface, you'll be able to edit them in the Properties tab here. Finally, the Objects and Timeline pane (#4) displays the structure of your XAML as a hierarchy.

Let's make some changes with Blend. First (as shown in Figure 2.14); select the "hello world" text in the designer.

FIGURE 2.14   Selecting an object in Blend

After it's selected, you can see that eight squares surround the selection. These are the handles with which you can change the size or location of the TextBlock. While this object is selected, the Objects and Timeline pane shows the item selected in the hierarchy; as well, the item is shown in the Properties tab so you can edit individual properties (as shown in Figure 2.15).

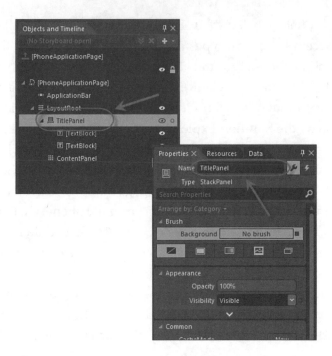

FIGURE 2.15   Selecting an object to edit in the Properties pane

If you type "text" into the search bar of the Properties pane, the properties that have that substring in them will appear (to temporarily reduce the number of properties in the Properties pane). You can change the title by changing the Text property, as shown in Figure 2.16.

FIGURE 2.16   Updating a property in Blend

After you're done changing the text, you might want to click the "X" in the Search bar to clear the search criteria. This will remove the search and show all the properties of the TextBlock again.

Selecting items and changing properties seems similar to what you can do in Visual Studio, but that's just where the design can start. Let's draw something. Start by selecting a container for the new drawing. In the Objects and Timeline pane, select the ContentPanel item. This will show you that it is a container that occupies most of the space below our "hello world" text on the phone's surface.

We can draw a rectangle in that container by using the left toolbar. On the toolbar is a rectangle tool (as shown in Figure 2.17). Select the tool and draw a rectangle in the ContentPanel to create a new rectangle (also shown in Figure 2.17). If you then select the top arrow tool (or press the V key), you'll be able to modify the rectangle.

FIGURE 2.17 Drawing in a container

The rectangle you created has eight control points (the small squares at the corners and in the middle of each side). In addition, the rectangle has two small control points in the upper-left side (outside the surface area of the rectangle). These controls are used to round the corners of rectangles. Grab the top one with your mouse and change the corners to be rounded slightly, as shown in Figure 2.18.

FIGURE 2.18   Rounding the corners

Now that you have rounded the corners, you can use the Properties pane to change the colors of the rectangle. In the Properties pane is a Brushes section showing how the various brushes for the rectangle are painted. The rectangle contains two brushes: a fill brush and a stroke brush. Selecting one of these brushes will allow you to use the lower part of the brush editor to change the look of that brush. Below the selection of brush names is a set of tabs for the various brush types, as shown in Figure 2.19.

FIGURE 2.19   Editing brushes

The first four tabs indicate options for brushes. These include no brush, solid color brush, gradient brush, and tile brush. Select the stroke brush, and then select the first tab to remove the stroke brush from the new rectangle. Now select the fill brush, and change the color of the brush by selecting a color within the editor, as shown in Figure 2.20.

FIGURE 2.20   Picking a color

Now let's put some text in the middle of our design to show some data. More specifically, let's put a TextBlock on our design. Go back to the toolbar and double-click the TextBlock tool (as shown in Figure 2.21). Although we drew our rectangle, another option is to double-click the toolbar, which will insert the selected item into the current container (in this case, the ContentPanel). The inserted TextBlock is placed in the upper left of our ContentPanel, as also shown in Figure 2.21.

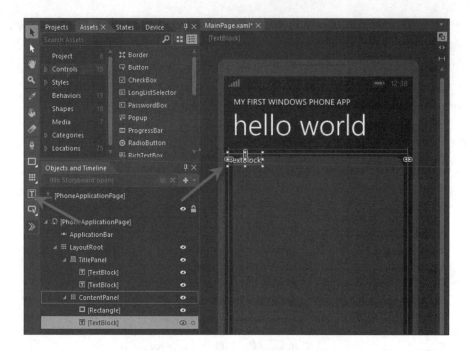

FIGURE 2.21   Inserting a TextBlock

After the new TextBlock is inserted, you can simply type to add some text. Type "Status" just to have a placeholder for some text we will place later in this chapter. You should use the mouse to click the Selection tool (the top arrow on the toolbar) so that you can edit the new TextBlock. You could use the mouse to place the TextBlock exactly where you like, but you could also use the Properties pane to align it. In the Properties pane, find the Layout section and select the horizontal center alignment and vertical bottom alignment, as shown in Figure 2.22. You might need to set your margins to zero as well to achieve the effect (because Blend might put a margin on your item depending on how you draw it).

Next you can edit the font and size of the TextBlock using the Text section of the Properties pane. You will likely need to scroll down to reach the Text section. From there, you can change the font, font size, and text decoration (for example, bold, italic, and so on). Change the font size to 36 points and make the font bold, as shown in Figure 2.23.

FIGURE 2.22 Centering the `TextBlock`

FIGURE 2.23 Changing the text properties

At this point our application does not do much, but hopefully you have gotten your first taste of the basics of using Blend for design. To get our first application to do something, we will need to hook up some of the elements with code. So we should close Blend and head back to Visual Studio.

When you exit Blend you will be prompted to save the project. Upon returning to Visual Studio, your changes will be noticed by Visual Studio; allow Visual Studio to reload the changes.

TIP

Blend is great at a variety of design tasks, such as creating animations, using behaviors to interact with user actions, and creating transitions. In subsequent chapters we will delve much further into using those parts of the tool.

Adding Code

This first Windows Phone application is not going to do much, but we should get started and make something happen with the phone. Because this is your first Windows Phone application, let's not pretend it is a desktop application but instead show off some of the touch capabilities.

First, if you look at the text of the XAML you should see that the first line of text shows the root element of the XAML to be a PhoneApplicationPage. This is the basic class from which each page you create will derive. The x:Class declaration is the name of the class that represents the class. If you open the code file, you will see this code was created for you:

```
<phone:PhoneApplicationPage x:Class="HelloWorldPhone.MainPage"
  . . .
```

> ■ **NOTE**
>
> The "phone" alias is an XML alias to a known namespace. If you're not familiar with how XML namespaces work, we will cover it in more detail in Chapter 3.

You will need to open the code file for the XAML file. You can do this by right-clicking the XAML page and picking View Code, or you can simply press F7 to open the code file. The initial code file is pretty simple, but you should see what the basics are. The namespace and class name match the x:Class definition we see in the XAML. This is how the two files are related to each other. If you change one, you will need to change the other. You should also note that the base class for the MainPage class is the same as the root element of the XAML. They are all related to each other. Here is the initial code file:

```
using System;
using System.Collections.Generic;
using System.Linq;
using System.Net;
using System.Windows;
using System.Windows.Controls;
using System.Windows.Navigation;
using Microsoft.Phone.Controls;
```

```csharp
using Microsoft.Phone.Shell;
using HelloWorldPhone.Resources;

namespace HelloWorldPhone
{
  public partial class MainPage : PhoneApplicationPage
  {
    // Constructor
    public MainPage()
    {
      InitializeComponent();

      // Sample code to localize the ApplicationBar
      //BuildLocalizedApplicationBar();
    }
  }
  // ...
}
```

These two files (the .xaml and the code files) are closely tied to each other. In fact, you can see that if you find an element in the XAML that has a name, it will be available in the code file. If you switch back to the .xaml file, click the TextBlock that you created in Blend. You will notice in the Properties window that it does not have a name (as shown in Figure 2.24).

FIGURE 2.24   Naming an element in the Properties window

If you click the text "<no name>", you can enter a name. Name the TextBlock "theStatus." If you then switch over to the code file, you will be able to use that name as a member of the class:

```
...
public partial class MainPage : PhoneApplicationPage
{
  // Constructor
  public MainPage()
  {
    InitializeComponent();

    theStatus.Text = "Hello from Code";
  }
}
...
```

At this point, if you run the application (pressing F5 will do this), you will see that this line of code is being executed as the theStatus TextBlock is changed to show the new text (as seen in Figure 2.25).

FIGURE 2.25   **Running the application**

There is an important fact you should derive from knowing that named elements in the XAML become part of the class: The job of the XAML is to build an object graph. The hierarchy of the XAML is just about creating the hierarchy of objects. At runtime, you can modify these objects in whatever way you want.

When you stop your application, the emulator will continue to run. You can leave the emulator running across multiple invocations of your application. You should not close the emulator after debugging your application.

Working with Events

Because you are building a phone application, let's show how basic events work. You can wire up events just as easily using standard language (for example, C#) semantics.[2] For example, you could handle the Tap event on theStatus to run code when the text is tapped:

```
...
public partial class MainPage : PhoneApplicationPage
{
  // Constructor
  public MainPage()
  {
    InitializeComponent();

    theStatus.Text = "Hello from Code";

    theStatus.Tap += theStatus_Tap;

    // Sample code to localize the ApplicationBar
    //BuildLocalizedApplicationBar();
  }

  void theStatus_Tap(object sender,
                     System.Windows.Input.GestureEventArgs e)
  {
    theStatus.Text = "Status was Tapped";
  }
}
...
```

---

2   For Visual Basic, you would just use the handles keyword instead of the C# event handler syntax.

When you tap on theStatus the Tap event will be fired (which is what causes the code in the event handler to be called). All events work in this simple fashion, but the number and type of events in Silverlight for Windows Phone vary widely.

Debugging in the Emulator

If clicking the user interface was not working the way we would like, it might help if we could stop the operation during an event to see what was happening during execution. We can do this by debugging our operation. We can use the debugger to set breakpoints and break in code while using the emulator. Place the text cursor inside the event handler and press F9 to create a breakpoint. When you run the application (again, press F5), you can see that when you click the theStatus TextBlock the debugger stops inside the event handler. You can hover your mouse over specific code elements (for example, theStatus.Text) to see the value in a pop-up (as shown in Figure 2.26).

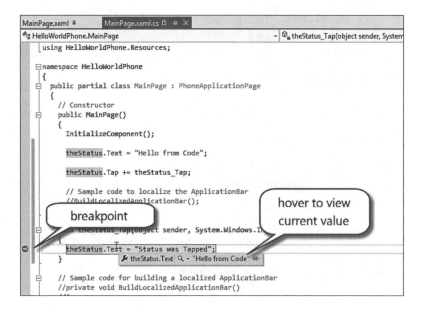

FIGURE 2.26　Using the Visual Studio debugger

Pressing the F5 key while stopped at a breakpoint will cause the application to continue running. There are other ways to walk through the code, but for now that should be sufficient to get you started. Using the emulator is the most common way you will develop your applications, but there are some interactions that are difficult to do with the emulator (for example, multitouch, using phone sensors, and so on) for which debugging directly on a device would be very useful. Luckily, debugging on the device is supported and works pretty easily.

Debugging with a Device

If you have a phone with which you want to do your development, you will need to be able to deploy and debug directly on the phone itself. First, you need to connect your phone to your development machine. All you need to do is connect your phone to your computer by a USB cable.

'Now that your device is connected, you can use it to browse to the directories for music, photos, and so on. However, before you can use a phone as a development device, you will need to register the phone for development. This lifts the requirements that applications be signed by Microsoft and allows you to deploy your applications directly to the phone so that you can debug applications.

Before you can enable your phone as a developer phone, you will need to have an account at the Windows Phone App Hub (http://developer. windowsphone.com). After you have done that, you can enable your phone to be used for development. To do this you will need the Windows Phone Developer Registration tool, which is installed when you install the Windows Phone SDK. When you run this application, it detects the device. You will need to ensure that the device is unlocked and turned on. At that point the Windows Phone Developer Registration tool will enable the Register button, as shown in Figure 2.27.

FIGURE 2.27　**Windows Phone Developer Registration tool**

Next, it will ask you for your Windows Live ID that you used to register with the developer portal, as shown in Figure 2.28.

If your phone is successfully attached to your computer, the Status area will tell you that it is ready to register your device for development. At this point, just click the Register button to register with the developer portal. After it registers the phone, it changes the status to show you that the phone is ready.

FIGURE 2.28 Signing in with your Microsoft ID

When you use a device to debug, you will find it much easier to change the default time-out of the device to be longer than the default (usually one minute, but it depends on the device manufacturer and carrier). To do this, go to the settings on your phone. In the settings is an option called "lock screen", as shown in Figure 2.29.

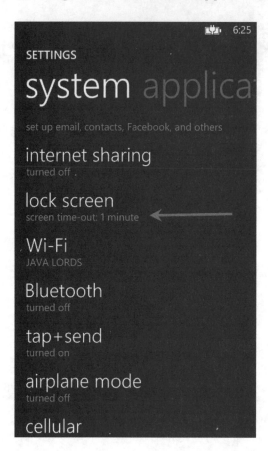

FIGURE 2.29 The Lock Screen option on the settings screen

When you're in this option, you can scroll down to find the "Screen times out after" option, open the option, and select the longest time-out you can tolerate (this will affect battery life when you're not debugging on the device, so be careful to choose a time-out you can live with if it's not a testing-only device). You can see this in Figure 2.30.

Now that you've registered your device, you can deploy and debug your applications using Visual Studio. The key to using the device instead of the emulator is to change the deployment using the drop-down list of deployment options. The drop-down is located in the toolbar of Visual Studio, as shown in Figure 2.31.

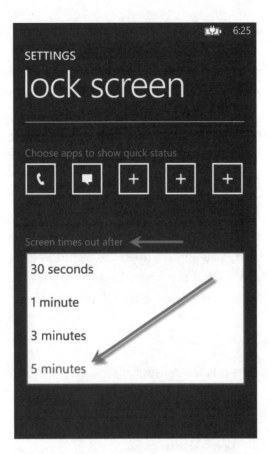

FIGURE 2.30   Changing the default device time-out

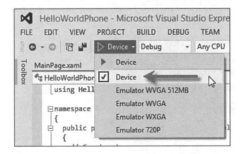

FIGURE 2.31   Changing the deployment to use a development phone

After you change the deployment target, you can debug just like you did with the emulator. When you run the application, it will deploy your application to the device and run it so that you can debug it in the same way as you did with the emulator.

Using Touch

Even though the touch interactions do fire mouse events, other events enable you to design your application for touch. Because touch is so important to how applications on the phone work, this first application should give you a taste of that experience. To show touch working, let's add an ellipse to the application that the user can move around by dragging it with her finger. To get started, you should open the MainPage.xaml file and add a new ellipse in the center of the page. To do this, find the TextBlock called theStatus and place a new Ellipse element after it, like so:

```
...
    <Grid x:Name="ContentGrid"
        Grid.Row="1">
      <Rectangle Fill="#FF7E0505"
                Margin="8"
                RadiusY="24"
                RadiusX="24" />
      <TextBlock HorizontalAlignment="Center"
                TextWrapping="Wrap"
                Text="Status"
                VerticalAlignment="Bottom"
                FontSize="48"
                FontWeight="Bold"
                Name="theStatus" />
      <Ellipse x:Name="theEllipse"
              Fill="White"
              Width="200"
              Height="200">
      </Ellipse>
    </Grid>
...
```

We need to be able to move the ellipse (named theEllipse) as the user drags it. To allow us to do this, we must use something called a **transform**. In XAML, a transform is used to change the way an object is rendered without having to change properties of the ellipse. Although we could change the margins and/or alignments to move it around the screen, using a transform is much simpler. You should use a `TranslateTransform` to allow this movement. A `TranslateTransform` provides `X` and `Y` properties, which specify where to draw the element (as a delta between where it originally exists and where you want it). You can specify this transform by setting the `RenderTransform` property with a `TranslateTransform` (naming it in the process):

```
...
<Ellipse x:Name="theEllipse"
         Fill="White"
         Width="200"
         Height="200">
  <Ellipse.RenderTransform>
    <TranslateTransform x:Name="theMover" />
  </Ellipse.RenderTransform>
</Ellipse>
...
```

Now that we have a way to move our ellipse around the page, let's look at dealing with touch. In Silverlight, there are two specific types of touch interactions that are meant to allow the user to change onscreen objects. These are when the user drags her finger on the screen and when she uses a pinch move to resize objects. These types of interactions are called **manipulations.** Silverlight has three events to allow you to use this touch information:

- `ManipulationStarted`
- `ManipulationDelta`
- `ManipulationCompleted`

These events let you get information about the manipulation as it happens. For example, let's handle the `ManipulationDelta` event to get information about when the user drags on the screen. This event is called as the manipulation happens, and it includes information about the difference between the start of the manipulation and the current state (for example, how far the user has dragged her finger):

```
...
public partial class MainPage : PhoneApplicationPage
{
  // Constructor
  public MainPage()
  {
    InitializeComponent();

    theStatus.Text = "Hello from Code";

    theStatus.Tap += theStatus_Tap;

    theEllipse.ManipulationDelta += theEllipse_ManipulationDelta;

    // Sample code to localize the ApplicationBar
    //BuildLocalizedApplicationBar();
  }

  void theEllipse_ManipulationDelta(object sender,
                                    System.Windows.Input.
                                    ManipulationDeltaEventArgs e)
  {
    // As a manipulation is executed (drag or resize), this is called
    theMover.X = e.CumulativeManipulation.Translation.X;
    theMover.Y = e.CumulativeManipulation.Translation.Y;
  }

  ...
}
...
```

The event is fired while the user either pinches or drags within the theEllipse element. In this case the code is only concerned with the dragging. In the event handler for ManipulationDelta, the ManipulationDeltaEventArgs object contains information about the extent of the manipulation. The CumulativeManipulation property of the event args has a property called Translation, which contains the extent of the drag operation (the complete delta). We are just changing theMover's properties to match the manipulation. This means we can now drag the theEllipse element around and see it change position under our dragging, as shown in Figure 2.32.

FIGURE 2.32   Dragging the ellipse

Working with the Phone

This first application is a program that can be pretty self-sufficient, but not all applications are like that. Most applications will want to interact with the phone's operating system to work with other parts of the phone. From within your application, you might want to make a phone call, interact with the user's contacts, take pictures, and so on. The Windows Phone SDK calls these types of interactions **tasks.** Tasks let you leave an application (and optionally return) to perform a number of phone-specific tasks. Here is a list of some of the most common tasks:

- CameraCaptureTask

- EmailAddressChooserTask

- EmailComposeTask

- PhoneCallTask

- SearchTask

- WebBrowserTask

These tasks allow you to launch a task for the user to perform. In some of these tasks (for example, CameraCaptureTask, EmailAddressChooserTask), after the task is complete the user expects to return to your application; while in others (for example, SearchTask), the user might be navigating to a new activity (and might come back via the Back key, but might not).

Let's start with a simple task, the SearchTask. Add a using statement to the top of the code file for Microsoft.Phone.Tasks to ensure that the SearchTask class is available to our code file. Next, create an event handler for the Tap event on theEllipse. Then, inside the handler for the Tap event, you can create an instance of the SearchTask, set the search criteria, and call Show to launch the task:

```
...
using Microsoft.Phone.Tasks;
...
public partial class MainPage : PhoneApplicationPage
{
  // Constructor
  public MainPage()
  {
    ...

    theEllipse.Tap += theEllipse_Tap;

  }

  void theEllipse_Tap(object sender,
                      System.Windows.Input.GestureEventArgs e)
  {
    SearchTask task = new SearchTask();
    task.SearchQuery = "Windows Phone";
    task.Show();
  }

  ...
}
```

If you run your application, you'll see that when you tap on the theEllipse element it will launch the phone's Search function using the search query you supplied (as shown in Figure 2.33). The results you retrieve for the search query can vary because it is using the live version of Bing for search.

FIGURE 2.33 The SearchTask **in action**

Although this sort of simple task is useful, the more interesting story is being able to call tasks that return to your application. For example, let's pick an email address from the phone and show it in our application. The big challenge here is that when we launch our application, we might get tombstoned (or deactivated). Remember that, on the phone, only one application can be running at a time. To have our task wired up when our application is activated (remember, it can be deactivated or even unloaded if necessary), we have to have our task at the page or application level and wired up during construction. So, in our page, we create a class-level field and wire up the Completed event at the end of the constructor for it, like so:

```
public partial class MainPage : PhoneApplicationPage
{

    EmailAddressChooserTask emailChooser =
      new EmailAddressChooserTask();

    // Constructor
    public MainPage()
    {
      ...

      emailChooser.Completed += emailChooser_Completed;
    }

    ...
}
```

In the event handler, we can simply show the email chosen using the MessageBox API:

```
...
void emailChooser_Completed(object sender, EmailResult e)
{
  MessageBox.Show(e.Email);
}
...
```

Now we need to call the task. To do this, let's hijack the event that gets called when the theEllipse element is tapped. Just comment out the old SearchTask code and add a call to the emailChooser's Show method, like so:

```
...
void theEllipse_MouseLeftButtonUp(object sender,
                                 MouseButtonEventArgs e)
{
  //SearchTask task = new SearchTask();
  //task.SearchQuery = "Windows Phone";
  //task.Show();

  // Get an e-mail from the user's Contacts
  emailChooser.Show();
}
...
```

After you run the application, a list of contacts will be displayed and you will be able to pick a contact (and an address, if there is more than one), as shown in Figure 2.34. The emulator comes prepopulated with several fake contacts to test with.

FIGURE 2.34　Choosing a contact to retrieve an email address via the `EmailAddressChooserTask`

After the user selects the contact, the phone returns to your application. You will be returned to your application (and debugging will continue). The event handler should be called when it is returned to the application, as shown in Figure 2.35.

FIGURE 2.35 **Showing the selected email in a** MessageBox

Where Are We?

You have created your first Windows Phone application using Silverlight. Although this example has very little real functionality, you should have a feel for the environment. Taking this first stab at an application and applying it to your needs is probably not nearly enough. That's why, in subsequent chapters, we will dive deep into the different aspects of the phone application ecosystem. You will learn how to build rich applications using Silverlight, services, and the phone itself.

▛ 3 ▪

XAML Overview

While phones used to be very utilitarian (for example, wow, I can make a phone call), things have changed dramatically over the past few years. Therefore, although you could try to create applications that are focused on functionality, they probably would not attract a large audience unless they had a great user interface. That is what draws people to an application. That means it's your job to figure out what people want and what makes an application easy to use and learn. Luckily, XAML comes with a way to design interfaces with a lot of control over the look and feel of the application. Creating dynamic applications that will wow your users is easier than ever. This chapter will show you how.

What Is XAML?

What is eXtensible Application Markup Language (XAML)? For Windows Phone, XAML is used to design the user interfaces (both the look and feel of applications). Although the actual XAML is the markup language, it is often used interchangeably for the framework for building applications (in Silverlight, Windows Phone, Windows 8, and WPF). The main thing to learn here is that XAML can be thought of as a serialization format that works well with tools. It enables us to declare the structure of a user interface.

Declaring the interface in this way makes it easy for tools to create the user interfaces and have applications consume the files at runtime.

What do I mean by a *serialization format*? XAML is quite simple; let's take a very basic piece of XAML:

```
<UserControl x:Class="WinningTheLottery.Sample"
    xmlns="http://schemas.microsoft.com/winfx/2006/xaml/presentation"
    xmlns:x="http://schemas.microsoft.com/winfx/2006/xaml">
  <Grid>
    <TextBlock Text="Hello" />
    <Rectangle Width="100"
               Height="100"
               Fill="Blue" />
  </Grid>
</UserControl>
```

XAML is an XML file that obeys basic XML rules (for example, single top-level container, case sensitivity). In this file we are declaring a UserControl root that contains a Grid element that contains two elements (a TextBlock and a Rectangle). This is the basic hierarchy of this simple user interface. When parsed, this XAML document is used to create that same hierarchy in memory. Literally, the name of the element ties itself to the name of a class. So when the XAML is parsed, the UserControl element informs the system to create a new UserControl instance. To be used here, all the classes must allow for empty constructors (in the .NET sense) so that the UserControl class can be created. After it creates the UserControl itself, it looks at its subelements (the Grid) and creates that element as a child inside the UserControl. Finally, it creates the TextBlock and Rectangle and places them as children inside the Grid. When the TextBlock is created, it sees the attribute (Text) and calls the property setter of the new TextBlock with the contents of the attribute. It does this with the multiple attributes of the Rectangle as well. In this way it uses the XAML to build an in-memory object graph that follows the same structure as the XAML. Understanding that the XAML you are using is the basis for your runtime design is very important in understanding how XAML works.

XAML Object Properties

Most objects' properties you will set in XAML are simple and string-based:

```
<Rectangle Fill="Blue" />
```

Not all properties can be set using the simple, string-based syntax, however. Under the covers, many properties (during XAML parsing) are attempting to convert a string attribute to a property value. For example, Fill is a property that accepts a Brush value, not a Color value as the markup implies. When Fill="Blue" is parsed as XAML, a conversion is done between the string (that is, "Blue") and a brush called a SolidColorBrush. For a more complex value type (like a Brush), there is a verbose syntax (called this Property Element Syntax) for setting property values:

```
<Rectangle>
  <Rectangle.Fill>
    <SolidColorBrush Color="Blue" />
  </Rectangle.Fill>
</Rectangle>
```

This verbose syntax is identical at runtime to the earlier example. By adding an element inside the Rectangle whose name is the name of the object, a dot, and the name of the property (for example, Rectangle.Fill), we can define the value for the property using XAML instead of being stuck using just strings. Because not all complex property values can be defined in such a way that a conversion can be made, this syntax allows for property values to be set when the value is a complex type that would be difficult or impossible to describe in a single string. For example, let's replace the SolidColorBrush with a LinearGradientBrush:

```
<Rectangle>
  <Rectangle.Fill>
    <LinearGradientBrush>
      <GradientStop Color="Blue" Offset="0" />
      <GradientStop Color="White" Offset="0.5" />
      <GradientStop Color="Blue" Offset="1" />
    </LinearGradientBrush>
  </Rectangle.Fill>
</Rectangle>
```

This example demonstrates that defining a fill by specifying the colors and offsets not only would be difficult in a simple string, but would make the XAML even harder to read. In this way, XAML allows you to set very complex properties without having to invent conversions. You will see how this is used in many places in XAML as we continue.

Understanding XAML Namespaces

Inside the root element are two namespaces. Namespaces in XAML are XML namespaces.[1] The default namespace (`xmlns`) declares that this is a XAML document. The second namespace (`xmlns:x`) brings in several elements and attribute types that are all prefixed with the x alias. So when you see `x:Class`, that is a convention that is defined in the second namespace.

You can think of the namespace aliasing as similar to namespaces in .NET. When you add a namespace, it brings in those new types of things that can be described in XAML. Unlike .NET, though, you have to use an alias (because all other namespaces are not the "default" namespace) and then use that alias everywhere you want to refer to information from that namespace. In the x alias's case, the alias here as "x" is just a convention that XAML tends to use. In the XML namespace sense, you can change the alias to whatever you want, but you would have to change it everywhere it's referenced as well. For example:

```
<UserControl foo:Class="WinningTheLottery.Sample"
    xmlns="..."
    xmlns:foo="...">
```

The alias is just that: an alias so that the parser can determine from which of the namespaces your element or attribute originates. When we changed the name of the alias, it is what you would use to alias that namespace in the rest of the document.

Although these namespaces represent the basic XAML namespaces, you can extend the XAML by using namespaces to bring in arbitrary .NET types as well. If you define a namespace that points at a .NET namespace and assembly, those types will also be available in the XAML:

---

1   http://shawnw.me/pFshpG

```
<UserControl x:Class="WinningTheLottery.Sample"
  xmlns="http://schemas.microsoft.com/winfx/2006/xaml/presentation"
  xmlns:x="http://schemas.microsoft.com/winfx/2006/xaml"
  xmlns:sys="clr-namespace:System;assembly=mscorlib">
  <Grid>
    <TextBlock>
      <TextBlock.Text>
        <sys:String>Hello</sys:String>
      </TextBlock.Text>
    </TextBlock>
  </Grid>
</UserControl>
```

In this example, the XAML "imports" the System namespace that exists inside the mscorlib.dll assembly. After that .NET namespace is imported, all the types in that namespace are creatable in the XAML. Any type that is created in XAML must conform to the following rules:

- Has an empty, public constructor
- Has public properties

If any .NET objects follow these rules, they are creatable in XAML (and therefore can be part of your initial object graph). You will see how this is used as we continue in this chapter.

Naming in XAML

Unlike other platforms, XAML does not require that every object in the XAML be specifically named. In fact, it is probably a bad idea to name every object in the XAML. Naming objects in the XAML becomes important after you need to refer to an object by name (for example, from code or via data binding). Naming objects in XAML takes the form of an attribute that can be applied to most XAML elements: x:Name. Here's an example:

```
<UserControl x:Class="WinningTheLottery.Sample"
    xmlns="http://schemas.microsoft.com/winfx/2006/xaml/presentation"
    xmlns:x="http://schemas.microsoft.com/winfx/2006/xaml">
  <Grid x:Name="LayoutRoot">
    <TextBlock Text="Hello"
               x:Name="theTextBlock" />
    <Rectangle Width="100"
               Height="100"
```

```
            Fill="Blue"
            x:Name="theRectangle" />
    </Grid>
</UserControl>
```

You will notice that the naming attribute starts with the x: prefix (or alias). As was explained in the namespaces discussion, this means that attribute is available through the x namespace included on the top of every XAML document (by default). After these objects are named, they will be available to other XAML elements by name or via code (both of which you will see in this chapter). The names used here must be unique. Each name can occur only once within a single XAML document. This simplifies the naming strategy but also means there is no sense of naming scope (like HTML has).

Visual Containers

If you consider the examples that have been shown, you might have missed the importance of XAML containers. The most obvious of these can be seen in the Grid element:

```
<UserControl x:Class="WinningTheLottery.Sample"
    xmlns="http://schemas.microsoft.com/winfx/2006/xaml/presentation"
    xmlns:x="http://schemas.microsoft.com/winfx/2006/xaml">
  <Grid>
    <TextBlock Text="Hello" />
  </Grid>
</UserControl>
```

The purpose of these containers is to allow other elements to be laid out in particular ways on the visual surface of XAML. The containers themselves typically don't have any user interface but simply are used to determine how various XAML elements are arranged on the screen. A number of layout containers are important to designing in XAML. Each of these can contain one or more child elements and lay them out in specific ways. You can see the common visual containers in Table 3.1.

TABLE 3.1   Visual Containers

Layout Container	Description	Supports Multiple Children?
Grid	Table-like layout of columns and rows; good for alignment o.r margin-oriented design	Yes
StackPanel	Horizontal or vertical stacking of individual elements.	Yes
Canvas	Position-based layout (via top and left positions).	Yes
ScrollViewer	Virtual container that can be larger than the contents to allow users to scroll through the container.	No
Border	To create a simple border around a single element.	No

These containers are important because they are used to determine how your elements are laid out. The most important of these is the Grid container, which is the one you use most often. The Grid is a container that supports dynamic, table-like layout using rows and columns. To define rows and columns, you set the Grid's ColumnDefinitions and/or RowDefinitions properties. These properties take one or more ColumnDefinition or RowDefinition elements, as shown in the following code:

```
<UserControl x:Class="WinningTheLottery.Sample"
    xmlns="http://schemas.microsoft.com/winfx/2006/xaml/presentation"
    xmlns:x="http://schemas.microsoft.com/winfx/2006/xaml">
  <Grid>
    <Grid.ColumnDefinitions>
      <ColumnDefinition />
      <ColumnDefinition />
    </Grid.ColumnDefinitions>
    <TextBlock Text="Hello" />
  </Grid>
</UserControl>
```

You create new columns and rows using the ColumnDefinitions and RowDefinitions properties. The code below shows how you would add columns by specifying the Grid.ColumnsDefinitions property and adding new ColumnDefinition objects inside the property. This allows you to specify that individual elements are in a particular row or column using the Grid.Column or Grid.Row attached properties (see the sidebar "What Are Attached Properties?"):

```
<UserControl x:Class="WinningTheLottery.Sample"
    xmlns="http://schemas.microsoft.com/winfx/2006/xaml/presentation"
    xmlns:x="http://schemas.microsoft.com/winfx/2006/xaml">
  <Grid>
    <Grid.ColumnDefinitions>
      <ColumnDefinition />
      <ColumnDefinition />
    </Grid.ColumnDefinitions>
    <TextBlock Text="Hello"
               Grid.Column="1" /> <!-- The Second Column -->
  </Grid>
</UserControl>
```

By using the attached property, the TextBlock is indicating that the TextBlock belongs in the second column (note that row and column numbers are zero-indexed). In this way, the Grid is creating columns or rows proactively by specifying the number of rows or columns up front. At first blush it might seem verbose to create row and/or column definitions this way, but it's important because the definitions contain other important information that can be set.

∎ What Are Attached Properties?

Some properties are not relevant until they exist in some specific scope. For example, when an object is inside a Grid, being able to tell the XAML which column or row you are in becomes critical. But that same element inside a StackPanel has no notion of a row or column. Attached properties are specific types of properties that are valid only in certain cases. Attached properties are defined by the name of the owning type and the name of the attached property (for example, Grid.Row). The information in attached properties is available to the class that exposes them because that is where they are typically used. Although in XAML it is common for these attached properties to be used in this way, attached properties are really for properties that are global in scope. So you can define a property that could be applied to any XAML object. Containers such as the Grid and the Canvas expose attached properties to explicitly let them handle layout and will probably be the first real use of attached properties for most developers who are new to XAML.

For example, in the Grid class, as the Grid object lays out the elements inside it, it will query for the attached property to determine in which row and/or column to place an element. The properties are attached at runtime, so the underlying element does not need to have unnecessary properties (such as Row and Column).

When creating rows and columns, you can define the height or width (respectively) in three ways, as shown in Table 3.2.

TABLE 3.2   Grid **Row and Column Sizing**

Type	Description	Example
Auto	Sizes row or column based on the contents. The size will be determined by the largest object in a respective row or column.	`<RowDefinition Height="Auto" />`
Pixel	Sets row or column to a specific size, in pixels. Larger objects will be clipped.	`<RowDefinition Height="100" />`

Type	Description	Example
Star	Proportionally sizes rows or columns based on the weighted value.	`<RowDefinition Height="*" />` `<RowDefinition Height="25*" />` `<RowDefinition Height="0.147*" />`

Auto and pixel sizing are pretty self-explanatory, but star sizing requires some explanation. Star sizing proportionally sizes rows or columns based on the values of the height or width. Here's an example:

```
<UserControl x:Class="WinningTheLottery.Sample"
    xmlns="http://schemas.microsoft.com/winfx/2006/xaml/presentation"
    xmlns:x="http://schemas.microsoft.com/winfx/2006/xaml">
  <Grid>
    <Grid.ColumnDefinitions>
      <ColumnDefinition Width="33*" />
      <ColumnDefinition Width="66*" />
    </Grid.ColumnDefinitions>
  </Grid>
</UserControl>
```

The width values are used as weighted proportions of the whole size. Although this looks similar to percentages (like you might be used to in web applications), the numbers are not part of an arbitrary 100% scale. For example, changing the values to "1*" and "2*" will yield the same 2-to-1 ratio as "33*" and "66*". In the case of using a star alone (for example, "*"), it is equivalent to "1*". By using Grid elements with a mix of auto, pixel, and star sizing, you can create elastic layouts (using star sizing for the flexible, sized elements and pixel/auto sizing for the more static parts of the design).

You have already seen that you can use attached properties to set the row and column of a specific element inside the Grid. The Grid class also supports the ability to specify RowSpan and ColumnSpan to signify that a particular element should span more than one row and/or column. This will give you extra flexibility to create your table-based designs, like so:

```
<Grid>
  <Grid.ColumnDefinitions>
    <ColumnDefinition Width="*" />
    <ColumnDefinition Width="*" />
    <ColumnDefinition Width="*" />
  </Grid.ColumnDefinitions>
```

```
<Grid.RowDefinitions>
  <RowDefinition Height="*" />
  <RowDefinition Height="*" />
</Grid.RowDefinitions>
<TextBlock Text="1" />
<TextBlock Text="1"
           Grid.Row="1" />
<TextBlock Text="1"
           Grid.Column="1" />
<TextBlock Text="Across All 3 Columns"
           Grid.ColumnSpan="3" />
<TextBlock Text="Across Both Rows"
           Grid.RowSpan="2" />
</Grid>
```

Although you can use the other layout containers in certain cases, you should become comfortable with the Grid because it is the container you will use most often.

Visual Grammar

XAML gives you the ability to draw shapes and colors on the surface of the phone itself. Although you might not imagine doing much actual drawing, it is important to understand how creating a design with the drawing primitives is important to the overall XAML story. As you start to use controls, you will learn that those controls are made up of more primitive elements, and when you want to change the way controls and other elements look, you will have to understand the drawing stack.

Shapes

The most basic drawing element is a Shape. The Shape element is a base class for a small number of shapes that are used for basic drawing. The basic shapes are

- Line
- Rectangle
- Ellipse
- Polygon
- Polyline
- Path

Each shape has basic attributes, such as Height, Width, Fill, and Stroke:

```
<Grid>
  <Rectangle Width="100"
             Height="100"
             Fill="Blue" />
  <Ellipse Width="200"
           Height="50"
           Stroke="Black" />
</Grid>
```

If you cannot compose the kind of shape you need with the first five shapes in the previous list, everything falls down to the Path shape. A Path is a powerful shape that can give you full power to design arbitrary shapes. The Path shape allows you to create open, closed, or compound shapes. The Path shape has a property called Data that specifies the elements of the shape. For example, you can specify a Path with an object graph, like so:

```
<Path Stroke="Black">
  <Path.Data>
    <PathGeometry>
      <PathFigure StartPoint="0,50">
        <BezierSegment Point1="50,0"
                       Point2="50,100"
                       Point3="100,50"/>
      </PathFigure>
    </PathGeometry>
  </Path.Data>
</Path>
```

By setting the Data attribute to a PathGeometry element that specifies a Path that contains a BezierSegment (from 0,50 to 100,50 with control points of 50,0 and 50,100 as the curves), you can draw a curved line, as shown in Figure 3.1.

The Data property contains a shorthand notation to simplify and shorten the size of the XAML. This shorthand is the same type of information but is stored in a single string. For example, the curve in Figure 3.1 can be simplified to:

```
<Path Stroke="Black"
      Data="M 0,50 C 50,0 50,100 100,50" />
```

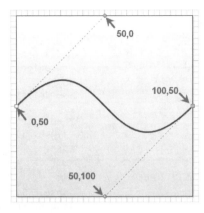

FIGURE 3.1   Path **explained**

This has the same information in it but in a shortened form: Move to the 0,50 position and do a Bezier curve using these three points. Usually `Paths` are created with tools (for example, Expression Blend) because the process can get terse, but the process does allow for very complex paths.

Brushes

In many of the examples so far, you have seen color names (for example, black, red) used in XAML to indicate with which color an object is displayed. In fact, those colors were a shortcut to creating an object called a *brush*. Brushes are always used to paint surfaces (for example, using fill, stroke, and background brushes). Several types of brushes are available to you, as shown in Table 3.3.

TABLE 3.3   **Brush Types**

Type	Description	Example
SolidColorBrush	Paints a solid color	`<Ellipse Fill="Blue" />`

LinearGradientBrush	Paints a gradient along a line	`<Ellipse>`
		`<Ellipse.Fill>`
		`<LinearGradientBrush>`
		`    <GradientStop Color="Blue"`
		`                 Offset="0" />`
		`  <GradientStop Color="Red"`
		`                  Offset="1" />`
		`  </LinearGradientBrush>`
		`</Ellipse.Fill>`
		`</Ellipse>`

RadialGradient Brush	Paints a gradient between a focal point and a circle on the outside of the shape	```
		<Ellipse>
		  <Ellipse.Fill>
		    <RadialGradientBrush>
		      <GradientStop Color="Blue"
		                   Offset="0" />
		      <GradientStop Color="Red"
		                   Offset="1" />
		    </RadialGradientBrush>
		  </Ellipse.Fill>
		</Ellipse>
		``

ImageBrush	Paints an image	``` <Ellipse> <Ellipse.Fill> <ImageBrush ImageSource="/ foo.jpg" /> </Ellipse.Fill> </Ellipse> ```
VideoBrush	Paints a MediaElement	``` <Ellipse> <Ellipse.Fill> <ImageBrush SourceName="theVideo" /> </Ellipse.Fill> </Ellipse> ```

Each property of a XAML element that accepts a brush object can take any of the various types of brushes.

Colors

XAML contains a set of built-in colors. You can use these 141 named colors to specify individual colors, like so:

```
<Grid>
  <Rectangle Fill="Blue"
             Stroke="Pink" />
</Grid>
```

In most cases, though, named colors end up being insufficient to handle the basics of colors. Because millions of colors are available, XAML needs a way to more effectively specify a color. XAML supports the HTML convention of an RGB hexadecimal string, like so:

```
<Grid>
  <Rectangle Fill="#0000FF"
             Stroke="#FF0000" />
</Grid>
```

In this format, the pound symbol (#) is followed by a set of hexadecimal numbers that represent the amount of red, green, and blue being used. Both the six- and three-digit formats are supported (for example, #FF0000 is equivalent to #F00). In addition, XAML extends the HTML syntax to include an eight-character version. In the eight-character version, the first two characters represent a hexadecimal number that indicates the alpha channel (or level of opaqueness):

```
<Grid>
  <Rectangle Fill="#800000FF"
             Stroke="#C0FF0000" />
</Grid>
```

In this example, the Fill is roughly 50% transparent and the Stroke is approximately 75% opaque (or 25% transparent).

Text

For basic drawing of text, the TextBlock class is the right tool. The TextBlock is a simple container for drawing text. It supports properties for basic font choices such as size, family, weight, foreground color, alignment, and so on:

```
<Grid>
  <TextBlock Text="Hello World"
             Foreground="White"
             FontFamily="Segoe WP"
             FontSize="18"
             FontWeight="Bold"
             FontStyle="Italic"
             TextWrapping="Wrap"
             TextAlignment="Center" />
</Grid>
```

Along with simple text, the TextBlock class also supports simple inline formatting using the LineBreak and Run constructs:

```
<Grid>
  <TextBlock TextWrapping="Wrap">
    Hello World. <LineBreak />This
    is the second line. The breaking of
    the lines in the XAML are
    <Run Foreground="Red">not significant</Run>.
  </TextBlock>
</Grid>
```

A LineBreak indicates where line breaks are going to occur without regard to the TextWrapping property. A Run is used to wrap some piece of text that needs to be formatted differently than other parts of the TextBlock. The Run supports the basic properties that a TextBlock allows but applies them only to the text inside the Run element as shown previously. The TextBlock is not a control to handle any sort of rich text or HTML-level text handling but will suffice in most cases for text manipulation.

Images

Although the simple vector drawing stack is invaluable to the design of your Windows Phone application, you will always need to use images in your application. The simple Image element is used to display images in your application:

```
<Image Source="http://wildermuth.com/images/headshot.jpg" />
```

The Image element supports JPEG and PNG files; it does not support GIF files. By specifying the Source attribute, the Image element shows the picture you specify in the URI of the source. Specifying an Internet URI, the Image element will attempt to download the image from the Internet location. The Source attribute supports a relative URI as well:

```
<Image Source="headshot.jpg" />
```

By using a relative URI, the Image element attempts to retrieve the image from the application itself. You can add an existing image to the Windows Phone project by simply selecting Add | Existing Item from the Project menu. After you have the image as part of the project, it will be packaged with your application. Therefore, you can simply use the relative URI to specify the Source attribute. The relative URI is relative to the root of the project. So if you were to place an image in a project folder, the URI would navigate to the path:

```
<Image Source="Images/headshot.jpg" />
```

Storing your images as part of the application is typical for static images (for example, button icons, backgrounds, and so on).

By default, the Image element is set to stretch the image to fit the size of the element. You can stretch images by specifying the Stretch attribute. The valid types of stretch include

- **None:** No stretching is performed.
- **Uniform:** Stretches the image, preserving the original aspect ratio, to fit within the frame of the **Image** element. This is the default.
- **UniformToFill:** Stretches the image, preserving the original aspect ratio, to fill the **Image** element. If the aspect ratio of the **Image** element is different from that image, the image will be clipped to accommodate the difference.
- **Fill:** Stretches the image to fill the **Image** element without preserving the aspect ratio.

Figure 3.2 illustrates examples of the various stretch types.

FIGURE 3.2   Image stretching

When creating Image elements, you can simply specify the Stretch attribute, like so:

```
<Image Source="Images/headshot.jpg" Stretch="UniformToFill" />
```

Because the `Image` element is just part of the design grammar, you can specify size either by using height and width or by using container properties like any other element (for example, `Grid.Row/Column`, `Margin`, `VerticalAlignment`, and so on).

Transformations and Animations

Now that you have the basic building blocks of designing the look of an application, let's talk about creating the "feel" of an application. The feel of an application is the way it interacts with the user. The level of interaction depends on the nature of the application, but many applications should feel alive to the user. Often this is accomplished with subtle feedback to the user, including changing the look of the user interface (UI) in reaction to the user's actions or using techniques such as haptic (for example, vibration) feedback. This feedback is important to help the user know he is doing something. A common example of this is the venerable button object. In a typical desktop operating system, when you move your mouse over a button it changes its look to indicate you're over the button. When you click it, it changes its look to give you the impression that it is actually pressed (like a real-world button). This feedback ensures that you can feel confident that clicking the button is doing what you expect. Some websites lack this feedback, which simply confuses users (often they don't know what is missing). This is where transformations and animations can help you polish your user interface design.

Transformations

Let's start with transformations. The idea of a transformation is to simply change the way an element is drawn on the screen. Let's take a simple rectangle:

```
<Grid>
  <Rectangle Width="100"
             Height="100"
             Fill="Red" />
</Grid>
```

As you would expect, this rectangle will be drawn as a simple square. Let's see what happens when we add a transform (by assigning it to the Rectangle's RenderTransform property):

```
<Grid>
  <Rectangle Width="100"
             Height="100"
             Fill="Red">
    <Rectangle.RenderTransform>
      <RotateTransform Angle="30" />
    </Rectangle.RenderTransform>
  </Rectangle>
</Grid>
```

By using a RotateTransform, you ensure that the object can remain a Rectangle, but when drawn, the transformation is applied (as shown in Figure 3.3).

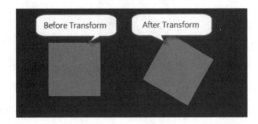

FIGURE 3.3 Showing the transformation

Using a transformation on a single element rarely is the right thing to do; usually a transformation is applied to an entire container to change the look of the container:

```
<Canvas>
  <Canvas.RenderTransform>
    <RotateTransform Angle="30"
                     CenterX="150"
                     CenterY="150" />
  </Canvas.RenderTransform>
  <Ellipse Width="300"
           Height="300"
           Stroke="Black"
           Fill="Yellow"
           StrokeThickness="2" />
```

```
<Ellipse Fill="Black"
        Width="50"
        Height="50"
        Canvas.Left="50"
        Canvas.Top="75" />
<Ellipse Fill="Black"
        Width="50"
        Height="50"
        Canvas.Left="200"
        Canvas.Top="75" />
<Path Stroke="Black"
     StrokeThickness="5"
     Data="M 50,200 S 150,275 250,200" />
</Canvas>
```

In this case the entire smiley face design is rotated (as shown in Figure 3.4).

FIGURE 3.4 **Entire container transformed**

Table 3.4 describes and provides examples of the different types of transformations.

TABLE 3.4 **Transformation Types**

Type	Description	Example
RotateTransform	Performs a two-dimensional rotation on an object or object tree	`<RotateTransform Angle="30" />`
SkewTransform	Performs a two-dimensional skew on an object or object tree	`<SkewTransform AngleX="30" AngleY="75" />`
ScaleTransform	Scales an object or object tree	`<ScaleTransform ScaleX="1.5" ScaleY=".75" />`

Type	Description	Example
TranslateTransform	Moves an object or object tree in two dimensions	`<TranslateTransform X="1.5" Y=".75" />`
CompositeTransform	Performs a mix of rotation, skewing, scaling, and transla-tion in a preferred order	`<CompositeTransform TranslateX= "150" Rotation="30" ScaleX="1.5"/>`

You can use the four basic types of transforms singularly or, if you need to mix transforms (for example, scale and rotate), you can use Composite-Transform to combine multiple transforms.

Animations

Although the idea of animations in applications might make you think of creating the next blockbuster animated feature, that's not what animations are for at all. Animations are simply a way to change properties of XAML elements over time. For example, a simple animation to change the width of a rectangle would look like this:

```
<DoubleAnimation Storyboard.TargetName="theRectangle"
                 Storyboard.TargetProperty="Width"
                 From="50"
                 To="250"
                 Duration="00:00:05" />
```

Animation elements tell a specific property how to change over time. This example shows how to change the width of an element named theRectangle from 50 to 250 over five seconds. The attached properties (Storyboard.TargetName and Storyboard.TargetProperty) hint at the fact that animations are not executed on their own but are housed in a container called a Storyboard. Here's an example:

```
<Grid.Resources>
```

```
<Storyboard x:Name="theStory">
  <DoubleAnimation Storyboard.TargetName="theRectangle"
                   Storyboard.TargetProperty="Width"
                   From="50"
                   To="250"
                   Duration="00:00:05" />
</Storyboard>
</Grid.Resources>
```

The Storyboard is embedded in a Resources section (usually at the main container or UserControl level) and named so that it can be executed and controlled via code. The unit of work for animations is the Storyboard. Storyboards can contain one or more animations, but all animations are executed concurrently (not consecutively). Therefore, if we expand this Storyboard to include two animations:

```
<Grid.Resources>
  <Storyboard x:Name="theStory">
    <DoubleAnimation Storyboard.TargetName="theRectangle"
                     Storyboard.TargetProperty="Width"
                     From="50"
                     To="250"
                     Duration="00:00:05" />
    <DoubleAnimation Storyboard.TargetName="theEllipse"
                     Storyboard.TargetProperty="Opacity"
                     From="1"
                     To="0"
                     Duration="00:00:03" />
  </Storyboard>
</Grid.Resources>
```

When this Storyboard is executed, both animations will execute at the same time (again concurrently), even though the animations themselves are against entirely different properties on different objects.

The animations you've seen so far have been of the type DoubleAnimation. These animations are used because the animation is changing a number (a double value). There are also animations to change colors (ColorAnimation) and vectors (PointAnimation). All three of these animation types change values over a consistent time frame (and are called **timeline animations**).

Sometimes you do not want to have animation consist purely of linear changes across the timeline of a before and after value. To change the way the values are interpolated, you can use one of two methods: **keyframe animations** and **easing functions**.

Like timeline animations, **keyframe animations** change properties over time, but the calculation is based on a value at a specific time in the animation. For example

```
<DoubleAnimationUsingKeyFrames Storyboard.TargetName="theRectangle"
                               Storyboard.TargetProperty="Height">
  <LinearDoubleKeyFrame KeyTime="00:00:00" Value="50" />
  <LinearDoubleKeyFrame KeyTime="00:00:01" Value="150" />
  <LinearDoubleKeyFrame KeyTime="00:00:03" Value="200" />
</DoubleAnimationUsingKeyFrames>
```

There are keyframe animations for each timeline animation (for example, double, point, and color), but they are named with the UsingKeyFrames postfix, as shown previously. The Storyboard attached properties are still used to signify the target of the animation, but instead of a simple To and From to specify the values of the animation, one or more keyframes are used. For example, the LinearDoubleKeyFrame element specifies at what time the value should be a specific numeric property.

In this case, the height should start at 50 at the start of the animation, move quickly over the first second to 150, and finally slow down and move to 200 over the last two seconds. The interpolation of the values between the keyframes depends on the type of keyframe. In this example the interpolation is linear. You can also use spline and discrete to achieve curved interpolation and stepped interpolation, respectively.

Alternatively, **easing functions** are applied against **timeline animations** to change the nature of the interpolation. For example

```
<Grid.Resources>
  <Storyboard x:Name="theStory">
    <DoubleAnimation Storyboard.TargetName="theRectangle"
                     Storyboard.TargetProperty="Width"
                     From="50"
                     To="250"
                     Duration="00:00:05">
      <DoubleAnimation.EasingFunction>
        <ExponentialEase Exponent="1.0"
                         EasingMode="EaseOut" />
      </DoubleAnimation.EasingFunction>
```

```
    </DoubleAnimation>
   </Storyboard>
 </Grid.Resources>
```

An easing function is applied on a timeline animation. In this example the **ExponentialEase** is applied to the **EasingFunction** property of the animation. **ExponentialEase** is one of a handful of types of easings that are supported. This easing function specifically increases the value of the double animation on an exponential curve. Each easing function has an easing mode to determine where the curve of interpolation should start (for example, **EaseOut** says to start slowly and end fast; **EaseIn** does the reverse). You should experiment with the easing functions to get comfortable with them because they are very handy to make pleasing animations with little effort.

With these tools in hand, you should be able to create the subtle interactive effects that give the user the impression that she is interacting with real-world objects.

XAML Styling

When writing code, it's customary to take common pieces of code and reuse them in a number of ways, including creating base classes, creating static classes, or even creating reusable libraries. XAML has the same need for creating reuse in the design. This reusability, though, is more about creating a consistent look for the application without having to copy the same code over and over. Consider this common XAML:

```
<TextBox x:Name="nameBox"
         FontSize="36"
         FontFamily="Segoe WP"
         FontWeight="Black"
         BorderBrush="Blue"
         Foreground="White"
         HorizontalAlignment="Stretch" />
<TextBox x:Name="emailBox"
         FontSize="36"
         FontFamily="Segoe WP"
         FontWeight="Black"
         BorderBrush="Blue"
         Foreground="White"
         HorizontalAlignment="Stretch" />
```

In this XAML many of the properties are copied from one of the TextBoxes to the other. If we change any of the properties of one, we will have to copy the change to the other to provide consistency of the UI. In addition, the Foreground and BorderBrush are using colors that could or should be part of an overall look and feel. It's likely that we would want the brushes used there to be consistent not only from TextBox to TextBox, but also across the entire application. That's where styling and resources come in.

▪ Phone Styling

In this section, you are learning how resources and styles work together to make your app look consistent. The phone itself has a set of built-in styles and resources that you should use. We cover this in more detail in Chapter 5, "Designing for the Phone."

Understanding Resources

The first level of consistency has to do with sharing common resources. When creating an application, you often will want to use common colors or brushes across the application. XAML allows you to create objects to be used in more than one area by specifying them in a Resources section and identifying the object with an x:Key attribute. For example, you could define a SolidColorBrush in a Resources section like so:

```
<Grid x:Name="LayoutRoot">
  <Grid.Resources>
    <SolidColorBrush x:Key="mainBrush"
                     Color="Blue" />
  </Grid.Resources>
  ...
</Grid>
```

Every class that derives from FrameworkElement (which means most XAML elements) supports a collection of Resources. We can refer to these named elements using the StaticResource markup extension[2], like so:

```
<Grid x:Name="LayoutRoot">
  <Grid.Resources>
    <SolidColorBrush x:Key="mainBrush"
                     Color="Blue" />
  </Grid.Resources>
  <TextBlock Foreground="{StaticResource mainBrush}"
             Text="Hello World" />
  ...
</Grid>
```

The StaticResource markup extension tells the XAML parser to replace the foreground with the main brush. You can use the resource in several places, which isolates it from changes so that later, when you change the main brush to a LinearGradientBrush, it cascades down to wherever the StaticResource was used.

The StaticResource markup extension looks up through the XAML document to find the resource with the correct name (through the hierarchy) and will continue beyond the beginning of the XAML document. Above the XAML document is the App.xaml file in the phone application project. Normally this is where you would place any application-wide resources. For example, if the App.xaml file looked like this:

```
<Application x:Class="PhoneControls.App"
             xmlns="..."
             xmlns:x="..."
             xmlns:phone="..."
             xmlns:shell="...">

  <!--Application Resources-->
  <Application.Resources>
    <SolidColorBrush x:Key="mainBrush"
                     Color="Blue" />
  </Application.Resources>

  ...

</Application>
```

---

2   Markup extensions are special, macro-like parts of XAML that allow for setting values via code. We will discuss several of them throughout this chapter.

the `mainBrush` would then be defined at the application level so that any XAML document that wanted to use the brush could do so, like so:

```
<Grid x:Name="LayoutRoot">
  <TextBlock Foreground="{StaticResource mainBrush}"
            Text="Hello World" />
...
</Grid>
```

Although this example shows a brush (which is a commonly shared resource), it is not limited to only brushes. Any creatable object can be used in this way. In addition, when you want to share these resources across projects, you can accomplish this with `ResourceDictionary` objects. **Resource dictionaries** are XAML files that contain shared resources that can be imported into App.xaml using merged dictionaries. These dictionaries can be flat XAML files or can be contained in separate assemblies that are referenced to your phone application. For more information on merged dictionaries, see the documentation.[3]

Understanding Styles

Although sharing resources can help you to define a common look and feel, the styling stack extends this idea by allowing you to specify the default properties for controls in a common place. The `Style` object allows you to create these default properties:

```
<Style TargetType="TextBox"
       x:Key="mainTextBox">
  <Setter Property="FontSize"
          Value="18" />
  <Setter Property="FontFamily"
          Value="Segoe WP Bold" />
</Style>
```

The `Style` object takes the type of object it can be applied to and then a set of `Setter` objects that define default values for properties. In this example, the `FontSize` and `FontFamily` for a `TextBox` are supplied. To apply

---

3 http://shawnw.me/Xw90bf

this style to an object, you can map it to the Style property on an element via the StaticResource markup extension, like so:

```
<TextBox Style="{StaticResource mainTextBox}" />
```

By setting this TextBox's Style property using the StaticResource markup extension, the default property values of the TextBox will be set using the Style. Styles are just named resources, so you would typically place them in the App.xaml file along with other resources. In addition, you can use resources inside your styles, like so:

```
<Application.Resources>
  <SolidColorBrush x:Key="mainBrush"
                   Color="Blue" />
  <Style TargetType="TextBox"
         x:Key="mainTextBox">
    <Setter Property="FontSize"
            Value="18" />
    <Setter Property="FontFamily"
            Value="Segoe WP Bold" />
    <Setter Property="Foreground"
            Value="{StaticResource mainBrush}" />
  </Style>
</Application.Resources>
```

In this way, the shared resources can cascade down into the styling stack. In addition, the Styles themselves can be cascaded by using the BasedOn property:

```
<Application.Resources>
  <SolidColorBrush x:Key="mainBrush"
                   Color="Blue" />
  <Style TargetType="TextBox"
         x:Name="baseTextBox">
    <Setter Property="FontSize"
            Value="18" />
    <Setter Property="FontFamily"
            Value="Segoe WP Bold" />
  </Style>
  <Style TargetType="TextBox"
         x:Key="mainTextBox"
         BasedOn="{StaticResource baseTextBox}">
    <Setter Property="Foreground"
            Value="{StaticResource mainBrush}" />
  </Style>
</Application.Resources>
```

Finally, styles can be polymorphic. In other words, the TargetType might apply to a base class and be applied to all objects of that type. For example

```xml
<Application.Resources>
  <SolidColorBrush x:Key="mainBrush"
                   Color="Blue" />
  <Style TargetType="Control"
         x:Name="baseControl">
    <Setter Property="BorderBrush"
            Value="Black" />
  </Style>
  <Style TargetType="TextBox"
         x:Key="mainTextBox"
         BasedOn="{StaticResource baseControl}">
    <Setter Property="FontSize"
            Value="18" />
    <Setter Property="FontFamily"
            Value="Segoe WP Bold" />
    <Setter Property="Foreground"
            Value="{StaticResource mainBrush}" />
  </Style>
</Application.Resources>
```

Because the TargetType of the base style was Control, it could be used as the BasedOn for any controls (or even the Style for any control that derived from the Control class).

Implicit Styles

Although you will often use named styles (and the StaticResource markup extension) to tie a Style to a XAML element (as shown in the preceding section), you can also create styles that apply to elements by default. These are called **implicit styles.** To create an implicit style, your style must not include a key. Here's an example:

```xml
<Application.Resources>
  <Style TargetType="TextBox">
    <Setter Property="FontSize"
            Value="18" />
    <Setter Property="FontFamily"
            Value="Segoe WP Bold" />
  </Style>
</Application.Resources>
```

By eliminating the x:Key on the Style, the style will apply to every element of the TargetType (for example, TextBox). If an element is specifically styled with an explicit (for example, named) style, the implicit style is completely replaced. Therefore, you can have either an implicit or an explicit style applied to a specific XAML element, not both. In most cases you will have an implicit style for the main style of a control, then specific explicit styles to handle specific use cases for controls.

One big difference in implicit styles is that the TargetType is not polymorphic, so it applies to only the specific type, not derived types. For instance, if you create an implicit style of type "Control," it will apply only to XAML elements of the Control class specifically; TextBox and Button elements (which derive from Control) will not use the style at all. The other rules for styles (for example, using base resources, cascading styles with BasedOn) all apply.

Where Are We?

This chapter introduced you to the basics of the XAML ecosystem in XAML for Windows Phone. Now you are ready to start designing the user interfaces for your applications. I have only touched the surface of the nature of XAML, so you should not assume that I described every element and every attribute in this chapter. Use the documentation to fill out your knowledge of XAML.

Whereas this chapter focused on understanding the textual representation of the XAML, the next chapter will introduce you to using controls in your applications to interact with users.

4

Controls

While the drawing grammar is useful for designing an exciting and dynamic application for the phone, most of the functionality users expect has to do with interacting with your application. That is where controls come in. **Controls** support direct interaction with users. The type of interaction depends on the control. For example, buttons and sliders use the touch interface; the TextBox uses a keyboard (onscreen or hardware). Using controls in your phone applications requires that you think differently about how you build applications. If you simply take any experience you have on the Web or in desktop applications and try to apply it to the phone, your application will not be easy to use. Taking the smaller screen and touch interface into account will help you build compelling applications using controls.

Controls in XAML

Controls are no different from any other XAML elements you have seen so far. For example, here is the TextBox control:

```
<Grid>
  <TextBox Text="Hello World" />
</Grid>
```

This TextBox will show up like the drawing elements but will support the user interacting with the control through touch (as evidenced by the cursor shown in Figure 4.1).

FIGURE 4.1   TextBox control example

Out of the box, XAML for Windows Phone supports these controls:

- Button
- CheckBox
- HyperlinkButton
- ListBox
- PasswordBox
- ProgressBar
- RadioButton
- RichTextBox
- Slider
- WebBrowser
- TextBox

These controls represent the main form of interaction with users. Although this list is somewhat abbreviated when compared to a typical development framework, these controls are specialized to support the Windows Phone touch interface. Most of these controls are built larger than you might imagine (and with large margins) to accommodate users touching them.

Most of the controls in XAML fit into one of three categories, which should help you to understand how the controls are expected to work:

- Simple controls
- Content controls
- List controls

Silverlight Controls

If you are coming to this book with existing Silverlight knowledge, you might be surprised by the abbreviated nature of the list of controls to be supported. Although many of the controls in Silverlight 4 (and the Silverlight Toolkit for Silverlight 4) will work with Windows Phone, Microsoft has not redesigned these controls to be easy to use with the phone. If you need these other controls, they are not forbidden; it is just up to you to change the way they look to conform to the Metro design language as well as make them work sufficiently with the touch-based input that is available on the phone.

The controls Microsoft chose have specific integration with the phone's touch interface. When you start to look at other controls (for example, ToolTip, Calendar, and so on), you will see that finding the right functionality for these controls in a touch environment is not simple. Therefore, you might want to stick with the built-in controls until you have a good feel for the way touch affects how users interact with the controls.

Simple Controls

The simple controls include TextBox, PasswordBox, Slider, and ProgressBar. These controls have a simple API in that they do a specific job and look a certain way. They are, in a word, simple:

```
<StackPanel>
  <TextBox Text="Hello" />
  <PasswordBox PasswordChar="*" />
  <Slider Value="5" />
  <ProgressBar IsIndeterminate="True" />
</StackPanel>
```

Using Keyboards

The TextBox and PasswordBox controls support text input by the user. For devices with physical keyboards this is simple, but for the majority of devices (that don't have physical keyboards) you must use a **software input panel (SIP).** A SIP is shown when either of these controls has received focus. You can see the default SIP in Figure 4.2 (both the portrait and landscape versions).

The SIP attempts to put the most common keys directly on the keyboard but also supports ways of getting at the rest of the characters. Figure 4.3 shows you these special keys. These include the Shift key (#1 in the figure), the &123 key (#2), and special long-hold keys (such as the period key, #3).

The long-hold keys offer a way to pop up commonly used keys without making the keyboard looked cramped. For example, in Figure 4.4 you can see the standard SIP's period key when the user holds it for more than two seconds.

FIGURE 4.2   Software input panel

FIGURE 4.3   Special SIP keys

FIGURE 4.4   **Long-hold keys**

This default look of the SIP is only one of many layouts that are supported on the phone. When you are building applications that require text input, you will need to tell the controls which SIP layout to use. Deciding on the features of the various SIP layouts is important. The faster users can enter data, the happier they will be.

Changing the look of the SIP is as simple as using something called an **input scope.** For example, you can specify that you want to have some chat features (such as a button for smiley faces) by using the chat input scope, like so:

```
<TextBox InputScope="Chat" />
```

This changes the SIP to be friendlier for a simple chat, as shown in Figure 4.5.

The chat input scope adds an emoticon button, as well as an Autocorrect panel, to help users more quickly type what they want to say. The items in the long-hold keys are also customized for the type of task that the input scope specifies. For example, when the user is typing on the SIP using the chat input scope, the exclamation point character is located in the period's long-hold list. But if the user is typing a URL, the colon and slash characters are in the long-hold keys.

FIGURE 4.5 Chat input scope

Although there are a large number of input scopes you can use, for most applications the InputScope values listed in Table 4.1 should help you pick the right one for your use.

TABLE 4.1 Common InputScope Values

Input Scope	Layout	Use Case
Default	QWERTY	When entering nondictionary words such as usernames
Text	QWERTY	When entering text that can be helped by autocorrect and capitalization (includes visual indicator of mis-spelled words)
Chat	QWERTY	When constructing chat messages (where abbreviations are more important) such as Twitter or SMS messages

Input Scope	Layout	Use Case
URL	QWERTY	When entering an Internet URL
EmailSmtpAddress	QWERTY	When entering an email address
TelephoneNumber	12-key	When entering phone numbers
Search	QWERTY	When the user wants to enter search phrases (includes visual indicator of misspelled words)
NameOrPhoneNumber	QWERTY	When entering names (for example, SMS messages) but quick access to a 12-key layout for phone number entry is desired
Date	QWERTY	When entering both numeric and character dates (for example, 12/12/2011 and December 12, 2011)
Maps	QWERTY	When entering addresses; simplifies entry by defaulting to numeric entry

RichTextBox Control

The Windows Phone SDK includes a specialized control for displaying formatted text called the RichTextBox. With the RichTextBox control, you can format text by using a simplified markup including paragraph, bold, italic, and hyperlink tags.

The format is meant to provide some level of formatting like HTML text allows without requiring the complexity (or power) of the full HTML stack. Here's an example:

```
<RichTextBox>-
  <Paragraph>You can use inline tags to format
    <Bold>bold</Bold> text and even add
    <Italic>italics</Italic>.
  </Paragraph>
  <Paragraph>Using this Markup you can add
    <LineBreak /> line breaks and even add
    <Hyperlink NavigateUri="/SomePage.xaml">hyperlinks</Hyperlink>!
  </Paragraph>
  <Paragraph>Also arbitrary XAML:
    <InlineUIContainer>
      <StackPanel>
```

```
        <Ellipse Fill="Red"
                  Width="25"
                  Height="25" />
        <TextBox />
      </StackPanel>
    </InlineUIContainer>
  </Paragraph>
</RichTextBox>
```

The `RichTextBox` control supports a number of tags, as shown in Table 4.2.

TABLE 4.2   RichTextBox Markup Tags

Tag	Description
Paragraph	Represents the main container for text information. The `RichTextBox` typically contains a collection of Paragraph tags.
Bold	Formats the text within the tag to be bold.
Italic	Formats the text within the tag to be italic.
Underline	Formats the text within the tag to be underlined.
Run	Contains unformatted text to add formatting to.
Span	Contains any elements to add formatting to. Cannot contain the Paragraph, InlineUIContainer, or Hyperlink tags in current version of Windows Phone.
LineBreak	Inserts an explicit break in the text formatting.
Hyperlink	Used to create arbitrary text that, when clicked, will open a new page.
InlineUIContainer	Allows arbitrary XAML to be inserted inline into the text of the `RichTextBox`.

▪ Silverlight Developers

For those of you who are using Silverlight for the desktop, the `RichTextBox` on the phone just supports read-only mode.

Content Controls

Content controls specifically allow you to contain arbitrary XAML inside them. The most common of these is the Button control. For example, to simply show a text message in a button you could just set the Content property, like so:

```
<StackPanel>
  <Button Content="Click Me" />
</StackPanel>
```

You can see that the content of the control ("Click Me") is now inside the button, as shown in Figure 4.6.

FIGURE 4.6 **Simple button with simple content**

But the content can take arbitrary XAML content as well:

```
<StackPanel>
  <Button>
    <Button.Content>
      <StackPanel>
        <Image Source="headshot.png"
               Width="100"/>
        <TextBlock>Hello</TextBlock>
      </StackPanel>
    </Button.Content>
  </Button>
</StackPanel>
```

This results in a button containing XAML, as shown in Figure 4.7.

FIGURE 4.7 **Button with XAML content**

Notice that the content is inside the button, not replacing the XAML that makes up the button. Setting the Content property allows you to specify what is inside the button (or in most content controls, what is inside some part of the control). A content control is any control that derives from the ContentControl class. These include Button, CheckBox, RadioButton, and HyperlinkButton.

List Controls

List controls support showing any arbitrary list of items. They do this by using a property called ItemsSource. This property takes any collection that supports IEnumerable or IList. This means any type of collection (from simple arrays to complex generic collections) is supported by the list controls. The ListBox defined in XAML is pretty standard:

```
<StackPanel>
  <ListBox x:Name="theList" />
</StackPanel>
```

The real trick is when you set some collection to the ItemsSource property:

```
public partial class MainPage : PhoneApplicationPage
{
  // Constructor
  public MainPage()
  {
    InitializeComponent();

    theList.ItemsSource = new string[] { "One", "Two", "Three" };
  }
}
```

Setting the ItemsSource will display the collection and allow individual items to be selected, as shown in Figure 4.8.

FIGURE 4.8   List box

Other list controls will follow this same interface (of setting the collection to an ItemsSource) to set the collection. By using these simple control sets, you should be able to create great experiences for your users.

Phone-Specific Controls

So far all the controls you've seen have existed in other versions of XAML (for example WPF, Silverlight, and Windows 8). But some controls are specifically for use on the phone. The two most obvious are the Pivot and Panorama controls that enable you to create multipanel controls in a cohesive way. First, we'll discuss the Panorama control.

Panorama **Control**

The Panorama control creates a virtual canvas of several panels that the user can scroll into view as she wants. The Panorama control allows you to build these virtual canvases out of one or more panels. You can see an example of a panorama application in Figure 4.9.

FIGURE 4.9   **Panorama application**

The Panorama control requires that you add a reference to the Microsoft. Phone.Controls assembly. Likewise, you must import the new namespace into your XAML document, as shown here:[1]

```
<phone:PhoneApplicationPage
   x:Class="MyFirstPanorama.MainPage"
   xmlns:ctrls="clr-namespace:Microsoft.Phone.Controls;
              assembly=Microsoft.Phone.Controls"
   xmlns="http://schemas.microsoft.com/winfx/2006/xaml/presentation"
```

After you have the new namespace you can use the Panorama and PanoramaItem elements to create the panorama:

```
<Grid x:Name="LayoutRoot"
        Background="Transparent">
   <ctrls:Panorama Title="my panorama">
     <ctrls:PanoramaItem Header="first">
       <Grid>
         <ListBox />
       </Grid>
     </ctrls:PanoramaItem>
     <ctrls:PanoramaItem Header="second">
       <Grid>
         <ListBox Width="500" />
       </Grid>
     </ctrls:PanoramaItem>
   </ctrls:Panorama>
 </Grid>
```

The Panorama element supports a Title attribute, which is used to display text that goes across the entire Panorama control. Inside the Panorama control you can use one or more PanoramaItem elements. Each PanoramaItem element represents one second in the panorama. The PivotItem's Header property controls what is shown above each PanoramaItem section. You can see the panorama in Figure 4.10.

The Panorama element's Title property is labeled #1 in Figure 4.10. You can see that the title is shown across all the panes, so it is never shown in its entirety. The two panorama items in the design are shown as individual

---

1   Note that the namespace has a line break in it before the "assembly" part of the namespace. This is for illustration. In your XAML, the entire contents of the namespace should have no line breaks.

panes. The area labeled #2 shows the first PanoramaItem element, and the area labeled #3 shows the second PanoramaItem. Notice that the next panorama item is hinted at on the right side of the screen.

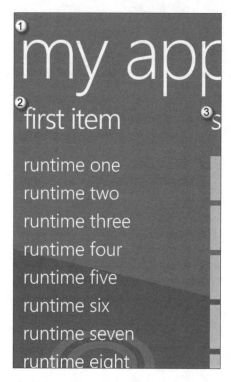

FIGURE 4.10 **Panorama explained**

Panoramas commonly have a background image that slides behind the panorama as the user moves from one panorama item to the next (using a parallax effect). To get that behavior, you can set the Background element of the panorama using an ImageBrush. For example, you would use the following code to paint the background with an image in the .xap file:

```
<ctrls:Panorama Title="my panorama">
  <ctrls:Panorama.Background>
    <ImageBrush ImageSource="/back.jpg"
                Opacity=".2" />
  </ctrls:Panorama.Background>
  ...
```

Although panorama sections (for example, `PanoramaItem` elements) are meant to take up most of a single screen on the phone, other sections can be larger than a single screen. You can see that the panorama is larger than a single screen, while the phone indicates that each pane of the panorama can be seen on the screen as the user navigates it. This is consistent with the design paradigm for the phone.

FIGURE 4.11   **Landscape sections**

To use landscape sections, you must make a couple of changes. By default, a panorama section will take up most of a single page. To get the larger panes, you must both size the `PanoramaItem`'s contents to be as large as necessary (using the `Width` attribute) as well as set the orientation of the `PanoramaItem` to `Landscape`, as shown with the second `PanoramaItem` in the code that follows:

```
<ctrls:Panorama Title="my panorama">
  <ctrls:Panorama.Background>
    <ImageBrush ImageSource="/back.jpg"
                Opacity=".2" />
  </ctrls:Panorama.Background>
  <ctrls:PanoramaItem Header="first">
    <Grid>
      <ListBox />
    </Grid>
  </ctrls:PanoramaItem>
```

```
<ctrls:PanoramaItem Header="second"
                    Orientation="Horizontal">
  <Grid Width="750">
    <ListBox />
  </Grid>
</ctrls:PanoramaItem>
<ctrls:PanoramaItem Header="third">
  <Grid>
    <ListBox Width="750" />
  </Grid>
</ctrls:PanoramaItem>
</ctrls:Panorama>
```

The design guidelines specify that you should have no more than four or five sections in your Panorama controls—fewer than that if you are using landscape sections. The general rule of thumb is for the entire panorama to be fewer than 2,000 pixels wide, although the smaller it is, the easier it will be for users to understand the intent.

Pivot **Control**

In addition to the Panorama control, there is another phone-specific control called a Pivot control. The Pivot control is also used to show multiple sections, but the Pivot control can handle a larger number of items than the Panorama control. The chief reason for this is that a pivot section takes the entire width of the page instead of having overlapping sections. For example, the phone's Search page uses a Pivot control, as shown in Figure 4.12.

In the Pivot control, headers at the top of the page show both the currently selected section (#1 in Figure 4.12) and other pages that are not currently selected (#2). The currently selected section is usually white with the other sections gray to indicate a difference between the sections. The Pivot control always displays the currently selected section's title at the upper left and scrolls the rest of the labels to the right (and off the screen typically). The user switches between sections by swiping left or right or by pressing on the section headers to go to that section automatically. As the section is changed, the content area (#3) is changed to reflect that change.

FIGURE 4.12   Pivot control

The Pivot control is in the same assembly and namespace as the Panorama control (Microsoft.Phone.Controls), so adding a reference to the assembly and XML namespace is required, as you saw earlier for the Panorama control. Building a Pivot control in XAML is similar to building a Panorama control in that the Pivot control can take one or more PivotItem elements, like so:

```xml
<ctrls:Pivot>
  <ctrls:PivotItem Header="first">
    <ListBox />
  </ctrls:PivotItem>
  <ctrls:PivotItem Header="second">
    <ListBox />
  </ctrls:PivotItem>
  <ctrls:PivotItem Header="third">
    <ListBox />
  </ctrls:PivotItem>
```

```
<ctrls:PivotItem Header="fourth">
  <ListBox />
</ctrls:PivotItem>
</ctrls:Pivot>
```

Like the `PanoramaItem` element, the `PivotItem` uses the `Header` property to specify the text on top of the `Pivot` control. The preceding XAML results in the page shown in Figure 4.13.

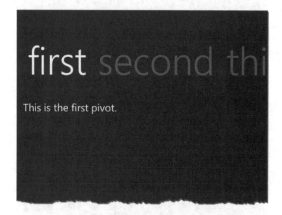

FIGURE 4.13   `Pivot` **control in action**

As the user clicks the headers or swipes, he can go to the other sections. As with the `Panorama` control, the sections loop, so when the user is on the last section, the first section is to the right of the last page, as shown in Figure 4.14.

FIGURE 4.14   **Looping pivot sections**

Data Binding

Writing applications for the phone will likely involve data of some sort. XAML's support for data binding helps you build your applications in a much more powerful way, but what is data binding exactly? **Data binding** is simply a way to take data from a source (for example, the value of a property on an object) and show it in a XAML element. If that XAML element is a control, it also supports pushing changes back to the source of the data. Although that is a pretty basic explanation, the explanation is correct. Data binding is profoundly simple. This simplicity makes it very powerful.

Simple Data Binding

At the most basic level, a **binding** is a connector to pull data from a data source and put it in an element's property. As you can see in Figure 4.15, a binding is in the middle of the data and the element (Control).

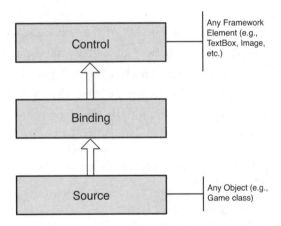

FIGURE 4.15   Simple data binding

Bindings are defined as a markup extension. For example, here is a TextBox bound to the Name property:

```
<TextBox Text="{Binding Name, Source={StaticResource myData}}" />
```

The Binding markup extension first takes a path to the property to be bound to and then a number of optional elements. As you can see in this example, the binding is pulling from a resource object called myData. When the data binding happens, it takes the source of the data binding and uses the property path (the Name in this case) to navigate to the data it needs to put in the TextBox's Text. The path to the property must be a public property because it uses reflection to call the getter of the public property to access the data from the source.

Having to specify the source for bindings is relatively rare, though, because when the source of an object changes, you would have to change it in a number of places. For example, this XAML would show a simple editor for some data:

```
<StackPanel>
  <TextBlock>Name</TextBlock>
  <TextBox Text="{Binding Name, Source={StaticResource myData}}" />
  <TextBlock>Phone Number</TextBlock>
  <TextBox Text="{Binding Phone, Source={StaticResource myData}}" />
  <TextBlock>BirthDate</TextBlock>
  <TextBox Text="{Binding BirthDay, Source={StaticResource myData}}" />
</StackPanel>
```

Imagine that if the source changed, all of the TextBoxes would need to be rebound. Instead, data binding uses a property called DataContext, which simply allows for the source of the data binding to exist along the hierarchy of the XAML. For example, if the DataContext were set at the StackPanel, all the controls that attempt data binding inside the StackPanel would get their data from the DataContext instead of needing specific sources:

```
<StackPanel DataContext="{StaticResource myData}">
  <TextBlock>Name</TextBlock>
  <TextBox Text="{Binding Name}" />
  <TextBlock>Phone Number</TextBlock>
  <TextBox Text="{Binding Phone}" />
  <TextBlock>BirthDate</TextBlock>
  <TextBox Text="{Binding BirthDay}" />
</StackPanel>
```

When the bindings pull their data, they will look for a source, and when they don't have one, they'll search for the first non-null data source in the hierarchy. In this case, they'll find it at the StackPanel level and will use that and the source for the data binding. The search for a DataContext will continue up the hierarchy until a valid DataContext is found. This walking of the XAML tree is not limited to the current XAML document. If the data binding is happening inside a control that is used on another XAML document, it will continue up through all the parents until it exhausts the entire object tree.

Data binding supports three modes, as described in Table 4.3.

TABLE 4.3   **Data Binding Modes**

Type	Description	Example
OneTime	Pulls data from a source after.	`<TextBox Text="{Binding Name,` `                  Mode=OneTime}" />`
OneWay	(Default) Pulls data from a source. As the source's data changes, it can pull those changes into the control.	`<TextBox Text="{Binding Name}" />`
TwoWay	Pulls data from a source and pushes changes back to the source as the data changes (normally on the control losing focus).	`<TextBox Text="{Binding Name,` `                  Mode=TwoWay}" />`

The pushing and pulling of changes is performed via reflection so that all binding modes work with any object. There are no requirements for that object to work with data binding. The one exception to that is if you want changes to the source object itself to be reflected in the controls via data binding. For that to work, your source classes must support a simple interface called INotifyPropertyChanged. When the source data changes, it notifies the binding that the data has changes that will cause the binding to reread the data and change the data in the control, as shown in Figure 4.16.

Using a DataTemplate

As you saw earlier in this chapter, list controls can show any list that supports IList or IEnumerable, but that's only part of the story. List controls also support the ability to use DataTemplates to customize the look of individual items in the list. You can use a DataTemplate to specify the `ItemTemplate` to use arbitrary XAML to define what is contained in a `ListBox`. For example:

```
<ListBox ItemsSource="{StaticResource theData}">
  <ListBox.ItemTemplate>
    <DataTemplate>
      <StackPanel>
        <TextBlock Text="{Binding Name}" />
        <Image Source="{Binding ImageUrl}" />
      </StackPanel>
    </DataTemplate>
  </ListBox.ItemTemplate>
</ListBox>
```

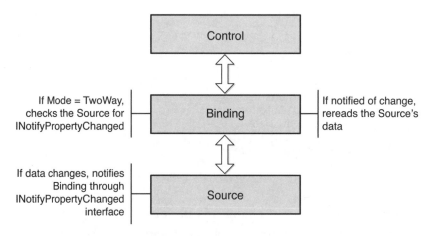

FIGURE 4.16   **Changes in the source**

Because this `ListBox` creates its individual items, it will use the `DataTemplate` as a factory to create the XAML that is contained inside. The `DataContext` for the created XAML becomes the individual item to be shown in the `ListBox` so that the data binding inside the `DataTemplate` works.

Improving Scrolling Performance

When binding against collections on the phone, you must be aware of the implications of how large amounts of data can affect the performance of the scrolling of list controls (for example, `ListBox`, `ScrollViewer`, `ItemsSource`, and so on). The two minor tweaks you can make to improve this performance are image creation and scroll handling.

For image creation, you can decide how images are actually loaded and decoded. Under the covers of the Image's source is a constructed object called a BitmapImage. The BitmapImage has a property called CreationOptions in which you can specify when an image is loaded. By default, the CreationOptions specify that images should be **delay-loaded.** This means images are not loaded until they can be seen on the surface of a page. In addition to delay-loading the image, you can also specify that an image is loaded on the background thread. Specifying these two things can improve the overall performance of images in a collection. To specify this, you would need to break out the Image.Source property and set a BitmapImage in the control template, like this:

```
<ListBox ItemsSource="{StaticResource theData}">
  <ListBox.ItemTemplate>
    <DataTemplate>
      <StackPanel>
        <TextBlock Text="{Binding Name}" />
        <Image>
          <Image.Source>
            <BitmapImage UriSource="{Binding ImageUrl}"
              CreateOptions="DelayCreation,BackgroundCreation" />
          </Image.Source>
        </Image>
      </StackPanel>
    </DataTemplate>
  </ListBox.ItemTemplate>
</ListBox>
```

You can see in this example that the Image is using the verbose XAML syntax to set the Source to a BitmapImage object. The UriSource takes the same binding the earlier example used for the Source. Finally, the CreateOptions is set to both DelayCreation and BackgroundCreation to improve the performance of loading this image in the user interface.

Additionally, you can improve the performance of scrolling by allowing the object responsible for scrolling in lists (the ScrollViewer class) to decide whether scrolling should be handled by the operating system (the default) or by the control. Although in general you should allow the operating system to manage the scrolling, in some cases you will want to be notified of scroll changes for specific needs. In other words, you need to have a very good reason to change scrolling responsibility. To change the manipulation mode, you can specify the ScrollViewer.ManipulationMode attached property on any list control (for example, ListBox, ItemsControl, ScrollViewer, and so on) to the value of Control, as shown here:

```
<ListBox ItemsSource="{StaticResource theData}"
         ScrollViewer.ManipulationMode="Control">
<ListBox.ItemTemplate>
  <DataTemplate>
    <StackPanel>
      <TextBlock Text="{Binding Name}" />
      <Image>
        <Image.Source>
          <BitmapImage UriSource="{Binding ImageUrl}"
            CreateOptions="DelayCreation,BackgroundCreation" />
        </Image.Source>
      </Image>
    </StackPanel>
  </DataTemplate>
</ListBox.ItemTemplate>
```

Binding Formatting

During the data binding process, you have the opportunity to format the data directly in the binding. Several binding properties allow you to specify what happens during binding. These include StringFormat, FallbackValue, and TargetNullValue. Each can affect what the user sees during data binding. For example, you can include these as additional properties inside the binding, as shown here:

```
<TextBox Text="{Binding ReleaseDate,
                StringFormat=d,
                FallbackValue='n/a',
                TargetNullValue='n/a'}" />
```

The StringFormat property is used to specify a .NET format string to be used during binding. This can be any .NET format string that matches the type. If the .NET format string contains spaces, you should surround it with single quotation marks. The StringFormat is used both to format the data when pushing it to the control as well as to parse the data going back to the source.

The FallbackValue is used to show a value when the binding fails. A binding can fail if it does not find a source (for example, source or data context is null) or when the source does not have a valid property to bind to.

Finally, the `TargetNullValue` is used to indicate that the binding succeeded, but the value of the bound result is null.

Element Binding

You can also create bindings that allow you to create a link between two XAML elements. This is called **element binding.** To use element binding, you can specify the `ElementName` as part of the binding syntax, like so:

```
<Slider Minimum="10"
        Maximum="36"
        x:Name="fontSizeSlider" />
<TextBox FontSize="{Binding Value, ElementName=fontSizeSlider}"
         Text="Make It Grow" />
```

The size of the font in the `TextBox` is being set based on the value of the `Slider` (named `fontSizeSlider`). In this way, you can use elements in the XAML to supply data to other elements in the XAML. A more conventional use of element binding is to set the data context of a container based on the selected value of a control, like so:

```
<ListBox ItemsSource="{Binding Games}"
         x:Name="theList" />
<StackPanel DataContext="{Binding SelectedItem,
                                  ElementName=theList}">
  <TextBlock>Name</TextBlock>
  <TextBox Text="{Binding Name}" />
  <TextBlock>Phone Number</TextBlock>
  <TextBox Text="{Binding Phone}" />
</StackPanel>
```

In this example, the `StackPanel` is setting its `DataContext` to whichever item is selected in the `ListBox`. In this way, you can show and/or edit the data in the `StackPanel` based on the selection of the `ListBox`.

Converters

Data binding takes properties from objects and moves them into properties on controls. At times, the types of the properties will not match or will need some level of manipulation to work. That is where converters come in. **Converters** are stateless classes that can perform specific conversions during the binding process. To be a converter, a class must implement the IValueConverter interface. This interface has two methods, Convert and ConvertBack, to allow for conversions in both directions during binding. For example, a simple converter to make dates display as short date strings looks like so:

```
public class DateConverter : IValueConverter
{

  public object Convert(object value,
                        Type targetType,
                        object parameter,
                        CultureInfo culture)
  {
    if (targetType == typeof(string) &&
        value.GetType() == typeof(DateTime))
    {
      return ((DateTime)value).ToShortDateString();
    }

    // No Conversion
    return value;

  }

  public object ConvertBack(object value,
                            Type targetType,
                            object parameter,
                            CultureInfo culture)
  {
    if (targetType == typeof(DateTime) &&
      value.GetType() == typeof(string))
    {
      DateTime newDate;

      if (DateTime.TryParse((string)value, out newDate))
      {
        return newDate;
      }
    }

    // No Conversion
    return value;
  }
}
```

Converters are created as resources (usually at the application level) like so:

```
<Application x:Class="PhoneControls.App"
             xmlns="..."
             xmlns:x="..."
             xmlns:phone="..."
             xmlns:shell="..."
             xmlns:my="clr-namespace:PhoneControls">
  <Application.Resources>
    <my:DateConverter x:Key="dateConverter" />
  </Application.Resources>
  ...
</Application>
```

By creating the converter at the application level, you can use it throughout the application. Finally, we can now use the converter directly in our data binding, like so:

```
<StackPanel DataContext="{Binding SelectedItem,
ElementName=theList}">
  <TextBlock>Name</TextBlock>
  <TextBox Text="{Binding Name, Mode=TwoWay}" />
  <TextBlock>Phone Number</TextBlock>
  <TextBox Text="{Binding PhoneNumber, Mode=TwoWay}" />
  <TextBlock>Phone Number</TextBlock>
  <TextBox Text="{Binding ReleaseDate,
                  Mode=TwoWay,
                  Converter={StaticResource dateConverter}}"
/>
</StackPanel>
```

During the conversion of the underlying data (in this case a DateTime), the DateConverter class is used. When moving the data from the source to the control, Convert is called; when the data is pushed back to the source, the ConvertBack method is called. As in this example, converters are often used just for formatting and not real conversion.

Data Binding Errors

By design, data binding errors do not cause exceptions. This behavior is desirable because the source of a data binding might enter a valid and an invalid state a lot during the life of your application. Let's take the example we saw earlier where we have a list of controls bound to the SelectedItem of a ListBox. When there is no selection in the ListBox, the data binding is failing. Throwing an exception in that case would be the wrong thing to do. So, as a developer, you will need a way to actually see data binding failures. Luckily, you can see them pretty clearly in the Visual Studio Output window. When running your application, you can use the View menu to show the Output window, as shown in Figure 4.17.

FIGURE 4.17 Output window

When data binding fails, it adds a debug message to the Output window. For example, if you used the wrong path in a Binding (for example, Title instead of Name) you could see this in the Output window, as shown in Figure 4.18.

Bad paths aren't the only binding errors that show up in the Output window; bad conversions (really, any exceptions) do as well. For example, if a user attempted to enter a bad date (for example, 2/31/2010) into a date field, the Output window would show that error, too, during data binding (as seen in Figure 4.19).

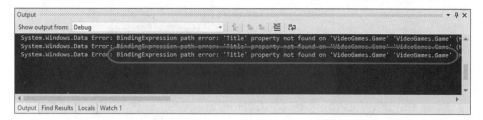

FIGURE 4.18 Binding error shown in the Output window

FIGURE 4.19 Conversion error shown in the Output window

Control Templates

Although property-based styling is very powerful, it might not let you change the look of the controls in dramatic ways. That is where control templates come in. Every control has XAML that defines how a control is drawn. For example, the humble button uses this XAML to draw itself:

```
<Grid Background="Transparent">
    ...
    <Border x:Name="ButtonBackground"
            BorderBrush="{TemplateBinding BorderBrush}"
            BorderThickness="{TemplateBinding BorderThickness}"
            Background="{TemplateBinding Background}"
            CornerRadius="0"
            Margin="{StaticResource PhoneTouchTargetOverhang}">
        <ContentControl x:Name="ContentContainer"
                        ContentTemplate="{TemplateBinding
                                                ContentTemplate}"
                        Content="{TemplateBinding Content}"
                        Foreground="{TemplateBinding Foreground}"
                        HorizontalAlignment="{TemplateBinding
                                        HorizontalContentAlignment}"
```

```
                    Padding="{TemplateBinding Padding}"
                    VerticalAlignment="{TemplateBinding
                                VerticalContentAlignment}" />
    </Border>
  </Grid>
```

Even though you think of controls as atomic elements, there is XAML inside the control to define the look and feel of the control. Control templates are used to redefine this XAML for any control.

Control templates are part of the style that is applied to a control. The ControlTemplate is the value of the Template property of any control. Here's an example:

```
<Style x:Key="ButtonStyle1"
        TargetType="Button">
  <Setter Property="Template">
    <Setter.Value>
      <ControlTemplate TargetType="Button">
        <Grid Background="Transparent">
          ...
        </Grid>
      </ControlTemplate>
    </Setter.Value>
  </Setter>
</Style>
```

The contents of the ControlTemplate contain the XAML that the particular control should use (Button in this case). As you define the XAML that makes up the look of a particular control, you can use a markup extension called a **template binding** to pull the value of a property into your XAML. For example:

```
<ControlTemplate TargetType="Button">
  <Grid Background="Transparent">
    <Border x:Name="ButtonBackground"
            BorderBrush="{TemplateBinding BorderBrush}"
            Background="{TemplateBinding Background}">
      ...
    </Border>
  </Grid>
</ControlTemplate>
```

By using template bindings, the natural value of the property will be used as the value inside the control template. This value could come from the default value in the control or from a style setter, or it could specifically be set on an instance of the control. Template bindings enable you to use whichever property value is supposed to be shown in the control.

For some controls, the XAML must have certain elements to ensure that the control still works. For example, the WebBrowser control requires that part of the XAML be a Border element named PresentationContainer. That way, the control knows where to show the web content. This contract between you and the control author is called a **template part** (many controls do not have any template parts). The template parts that are required are documented as attributes on the controls themselves (as shown in Figure 4.20).

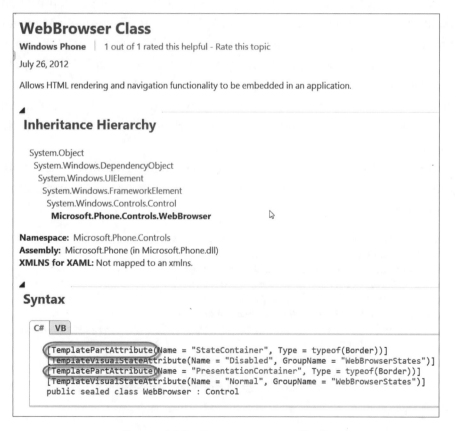

WebBrowser Class

Windows Phone | 1 out of 1 rated this helpful - Rate this topic

July 26, 2012

Allows HTML rendering and navigation functionality to be embedded in an application.

◢
Inheritance Hierarchy

System.Object
  System.Windows.DependencyObject
    System.Windows.UIElement
      System.Windows.FrameworkElement
      System.Windows.Controls.Control
        Microsoft.Phone.Controls.WebBrowser

Namespace: Microsoft.Phone.Controls
Assembly: Microsoft.Phone (in Microsoft.Phone.dll)
XMLNS for XAML: Not mapped to an xmlns.

◢
Syntax

C# | VB

```
[TemplatePartAttribute(Name = "StateContainer", Type = typeof(Border))]
[TemplateVisualStateAttribute(Name = "Disabled", GroupName = "WebBrowserStates")]
[TemplatePartAttribute(Name = "PresentationContainer", Type = typeof(Border))]
[TemplateVisualStateAttribute(Name = "Normal", GroupName = "WebBrowserStates")]
public sealed class WebBrowser : Control
```

FIGURE 4.20 TemplatePart **attribute**

The structure of the XAML in a control template represents the look of the control, but in addition you can specify the feel of an application. The feel of an application is the way the control can interact with the users. For instance, the Button class changes its appearance when pressed to give feedback to the user that she has correctly pressed the button. This is how the feel of an application works.

You can create the feel of an application using a structure called the **Visual State Manager.** With the Visual State Manager you can define animations that represent individual states for the control. For example, you might use the Visual State Manager to specify states for "selected" and "unselected." As the control changes this state, the visual look of the control could be changed based on the animation values in the Visual State Manager.

These states are broken up into groups so that a single control can be in more than one state. For example, two of the Visual State Manager groups that the TextBox has are CommonStates (which represents states such as Disabled and ReadOnly) and FocusStates (which represents whether the control has focus). The groups define a set of states where only one state can be active at a time. For example, you can have your control be Disabled and Focused but not Disabled and ReadOnly. The states in a group are mutually exclusive.

To define the groups and states for the Visual State Manager, the XAML can contain a VisualStateManager.VisualStateGroups property (as an attached property):

```
<ControlTemplate TargetType="Button">
  <Grid Background="Transparent">
    <VisualStateManager.VisualStateGroups>
      <VisualStateGroup x:Name="CommonStates">
        <VisualState x:Name="Normal" />
        <VisualState x:Name="MouseOver" />
        <VisualState x:Name="Pressed">
          <Storyboard>
            <ObjectAnimationUsingKeyFrames
                Storyboard.TargetProperty="Foreground"
                Storyboard.TargetName="ContentContainer">
```

```
            <DiscreteObjectKeyFrame KeyTime="0"
                                    Value="{StaticResource
                                            PhoneBackgroundBrush}" />
          </ObjectAnimationUsingKeyFrames>
          ...
        </Storyboard>
      </VisualState>
      <VisualState x:Name="Disabled">
        <Storyboard>
          <ObjectAnimationUsingKeyFrames
                Storyboard.TargetProperty="Foreground"
                Storyboard.TargetName="ContentContainer">
            <DiscreteObjectKeyFrame KeyTime="0"
                                    Value="{StaticResource
                                            PhoneDisabledBrush}" />
          </ObjectAnimationUsingKeyFrames>
          ...
        </Storyboard>
      </VisualState>
    </VisualStateGroup>
  </VisualStateManager.VisualStateGroups>
  ...
</Grid>
</ControlTemplate>
```

As this example shows, the VisualStateManager.VisualStateGroups attached property contains one (or more) VisualStateGroup objects. Inside the group is a list of VisualState objects that represent a storyboard that shows how to go to a specific state. The empty VisualState objects mean the state should look exactly like the natural state of the object.

The visual states and groups that a control supports are also specified as attributes on the control classes, as shown in Figure 4.21.

When creating your own control templates, you will need to be aware of the template parts and template visual states because that is the contract between you and the control author. You must implement these states and parts if you expect the controls to continue to operate correctly.

FIGURE 4.21   `TemplateVisualState` **attribute**

Windows Phone Toolkit

In addition to the controls that are part of the Windows Phone SDK, there is another download called the Windows Phone Toolkit. The version of the Toolkit for the phone includes a set of controls specific to the phone to help you create compelling applications. You should install the Windows Phone Toolkit to add these controls (and other features you'll learn about in subsequent chapters) to your applications. You can download the Windows Phone Toolkit directly from the CodePlex site at http://phone.codeplex. com. You can download only the installer, or you can opt to download the source code and other assets if you're interested in how these controls have been built. The entire project is open source.

The Windows Phone Toolkit includes the following controls:

- AutoCompleteBox
- ContextMenu
- DatePicker
- TimePicker
- ListPicker
- LongListSelector[2]

- ToggleSwitch
- ExpanderView
- PhoneTextBox
- Rating
- CustomMessageBox
- WrapPanel

We will discuss these controls in the subsections that follow.

Before you can get started using the Windows Phone Toolkit, you will need to add it to your project. Visual Studio Express 2012 for the Windows Phone Developers includes built-in support for a package management system called NuGet. With NuGet you can easily add the Toolkit to your project by right-clicking the project and selecting "Manage NuGet Packages." The dialog box that opens lets you add any of a number of Microsoft or community contributes packages to your project. Figure 4.22 shows how you can select the Online packages and simply search for "wptoolkit" to locate the Windows Phone Toolkit. Clicking the Install button will add it to your project.

AutoCompleteBox **Control**

First up is the AutoCompleteBox. The purpose of this control is to enable you to suggest selections as a user types into the control. The control is styled to look just like the TextBox, but as the user types, the control can show a list of possible options. For example, in Figure 4.23 when the user types "S," the control shows a pop-up with all options that start with the letter *S*.

---

2   This control is part of the phone controls in Windows Phone 7. It was moved from the Windows Phone Toolkit to the main Windows Phone runtime for Windows Phone 8.

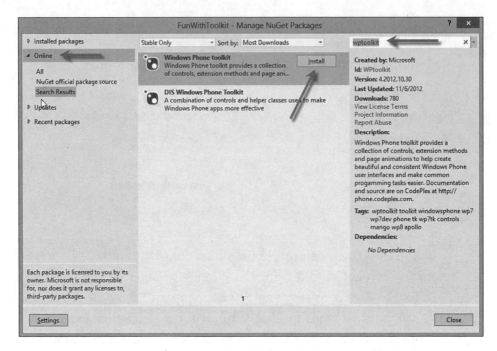

FIGURE 4.22   **Using NuGet to add the Windows Phone Toolkit**

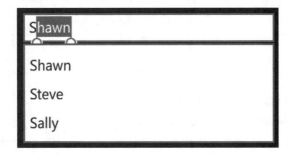

FIGURE 4.23   AutoCompleteBox **example**

The control is a list control, so you can assign an arbitrary list to the ItemsSource property:

```
theBox.ItemsSource = new string[]
{
  "Shawn",
  "Steve",
  "Sally",
```

```
    "Bob",
    "Kevin"
};
```

You can customize the control using XAML attributes in a number of ways, including specifying whether text completion is enabled and what type of filtering to support (StartsWith is the default, but you can have the suggestions based on Contains or Equals as well):

```
<toolkit:AutoCompleteBox x:Name="theBox"
                         IsTextCompletionEnabled="True"
                         FilterMode="Contains" />
```

A common approach with the AutoCompleteBox is to support a list of values that are not known at development time. This is how the Bing and Google search boxes work on the Web. You can achieve this by handling the TextChanged event and then filling in the ItemsSource as the text changes:

```
// Constructor
public MainPage()
{
  InitializeComponent();

  theBox.TextChanged += theBox_TextChanged;
}

void theBox_TextChanged(object sender, RoutedEventArgs e)
{
  // Go retrieve a list of items from a service
}
```

ContextMenu **Control**

The purpose of the ContextMenu control is to allow users to long-click on parts of your application to get a list of options. The control by default shows itself large enough to be obvious to the user. You can see the ContextMenu control in action with three menu items and a separator in Figure 4.24.

The structure of the ContextMenu control consists of a ContextMenu element with a collection of one or more items inside the ContextMenu. There is only a single level of menu items, so no submenus are supported. The two types of items are MenuItem elements and Separator elements:

```
<toolkit:ContextMenu>
  <toolkit:MenuItem Header="Add" />
  <toolkit:MenuItem Header="Remove" />
  <toolkit:Separator />
  <toolkit:MenuItem Header="Cancel" />
</toolkit:ContextMenu>
```

FIGURE 4.24 ContextMenu **example**

To add a context menu to a XAML element, you use the ContextMenu attached property to apply it to your design, like so:

```
<Grid>
  <toolkit:ContextMenuService.ContextMenu>
    <toolkit:ContextMenu>
      <toolkit:MenuItem Header="Add" />
      <toolkit:MenuItem Header="Remove" />
      <toolkit:Separator />
      <toolkit:MenuItem Header="Cancel" />
    </toolkit:ContextMenu>
  </toolkit:ContextMenuService.ContextMenu>
  ...
</Grid>
```

After the menu is attached to the element, a user touch-hold will cause the menu to be displayed. The individual `MenuItem` elements can launch code either via an event or via a `Command` binding:[3]

```
...

<toolkit:MenuItem Header="Add"
                  Click="MenuItem_Click" />
<toolkit:MenuItem Header="Remove"
                  Command="{Binding RemoveCommand}" />
...
```

> ### ■ Should You Use a `ContextMenu`?
>
> Although the `ContextMenu` is a powerful control and useful in many situations, you should avoid the use of this control. The reason is that a context menu isn't very discoverable by the user. Adding functionality via the `ContextMenu` means only a small number of your users might find the functionality. A common approach is to use the `ContextMenu` for quick access to features that are available in other parts of the application so that power users might use it but features aren't hidden from normal users.

DatePicker **and** TimePicker **Controls**

If you've designed desktop or web applications before, you probably are used to finding a calendar control to allow users to pick dates. The problem with a calendar control on the phone is that the interface is not very touch-friendly. Instead, the phone supports a control for choosing dates: `DatePicker`. Using the `DatePicker` is as simple as using the XAML element:

```
...
<TextBlock>Pick Date</TextBlock>
<toolkit:DatePicker />
...
```

---

3 Command binding is not covered in this book but is a useful technique for separating the XAML from the code. Please see the Silverlight documentation for the `ICommand` interface for more information.

The `DatePicker` looks like a simple `TextBox` that accepts a date. The difference is that when a user taps the control, it launches a full-screen date-picking user interface, as shown in Figure 4.25.

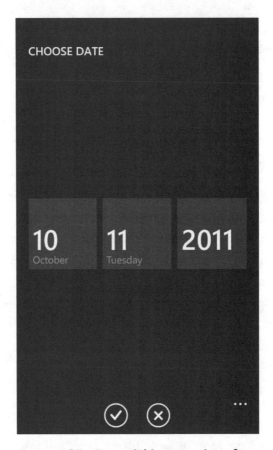

FIGURE 4.25 Date-picking user interface

The date-picking user interface allows the user to pan and flick to pick the date. This interface works really well with a touch interface. The `DatePicker` control defaults to `DateTime.Now`, which is why the current date is shown. You can specify a date using the `Value` property:

```
<toolkit:DatePicker Value="04/24/1969" />
```

The `TimePicker` works in exactly the same way as the `DatePicker` but uses the time portion of the `DateTime` structure:

```
...
<TextBlock>Pick Time</TextBlock>
<toolkit:TimePicker Value="12:34 PM" />
...
```

The user interface for picking the time is similar to the DatePicker, but it enables you to specify the time instead, as shown in Figure 4.26.

FIGURE 4.26   Time-picking user interface

ListPicker **Control**

I know developers love ListBoxes. For the phone, sometimes the ListBox is just the wrong tool. For very short lists of options, ListBoxes take up too much screen real estate. As an alternative, the toolkit gives you the ListPicker. The ListPicker is closer to the ComboBox control that is commonly used on websites and desktop applications.

The ListPicker control is a good solution when you have a short list from which the user must select one item. In fact, the ListPicker could also be used to replace radio buttons. The ListPicker shows the currently selected item in a box much like a TextBox, as shown in Figure 4.27.

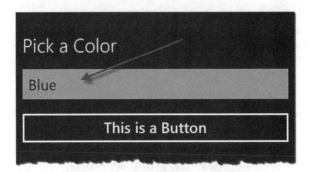

FIGURE 4.27   `ListPicker` **example (closed)**

When the user touches the `ListPicker`, it opens in one of two ways. If the list is short (five items or less), it expands the control to show the options, as shown in Figure 4.28.

FIGURE 4.28   `ListPicker` **example (opened)**

If the list has more than five options, it pops up a full-screen list of options from which to choose, as shown in Figure 4.29.

To create a `ListPicker`, you can create it as a simple XAML element, like so:

```
<TextBlock Style="{StaticResource PhoneTextLargeStyle}"
Text="Pick a Color" />
<toolkit:ListPicker x:Name="thePicker" />
<Button Content="This is a Button" />
```

FIGURE 4.29 ListPicker **example (full screen)**

Because the ListPicker is a list control, you can use the ItemsSource to specify the list:

```
...
thePicker.ItemsSource = new string[]
{
  "Blue",
  "Green",
  "Red",
  "Orange",
  "Purple",
  "Cyan",
  "Brown",
  "Gray",
  "Light Green"
};
...
```

LongListSelector **Control**

As an alternative to using the ListBox for very long lists, the Toolkit also supplies you with the LongListSelector control[4] that lets users look at large numbers of options. The phone uses this when you select a phone number from your address book. Because the list of people could be quite long, it categorizes the people by the first letter of their first or last name. Although it supports three modes, the real gem is the capability to have a pop-up list of groups to help users locate the items they're looking for. Although this type of control is used for the address book, that application uses the first letter for grouping; it's completely up to you how you decide to group the objects in the LongListSelector. For example, Figure 4.30 shows a list of games grouped by genre.

FIGURE 4.30 LongListSelector **with groups**

---

4   If you are using the LongListSelector on Windows Phone 8, you should use the built-in version. The Windows Phone Toolkit continues to include it for apps that are migrated from Windows Phone 7 and 7.1.

This shows the groups to the user and lets him tap on the group to pop up an overlay of groups to help him navigate large lists effectively, as shown in Figure 4.31.

FIGURE 4.31   `LongListSelector`**'s pop-up groups**

To use this control, you have to lean on data binding to set up three elements of your control:

- **ItemTemplate:** This is the contents of the individual data for an item in the `LongListSelector` (a "Game" in the preceding example).
- **GroupHeaderTemplate:** This is the item above the list of grouped objects (the "Genre" in the preceding example) shown in the main UI of the `LongListSelector`.
- **GroupItemTemplate:** This is the display for a group in the pop-up.

It is common to use the same template for the group item and the group header. Here is an example of the XAML to create a `LongListSelector`:

```xml
<Grid x:Name="LayoutRoot"
      Background="Transparent">

  <Grid.Resources>

    <DataTemplate x:Key="letterTemplate">
      <Border Background="{StaticResource PhoneAccentBrush}"
              Margin="4">
        <TextBlock Text="{Binding GroupName}"
               VerticalAlignment="Center"
               HorizontalAlignment="Center"
               Style="{StaticResource PhoneTextGroupHeaderStyle}" />
      </Border>
    </DataTemplate>

  </Grid.Resources>

  <phone:LongListSelector x:Name="theSelector"
              GroupHeaderTemplate="{StaticResource letterTemplate}"
              GroupItemTemplate="{StaticResource letterTemplate}">
    <phone:LongListSelector.ItemTemplate>

      <DataTemplate>
        <StackPanel Orientation="Horizontal">
          <Image Height="75"
                 Source="{Binding ImageUrl}" />
          <TextBlock Text="{Binding Name}"
                 Style="{StaticResource PhoneTextNormalStyle}"/>
        </StackPanel>
      </DataTemplate>

    </phone:LongListSelector.ItemTemplate>
  </phone:LongListSelector>
</Grid>
```

Notice first that the XAML stores a `DataTemplate` for the group in a resource. It does this so that we can use the same template for both the `GroupHeaderTemplate` and the `GroupItemTemplate`. Next, the `ItemTemplate` is specified inline. This works much like the `ListBox` examples earlier in this chapter. The grouping is what really changes the nature of how this control works.

When you apply data to the control, you can assign the `ItemsSource` like any other list control. The problem is that to make the control work, it expects your data to be in a specific format. This format is a collection of groups. A **group** is just a collection that often has something that describes it (such as the name of the genre in our example). The Windows Phone SDK already has something like this called the `IGrouping<T,T>` interface. You might try to just use the grouping semantics in LINQ to accomplish this, like so:

```
// THIS DOES NOT WORK

// Use LINQ to Group
var games = new GameList();
var qry = from g in games
          orderby g.Genre, g.Name
          group g by g.Genre into genres
          select genres;

// Bind the collection of Groups into the control
var result = qry.ToList();
theSelector.ItemsSource = result;
```

This LINQ query sorts the games by the name of the genre and the name of the game and then groups that result into collections of names by genre. This sounds very much like what we need for the control. Unfortunately, the underlying class that handles the grouping does not support data binding because the name of the group is not public.[5] To solve this, you can use a simple wrapper for the grouping, like so:

```
public class Group<T> : List<T>
{
  public Group(IGrouping<string, T> group)
  {
    GroupName = group.Key;
    this.AddRange(group);
  }
  public string GroupName { get; set; }
}
```

This class adds a public property for the name of the group and constructs itself from an `IGrouping<T,T>` object that LINQ uses (although it assumes a string-based key). Remember, not only does this group have a `GroupName` property to identify the group to the user, but also *is* a collection of the underlying objects. This is the data format this control requires, which is

---

5   As noted in the "Data Binding" section, data binding uses reflection and Windows Phone 8 does not
    support non-public reflection.

why we needed this class. This way, you can modify the LINQ query to construct these instead of returning the raw IGrouping<T,T> interface:

```
// Use LINQ to Group
var qry = from g in games
          orderby g.Genre, g.Name
          group g by g.Genre into genres
          select new Group<Game>(genres);
```

This works because our grouping data template uses the GroupName we specified in the Group<T> class to do the data binding:

```
<DataTemplate x:Key="letterTemplate">
  <Border Background="{StaticResource PhoneAccentBrush}"
          Margin="4">
    <TextBlock Text="{Binding GroupName}"
               VerticalAlignment="Center"
               HorizontalAlignment="Center"
               Style="{StaticResource PhoneTextGroupHeaderStyle}" />
  </Border>
</DataTemplate>
```

The LongListSelector supports other templates and properties to control the way you present this to the user, but understanding the basics of how to get a simple version of the control working will help you get started with the control.

PerformanceProgressBar **Control**

The built-in ProgressBar control has some known performance problems, including the fact that it renders on the wrong thread (making it appear jumpy) and the fact that the animations continue even if the control is stopped. This means if you want to use a progress bar in your application, you should use the PerformanceProgressBar control[6] from the Toolkit instead. This control existed because the Toolkit has much shorter release cycles and pushing a new progress bar to all phones would require an operating system update. Releasing this in the Toolkit means users can get the performance gains without waiting for the next phone update.

---

6 This control continues to be available in the Windows Phone Toolkit but these same changes were made to the built-in control, therefore making this control unnecessary except for backward compatibility with Windows Phone 7 and 7.1 applications.

You can simply use this control as your progress bar, instead of the built-in one, wherever you might expect to put the ProgressBar, like so:

```
<ProgressBar IsIndeterminate="{BindingIsBusy}" />
```

Replace this with the Toolkit version, like so:

```
<toolkit:PerformanceProgressBar IsIndeterminate="{BindingIsBusy}" />
```

ToggleSwitch **Control**

Although the phone includes a CheckBox control, clicking a box to enable something is not necessarily a good touch-based metaphor. In its place is a Toolkit control called a ToggleSwitch, as shown in Figure 4.32.

FIGURE 4.32 ToggleSwitch **example**

The ToggleSwitch allows users to either tap the switch to change its value or actually slide it to the right to enable the option (or to the left to disable it). The ToggleSwitch is made up of three sections, as shown in Figure 4.33.

FIGURE 4.33 ToggleSwitch **components**

The Header property controls what is in the section labeled #1 in Figure 4.33. The Content property controls what is in the section labeled #2. And the switch itself is shown in the section labeled #3. The Content of the control is usually changed as the state of the control is changed (for example, the default is On for checked and Off for unchecked). You can see the creation of a ToggleSwitch in the following XAML:

```
<toolkit:ToggleSwitch Header="This one is enabled"
                      Content="On"
                      IsChecked="true"/>
<toolkit:ToggleSwitch Header="This one is disabled"
                      Content="On" />
```

ExpanderView **Control**

The limited size of the display on the phone means that you might want to conserve the space on the screen as much as possible. One control that will help is the ExpanderView control. This control enables you to set up content that is hidden except when the user clicks the header to show the hidden content. The control consists of a header and content that can be shown when the control is tapped (see Figure 4.34).

FIGURE 4.34　ExpanderView **in action**

To use the control, you need an instance of the ExpanderView in your XAML. There are two parts to the control: the header and the items. The header is the part of the control that is always shown, and the items contain the content that is shown after the user taps on the header. For example:

```
<toolkit:ExpanderView Header="Click here to Expand">
  <TextBlock>This is hidden by default</TextBlock>
</toolkit:ExpanderView>
```

The Header property can be text (as is shown in the previous example), or it can be a more complex control using the expanded XAML syntax:

```
<toolkit:ExpanderView x:Name="theExpander">
  <toolkit:ExpanderView.Header>
    <TextBlock FontWeight="Bold"
```

```
               Margin="4">Click here to expand</TextBlock>
   </toolkit:ExpanderView.Header>
</toolkit:ExpanderView>
```

For the content, you can just include a list of controls to show simple content or use the ItemsSource to specify a collection (much like the way a ListBox works):

```
public partial class MainPage : PhoneApplicationPage
{
  // Constructor
  public MainPage()
  {
    InitializeComponent();

    expander.ItemsSource = new string[]
      { "Blue", "Red", "Green", "Orange" };
  }
}
```

Like the ItemsSource property, you can also use data templates (like the ItemTemplate) to control what each item looks like in the ExpanderView. You should think of the ExpanderView as similar to other list controls (detailed earlier in this chapter).

PhoneTextBox **Control**

The built-in TextBox is useful but is missing some features that would make it more useful in some scenarios. It would be nice if the TextBox supported hints (for example, showing a text watermark of what belongs in a text box before it contains text), length indication, pressing the Return key to create multiple lines of text, and icons to perform actions on the text box. The PhoneTextBox fills those needs. Figure 4.35 shows the PhoneTextBox when it does not have focus. Notice the watermark ("Enter Tweet") and the action icon on the right that you can hook up events to.

FIGURE 4.35 PhoneTextBox **with the** Hint **and** ActionIcon **shown**

To specify these, you can simply instantiate the control and specify the Hint attribute and the ActionIcon attribute as necessary:

```
<toolkit:PhoneTextBox x:Name="tweetText"
  ActionIcon="Toolkit.Content/ApplicationBar.Cancel.png"
  Hint="Enter Tweet" />
```

The PhoneTextBox includes an event to use when the ActionIcon is tapped. This event is called ActionIconTapped:

```
public partial class MainPage : PhoneApplicationPage
{
  // Constructor
  public MainPage()
  {
    InitializeComponent();

    tweetText.ActionIconTapped += tweetText_ActionIconTapped;
  }

  private void tweetText_ActionIconTapped(object sender, EventArgs e)
  {
    tweetText.Text = "";
  }
}
```

This example shows clearing the PhoneTextBox when the user clicks the cancel icon. This is a common usability improvement over the standard TextBox.

The PhoneTextBox also supports the ability to show the user how many characters she has typed. As the user types in the control, it can show the number of characters (as well as the maximum number of characters that will be allowed), as shown in Figure 4.36.

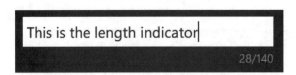

FIGURE 4.36 PhoneTextBox**'s length indication support**

The length indicator is supported by setting the `LengthIndicatorVisible` attribute to `True`. The `LengthIndicatorThreshold` attribute is also used to indicate how many characters have to be shown before the indicator is shown. This enables you to not show the indicator until the user is approaching the maximum number of characters. Finally, the `DisplayedMaxLength` attribute is used to indicate the maximum number in the indicator. Note that this does not limit the length of the field, but simply shows the maximum number in the indicator (which is why it's called `DisplayedMaxLength`). You can see the XAML where these are specified here:

```
<toolkit:PhoneTextBox x:Name="tweetText"
                      DisplayedMaxLength="140"
                      LengthIndicatorVisible="True"
                      LengthIndicatorThreshold="20" />
```

Lastly, you can also indicate that the control should support pressing the Return key to expand the text box to include multiple lines of text. When the user uses this functionality, pressing Enter on the keyboard (or the SIP) will expand the `PhoneTextBox` to include the multiple lines (see Figure 4.37).

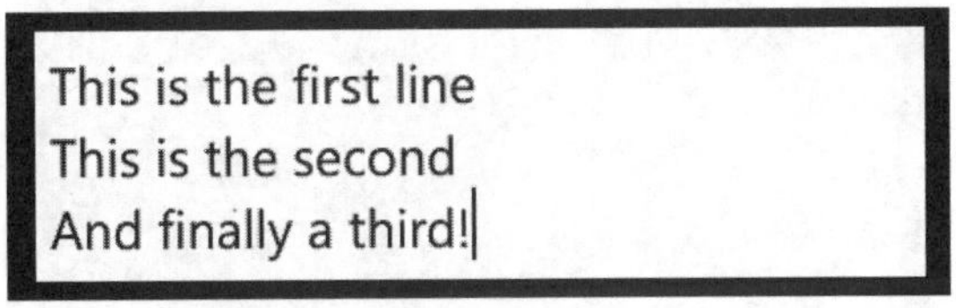

> This is the first line
> This is the second
> And finally a third!|

FIGURE 4.37 PhoneTextBox's AcceptReturn **functionality**

You specify this by using the `AcceptsReturn` attribute as shown here:

```
<toolkit:PhoneTextBox x:Name="tweetText"
                      AcceptsReturn="True" />
```

CustomMessageBox

Inside the toolkit is a special type of control for getting feedback from the user. Although there is a built-in `MessageBox` class, it is simple and doesn't allow you to customize the experience. Unsurprisingly, the `CustomMessage-Box` class from the Toolkit attempts to remedy this.

To use the CustomMessageBox, you simply create an instance of the class and set certain properties. At a minimum you should set the Caption, Message, and Button content properties, like so:

```
var myMessage = new CustomMessageBox()
{
  Caption = "A Custom MessageBox",
  Message = "This is a custom MessageBox example.",
  LeftButtonContent = "cancel",
  RightButtonContent = "ok",
};

myMessage.Show();
```

Running this code results in a message box at the top of the screen, as shown in Figure 4.38.

FIGURE 4.38 Simple CustomMessageBox

The underlying page is obscured with a semitransparent overlay. The Caption property is shown in larger text at the top of the message box, and the Message is shown in smaller text. The Caption should be the title of the message box, and the Message is used to hold a longer set of text to convey the information to the user.

In addition to the simple Caption and Message, you can also specify the Content of the message box to show specialized controls as necessary. For example, you could have a `HyperlinkButton` that enables the user to navigate to a specified page:

```
var link = new HyperlinkButton()
{
  Content = "About...",
  NavigateUri = new Uri("http://wp7book.com")
};

var myMessage = new CustomMessageBox()
{
  Caption = "A Custom MessageBox",
  Message = "This is a custom MessageBox example.",
  LeftButtonContent = "cancel",
  RightButtonContent = "ok",
  Content = link,
};

myMessage.Show();
```

In this case, creating a complex control (for example, `HyperlinkButton`) and then assigning it to the `Content` of the control places it after the `Message`, as shown in Figure 4.39.

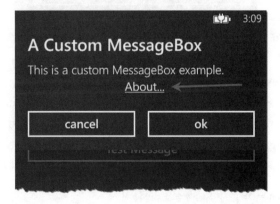

FIGURE 4.39   **Using** `Content` **in the** `CustomMessageBox`

You can also specify that the `CustomMessageBox` is a full-screen message box by specifying the `IsFullScreen` property. You can see this same message box with the `IsFullScreen` flag enabled in Figure 4.40.

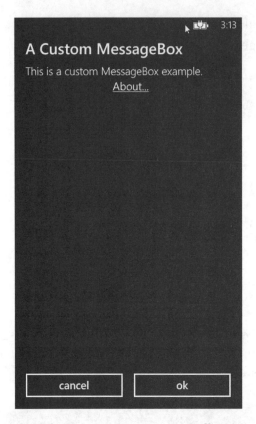

FIGURE 4.40 The CustomMessageBox **in Full Screen Mode**

The CustomMessageBox class has the concept of a left and right button. When the user selects either of these, the message box is closed. The user can also press the back button to close the message box without selecting a button. You will want to be able to know which button (if any) was pressed. To deal with this, you'll need to handle the Dismissed event as shown:

```
var myMessage = new CustomMessageBox()
{
  Caption = "A Custom MessageBox",
  Message = "This is a custom MessageBox example.",
  LeftButtonContent = "cancel",
  RightButtonContent = "ok",
};

myMessage.Dismissed += myMessage_Dismissed;

myMessage.Show();
```

The event handler will be passed however the user actually dismissed the message box. You can test this by checking the event arguments of the event:

```
void myMessage_Dismissed(object sender, DismissedEventArgs e)
{
  switch (e.Result)
  {
    case CustomMessageBoxResult.RightButton:
      results.Text = "Right";
      break;
    case CustomMessageBoxResult.LeftButton:
      results.Text = "Left";
      break;
    case CustomMessageBoxResult.None:
    default: // Back button or escape
      results.Text = "None";
      break;
  }
}
```

The DismissedEventArgs contains a property called Result that contains the type of dismissal the message box handled. As the code here shows, you can see whether the left or right button was pressed. If neither was pressed, the result will contain the CustomMessageBoxResult.None as the value. In this way, you can handle the dismissal correctly.

WrapPanel Layout Container

The last XAML element included in the toolkit is a new layout container called the WrapPanel. This element is not a control but a layout container (for example, Grid, StackPanel). The purpose of the WrapPanel is to lay out elements left to right, and when they don't fit horizontally, it wraps them onto a new line. For example, if you place nine buttons in a StackPanel like so:

```
<StackPanel>
  <Button Content="1" />
  <Button Content="2" />
  <Button Content="3" />
  <Button Content="4" />
  <Button Content="5" />
  <Button Content="6" />
  <Button Content="7" />
```

```
  <Button Content="8" />
  <Button Content="9" />
</StackPanel>
```

the StackPanel will simply stack them vertically, as shown in Figure 4.41.

FIGURE 4.41   Buttons in a StackPanel

But if you change the XAML to replace the StackPanel with a WrapPanel, like so:

```
<toolkit:WrapPanel>
  <Button Content="1" />
  <Button Content="2" />
  <Button Content="3" />
  <Button Content="4" />
  <Button Content="5" />
  <Button Content="6" />
  <Button Content="7" />
  <Button Content="8" />
  <Button Content="9" />
</toolkit:WrapPanel>
```

the WrapPanel will stack the items horizontally and then wrap to a "new line" when the items no longer fit, as shown in Figure 4.42.

FIGURE 4.42   Buttons in a WrapPanel

You can also change the Orientation attribute to Vertical to have the control stack vertically:

```
<toolkit:WrapPanel Orientation="Vertical">
    <Button Content="1" />
    <Button Content="2" />
    <Button Content="3" />
    <Button Content="4" />
    <Button Content="5" />
    <Button Content="6" />
    <Button Content="7" />
    <Button Content="8" />
    <Button Content="9" />
</toolkit:WrapPanel>
```

This is shown in Figure 4.43.

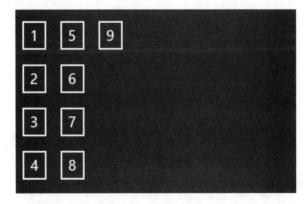

FIGURE 4.43   Buttons in a vertical WrapPanel

Where Are We?

The control set for Windows Phone is quite extensive. Combining standard XAML controls, special controls specific to the phone, and the controls Microsoft has released as part of the Windows Phone Toolkit will give you a compelling way to build your applications. The most important lesson here is to keep in mind that you're building applications for the phone. Touch is the first-class citizen. This means you have to let go of your old biases of which controls to use where and try to understand the differences in both touch and real estate.

▗ 5 ▖
Designing for the Phone

U P TO THIS POINT YOU HAVE LEARNED about the phone, worked your way through a simple walkthrough of an application, and learned the basics of XAML. Now you should be starting to think about the nature of the application you want to write. Although it is easy to think of this as just another XAML platform, it's not nearly that simple. In this chapter we talk about the nature of designing for Windows Phone to help you make those hard decisions.

The Third Screen

Microsoft has pushed an idea it calls "three screens and a cloud"[1] since the earliest announcements of Windows Phone (and possibly before). Essentially this is the idea that an application or service should support three fundamental user experiences: computer, TV, and phone. Although this idea of three screens that are all supported by a common infrastructure has evolved (for example, are tablets considered phones or computers?), it still represents a strong story for you to determine what your phone applications should allow the user to do.

---

1 http://tinyurl.com/3screensandthecloud

Your job in designing the experience for the phone involves more than fitting your web/desktop experience onto the small screen; it really involves crafting what a user will want to do on the device. For example, let's assume you work for a bank. Should the phone experience include doing things like downloading bank statements? Probably not. But users *will* want to be able to check balances and perhaps see several days' worth of transactions. The web story for your application may be very feature-driven, whereas the phone version should pick and choose the right experience for the form factor and use cases.

But the experiences you think about are not just a subset of web experiences; they might be very different. Consider the Foursquare website (http://foursquare.com) shown in Figure 5.1.

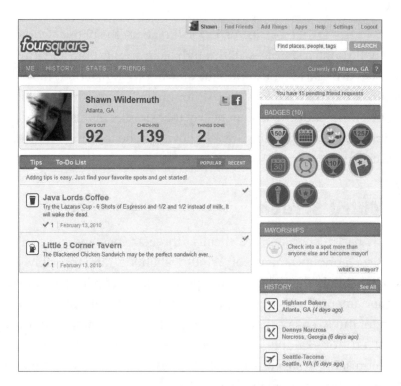

FIGURE 5.1   Foursquare.com

The user experience on the website is heavily geared toward seeing the status of a user; seeing the mayorships, history, and badges is a common task on the website. As a user, I might also be interested in some of the additional data presented to me in this larger format. In fact, there is quite a lot of functionality here that I might be interested in. But just how much of this is interesting on a smaller device? The user's attention span is hampered on a smaller device, so deciding what a user will do (and how long the user is expected to stay in your application) becomes crucial to a successful third screen for your offering. Let's take that site and see how the phone screen might help us pick some functionality (as shown in Figure 5.2).

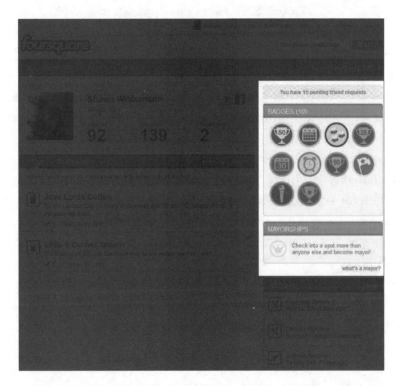

FIGURE 5.2   Phone-sized application

The problem with this approach is that it's unlikely that picking a phone-sized part of the application would make much sense. Your next thought might be to try to pack all that functionality in with a panorama application (as shown in Figure 5.3).

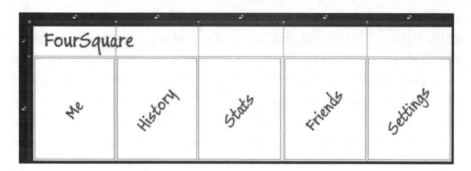

FIGURE 5.3   **Panorama application**

Although Windows Phone would allow this, it's important for you to look at what your third screen will be used for. How long do you expect users to work with the application? Even if users want all that functionality, is a large scrollable application the right idea? When I look at Foursquare, I am most interested in check-in (something that is an uncommon task on the website) and seeing where my friends are checked in; the rest of the functionality is purely "nice to have." In fact, the official Foursquare application for Windows Phone[2] is a mix of this standard Windows Phone paradigm by going with a panorama application but focusing exclusively on the places you visit instead of an all-in one approach (as shown in Figure 5.4).

Determining the right experience for your users is your first challenge. After you have a sense of what you should accomplish, the next challenge is to create an application that works well on a device.

It Is a Phone, Right?

Developing the right strategy for determining what your application does is only half the battle. The other half is to understand that you are working with a phone. Why does it matter that you're writing for a phone? It matters because the hardware, performance characteristics, and usability are completely different from a desktop or website. For example, the Application Certification Requirements for the Windows Phone[2] have limitations about consuming memory.

---

2   http://shawnw.me/wpcertreq

FIGURE 5.4   A sample Foursquare account on Windows Phone

■ Memory Consumption

The Application Certification Requirements specifically say "The application must not exceed 90MB of RAM usage, except on devices that have more than 256MB of memory." Because you can't dictate which devices it's available on, you must be ready to test for the memory in your app. The `DeviceStatus` class can be used to query the amount of memory on the device and modify the application behavior at runtime to take advantage of additional memory. For more information, see the `DeviceStatus` class in MSDN.

Therefore, you will need to design your application to work well within limitations on a number of fronts:

- Limited screen real estate
- Limited CPU speeds
- Limited battery life
- Limited memory
- Completely different input mechanism (for example, touch versus mouse)

If you're a seasoned mobile developer, none of this is new to you. But if you're a developer who is coming from the Web or the desktop world, you have to change your thinking substantially to fit your applications onto the phone. You will need to start with a clean slate and think about resources in a whole new way.

In addition, on the phone users run apps for very different reasons and expect very different experiences. Typically an application (not necessarily a game) is run frequently, but for very short periods of time. And the user experience is very touch-driven instead of keyboard- and mouse-driven. Designing an application to meet this different set of requirements means you really need to dig into how you expect the application will be used.

Deciding on an Application Paradigm

The Windows Phone style guide makes some specific recommendations about several styles of applications that look like the rest of the phone. When you design your application, you will have to look at these styles and determine whether any of them make sense with your application. Alternatively, you can just start from scratch and create a new workflow for your application without regard for Metro. Although these application styles are typical, it is not a requirement that your application follow any of these usability paradigms. In fact, some of the built-in apps already do this (for example, Music and Video).

Much more typical than having a single paradigm for your application is to determine the right mix of these UI metaphors to use in your applications. All Windows Phone applications use a navigation pattern in which you can have multiple pages that support the Back button on the phone (called the hub-and-spoke model). This pattern should match users' expectations as it is borrowed from the web pattern. A simple application can be made up of several pages that can be navigated to and from. For example, Figure 5.5 shows a simple blood sugar-monitoring application that mixes the different paradigms.

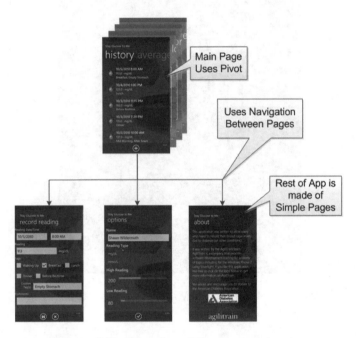

FIGURE 5.5 Sample application navigation

When you look at the design of your application, you will need to consider the various ways to create individual pages using the different styles of control, but you should never get away from the idea that Windows Phone revolves around page navigation. Of course, you can build your application as a single page, but that would likely be a simple application, such as the Moon Phaser application shown in Figure 5.6.

Let's look at some of the page design styles.

FIGURE 5.6   Single-page Windows Phone application

Panorama

The basic construction of the panorama page is an endless canvas of several panes. For example, let's take a simple application with a couple parts of the application, as shown in Figure 5.7.

This page will have two pieces of functionality ("first item" and "second item"). The panorama will show the first pane and hint at the second pane. So, this application in the emulator will look like Figure 5.8.

FIGURE 5.7   Sample panorama application

FIGURE 5.8   Panorama in the emulator

In the emulator, you can see that the first pane is shown, but it also hints that there is more to be seen. If the user swipes to the left (to move to the right), the second piece of functionality appears. Although the user is on the second pane, the first pane is shown again as a preview on the right. This is the magic of the panorama in that it implies an infinite canvas for the different parts of the application. This avoids the typical problem you would have with applications composed of several parts (or panes) and having to develop a way to navigate to them. The panorama makes it natural to get to the information the application is supplying. The background image also is stretched over the panes and slides along with the panes (although at a different speed to give a parallax look to the control). Although this example shows two panes, a panorama doesn't typically have more panes. The general rule of thumb is that you should use no more than five panes for a panorama.

Many of the built-in applications use the panorama style to enable different parts of their functionality (for example, People, Images, Music, and Video). It can be seductive to try to make your application use a panorama because other parts of the phone use that style, but you should choose this type of application only when you really do have multiple pieces of separate functionality. Each pane of the panorama is not meant to be a master-detail type of page. In fact, you should think of the panorama as the table of contents for your application. If you look at the built-in applications on the phone, you'll see that they often use a panorama as the landing page but then use other patterns (like the pivot discussed next) to show other information in the application. The individual panes are separate pieces of functionality, similar to the Foursquare example in Figure 5.3. Panorama applications also tend to require more horsepower from the phone, as all panes are live throughout the lifecycle of the application.

Pivot

Originally designed for Zune (the software and the device), the pivot-style page is a key style you will see on Windows Phone. It is used in the Music picker (in the Music and Video section) and is a common way to think of displaying the same information in different "views" (that is, by artist, by album, and so on).

The pivot is similar to the panorama, but use of the pivot is more straightforward. The pivot is also based on the idea of an infinite canvas, but unlike the panorama, the pivot is made of individual tabs and does not require that the next pane shows as a preview. The user can either swipe or tap on the headings (the next heading is previewed) to move to that pane. Figure 5.9 shows a typical pivot application.

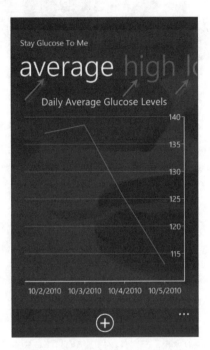

FIGURE 5.9   Pivot example

With the pivot, each pane takes up an entire page. The pivot works in a lot of places where a panorama would be too large and cumbersome. The biggest difference between a panorama and a pivot is that the pivot can handle a larger number of panes. As stated earlier, a panorama application really should be no more than five panes. You can use more than five panes in a pivot, but you cannot use an unlimited number of them; in addition, you should have a very good case to use a lot of pivot panels.

The pivot style of application is a good choice when you have the same or similar data that needs to be displayed in different views. For example, in the blood-monitoring app that contains a pivot, each page shows the data from the first page in different ways (different graphs or just a list of the data), as shown in Figure 5.10.

FIGURE 5.10   Pivot pages

Although the basic metaphor is about showing the same information in different ways on the pivot, you are ultimately in control and could have different functionality on each pivot page. What is important is to not surprise your users.

▪ Panorama or Pivot?

In principle you can think of Pivot and Panorama controls as similar in functionality (for example, they both show panes of information). In general, however, their use is pretty different. The Panorama control is typically used for a small number of panes and encourages a "discovery" type of experience in that the previewing of other panes means users will discover the rest of the functionality more naturally. But this pattern breaks down after four or five panes. The Panorama control also is heavier because there is no control over the display of the panes.

The Pivot control, on the other hand, is generally for when you want to show the same or similar data in different ways. For example, a common use of the Pivot control is in the Music library where you can view the music by artist, genre, and so on. The same information is in different panes but is organized differently.

More common is to actually use both. Using a panorama for the landing page and then using pivots for details is such a common practice that you'll see this pattern repeated in many of the built-in applications.

▪ Common Mistake

You should never use the Panorama and Pivot controls for master-detail interfaces (for example, one pane used for selection and the rest of the panes used for details of the selected item).

Simple Pages

Sometimes the different page styles just get in the way. That's where typical pages come in. Although Microsoft is encouraging some design paradigms with the Metro style, you don't have to choose one of them. Whether you're building a news application, a casual game, or even a custom video player, you can build it the way you want. The Metro design language should be your guide and should not deter you from creating the application that users will love.

Microsoft Expression Blend

The Windows Phone SDK includes a free version of Microsoft's Expression Blend tool for creating your Windows Phone application. You should get comfortable with this tool because it is an important way to design your applications. Blend has been around for a while for use with WPF and Silverlight applications, so it has had time to mature before the birth of Windows Phone.

Creating a Project

When starting a new application in Blend, you will be presented with a dialog box that includes several project types, as shown in Figure 5.11.

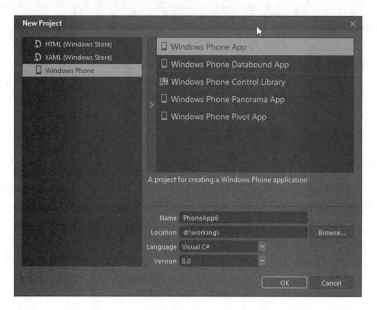

FIGURE 5.11 **Blend New Project dialog box**

There are separate project types for different starting project types. The first four of these project types are for creating new Windows Phone applications, and the last one is for a library to hold controls for other applications to use. Table 5.1 shows the various application projects.

TABLE 5.1 **New Project Types in Blend**

Project Type	Description
Windows Phone Application	Creates a simple, page-based application for Windows Phone
Windows Phone Databound Application	Creates a list-based application with sample date prewired into the user interface for Windows Phone
Windows Phone Panorama Application	Creates a Panorama control-based application for Windows Phone

| Windows Phone Pivot Application | Creates a `Pivot` control-based application for Windows Phone |
| Windows Phone Control Library | Creates a library to hold reusable controls that are used in Windows Phone applications |

A Tour Around Blend

Creating a new application will generate a new project with a base user interface on which you can start your design. This is usually the starting point for designing with Blend. To begin, let's look at the standard user interface layout of Blend to get comfortable with the various elements. The starting user interface contains several elements, as shown in Figure 5.12.

The basic interface of Blend is made up of five main areas (labeled #1 through #5 in Figure 5.12):

1. **Toolbar:** Commonly used tools live here.
2. **Common panels:** These include Project, Assets, and other panels.
3. **Objects and Timeline panel:** This is the basic layout/navigation panel.
4. **Artboard:** This is the basic design surface for Blend.
5. **Item panels:** These include the Properties, Resources, and Data panels.

As you start using Blend, you'll need to become pretty familiar with how each section can help you. The first area to get comfortable with is the toolbar. The toolbar contains many of the basic tools you will use to create your design. You can see the toolbar (and its submenus) in Figure 5.13.

FIGURE 5.12   Blend user interface

The basic toolbar is divided into five sections. Some of the individual toolbar buttons support holding them down to show a list of other toolbar buttons (as shown in the items labeled A–F in the figure). You can tell that a toolbar button supports multiple options by the small rectangle in the lower-right side of the button. The various toolbar sections are as follows:

1. **Selection tools:** Selection and Direction Selection
2. **View tools:** Hand and Zoom
3. **Brush tools:** Eye Dropper, Paint Bucket, Gradient tool, and Brush Transform (see A)
4. **Object tools:** A variety of tools to create different objects on the design surface (as shown in B–F)
5. **Asset tools:** The Asset button and Last Asset Used button

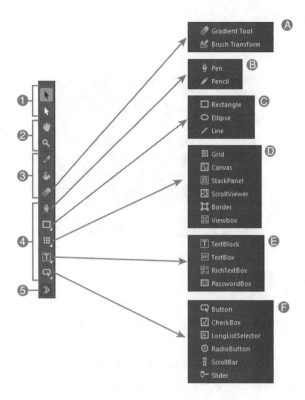

FIGURE 5.13 Blend toolbar

The Common Panel section of the Blend UI contains several commonly used panels. The two that you will interact with the most are the Projects panel and the Assets panel. The other three panels have specific uses that we will discuss later in this chapter.

The Projects panel provides a list of all the projects and files in a Blend project. If you are a designer and are new to Blend, one of the biggest changes you will need to get comfortable with is the idea that you are working with a project with multiple files, not just a single design file. The Projects panel (shown in Figure 5.14) shows all the files in the current project.

The Projects panel contains the solution file that contains one or more projects. In this example there is only one project, but you could have additional projects listed, such as libraries of shared designs or code. This panel is also where you would add other assets (for example, fonts, images, and so on) to the project. Everything in the project can be merged into the resultant phone application.

FIGURE 5.14   Projects panel

Another important panel is the Assets panel. Whereas the toolbar buttons give you access to the most common design elements (drawing shapes, containers, and controls), the Assets panel includes all the design elements you can add to a Windows Phone application. The Assets panel is made up of three sections, as shown in Figure 5.15.

As you will see in other parts of Blend, the panel starts with a search bar (#1 in Figure 5.15). Because the Assets panel can contain quite a lot of controls and other assets, searching for assets is often the quickest way to find the asset you are looking for. The categories on the left (#2) separate the different types of assets by individual categories. Notice the small triangles that indicate that some of the asset categories have subcategories. By making a selection in a category, you will display all the controls that fit in that category (or subcategory). As you can see in Figure 5.15, the categories are a mix of asset type (for example, Media, Controls, and Shapes) as well as location (for example, Locations and Project). This means an asset could be in more than one category. When a category is selected, the asset list (#3) shows the controls in that particular category or subcategory.

The next section of the user interface to look at is the Objects and Timeline panel. This panel lets you review the hierarchy of the objects in your design as well as facilitates the animation design process. Dealing with your object graph is the main purpose of this panel; we will discuss the animation features later in this chapter. For managing the object graph, the Objects and Timeline panel has several key parts, as shown in Figure 5.16.

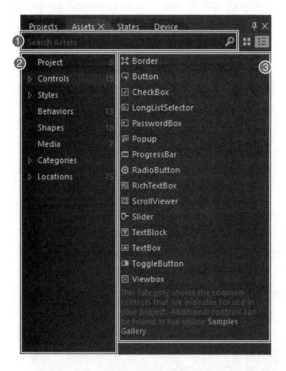

FIGURE 5.15   Assets panel

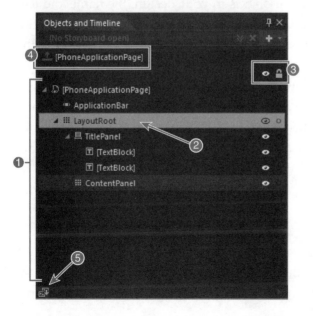

FIGURE 5.16   Objects and Timeline panel

The object graph (#1 in Figure 5.16) shows all the objects in your design. In this example you can see the Page; the ApplicationBar; and the Grid (called LayoutRoot), which contains a couple of other objects. This object graph is the same as the hierarchy of the XAML. The symbol on the left side of each object indicates the object type (they match the icons on the toolbar and Assets panel). For named members, the name is shown in the hierarchy; if an object is not named, it will be the object type surrounded by brackets (as seen for the PhoneApplicationPage).

When adding new elements to your design, it can be helpful to know what the current container is (which will tell you where new elements will be added). You can see the current container directly in the Objects and Timeline panel because that container will have a blue rectangle around it (#2 in Figure 5.16).

For every element in the object graph, the panel allows you to decide whether to hide or lock the object. The area toward the top-right (#3 in Figure 5.16) defines a column for both hiding and locking an object (or a container and its children). Clicking the icons to the right of the objects in the hierarchy will change whether they are shown or locked on the design surface. These changes are purely design-time and have no effect on the runtime look and feel of the objects.

As you move from different objects in your design, the name and icon (#4 in Figure 5.16) give you the ability to move back up to the last editing space. When we talk about styling using Blend, I will show you how this control comes into play.

Lastly, the icon on the lower-left of the screen (#5 in Figure 5.16) gives you the ability to flip the object graph order. This button only affects how the graph is displayed in the Objects and Timeline panel. Although XAML is written top-down (like HTML), the object graph will show that order. If you click the icon, it will flip this order. This reverse order is easier for people who are used to Photoshop or other design tools where the drawing order looks bottom-up.

Moving on to the artboard, shown in Figure 5.17, the main element (#1) of the artboard is much like any other design tool (even Microsoft Paint) in that it enables you to drop and manipulate objects directly. It uses the same handles metaphor as most other design tools as well (for example, the small squares on the sides and corners allow you to grab and resize anything on the artboard). Only the selected object(s) on the artboard will show its handles.

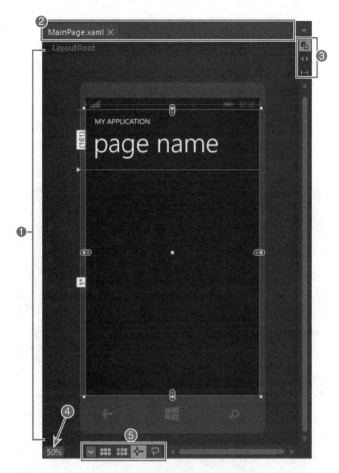

FIGURE 5.17   Artboard

On the top of the artboard (#2) are document tabs. For each document (for example, XAML file) you have open, a tab is created. Clicking individual tabs enables you to switch to that document. The view buttons (#3) allow you to switch from the design view to a XAML textual view or to a split view showing both the design and the XAML.

Immediately below the document tags is an indicator of the selected item on the design surface. This can be a drop-down (#4) for objects that have contextual menu items (for example, controls), or it might be a flat box with the type of control selected. This area will also show a breadcrumb of the different subobject design surfaces (for example, when editing a style or template) to ease the navigation back to the original design surface.

Lastly, the artboard has a zoom drop-down box (#5) to enable you to change the zoom level and a number of design option buttons that can be toggled on or off to show annotations, show gridlines, and enable rendering of effects.

The last section of the main Blend user interface is the Item Tools panel. This section is made up of several important panels, as shown in Figure 5.18.

FIGURE 5.18   Item Tools panel

This section provides tabs for several panels including (typically) Properties, Resources, and Data (#1). The main panel you will use while you are designing your Windows Phone application is the Properties panel. The main section (#2) of the Properties panel is the list of properties. If you are coming from Visual Studio, the organization and look of the Properties panel is quite different. The properties are sorted into logical groups—for example, Brushes (#3), Appearance, and so on. These groups are collapsible sections that will help you find related properties. Near the end of most of the groups will be a further collapsed section (#4) of less commonly used properties. You can click this arrow icon to open more properties.

Near the top of the Properties panel is an indicator of the name and type of control (#5). If you want or need to name an element, you can simply type it in here. Under the name/type section is the search bar (#6) that lets you search for property names. This is useful for finding property names because most of the controls have large numbers of properties. The search is a straight substring match, so, for example, typing "vis" in the search bar will result in both "Visibility" and "IsHitTestVisible," as shown in Figure 5.19.

Lastly, the Properties panel also has a switch (#7) to change between showing properties and events. Now that you have taken a basic tour of the Blend user interface, let's look at some common tasks using Blend for your design.

FIGURE 5.19 Searching in the Properties panel

Blend Basics

Much like any activity, learning Blend is a matter of performing tasks and repeating them. The more you do, the more the muscle memory of Blend will take over and allow you to create great applications.

Layout

The most basic layout task you will accomplish is simply drawing elements on the screen. With a new application project, if you draw a control (for example, Button) on the page, you will notice that the size of the control will be shown as you drag, as shown in Figure 5.20.

FIGURE 5.20   **Dragging a new control**

When you let go of the mouse button, you will notice that the control includes eight handles for resizing the control. Just outside these handles are lines that radiate outward from the control with small numbers near them. The usual way that XAML (and Blend) handles layout is by converting your object size to a margin from the side of the container (in this case a grid). So in Figure 5.21, you can see a "25" near the top and both sides of the new button. This indicates that the top, right, and left margins are 25 in size. Near each number is a small closed chain icon that indicates that the object is tied to these edges of the container. The bottom of the button has a dotted line that leads to an open chain icon that indicates that the button is not tied to the bottom. Because it is not tied to the bottom of the container, the margin doesn't appear either (because the margin wouldn't matter in this case). Using this metaphor of chaining to an edge can let you infer the alignment (top vertical aligned and stretch aligned horizontally). You can see the actual alignment and margins in the Properties panel that match this information. You can change these margins and alignments either directly on the artboard or by using the Properties panel.

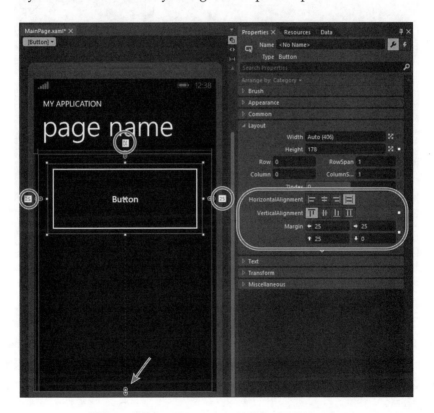

FIGURE 5.21   Margin and alignment layout

Most of the dynamic containers (Grid, StackPanel, and WrapPanel) all handle layout in this simple manner. The container in this example is the Grid. The Grid is different (and probably the most common of the containers) in that it enables you to create rows and columns. Blend makes it easy to create these rows and columns.

In a new simple Windows Phone application, Blend creates three Grids (LayoutRoot, TitlePanel, and ContentPanel). If you expand the LayoutRoot and select the ContentGrid in the Objects and Timeline panel, you will see that Blend shows a top- and left-side gutter for the grid, as shown in Figure 5.22.

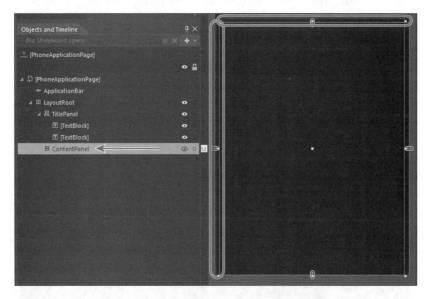

FIGURE 5.22   Column and row gutters

These gutters are important as you can click them to create columns and rows. Clicking the grid will create a split in the container that indicates where two rows or columns are separated. For example, if you click the left gutter about halfway down you'll see two rows created, as shown in Figure 5.23.

After the grid is split into two rows, you should notice the text indicators next to each row that indicate the way the row (or column) is sized. As you read in Chapter 3, "XAML Overview," there are three types of sizing: auto, fixed, and star sizing. The text indicator in Figure 5.23 shows that the two rows are star sized (as they are post-pended with an asterisk). When you hover on the text indicator, it shows a drop-down (see Figure 5.24).

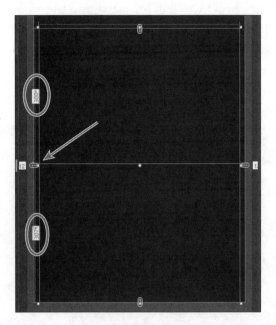

FIGURE 5.23 Splitting the grid into rows

FIGURE 5.24 Row/Column modification drop-down

You can use this drop-down to change the type of row or column to an auto-sized or fixed-sized column/row. You can also choose to select the row or add or remove columns/rows.

When working with multiple columns and rows, Blend draws only what you like, but because you are creating applications that have to deal with different screen sizes, this it potentially hazardous. The problem is that fixed sizes are notoriously finicky with fixed sizes, and the recommendation is to make your applications just adjust size with the screen size. The best way to do this is to use what Blend calls "quadrant sizing." To ensure this, go to the Blend Options (for example, use the Tool menu and pick Options). In Figure 5.25, this option is turned on.

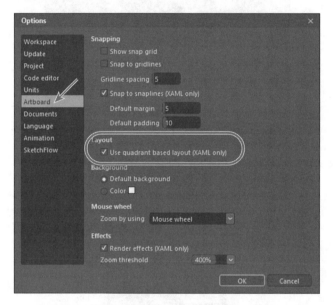

FIGURE 5.25   Enabling Quadrant Sizing

With quadrant sizing enabled, you can stretch objects across the row and column boundaries. Blend will do its best to help you determine which columns and rows you want to be a part of, but it is just guessing your intent. For example, you can see in Figure 5.26 that when an item just enters a second row, it handles this with a negative margin value.

FIGURE 5.26 Sizing across rows

But if you stretch that more, Blend assumes you want to span the two rows, as shown in Figure 5.27.

You will often need to manipulate the Row, Column, RowSpan, ColumnSpan, Alignment, and Margin entries manually in the Properties panel to get the exact behavior you want. In many cases you might not want to use margins at all, but rather make your object a fixed size. You can do this by ensuring that your object is not set to Stretch alignment (vertically and horizontally). Then the Margin box will indicate where to draw your element, but not how to size your element.

FIGURE 5.27   **Sizing across rows with** RowSpan

Brushes

Another common task in Blend is to select how to "paint" a particular element of your design. As you saw in Chapter 4, "Controls," XAML uses brushes to paint surfaces, and Blend supports this through the Brushes section of the Properties panel, as shown in Figure 5.28.

The Brushes section of the Properties panel is made up of a number of sections you will want to become familiar with. The first section (#1 in Figure 5.27) lists the brushes the particular object supports. In this example it's a simple Rectangle object, so you can set the brush for both the Fill and the Stroke of the Rectangle. This is like a small ListBox, so picking a brush will let you pick the properties for that brush in the lower part of the Brushes section. The second section (#2) lists the available brush types. This section takes the form of a set of tabs for each type of brush. Table 5.2 lists the brush editors.

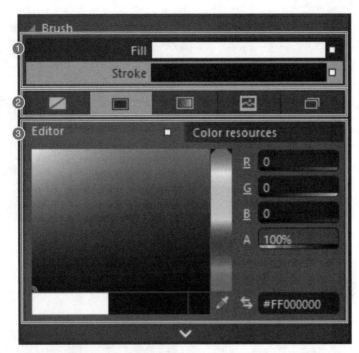

FIGURE 5.28 Brushes in the Properties panel

TABLE 5.2 Brush Editors

Brush Type	Description	Editor
None	No brush will be drawn.	No editor is shown.
Solid color	Used to create solid color brushes. At #1 in the figure to the right there is a tab to allow you to design colors. The second tab is used to reuse resource-based colors. You can create resource-based colors by using the square context menu on the editor tab. At #2 is a simple color picker with a mix between white, black, and the selected tint. At #3 is where you can specify the red, green, blue, and alpha (transparency) manually. The bar at #4 allows you to pick the current tint that the mixer (#2) uses. The control at #5 allows you to specify or copy the specific color text. You can paste web values here to match colors (for example, from CSS). The last four elements are the initial color (#6), current color (#7), the last color used (#8), and the eyedropper to pick a color (#9).	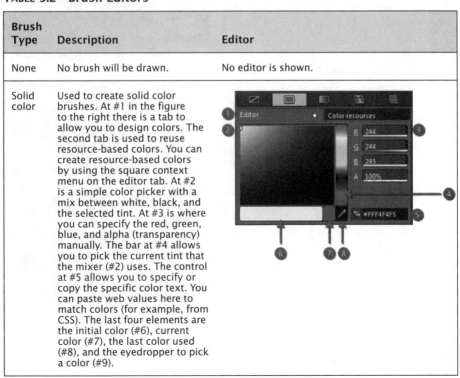

Gradient	At #1 in the figure to the right, the gradient brush editor supports a bar that contains all the stops of a gradient brush. Clicking on the bar will create a new stop. The current stop is always drawn with a black background. When editing a stop on the gradient, the solid color editor (#2) is used to change the color at that stop. The only difference between the color editor and the gradient editor is that the simple eyedropper has been replaced with a gradient eyedropper (#3) to copy existing gradients. The editor rounds out with several controls on the bottom, including the switch between linear and gradient brushes (#4), the reverse stops button (#5), the stop navigator (#6), and the manual entry of a stop's offset (#7).	
Image	The image brush editor allows you to specify the source of the image brush (#2 in the figure to the right) as well as how the image is fit to the source (for example, Stretch) as seen in #1. There is also a preview of how the image will be stretched (#3).	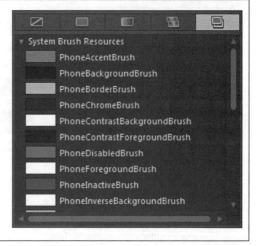
Resource	The resource brush editor lists named brushes (both from your project and from the Windows Phone standard system brushes). You can simply pick from the list to pick a brush.	

Within the brush editor you can directly create two types of resources: color resources and brush resources. These are created in different ways, but both originate on the brush editor. First, let's create a color resource. We can do this by clicking the small square next to the color picker, as shown in Figure 5.29.

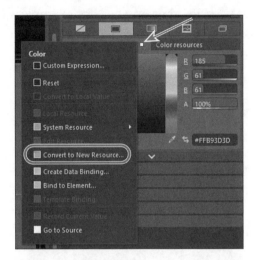

FIGURE 5.29 Converting a color to a resource

Selecting Convert to New Resource opens a dialog box where you can create a new named resource that will show up in the Resources list in the color editor, as shown in Figure 5.30.

FIGURE 5.30 Creating a color resource

After you name the resource, you will also need to specify where to define the resource. Your options are labeled Application, This Document, and

Resource Dictionary. Typically you would choose Application or Resource Dictionary if you have one. Defining a resource at the application level allows the resource to be used on any page in your application. Defining this resource enables you to specify it by name, and if it's changed later in the design workflow, the change affects every use of this color. This color resource can also be used in other brushes (for example, gradient brushes). After you have a color resource, you can use it via the Color Resources tab, as shown in Figure 5.31.

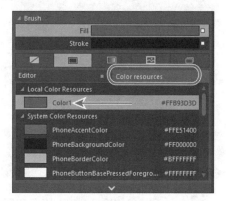

FIGURE 5.31 Applying a color resource

The other type of resource is a brush resource. This is different because, instead of defining a color to be used in a brush, you can define an entire brush (for example, image, gradient, or solid color brush). This way, you can define a named brush so that if you later change a brush from a solid color brush to a gradient brush, the change cascades to all uses. You can create a brush resource like you created a color resource, but the context menu is in a different location. This time you will use the small square to open the context menu on the brush itself instead of the color, as shown in Figure 5.32.

Applying the brush resource is similar, too. You would show the Resource Brush tab and pick the local brush resource you want to use, as shown in Figure 5.33.

Dealing with brushes is a pretty typical task. Using these techniques, you'll be up to speed in using Blend to create your Windows Phone applications quickly.

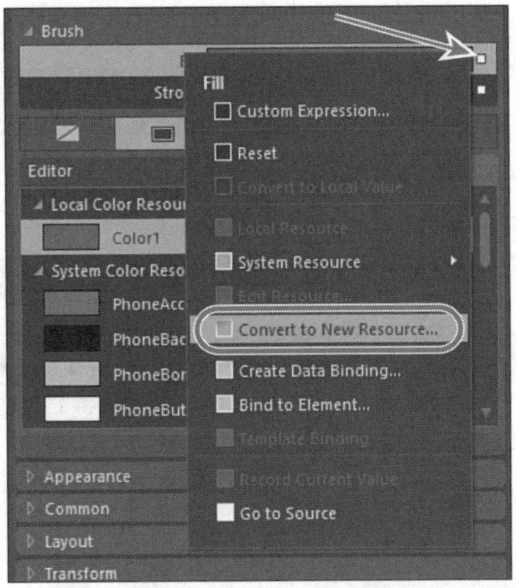

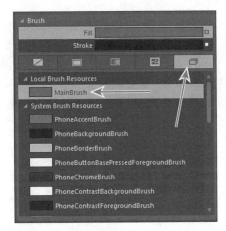

FIGURE 5.32   Creating a brush resource

FIGURE 5.33   Applying a brush resource

Creating Animations

In Blend, the panel you use most often is the Objects and Timeline panel. It might not be obvious yet why it has this long name. The "Timeline" part of the name indicates that it is also where you can build your animations as part of your overall design. Timelines are the basic building blocks of animations.

To begin, take a look at Figure 5.34. At the top of the Objects and Timeline panel is a bar that controls the creation of storyboard objects. A **storyboard** is a container that can hold animations of objects in your design. The + button in the bar enables you to create a new storyboard to contain animations.

FIGURE 5.34   Storyboard basics

When you click the + button to start a storyboard, you're asked to name your new storyboard. This name will be used later to execute the storyboard (that is, cause the animations to run), as shown in Figure 5.35.

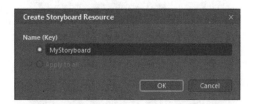

FIGURE 5.35   Creating a storyboard

After you've created a storyboard, the Objects and Timeline panel shows a timeline next to each element in the object tree. Figure 5.36 shows the metamorphosis to this new look.

You can see and change which storyboard is the current one, using the panel below Objects and Timeline in Figure 5.36. The animation pane to the right shows the new storyboard of animations. The VCR-like controls at the upper-left corner of this pane allow you to play, pause, or move the current marker (the line currently positioned at 0) in the animation. You can also move the current marker by simply clicking at the top of the numbered timeline (these are in seconds).

To create your first animation, you can simply click the timeline to change the current time in the animation to one second. Also select the ellipse object in your object tree. After you do that, you can change the properties of your ellipse and those changes will be reflected in the form of an animation. You can see how this looks in the Objects and Timeline panel, as shown in Figure 5.37.

FIGURE 5.36   Objects and Timeline panel with animation

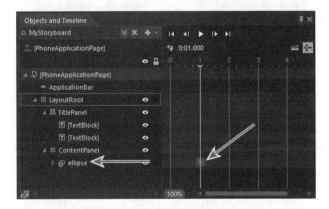

FIGURE 5.37   Picking the animation point

At this point, you will notice that there is a red rectangle (shown with the top right arrow in the figure) around the entire artboard to indicate that you are in animation mode and recording an animation (instead of just modifying objects normally). You can see this in Figure 5.38.

When you are in animation mode and you modify objects (through either the artboard or the Properties panel), your changes will be reflected in the storyboard. For this example, change the opacity of the ellipse to zero. This will cause the animation to move for one second (where our marker currently is set) and become transparent. You can see the state of the ellipse over the time of the animation (at zero, one-half, and one second) in Figure 5.39.

FIGURE 5.38   Animation mode on the artboard

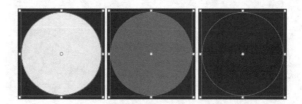

FIGURE 5.39   The ellipse animated

Back in the Objects and Timeline panel you can see that the ellipse now has a little red circle on it (to indicate it's part of this animation). It also shows an indicator at the one-second mark to show that the ellipse has a value at that part of the animation. If you open the arrow next to the ellipse, you will see that there is now a sub-object that represents the property that was animated (for example, opacity). If more than one property was affected, there would be a line for each of them. This is shown in Figure 5.40.

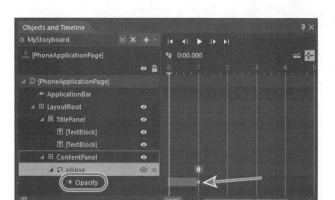

FIGURE 5.40   Animation values in the Objects and Timeline panel

Instead of changing a property, you might decide to change the location or size of an object on the artboard. When you do this, Blend attempts to do what you want. To make it easy to animate, Blend usually incorporates render transforms so that moving or sizing an element is based on the transform (instead of moving the margin and/or size of an element). If you move and resize your ellipse, you will see that Blend creates a RenderTransform and then creates values for the RenderTransform's properties, as shown in Figure 5.41.

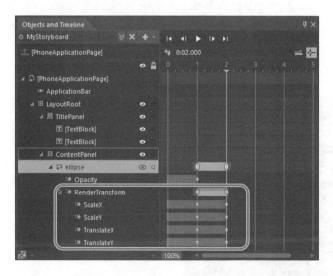

FIGURE 5.41   RenderTransform in an animation

By adding these together, you can create complex animations and then use the VCR-like controls to test them. When you get the style you want, you can save and close the animation by clicking the X button, as shown in Figure 5.42.

FIGURE 5.42   Closing a storyboard

Although you can create individual animations this way, you will find that using the visual state manager (often called the VSM) to create the state of a control or object is much more common. See the Blend documentation about the States panel for more information on the VSM.

Working with Behaviors

Although most of our discussion about design has focused on structure, some parts of a design should focus on performing actions. This is where behaviors come into play. A **behavior** is an object that can be activated based on an event in the design to perform some action. For example, you could have an animation fire when an item is acted upon. Figure 5.43 shows the various behaviors that ship with Blend.

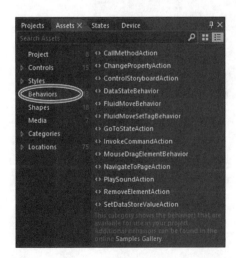

FIGURE 5.43   Behaviors in the Assets panel

Table 5.3 explains the built-in behaviors.

TABLE 5.3   Blend Behaviors

Behavior	Description
CallMethodAction	Allows you to call a method on an object
ChangePropertyAction	Allows you to change a property value based on user input
ControlStoryboardAction	Allows you to change the state of an animation (usually start it)
DataStateBehavior	Changes the a VisualStateManager .VisualStates of an object based on some specific data on the object
FluidMoveBehavior	Animated changes to layout within a container to be smooth (or fluid)
FluidMoveSetTagBehavior	Same as FluidMoveBehavior but affects only objects with a specific Tag value
GoToStateAction	Controls a VisualStateManager .VisualStates to move to a specific state
InvokeCommandAction	Invokes an ICommand object based on an event
MouseDragElementBehavior	Allows movement of an object when dragged by the user
NavigateToPageAction	Allows navigation to different pages within the Navigation Framework
PlaySoundAction	Causes a specific sound to be played when an action occurs
RemoveElementAction	Removes a specific child of a container when an action occurs
SetDataStoreValueACtion	Changes the value of a property based on an event

To use behaviors, you simply drag them onto an object in the Objects and Timeline panel or onto the artboard. For example, if you drag a

`ControlStoryboardAction` object onto the ellipse, it creates the new behavior on the ellipse, as shown in Figure 5.44.

FIGURE 5.44   Applying a behavior

After the behavior is created, you'll see the behavior properties in the Properties panel. The top half (the trigger) is where you can select the event that causes the behavior to fire. In this case we are executing it when the Tapped event is fired, which also happens when a user presses the screen of Windows Phone. The top half is the same for most behaviors.

The bottom half is different for different behaviors. In this case we are choosing what to do to a storyboard (for example, play, pause, and so on) and which storyboard to affect. The drop-down will show you all the animations you've created (as shown in Figure 5.45).

FIGURE 5.45   Changing behavior properties

You can have multiple behaviors on objects in the Objects and Timeline panel. In fact, you can have multiple behaviors with the same trigger. You can see the behaviors directly in the object tree, as shown in Figure 5.46.

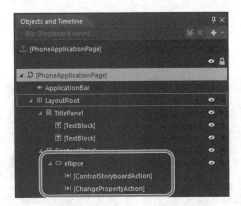

FIGURE 5.46 Multiple behaviors

Behaviors do not replace the need for typical code, but they do represent a way to perform UI-specific operations (for example, actions). For instance, you might have a fly-out panel that is shown when a button is pressed. It is not necessary to get code involved to show and hide the panel because there is no logic in this operation. It's purely a UI operation. Behaviors allow you to have XAML that represents a unit of the UI. Anytime you put real logic (for example, validation or other behavior) in the design, you're probably making a mistake and should do that sort of work in code.

Phone-Specific Design

Although designing an application using Blend should be similar whether you are building a traditional XAML application or a Windows Phone application, some things are applicable only to the phone. These include the ApplicationBar, the Panorama control, the Pivot control, and launching the emulator.

The ApplicationBar in Blend

Although having a user interface that compels users to move, swipe, and pan their way to getting the most from your application is nice, sometimes users need simple operations. This is where the ApplicationBar comes in. The ApplicationBar is a standard part of many applications. A mix of a menu and a toolbar, the ApplicationBar can hold both icons (like a toolbar) and menu items. The ApplicationBar starts in a minimized (or closed) state and can be opened by the user to reveal more information, as shown in Figure 5.47.

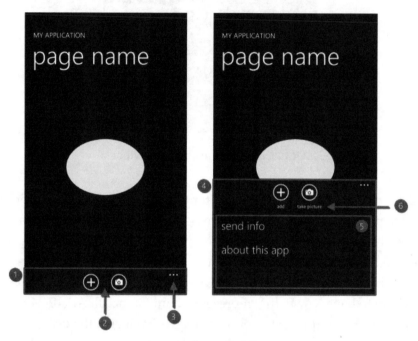

FIGURE 5.47   ApplicationBar explained

By default, the ApplicationBar takes up a small portion of the user interface (labeled #1 in Figure 5.47). On the ApplicationBar are icons that can perform certain tasks. In this mode only the icons are visible; the menu items are not. You can see the icons in the ApplicationBar (#2). To the right of the icons is an ellipse (#3) that alerts the user that pressing it will open the ApplicationBar (#4). In this open view, the menu items are shown below the icons (#5). Finally, you should notice that, when opened, the icons have text associated with them (this is not visible when closed but is shown when the application bar is opened, as shown in #6). In this example, all the text is lowercase. The ApplicationBar forces any text in the menu items or icon text to be lowercase (to preserve the Metro-style guide).

You can add an ApplicationBar to a XAML file with the context menu on the PhoneApplicationPage element in the Objects and Timeline panel, as shown in Figure 5.48.

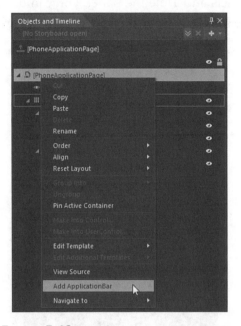

FIGURE 5.48 Adding an ApplicationBar

This adds the bar to your application as just another part of your object tree. From that point, you can use the context menu to add both icons and menu items, as shown in Figure 5.49.

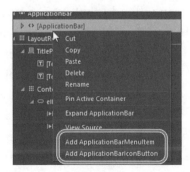

FIGURE 5.49 Adding items to the ApplicationBar

Adding an `ApplicationBarIconButton` creates the icons you see on the bar (whether closed or opened). Blend supports a number of built-in icons you can choose, or you can supply your own. With an `ApplicationBarIconButton` selected in the Objects and Timeline panel, you can use the drop-down to pick an icon to use for your application, as shown in Figure 5.50.

FIGURE 5.50 Selecting a built-in icon for an `ApplicationBar` **icon**

Selecting a built-in icon will add that icon to your project (in an Icons folder). You can simply supply your own `IconUri` to point to an icon of your choosing (located in your project). The built-in icons are useful, but be careful not to reuse a built-in icon for a use that is not natural. It will confuse users if you reuse an icon that is commonly used for some other function.

Typically, these should follow the Metro style and be monochrome (for example, white on black or black on white) in the PNG format. If you choose white with PNG transparency, Windows Phone will change your icons to black on white when the user switches his theme to a light theme. Otherwise, you will need to modify the icon at runtime manually.

Using the Panorama **Control in Blend**

On Windows Phone, you are not limited to the size of the screen. As we discussed earlier in this chapter, the Panorama control in an application enables you to use a larger virtual space. Although you can use a Panorama control directly, one of the most common scenarios is to start with a new panorama application, as shown in Figure 5.51.

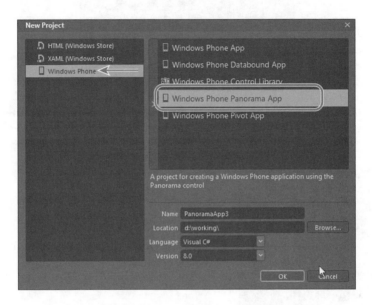

FIGURE 5.51   **New panorama application**

After you create a new panorama application, your main page (MainPage.xaml) will consist primarily of a virtual area that contains one or more PanoramaItems. You can see this if you drill down into the Objects and Timeline panel for the panorama, as shown in Figure 5.52.

The Panorama control user interface is made up of several parts, labeled 1–4 in Figure 5.53.

The control itself is sized to contain all panorama items. This means the control is much larger than the screen but indicates to the user that more content is available (via the other panes overlapping on the side of the page), as indicated by the #1. The header (#2) shows the header for the current PanoramaItem. The #3 indicates the content area of an individual item. Lastly, the next item (#4) is shown to the right of the current item.

This user experience is meant to help users learn your user interface by exploring the parts they can't see in the virtual space on the phone.

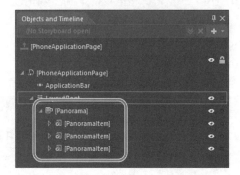

FIGURE 5.52   PanoramaItems **in the Objects and Timeline panel**

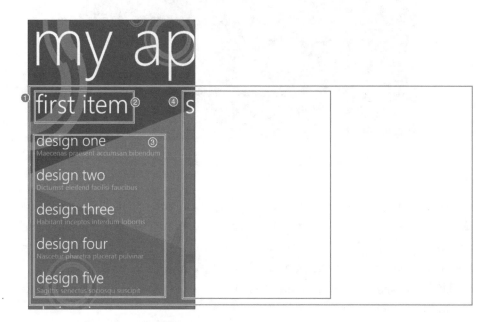

FIGURE 5.53   Panorama **control user interface**

In Blend, you can view each PanoramaItem as the "current" item by simply selecting it in the Objects and Timeline panel, as shown in Figure 5.54.

FIGURE 5.54 PanoramaItem **selection**

As the individual PanoramaItem is selected, you can manually edit the contents as you would in any other container (for example, Grid, Canvas, and so on). The actual PanoramaItem contains both a header and content. The header (usually just lowercase text) indicates to the user what the PanoramaItem contains. The content is the control(s) that represents the content of the PanoramaItem.

Adding new PanoramaItems to your Panorama control is just as easy as using the context menu, as shown in Figure 5.55.

By adding multiple PanoramaItem objects to the Panorama control, you will be creating an increasingly larger virtual area for your application. As stated earlier, the rule of thumb is to only have four or five PanoramaItems in a Panorama control.

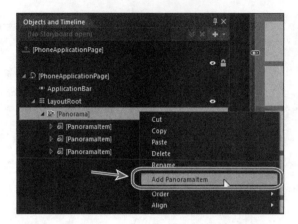

FIGURE 5.55   Adding a `PanoramaItem`

Using the `Pivot` **Control in Blend**

Much as you can with the `Panorama` control, you can use the `Pivot` control in an existing project or as the basis for a brand-new Windows Phone application. When creating a new project in Blend, you are given the option to create a new pivot application, as shown in Figure 5.56.

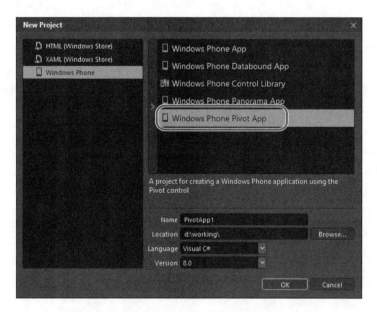

FIGURE 5.56   Creating a pivot application

After you create the pivot application, your main application is made up of a single Pivot control (much like the preceding panorama). The Pivot has PivotItem objects that represent a container for each pane in the Pivot control, as shown in Figure 5.57.

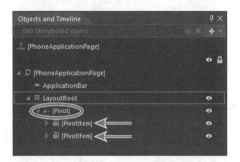

FIGURE 5.57 A pivot application

The user interface of the Pivot control is different from the Panorama control UI in that it is optimized for the screen, and navigating to the different items is accomplished via swipes or via the list of items at the top of the Pivot control. You can think of the Pivot as a view manager or even a tab control. The Pivot control UI consists of multiple parts, as shown in Figure 5.58.

The section labeled #1 shows a header for each item of the Pivot control. Each item has a header (usually text) that the user can tap on to make that view the current view. The current view's header is shown on the left of this section and is typically highlighted (#2). Lastly, the main content of an individual item of the Pivot can contain any user interface that fits with the design (#3). Unlike the Panorama, the only indication that there is more information to view is the list of headers at the top.

Just like the Panorama control, you can edit the Pivot control's individual items (PivotItems) in Blend by simply selecting the appropriate PivotItem, which makes that item the current container in which you can do your design, as shown in Figure 5.59.

At this point you can think of each PivotItem as just another container in your design.

FIGURE 5.58   Pivot control parts

FIGURE 5.59   Editing a PivotItem

Previewing Applications

As you are working on the design of your application, you might want to test the look of the application. You can do this by using the Project menu (Project, Run Project). The Visual Studio hotkeys for this also match (F5 or Ctrl+F5) to launch your project. To facilitate previewing your application in a variety of scenarios, there is a Device panel in Blend that enables you to specify how to run your application. Figure 5.60 shows this panel.

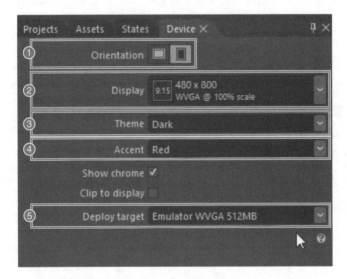

FIGURE 5.60   Changing device properties

The Device panel contains just three types of options. You can pick the orientation to choose when the application starts (#1), you can specify the screen size to show on the artboard (#2), you can show the application theme (#3), or you can select the theme and accept the color (#4). The theme can be dark or light, and the color is the chosen accent color to set on the device/emulator. Lastly, you can specify whether to preview your application via the emulator (the default) or on a device (#5). To test it on a device, you have to go through a couple of steps, including registering the phone with Microsoft as a development device. These steps are covered in Chapter 2, "Writing Your First Phone Application."

Designing with Visual Studio

Although Blend provides the strongest tooling for design including the features we've seen like animations and visual state manager support, at times switching to Blend is unnecessary for smaller layout and property changes. Starting in Visual Studio 2012, the XAML designer is powered by Blend's design surface. This means most of the techniques you've learned to use in Blend earlier in this chapter will apply directly to Visual Studio.

If you start with a new project, your XAML is shown in a split view, as shown in Figure 5.61.

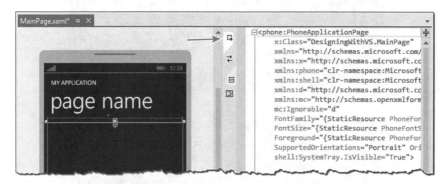

FIGURE 5.61   Showing just the design view

In this split view, you can simply double-click the designer icon (where the arrow is pointing) to show only the design view (which I find easier). After you have the design view opened, you can see the Properties pane is similar to the Blend pane (in that it's collapsible and uses the same editors as Blend), as shown in Figure 5.62.

The missing piece here for most of the Blend-like design is the Objects and Timeline pane. In Visual Studio, this is called the Document Outline. As Visual Studio can't do animations, this pane includes only the object graph you used earlier in this chapter. You can click the dedicated Document Outline button to show this pane (see Figure 5.63).

When you have this view, you can simply work with the design surface exactly like you would in Blend. The underlying code for this design surface is the same one used in Blend. For example, you can simply right-click the ApplicationBar section of the Document Outline to add an `ApplicationBar` to your design, as shown in Figure 5.64.

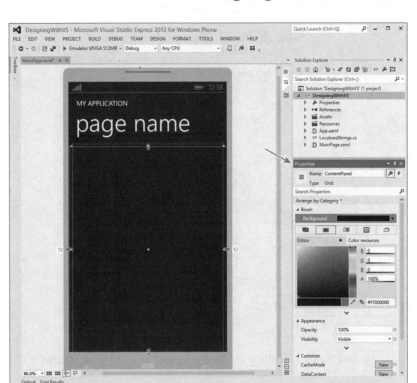

FIGURE 5.62   The Blend-like Properties pane in Visual Studio

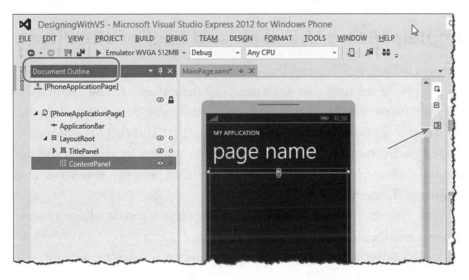

FIGURE 5.63   Showing the Document Outline

FIGURE 5.64   Adding an `ApplicationBar` in Visual Studio

So for those simple XAML changes, Visual Studio can be a faster way to modify your design.

Implementing the Look and Feel of the Phone

In this chapter, you've seen that building an application that works well on the phone requires you to understand the nature of how applications are used on phones. Driving this change in how you design the interaction with your applications doesn't have to be that difficult. The Windows Phone platform can help you with built-in resources for many of the user interface elements. These resources are called **system resources** (also known as theme resources).

The system resources can change to accommodate different-sized screens and themes on the phone. For example, a newly created Windows Phone application contains use of these system resources by default:

```
<phone:PhoneApplicationPage ...
  FontFamily="{StaticResource PhoneFontFamilyNormal}"
  FontSize="{StaticResource PhoneFontSizeNormal}"
  Foreground="{StaticResource PhoneForegroundBrush}"
  ...>
  <Grid x:Name="LayoutRoot"
        Background="Transparent">
    <Grid.RowDefinitions>
      <RowDefinition Height="Auto" />
      <RowDefinition Height="*" />
    </Grid.RowDefinitions>

    <StackPanel x:Name="TitlePanel"
                Grid.Row="0"
                Margin="12,17,0,28">
      <TextBlock Text="MY APPLICATION"
                Style="{StaticResource PhoneTextNormalStyle}"
                Margin="12,0" />
      <TextBlock Text="page name"
                Margin="9,-7,0,0"
                Style="{StaticResource PhoneTextTitle1Style}" />
    </StackPanel>

    <!--ContentPanel - place additional content here-->
    <Grid x:Name="ContentPanel"
          Grid.Row="1"
          Margin="12,0,12,0">

    </Grid>
  </Grid>
</phone:PhoneApplicationPage>
```

The system resources are part of the core framework and are not contained as code you would include in your project directly. These system resources actually change as the user picks the theme on his phone. For example, the PhoneBackgroundColor resource is a dark gray color (almost black) on a typical phone application. But if the user changes to the light theme (black text on white background), the PhoneBackgroundColor becomes white.

There are system resources of various kinds, including the following:

- Colors (for example, PhoneBackgroundColor)
- Brushes (for example, PhoneForegroundBrush)
- Font Faces (for example, PhoneFontFamilyNormal)

- Font Sizes (for example, PhoneFontSizeLarge)
- Thickness (for example, PhoneMargin)
- Text Styles (for example, PhoneTextNormalStyle)
- Theme Visibility (for example, PhoneDarkThemeVisibility)

You can find a complete list of the system resources in the documentation:

http://shawnw.me/wptheming

To use the system resources, you can use either Blend or Visual Studio. In both cases you can simply select the resource instead of using fixed values (see Figure 5.65).

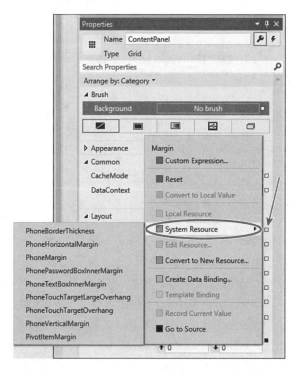

FIGURE 5.65 **Using theme resources (for example, system resources)**

By clicking the small square next to a value, an option for System Resource displays that will show you the valid system resources that match the data-type you have selected. In Figure 5.65, the margin was selected and therefore the system resources available are all in the "thickness" category.

One system resource you should get comfortable working with is the PhoneAccentBrush. This particular system resource replaces the brush with the selected accent brush the user has chosen for the phone. In general, you should use the PhoneAccentBrush anywhere you want to show a selection (instead of relying on bolding or a custom color).

▪ System Resources Best Practices

In general, you should always use a system resource when one is available. By using the system resource for resource types such as thickness and font sizing, you can be sure that your application will adhere to the Windows Phone style guide. You can certainly use your own judgment when using the system resources or not, but by deviating, you'll have to handle the different themes and phone sizes manually.

Where Are We?

Design is an important part of any software project, but when you're writing for Windows Phone, you should treat design of the user experience as a crucial part of the process. Choosing the right user paradigm is important because the user cannot drop down into a richer set of input mechanisms (for example, keyboard or mouse). Touch changes the way applications should work. In addition, applications should thrive on users' curiosity; compelling users to want to learn what your application is capable of is an important dynamic. Lastly, any design that does not make it clear from the start both what it is used for and how to use it is doomed to fail. When it comes to achieving your vision, Expression Blend is a great tool. It's important to realize that even if you're a developer, Blend is a *design* tool, not a *designer's* tool. Learning how to navigate it can really help you not only design great applications, but also accomplish the task in a shorter timeframe. Angle brackets are cool, but creating a complex design with a real tool (like Blend) lets you focus on the parts of the application authoring process you love—whether that is the user interface, the business logic, or the back end.

Although this chapter just scratched the surface of real design, ideally it has given you a sense of what is required to get your vision onto the phone. You might want to augment this book with other design resources to elevate your applications to true experiences.

6

Developing for the Phone

T HUS FAR IN THE BOOK WE HAVE FOCUSED on building experiences. Although creating the appropriate design for your application is crucial to being successful, the development process on the phone is what brings it all together. Developing your application for the phone requires that you understand how developing for the phone is different from other .NET platforms (such as WPF, Windows 8 Store applications, and desktop development). That is what you will learn in this chapter.

Application Lifecycle

When you create a new Windows Phone project, the project contains all the files you need to get started building a phone application. There are several key files, but let's start with the XAML files. As you can see in Figure 6.1, the App.xaml and MainPage.xaml files have code files associated with them (they have a ".cs" extension because this project is a C# project).

These code files represent the code that goes with the main page and the application class, respectively. As we discussed in Chapter 2, "Writing Your First Phone Application," the App.xaml file is where we can store application-wide resources. The class that goes with the App.xaml file represents the application itself. In fact, when your application is started it is this file (not MainPage.xaml's class) that starts up first. This class is called the App class, and it derives from the Application class:

```
public partial class App : Application
{
  // ...
}
```

FIGURE 6.1   **Important files in a new project**

This class is used to store application-wide code/data. For example, the App class stores the main frame for your entire application. This RootFrame property exposes the frame in which all your pages will display:

```
public partial class App : Application
{
  /// <summary>
  /// Provides easy access to the root frame
  /// of the Phone Application.
  /// </summary>
  /// <returns>The root frame of the Phone Application.</returns>
  public PhoneApplicationFrame RootFrame { get; private set; }

  // ...
}
```

Although the App class represents your running application, it is exposed as a singleton via the Application class's Current property. For example, to get at the current application class anywhere in your code, you would call the static Current property on the App class:

```
Application theApplication = App.Current;
```

You should notice that the Current property returns an instance of the Application class (the base class). If you want to access properties on the App class instance itself, you must cast it to the App class, like so:

```
App theApplication = (App)App.Current;
var frame = theApplication.RootFrame;
// ...or...
frame = ((App)App.Current).RootFrame;
```

During initialization of the App class, the RootFrame is created and shown to the user of the phone. But if you look through the code for the App class, it might not seem obvious how the MainPage.xaml is actually shown. The trick is in the third file I highlighted in Figure 6.1: WMAppManifest.xml.

When you open the WMAppManifest.xml file (by double-clicking it), it opens an editor that enables you to change information about the phone app. You can see this editor shown in Figure 6.2.

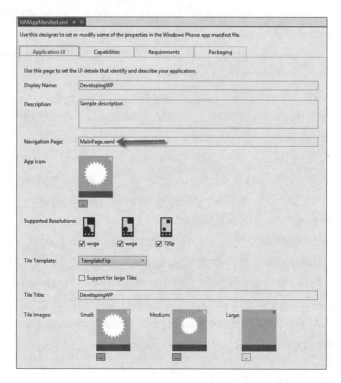

FIGURE 6.2   The WMAppManifest.xml Editor

Highlighted in Figure 6.2 is the item called Navigation Page; this is the URI to the starting page of your application. The manifest file contains a variety of settings that help the phone (and the Marketplace) determine information about your application.

After an instance of the App class is created and initialized, the application is told to navigate to the page in the Navigation Page element of the WMAppManifest.xml file. This is how your MainPage.xaml is shown.

■ Changing the Name of the XAML File

If you decide to change the name of the XAML file (and the underlying class file), you must be sure to change the name in the x:Class declaration as well.

Using a mix of the application class and the manifest file, your application gracefully starts up with your first page being shown. This is similar to how running a typical desktop application starts as well, but the lifecycle of your phone application is actually much different from that.

Navigation

Your application does not have a window. This is an important indication that, although it is called Windows Phone, the "Windows" in the name is not an indication that *Windows* is the operating system. You will have to get used to a different style of development. The entire application model is built around the concept of page-based navigation, which should be comfortable to any user of the Web.

When you start an application, it navigates to a particular page (as dictated in the WMAppManifest.xml file's default task). As the user navigates to other pages, the stack of pages grows. The user can press the Back button on the phone to return to the last page within your application. If the user is at the first page of your application, pressing the Back button will exit your application, as shown in Figure 6.3.

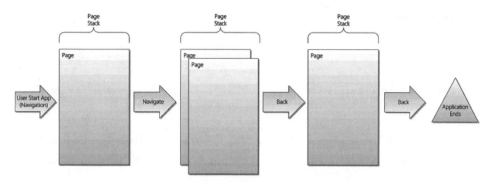

FIGURE 6.3   **Page navigation explained**

If you need to explicitly exit your application, you can use the Application. Terminate method to do so. Although pressing back on the first page of your application will terminate the application, the Application.Terminate method will enable you to specify exit anywhere in the application that makes logical sense.

Programmatically, you can interact with the navigation facility using the NagivationService class. To get access to the application's instance of the NavigationService class, you have two options to find the navigation APIs:

- NavigationService property on classes that derive from Phone-ApplicationPage (for example, MainPage.xaml or other "Page" project items added to your project).

- PhoneApplicationFrame class, which has all the navigation functionality of the NavigationService class. This frame is ordinarily a member of your application's App class.

Although they are functionally the same, these two implementations do not depend on a common base class or an interface to enforce them. They are identical by convention only.

The NavigationService class has a number of useful methods, but the most common usage includes Navigate and GoBack. The Navigate method starts a navigation to a new "page," like so:

```
NavigationService.Navigate(new Uri("/Views/SecondPage.xaml",
                                    UriKind.Relative));

// or

NavigationService.Navigate(new Uri("/Views/SecondPage.xaml?id=123",
                                    UriKind.Relative));
```

The URI in the `Navigate` call specifically searches for a file in the .xap file, and this is typically mimicked by your project structure, as shown in Figure 6.4.

FIGURE 6.4   URI mapping to the files in the project

`HyperlinkButtons` are automatically wired to use the `NavigationService`, so this works fine in your XAML:

```
<HyperlinkButton NavigateUri="/Views/SecondPage.xaml"
                 Content="Go to 2nd Page" />
```

Conversely, the `NavigationService` class's `GoBack` method goes back to the top page on the navigation page stack (or back stack, explained in the next paragraph). This method mimics the user pressing the Back button:

```
NavigationService.GoBack();
```

As you navigate through an application, this `NavigationService` class keeps track of all the pages, so `GoBack` can walk through the pages as necessary. This stack of pages is called the **back stack.** The `NavigationService` provides read-only access to the back stack by providing a property:

```
IEnumerable<JournalEntry> backStack = NavigationService.BackStack;
```

The `backStack` property enables you to iterate through the back stack and interrogate the source of each page, but not change it:

```
// Iterate through the BackEntries
foreach (var entry in NavigationService.BackStack)
{
  Uri page = entry.Source;
}
```

The only change that the `NavigationService` allows is to remove the last entry in the `backStack`. You can do this with `RemoveBackEntry`, which removes only the current page from the `backStack`:

```
// Remove the last page from the navigation
NavigationService.RemoveBackEntry();
```

When navigation occurs (even at the start of an application), the class that represents the page has an opportunity to know it is being navigated to. This is implemented as overrideable methods on the `PhoneApplicationPage` class. The first of these overrideable methods is the `OnNavigatedTo` method:

```
public partial class MainPage : PhoneApplicationPage
{

  // ...

  // I was just navigated to
  protected override void OnNavigatedTo(NavigationEventArgs e)
  {
    base.OnNavigatedTo(e);

    var uri = e.Uri;

  }
}
```

Additionally, there are overrideable methods for navigating away from a page (`OnNavigatingFrom` and `OnNavigatedFrom`):

```csharp
public partial class MainPage : PhoneApplicationPage
{

  // …

  // Navigation to another page is about to happen
  protected override void OnNavigatingFrom(NavigatingCancelEventArgs e)
  {
    base.OnNavigatingFrom(e);
  }

  // Navigation to another page just finished happening
  protected override void OnNavigatedFrom(NavigatingCancelEventArgs e)
  {
    base.OnNavigatedFrom(e);
  }
}
```

The NavigationService also has events if you want to react to changes in the navigation as they happen, including Navigating, Navigated, and NavigationFailed. These events can be useful in globally monitoring navigation.

■ Accidental Circular Navigation

Be careful when doing navigation in your application because you can accidentally get into circular navigation by using the NavigationService's Navigate method when you meant to use the GoBack method.

For example, you might want to go to an Options page in your application. When the user is finished changing options, it might be tempting to use Navigate() to return to the last page, but doing that leaves the last page in the page stack twice. Using GoBack() is the right way to return to the prior page.

As shown earlier, the URI you navigate to can contain query string information. You could get the URI in your OnNavigatedFrom method and try to parse the query string manually, but this is unnecessary. The NavigationContext class supports simple access to the query string. For example, if you wanted to get the ID from the query string, you could simply use the NavigationContext instead:

```
protected override void OnNavigatedTo(NavigationEventArgs e)
{
  base.OnNavigatedTo(e);

  if (NavigationContext.QueryString.ContainsKey("id"))
  {
    var id = NavigationContext.QueryString["id"];
    // Use the id
  }
}
```

By using the NavigationService, NavigationContext, and PhoneApplicationPage classes, you can control the navigation of different parts of your application as well as give users a more intuitive experience.

During the OnNavigatedTo method, you can also discern the mode of the navigation. This can help determine how to deal with the navigation to a particular page. The mode of the navigation has to do with how the page is being launched. If the page was reached by pressing back on a deeper page in the navigation stack, you can think of the navigation as being a "back" navigation. The NavigationEventArgs object that is passed into the OnNavigatedTo method contains the mode of the navigation, as shown here:

```
protected override void OnNavigatedTo(NavigationEventArgs e)
{
  base.OnNavigatedTo(e);

  if (e.NavigationMode == NavigationMode.Back)
  {
    // Get changes from other page
  }
  else if (e.NavigationMode == NavigationMode.Forward)
  {
    // Initialize for a clean navigation
  }
}
```

You can also check for NavigationMode from within the OnNavigatingFrom method:

```
protected override void OnNavigatingFrom(NavigatingCancelEventArgs e)
{
  base.OnNavigatingFrom(e);

  if (e.NavigationMode == NavigationMode.Back)
  {
    // Handle Back
  }

}
```

In addition to the mode, you can determine whether your application initiated a particular navigation. This is useful for when you want to see whether the navigation to a particular page started from inside your application or elsewhere (for example, from a deep link). You can test this by checking the IsNavigationInitiator property both in the OnNavigatedTo and the OnNavigatingFrom methods. For IsNavigationInitiator to be true, both the origin of the navigation and the destination must both be within the application. If you are navigating from a shortcut or navigating to an external app (that is, a web browser), this property will be false:

```
protected override void OnNavigatedTo(NavigationEventArgs e)
{
  base.OnNavigatedTo(e);

  if (e.IsNavigationInitiator)
  {
    MessageBox.Show("We initiated the navigation");
  }
}

protected override void OnNavigatingFrom(NavigatingCancelEventArgs e)
{
  base.OnNavigatingFrom(e);

  if (e.IsNavigationInitiator != true)
  {
    // Prepare to head outside the app
  }
}
```

When you are handing the OnNavigatingFrom method, there are times when this navigation is cancellable. You could imagine if a user isn't done filling out a form or data and you don't want him to lose what he's filled in. The NavigatingCancelEventArgs parameter contains a couple of properties that will let you see whether a navigation is cancellable and enable you to mark it as cancelled if necessary, as shown:

```
protected override void OnNavigatingFrom(NavigatingCancelEventArgs e)
{
  base.OnNavigatingFrom(e);

  if (e.IsCancelable)
  {
    e.Cancel = true;
    return;
  }
}
```

Setting the Cancel property to true is valid only if the IsCancelable property is also true. You could imagine that some navigations will not support cancellation such as the user hitting the Windows button or answering a phone call. Those types of operations are always given precedence to your application's requirements.

Tombstoning

As you saw back in Chapter 1, "Introducing Windows Phone," the phone supports a concept called **tombstoning**. The idea of tombstoning is essentially to give the illusion of multitasking without the touch realities of running multiple applications at the same time. To achieve this illusion, your application can move between running, dormant, and suspended states, as shown in Figure 6.5.

When your application is on the screen (visible to the user), your application is in a running state. But a number of things can interrupt your application, including a phone call, a "toast" alert, or even the user pressing the Start or Search keys. When something interrupts your application, your application is notified that it is being **deactivated.** During deactivation you can save certain data (or state) about your application. After deactivation is complete, your process is moved to a **dormant** state. In this state all the threads are suspended and no processing continues to take place. If the operating system determines that it needs the memory your dormant application is using, it will remove it from memory (called the **suspended** state) but will retain any data (state) you saved during deactivation. If the user returns to your app (usually via the Back button), your application is notified that it is being **activated.** During the activation process, you will determine whether the phone was activated from the dormant or suspended state, and either just restart the application or use the saved state to return your application to its original state. As far as the user is concerned, the application should act just like it was running in the background.

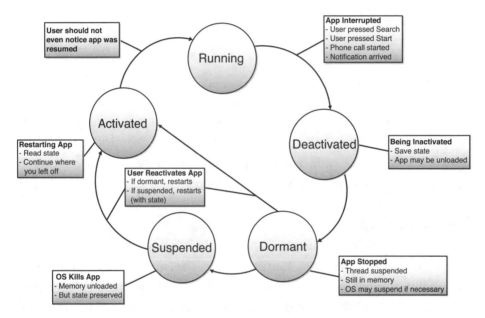

FIGURE 6.5 How tombstoning works

■ Why Tombstoning?

Tombstoning gives the illusion of multitasking without the overhead. It enables the operating system to load and unload your application as if it were running in the background. The user should be oblivious that your application was stopped or unloaded. It should "just work."

This process is exposed to you via the PhoneApplicationService class. An instance of this class is created in the App.xaml file of your project by default:

```
<Application ...>

  <!--Application Resources-->
  <Application.Resources>
  </Application.Resources>

  <Application.ApplicationLifetimeObjects>
    <shell:PhoneApplicationService
      Launching="Application_Launching"
      Closing="Application_Closing"
      Activated="Application_Activated"
      Deactivated="Application_Deactivated" />
  </Application.ApplicationLifetimeObjects>

</Application>
```

The PhoneApplicationService class is created to have the same lifetime as the Application class we discussed earlier. When it is created, it wires it up to four events in the Application class itself. The default Windows Phone Application template creates this object and wires it up for you. If you look at the App.xaml.cs/vb file (where the Application class is defined), you will see the corresponding methods that are mentioned in the App.xaml class:

```
public partial class App : Application
{
  // ...

  private void Application_Launching(object sender,
                                LaunchingEventArgs e)
  {
    // ...
  }

  private void Application_Activated(object sender,
                                ActivatedEventArgs e)
  {
    // ...
  }
```

```
private void Application_Deactivated(object sender,
                                     DeactivatedEventArgs e)
{
  // ...
}

private void Application_Closing(object sender,
                                 ClosingEventArgs e)
{
  // ...
}

// ...
}
```

These boilerplate functions are called as the state of your application changes. The first and last ones (Launching and Closing) only happen when your application is first launched directly by the user (for example, by clicking an application icon or responding to a toast notification) and when the user closes the application (for example, by pressing Back from the first page of the application). But for tombstoning, the real magic happens in the other two handlers: Activated and Deactivated. These handlers are called during tombstoning to enable you to save and load state into your application.

To save your state, the PhoneApplicationService class gives you access to a property bag to store data into. This class supports a State property, which is an IDictionary<string, object> collection that is used to store serializable objects by name. To use the class, simply use the class's static Current property to get at the current service object and use the State property from there. Here is an example of storing a simple object (a color) into the State property:

```
private void Application_Deactivated(object sender,
                                     DeactivatedEventArgs e)
{
  PhoneApplicationService.Current.State["favoriteColor"] = Colors.Red;
}
```

> ■ **NOTE**
>
> If you are new to .NET, the concept of serializable objects means whether an in-memory version of an object is compatible with being written out in a format for temporary or permanent storage. This storage is typically used to take objects in memory and store them for rehydration back to memory objects. Serialization is used when you're storing objects in the PhoneApplicationService's State collection, but it is also used when storing data to memory on the phone, or even when you want to save data across a network connection.

The application is a common place to store this state, but because the PhoneApplicationService class is where the real magic happens, you can handle that state wherever you want. For example, in a single-page application, you might use the PhoneApplicationService class to store data as the page is navigated from (which happens during tombstoning as well):

```
protected override void OnNavigatingFrom(NavigatingCancelEventArgs e)
{
  base.OnNavigatingFrom(e);

  PhoneApplicationService.Current
                    .State[MoodKey] = moodPicker.SelectedItem;
}
```

Because the PhoneApplicationService's Current method always points to the current service for the application, you can use this state class anywhere.

■ **Saving Tombstone State**

Although tombstoning gives you the opportunity to save state, you should only save transitory state here. Tombstoning state should be just enough to restart the application. You can save longer-lived or nonvolatile state into isolated storage (discussed in Chapter 9, "Databases and Storage") or in the cloud. The tombstoning state's lifetime is owned by the operating system and can go away without your control. It is not an exceptional case for the operating system to eliminate this state, and you should be prepared for your application to relaunch instead of recovering from tombstoning. Therefore, the tombstone state should be only for the minimum state required to have your application "wake up" from being suspended. The larger the tombstone state, the longer it will take you to wake up from tombstoning. Because the user shouldn't notice tombstoning, minimizing this state is important.

When your application is activated, you can check the event argument's IsApplicationInstancePreserved property to detect whether your application was dormant or actually suspended. If it was suspended, you will need to recover the state saved during the Deactivated event:

```
private void Application_Activated(object sender,
                                          ActivatedEventArgs e)
{

  if (e.IsApplicationInstancePreserved)
  {
    // Nothing to do as your application was just 'Dormant'
  }
  else
  {
    // Recover State and resurrect your
    // application from being 'Suspended'
    var stateBag = PhoneApplicationService.Current.State;
    var state = stateBag["favoriteColor"];
    var color = (Color)state;
  }
}
```

During activation you have a full 10 seconds to process your data. Ten seconds ends up being a really long time and should not be used as the benchmark. Users will give up way before that. In general, tuning this to be as fast as possible will give you a better user experience.

The Navigation Framework is part of an application's tombstone state by default, so when an application is acti

vated, the first page navigated to will be the last page the user was on. In addition, the page stack is also preserved, so you do not have to save this information manually. The applications will be activated in the exact same place (navigation-wise) from which they were deactivated. At this point, you should understand how the life of a phone application works. Knowing that your application will need to deal with a mix of navigation, tombstoning, and startup/shutdown behaviors should equip you with the knowledge to build your application for the phone.

The Phone Experience

Phones are different. Yes, we've covered that already in this book, but it deserves to be reiterated. Phones are different. The development experience is different, too. While developing your application, you will have to deal with several facilities that relate to the user's experience on the phone: phone orientation, touch input, phone-specific controls, the application bar. In this section you will learn how to deal with these different areas of functionality.

Orientation

The phone supports three main orientations: portrait, landscape left, and landscape right, as shown in Figures 6.6, 6.7, and 6.8. These orientations are supported on all the phones. You can control which orientation(s) your application supports as well as switching between them.

On the `PhoneApplicationPage` class, you can specify which orientations you expect your application to support:

```
<phone:PhoneApplicationPage
        ...
        SupportedOrientations="PortraitOrLandscape">
```

FIGURE 6.6   **Portrait orientation**

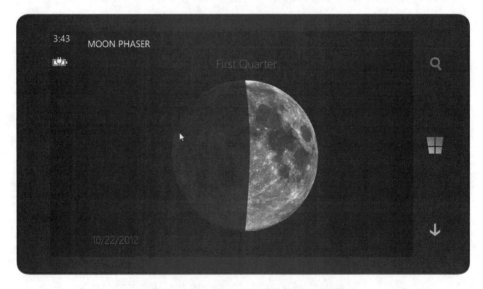

FIGURE 6.7   **Landscape left orientation**

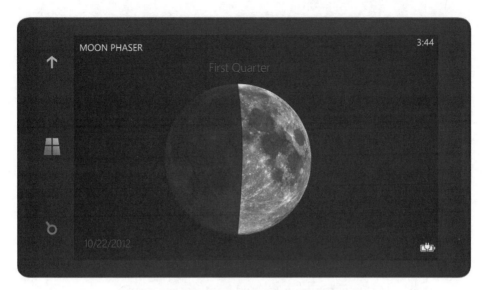

FIGURE 6.8 Landscape right orientation

The `SupportedOrientations` accepts one of the values in the `SupportedPageOrientation` enumeration: `Landscape`, `Portrait`, or `PortraitOr-Landscape`. By specifying `PortraitOrLandscape`, you are telling the phone that you want to enable the orientation to change as the phone is turned. By default, the phone will simply attempt to display your page using the new orientation. Because the default project template creates a page that is essentially just a grid within a grid, often this works. But in many cases you will want to customize the experience when the user changes the orientation. The `PhoneApplicationPage` class supports an `OrientationChanged` event that is fired when the orientation changes, and this is a common way to change the user interface:

```
public partial class MainPage : PhoneApplicationPage
{
  // ...

  // Constructor
  public MainPage()
  {
    InitializeComponent();
```

```
    // Change size of app based on changed orientation
    OrientationChanged += MainPage_OrientationChanged;
  }
}
```

This will give you a chance to change your application as necessary. For example, if you just wanted to resize some of your user interface, you could scale the application depending on the orientation:

```
void MainPage_OrientationChanged(object sender,
                                 OrientationChangedEventArgs e)
{
  if ((e.Orientation & PageOrientation.Landscape) ==
                            PageOrientation.Landscape)
  {
    theScaler.ScaleX = theScaler.ScaleY = .86;
  }
  else if ((e.Orientation & PageOrientation.Portrait) ==
                            PageOrientation.Portrait)
  {
    theScaler.ScaleX = theScaler.ScaleY = 1.16;
  }
}
```

Although using a rendering transformation will help you change your user interface, you might decide to rearrange your design dramatically for the change in orientation, or even use a different view. The amount of change is completely up to you.

■ Changing the Orientation Design in Blend

Jaime Rodriguez has a great presentation on some sample behaviors he has created for Blend that can enable you to change the layout of your application using behaviors. See his video at http://channel9.msdn.com/blogs/jaime+rodriguez/windows-phone-design-days-blend.

Designing for Touch

The primary input on the phone is touch. It is the main reason that designing for the phone is so different from designing for other applications. At this point in the book you should have a good idea about the difference in the design metaphor, but programming against that metaphor is a different story.

If you are coming to Windows Phone development from Microsoft platforms (for example, Silverlight, .NET, and so on), it might seem obvious to handle touch by using the built-in mouse events. The touch interface is mimicked in the mouse events, as you might expect. For example, to handle tapping on the surface of an application, you can simply handle the mouse event:

```
public partial class MainPage : PhoneApplicationPage
{
  // Constructor
  public MainPage()
  {
    InitializeComponent();

    ContentPanel.MouseLeftButtonUp +=
      new MouseButtonEventHandler(ContentPanel_MouseLeftButtonUp);

  }

  void ContentPanel_MouseLeftButtonUp(object sender,
                                      MouseButtonEventArgs e)
  {
    theText.Text = "Content Panel Tapped";
  }

  // ...
}
```

Although the built-in mouse events do work, they are often not fine-grained enough for a rich user experience, so it is recommended that you not use them unless you have a very specific reason. Touch is different because we tend to drag, swipe, and pinch the screen very differently than we did (or could) with the mouse. The phone supports four points of touch so that the mouse events end up falling down on any input that enables more than one finger. Instead of relying on the mouse events, you should use one of the other methods for working with touch (as shown in the following).

> ■ **Best Practice**
>
> You should not use mouse events for implementing touch in your applications. You should instead use the touch APIs (for example, Tap, Hold, and so on), the Manipulation events, or the Touch class for the highest level of control to implement touch in your application.

To help with touch, the phone has several layers of APIs to help you get to the touch surface. At the lowest level, the Touch class can report every touch interaction the user does. Windows Phone's Touch class is most useful when you want to get as close to the metal as possible. The Touch class has a static event called FrameReported, which is called as touch interaction is happening. With it you can get information about how many touch points are being used (for example, how many fingers are on the touch surface) as well as where the touch points are. The event contains an argument that enables you to get at the point information. Here is an example using the FrameReported event to show where the touch is being dragged on the surface of the phone:

```
public partial class MainPage : PhoneApplicationPage
{
  // Constructor
  public MainPage()
  {
    InitializeComponent();

    Touch.FrameReported += Touch_FrameReported;
  }

  void Touch_FrameReported(object sender, TouchFrameEventArgs e)
  {
    var mainTouchPoint = e.GetPrimaryTouchPoint(this);
    if (mainTouchPoint.Action == TouchAction.Move)
    {
      theText.Text = string.Concat("Moving: ",
                                   mainTouchPoint.Position);
    }
```

```
    }

    // ...
}
```

The TouchFrameEventArgs class has several pieces of functionality. The two that are most important are the GetPrimaryTouchPoint and GetTouchPoints methods. The GetPrimaryTouchPoint method is used to retrieve a TouchPoint object that is relative to a particular-UIElement of the design. The primary touch point is determined by the first thing that touches the screen. Being **relative** means that all touch positions will be relative to that UIElement. The TouchPoint class can tell you the position and action that are occurring, as shown in the following code sample:

```
void Touch_FrameReported(object sender, TouchFrameEventArgs e)
{
  // Get the main touch point (relative to a UIElement)
  TouchPoint mainTouchPoint = e.GetPrimaryTouchPoint(ContentPanel);

  // Get the position
  Point position = mainTouchPoint.Position;

  // Get the Action of the Touch
  switch (mainTouchPoint.Action)
  {
    case TouchAction.Move:
      theText.Text = "Moving";
      break;
    case TouchAction.Up:
      theText.Text = "Touch Ended";
      break;
    case TouchAction.Down:
      theText.Text = "Touch Started";
      break;
  }
}
```

The GetTouchPoints method also retrieves touch information that is relative to a UIElement, but in this case all the current touch points are returned as a collection of TouchPoint objects:

```
void Touch_FrameReported(object sender, TouchFrameEventArgs e)
{

  // Get all the touch points
```

```
TouchPointCollection points = e.GetTouchPoints(ContentPanel);

theText.Text = string.Concat("#/Touch Points: ", points.Count);

}
```

Each `TouchPoint` object in the collection represents a single touch point on the phone. All phones support at least four points of touch. The way you work with the individual touch points from the collection is identical to the `TouchPoint` you retrieved from the `GetPrimaryTouchPoint` method.

Although the `Touch.FrameReported` event will give you a lot of control, you might want something higher-level so that you can handle simple movement or sizing behavior. To fill that need, Windows Phone also supports manipulations. The concept behind manipulations is to be able to easily interact with common manipulations of objects on the screen. These include sizing and moving of objects. The `UIElement` class supports these directly by supporting three events, as described in Table 6.1.

TABLE 6.1 **Manipulation Events**

Event	Description
ManipulationStarted	Occurs when a manipulation (pinch or drag) begins on the UIElement
ManipulationCompleted	Occurs when a manipulation (pinch or drag) is complete on the UIElement
ManipulationDelta	Fires as a manipulation (pinch or drag) is occurring on the UIElement

These events are used to support manipulation of objects on the screen, more than just touch. The basic idea of a manipulation is to be notified about attempts to change objects on the phone by dragging or resizing. For example, the `ManipulationDelta` event sends information about the manipulation while it is happening in the form of a `ManipulationDeltaEventArgs` object argument. This argument includes both the cumulative amount of manipulation and the difference between the last delta and the current one. The manipulation amount is defined in a class called `ManipulationDelta`. The `ManipulationDelta` class contains two pieces of information: translation and scale. These pieces of information correlate directly to the idea of how transforms in XAML work (for example, `TranslateTransform` and `ScaleTransform` specifically). The amount of translation indicates how far an item has been dragged (or moved). The scale indicates how much the item has been sized using the pinch touch gesture. For example, to move an object using a manipulation, you might add a `TranslateTransform` to your design:

```xml
...
<Ellipse Fill="Red"
          Width="200"
          Height="200"
          x:Name="theCircle">
  <Ellipse.RenderTransform>
    <TranslateTransform x:Name="theTransform" />
  </Ellipse.RenderTransform>
</Ellipse>
...
```

With the transform in place, you can handle the `ManipulationDelta` event and use the `TranslateTransform` to move the element in response to dragging:

```csharp
public partial class MainPage : PhoneApplicationPage
{
  // Constructor
  public MainPage()
  {
    InitializeComponent();

    ManipulationDelta += MainPage_ManipulationDelta;
  }

  void MainPage_ManipulationDelta(object sender,
                                  ManipulationDeltaEventArgs e)
  {

    // Move (for example Translate) the ellipse based on delta
    ManipulationDelta m = e.CumulativeManipulation;
    theTransform.X = m.Translation.X;
    theTransform.Y= m.Translation.Y;

  }

  ...

}
```

In this particular example, the CumulativeManipulation is used to get the entire touch manipulation. The Manipulation's Translation property contains the amount of the translation, but we cannot be sure this manipulation is about a particular element on our page (as we registered for the page's ManipulationDelta event). We could register just for our ellipse's manipulation, but alternatively we could also test to see which container was being manipulated by testing the ManipulationContainer like so:

```
void MainPage_ManipulationDelta(object sender,
                              ManipulationDeltaEventArgs e)
{
  if (e.ManipulationContainer == theCircle)
  {
    // Move (for example Translate) the ellipse based on delta
    ManipulationDelta m = e.CumulativeManipulation;
    theTransform.X = m.Translation.X;
    theTransform.Y = m.Translation.Y;
  }

}
```

Using pinch and zoom touch gestures works in the same way you can use a ScaleTransform to change the size instead of the TranslateTransform:

```
<Ellipse Fill="Red"
         Width="200"
         Height="200"
         x:Name="theCircle">
  <Ellipse.RenderTransform>
    <ScaleTransform x:Name="theTransform"
                    CenterX="100"
                    CenterY="100"/>
  </Ellipse.RenderTransform>
</Ellipse>
```

Then, in the manipulation events, you can simply use the scale properties in the ManipulationDelta instead of Translate, like so:

```
void MainPage_ManipulationDelta(object sender,
ManipulationDeltaEventArgs e)
{
  if (e.ManipulationContainer == theCircle)
  {
    // Size (for example Scale) the ellipse based on delta
    ManipulationDelta m = e.CumulativeManipulation;
```

```
    theTransform.ScaleX = m.Scale.X;
    theTransform.ScaleY = m.Scale.Y;
  }
}
```

Manipulations also include information about the **inertia** of the touch gestures. The idea behind inertia is to be able to tell whether the user was still moving when the manipulation ended. The inertia information becomes important to making more organic interactions with users. If you have seen how flicking a list box on the phone makes the list scroll up even when the user is no longer touching the phone, this is accomplished using inertia.

For example, on the `ManipulationCompleted` event you can test for `IsInertial` to see whether the manipulation contains inertial velocity information:

```
void MainPage_ManipulationCompleted(object sender,
                                    ManipulationCompletedEventArgs e)
{
  if (e.IsInertial)
  {
    var m = e.TotalManipulation;
    var velocity = e.FinalVelocities;
    theTransform.X =
      m.Translation.X + (velocity.LinearVelocity.X / 100);
    theTransform.Y =
      m.Translation.Y + (velocity.LinearVelocity.Y / 100);
  }
}
```

After the code determines it is inertial, it can use the `FinalVelocities` to change the outcome of the translation (in this example). You could also see whether the `LinearVelocity` is greater than some threshold to determine whether it is a "flick" :

```
void MainPage_ManipulationCompleted(object sender,
                                    ManipulationCompletedEventArgs e)
{
  if (e.IsInertial)
  {
    var velocity = e.FinalVelocities;
```

```
    // Is it a Right Flick?
    if (velocity.LinearVelocity.X > 100)
    {
      // ...
    }
  }
}
```

The manipulation events are used specifically to handle the drag and scale, but as we discussed before, there are a number of types of touch gestures. Although having access to manipulations and lower-level access with the Touch class helps, for most of your touch interface, you'd like to access events for those gestures directly.

The UIElement class has access to the most common types of touch gestures. You can see the touch events the UIElement class exposes in Table 6.2.

TABLE 6.2 UIElement **Touch Events**

Event	Description
Tap	Occurs when a user touches a UIElement and lifts her finger fairly quickly
Double-tap	Occurs when a user taps a UIElement twice in quick succession
Hold	Occurs when a user touches and holds her finger over a UIElement

Wiring up to these events is as simple as wiring up the event:

```
public partial class MainPage : PhoneApplicationPage
{
  // Constructor
  public MainPage()
  {
    InitializeComponent();

    var listener = theCircle.Hold += theCircle_Hold;
  }

  void theCircle_Hold(object sender, GestureEventArgs e)
  {
```

```
    // Do a hold
  }
}
```

The UIElement class represents any visual element on a page, so you can wire up these events on any object (for example, Button, ListBox, Grid, Ellipse, and so on). As you work with touch, you will use a variety of these touch-based APIs in your application. When working with common gestures, the element approach is easiest, but because you want more control over the nature of the touch surface, you will have to delve further down into the stack of APIs.

Application Client Area

As the basis for the entire application, the shell is responsible for hosting your pages. This also means certain responsibilities are given to a set of classes that exist in the Microsoft.Phone.Shell namespace; it is where you can make some decisions about how your application is displayed. As explained in Chapter 1, the application area is broken up into a system tray, the logical client area, and the application bar (as shown in Figure 6.9).

FIGURE 6.9 Application client area

You can decide to hide the system tray (entering a sort of "full-screen mode") via the SystemTray class, as shown here:

```
void MainPage_Loaded(object sender, RoutedEventArgs e)
{
  SystemTray.IsVisible = false;
}
```

Using the SystemTray class enables you to change this to meet your needs. You do not have to set this in code, but doing so is supported via an attached property in XAML:

```
<phone:PhoneApplicationPage ...
  xmlns:shell=
    "clr-namespace:Microsoft.Phone.Shell;assembly=Microsoft.Phone"
  shell:SystemTray.IsVisible="True">
```

In addition, you can also specify the color and opacity of the SystemTray to better match any branding your application uses:

```
<phone:PhoneApplicationPage x:Class="DevelopingWP.MainPage"
                            shell:SystemTray.IsVisible="True"
                            shell:SystemTray.BackgroundColor="White"
                            shell:SystemTray.ForegroundColor="Blue"
                            shell:SystemTray.Opacity="0.8">
```

When you show the SystemTray, it reduces the size of your application. The only exception to this is when you reduce the opacity of the SystemTray. By using an opacity of less than 1, the SystemTray will be swipeable (to show it over your application). It is suggested that all applications show the SystemTray but use the opacity to enable the user to optionally show the SystemTray as needed.

Several operations on the phone also will show over some part of your application (but not navigate away from your application). Receiving a phone call, alarms, and the lock screen are common examples of this. When the phone shows these over your application, it is **obscuring** your application. You can react to these activities by handling the PhoneApplicationFrame's Obscured and Unobscured events:

```
var rootFrame = ((App)App.Current).RootFrame;

rootFrame.Obscured += RootFrame_Obscured;

rootFrame.Unobscured += RootFrame_Unobscured;
```

These events will enable you to react to the obscuring of your application. A common usage is to enter a pause screen when you are writing a game for the phone.

Application Bar

Another part of the normal screen real estate is the application bar. This bar is a mix of a toolbar and a menu. Although you can create an application bar using Blend (that is, XAML), programming against application bars presents a couple of small inconveniences. In fact, the ApplicationBar is part of the operating system, and when you add an ApplicationBar to your XAML, you're simply instructing the underlying operating system to show the application bar with your items on it. This means you won't be able to draw directly onto the application bar but simply supply items to the operating system.

As I explained before, the ApplicationBar supports ApplicationBarIcon-Button and ApplicationBarMenuItem objects to enable users to interact with the application:

```
<phone:PhoneApplicationPage.ApplicationBar>
  <shell:ApplicationBar IsVisible="True"
                        IsMenuEnabled="True">
    <shell:ApplicationBarIconButton
      IconUri="/icons/appbar.add.rest.png"
      Text="add" />
    <shell:ApplicationBarIconButton
      IconUri="/icons/appbar.back.rest.png"
      Text="revert" />
    <shell:ApplicationBar.MenuItems>
      <shell:ApplicationBarMenuItem Text="options" />
      <shell:ApplicationBarMenuItem Text="about" />
    </shell:ApplicationBar.MenuItems>
  </shell:ApplicationBar>
</phone:PhoneApplicationPage.ApplicationBar>
```

Wiring up the Click events in XAML is possible and works the way you expect:

```
<shell:ApplicationBarIconButton
  IconUri="/icons/appbar.add.rest.png"
  x:Name="addIconButton"
  Click="addIconButton_Click"
  Text="add" />
```

But the application bar is different from typical buttons or similar controls. The menu and icon button objects don't support commanding (like ButtonBase-derived controls), so you can't use data binding with the commanding support. Even if you name elements in the ApplicationBar (like previously shown). the resultant wired-up member of the code-behind is null, so the event wiring will fail:

```
public partial class MainPage : PhoneApplicationPage
{
  // Constructor
  public MainPage()
  {
    InitializeComponent();

    // Doesn't work because addIconButton is null!
    addIconButton.Click += addIconButton_Click;
  }
...
}
```

There is a technical reason this does not work,[1] but more important than understanding the reason is to understand that when you need to refer to the icon buttons or menu items in code, you will need to retrieve them by ordinal from the ApplicationBar property on the PhoneApplication-Phone class. Although this is fragile and painful, it's the only way this will work currently. Here is how to do it:

```
public partial class MainPage : PhoneApplicationPage
{
  // Constructor
```

---

1 The ApplicationBar is applied to the PhoneApplicationPage class via an attached property. This means the named elements are not part of the namescope, so calling the FrameworkElement class's FindName method that the generated partial class uses does not find the icon buttons or menu items.

```
public MainPage()
{
  InitializeComponent();

  // Wire-up the button by ordinal
  addIconButton =
    (ApplicationBarIconButton)ApplicationBar.Buttons[0];

  // Wire-up the menu by ordinal
  optionMenuItem =
    (ApplicationBarMenuItem)ApplicationBar.MenuItems[0];

  // Works now that the manual wire-up was added
  addIconButton.Click += addIconButton_Click;
}
...
}
```

Understanding Idle Detection

The Windows Phone operating system automatically detects when a user has stopped using the phone and locks it. The phone will go to a lock screen, which can either display a pass code to open the lock screen or just instruct the user to slide up the wallpaper screen to get back to the phone.

Sometimes when you're building certain types of applications, you want your application to continue to run regardless of whether the phone has input. There are two types of idle detection modes: application and user.

The easier of these to understand is the **user idle detection mode.** On the PhoneApplicationService class is a property called UserIdleDetectionMode; it is enabled by default. This means that if no touch events are detected, it will let the phone go to the lock screen. You can change this behavior (to enable your application to continue to run as the main running application even if the user isn't interacting with your application) by disabling this detection mode, like so:

```
// Allow application to stay in the foreground
// even if the user isn't interacting with the application
PhoneApplicationService.Current.UserIdleDetectionMode =
  IdleDetectionMode.Disabled;
```

Disabling the user idle detection mode is useful when you are doing things that engage the user but do not require input (for example, showing a video, displaying a clock, and so on).

In contrast, the **application idle detection mode** is not about preventing the lock screen but determining what the application should do when the lock screen is enabled. By default, the application idle detection mode is enabled, which means that when the lock screen appears the application is paused (as though it was being tombstoned). By disabling the application idle detection mode, you allow your application to continue to run under the lock screen. To disable the application idle detection mode, you also use the PhoneApplicationService class:

```
// Allow your application to continue to run
// when the lock screen is shown
PhoneApplicationService.Current.ApplicationIdleDetectionMode =
  IdleDetectionMode.Disabled;
```

The Tilt Effect

In many places on the phone, a subtle but effective feedback mechanism is employed when selecting items in a list or other controls. This is called the **tilt effect.** In Figure 6.10, you can see that the second item in the list is not being interacted with via touch; however, in Figure 6.11 you can see that the second item is subtly tilted to give the user feedback that she is touching the item. In fact, it's hard to see here in static images, but the tilt actually interacts with where the user is touching the item.

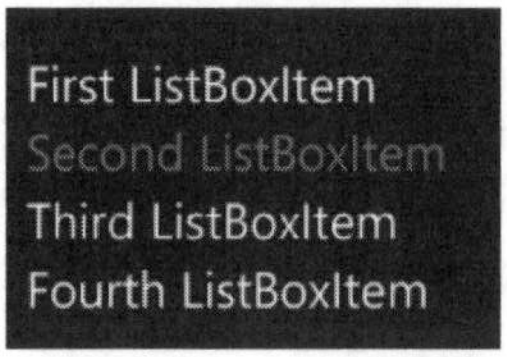

First ListBoxItem
Second ListBoxItem
Third ListBoxItem
Fourth ListBoxItem

FIGURE 6.10   Untilted

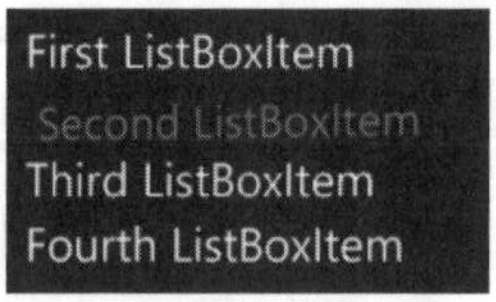

First ListBoxItem
Second ListBoxItem
Third ListBoxItem
Fourth ListBoxItem

FIGURE 6.11   Tilted

Unfortunately, this effect is not built into the framework, but it is available in the Windows Phone Toolkit. When you include the Toolkit's XML namespace declaration in your XAML file, you can specify it at any level to enable or disable this behavior. The namespace required is the same one that is used to include Windows Phone Toolkit controls (as shown in Chapter 5, "Designing for the Phone"). Typically you would include it at the page level to support the tilt effect in all controls, like so:

```
<phone:PhoneApplicationPage ...
    xmlns:toolkit="clr-namespace:Microsoft.Phone.Controls;
                    assembly=Microsoft.Phone.Controls.Toolkit"
    toolkit:TiltEffect.IsTiltEnabled="True">
```

The `TiltEffect.IsTiltEnabled` property can be applied to any individual control as well if you want to apply the effect to specific controls instead of at the page or container levels. The other attached property is `TiltEffect.SuppressTilt`. This attached property enables you to turn off the tilt effect on particular controls where the `TiltEffect.IsTiltEnabled` attached property is enabled at a higher level. For example:

```
<Grid x:Name="ContentPanel"
      Grid.Row="1"
      Margin="12,0,12,0"
      toolkit:TiltEffect.IsTiltEnabled="False">
  <ListBox FontSize="28"
           Name="listBox1"
           toolkit:TiltEffect.SuppressTilt="True"
           ItemsSource="{Binding}" />
</Grid>
```

Because these are attached properties, you can set them in code as well:

```
using Microsoft.Phone.Controls;

public partial class MainPage : PhoneApplicationPage
{
  // Constructor
  public MainPage()
  {
    InitializeComponent();

    listBox1.SetValue(TiltEffect.SuppressTiltProperty, false);
  }
}
```

Localizing Your Phone Application

When creating applications for the global market, it becomes important to be able to allow users to use your application in their native language. Because the Windows Phone uses the .NET Framework, many of the same techniques can be used.

Many of these changes are supported in the templates. If you create a new phone application, by default a string resource file (AppResources.resx file) is created with some basic string localization. This generates a new class called AppResources that provides access to the localized resources based on the current culture of the app. The template also generates a class called LocalizedStrings that wraps the AppResources class so you can use it in data binding, but we'll get to how that works in a minute. If you look at Figure 6.12, you can see the AppResources.resx file and the LocalizedStrings.cs file:

FIGURE 6.12   **AppResources.resx and LocalizedString.cs in the project**

If you double-click the AppResources.resx file, you'll see the string table shown in an editor that will let you modify, add, and remove specific strings, as shown in Figure 6.13.

The default AppResources.resx file contains resources for the default language (for example, U.S. English). The name column specifies the identifier that you will use to access the resource. The second column is the localized value (U.S. English is this default resource file). Finally, the comment column is to document the resource if necessary.

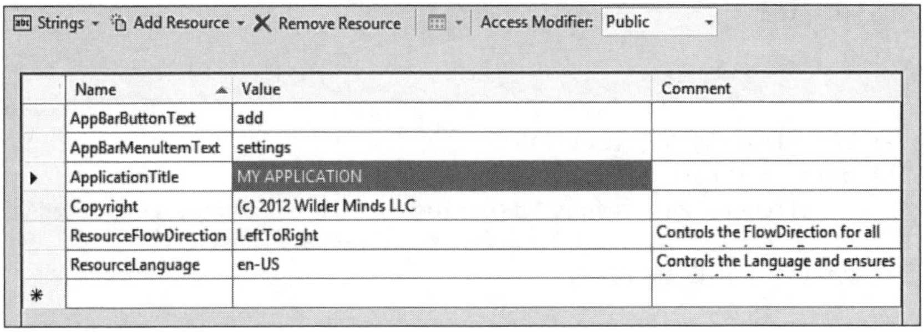

	Name ▲	Value	Comment
	AppBarButtonText	add	
	AppBarMenuItemText	settings	
▶	ApplicationTitle	MY APPLICATION	
	Copyright	(c) 2012 Wilder Minds LLC	
	ResourceFlowDirection	LeftToRight	Controls the FlowDirection for all
	ResourceLanguage	en-US	Controls the Language and ensures
✳			

FIGURE 6.13 Editing the `AppResources.resx` file

To access the resources, you can just use the static methods and properties on the generated `AppResource` class. For example, to set the text of a `TextBlock` via code:

```
void MainPage_Loaded(object sender, RoutedEventArgs e)
{
  contentBlock.Text = AppResources.Copyright;
}
```

Because you're building applications with XAML, it would be useful if this same technique can be used via data binding. The problem is that data binding does not work against static classes. So to solve that, the template creates a simple wrapper class that exposes the entire `AppResources` static class:

```
public class LocalizedStrings
{
  private static AppResources _localizedResources =
    new AppResources();

  public AppResources LocalizedResources
  {
    get { return _localizedResources; }
  }
}
```

To enable all the XAML to access this class, the template adds an instance of this class in the `app.xaml` file:

```
<Application x:Class="LocalizedApp.App"
  ...
>

  <!--Application Resources-->
  <Application.Resources>
    <local:LocalizedStrings xmlns:local="clr-namespace:LocalizedApp"
                            x:Key="LocalizedStrings" />
  </Application.Resources>

  // ...

</Application>
```

Because this is exposed in the App.xaml file, you can use this object utilizing a StaticResource. For example:

```
<TextBlock Text="{Binding LocalizedResources.ApplicationTitle,
                  Source={StaticResource LocalizedStrings}}"
           Margin="12,0" />
```

The binding walk down the LocalizedResources object (as named in the app.xaml resource) and then the property (which is just the name in the AppResource.resx file).

Bindings works with most types of controls, but unfortunately because the ApplicationBar control doesn't support data binding in a real way, you can't use this binding technique to handle localization of the ApplicationBar. Instead, the project template creates a localized ApplicationBar for you in code but leaves it commented out. Like the earlier example, this template code just uses the AppResources class to set the localized text:

```
private void BuildLocalizedApplicationBar()
{
  // Set the page's ApplicationBar
  ApplicationBar = new ApplicationBar();

  // Create a new button and set the text value
  ApplicationBarIconButton appBarButton =
    new ApplicationBarIconButton(
      new Uri("/Assets/ApplicationIcon.png", UriKind.Relative));

  appBarButton.Text = AppResources.AppBarButtonText;
  ApplicationBar.Buttons.Add(appBarButton);

  // Create a new menu item with the localized string
  ApplicationBarMenuItem appBarMenuItem = new
```

```
          ApplicationBarMenuItem(AppResources.AppBarMenuItemText);
        ApplicationBar.MenuItems.Add(appBarMenuItem);
}
```

This `ApplicationBar` code is similar to code you saw in Chapter 5. The change is that you're now using localized resources to set the text elements.

> **▪ NOTE**
>
> The image URI the template code uses doesn't point to an actual image so that the example out of the box in the template will simply not show an icon in the button.

The real magic happens when you add more language support. After you have your app written, you can simply go to the properties of the project and look at the Supported Cultures list; you'll see all the possible supported languages, as shown in Figure 6.14.

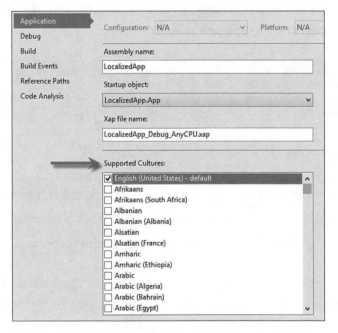

FIGURE 6.14 Adding supported cultures

If you click one of the languages and save the changes, a new resource file will be created specific to that language, as shown in Figure 6.15.

FIGURE 6.15   New language-specific resource file

The name of the new file is still AppResource but before the .resx extension is the name of the language (for example, "es" signifies that I chose generic Spanish). The new resource file copies all the strings from the original AppResource.resx file. It leaves the values that were in the original. You would change the values for the Spanish version of your app. You can see the strings converted to Spanish in Figure 6.16.

Name	Value	Comment
AppBarButtonText	añadir	
AppBarMenuItemText	ajustes	
ApplicationTitle	MI APPLICATION	
Copyright	(c) 2012 Wilder Minds LLC	
ResourceFlowDirection	LeftToRight	Controls the FlowDirection for all
ResourceLanguage	es	Controls the Language and ensures that

FIGURE 6.16   Spanish version of the resources

Now that you have Spanish resources, you can change the emulator to use Spanish as the primary language. To do this, go to the Settings apps (either on a device or in the emulator) and find the Languages and Region section, as shown in Figure 6.17.

After you change the language, you will have to restart the phone. You can see the language drop-down and the restart button in Figure 6.18.

FIGURE 6.17 The languages and region settings

FIGURE 6.18 Changing the language on the phone

Finally, if you run the application, you'll see that the new Spanish application name is shown. Note that no code was required—all the magic is happening in the `AppResources` class. You can see the app shown with Spanish resources in Figure 6.19.

Not all resources you want to use will have replacements in other languages. The default language is used as a fallback for any resources that aren't implemented in other languages. For example, because the *Copyright* string does not need to be localized, you can remove it from the Spanish resources. When it is missing in the Spanish resources, the `AppResources` class just falls back to using the default (for example, English) resource.

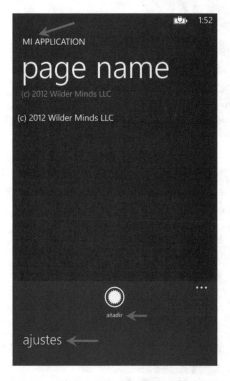

FIGURE 6.19   **The app with Spanish resources**

Where Are We?

At this point in the book you have only just begun to understand the basics of how to write code for the phone, but you should be comfortable with the lifecycle of phone applications, as well as simple tasks for interacting with the user with touch and events. This chapter focused on showing you the fundamentals of developing for the Windows Phone, including the differences in how applications work on the phone versus the desktop or web applications. By applying the basics of tombstoning, navigation, touch interactions, and localization, you should be able to build compelling user interfaces at this point.

7

Phone Hardware

BUILDING APPLICATIONS FOR WINDOWS PHONE is a compelling experience. So far you have seen ways to bring the desktop or web experience to a different form factor: the phone. But the phone has a number of device-specific features you will need to become familiar with if you are to succeed in building compelling phone applications.

Using Vibration

Unlike computers, phones are held in the hand. This makes vibration a useful mechanism to alert users that something is happening with their phones. This is called **haptic feedback.** Although haptic feedback is useful in some scenarios, its overuse is discouraged. Use of vibration can affect battery life, so vibrating the phone with every button click or other action isn't recommended. In general, using vibration is recommended for actions for which it can be difficult to use a visual cue. Small touch points are a common place for this, as the user cannot see the visual cue because his finger is often in the way.

Combining vibration with visual cues can really round out the user experience. To use haptic feedback, Windows Phone provides a simple class called `VibrateController` (in the `Microsoft.Devices` namespace):

```
private void theButton_Click(object sender, RoutedEventArgs e)
{
  VibrateController.Default.Start(TimeSpan.FromMilliseconds(100));
}
```

As you can see, the VibrateController class provides a static property to access the default controller. From there, you can start or stop the vibration. Typically, you would just call Start with a short amount of time to give the user that haptic feedback. You can also use the Stop method to cancel a long vibration, but in almost all cases you're just creating a very short vibration for the user to know he performed some action in your application.

> **■ Emulator Tip**
>
> VibrateController will run in the emulator, but you won't be able to tell it is working. That means the window won't vibrate—really!

Using Motion

Every Windows Phone also has an accelerometer built in. The **accelerometer** is a sensor that helps determine the phone's speed and direction based on its relationship to gravity. This means you can determine not only its position in three dimensions (which is how the phone determines when to change orientation), but also how much force is applied in each direction. As a result, you can determine the direction as well as the force in that direction. This is how some applications can test for shaking or other movements of the phone. Phones starting with the 7.1 version of Windows Phone OS also have a gyroscope to increase the sensitivity of this functionality.

The accelerometer works by showing the force against gravity. The force is separated into three axes to allow you to determine the location and force on the phone based on its relative position to gravity. These axes (x, y, and z) relate to the phone's position, and each will typically be in the range of -1 to +1 based on its position. If force is applied to the phone, these ranges can increase to detect the amount of force. For example, when you shake the phone the range will typically be greater than 1 or less than -1 to reflect that you are applying a force to the phone greater than that of gravity.

You can use this information to determine the amount of tilt applied to the phone. You can determine the tilt by comparing the value of each axis. These axes are mapped to the phone itself, as shown in Figure 7.1 (using the emulator).

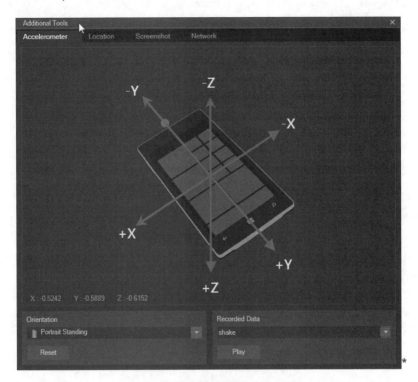

FIGURE 7.1   Accelerometer axes

Each axis has a negative and positive direction. For example, when you are holding the phone in portrait mode, exactly level with the ground, the y-axis will be -1 to represent that the top of the phone is up. In that case, the x-axis will be zero because it is halfway between lying down horizontally in either direction. This is the case with the z-axis as well, because the front and back of the phone are neither up nor down. Conversely, if you lay the phone (face-up) on a perfectly flat table, the z-axis will be -1 and the other axes will be zero. You can use the emulator to emulate moving the phone in three-dimensional (3D) space to see how it can be affected.

On the phone, there are actually two different Accelerometer classes. One is from WinRT, and one is for use on the phone. Be sure to use the

Accelerometer class from the `Microsoft.Devices.Sensors` namespace (not the one in `Windows.Devices.Sensors`). To use the class, you create an instance of it and register for the `CurrentValueChanged` event, like so:

```
public partial class MainPage : PhoneApplicationPage
{
  Accelerometer _theAccelerometer = new Accelerometer();

  // Constructor
  public MainPage()
  {
    InitializeComponent();

    _theAccelerometer. CurrentValueChanged +=
      _theAccelerometer_CurrentValueChanged;
  }
```

You will also want to determine how often you want updates. This allows the accelerometer to notify you only as often as necessary for your application. For example, if you're writing a tilt-based game, updates might be frequent (for instance, 100ms range). You can set this by setting the `TimeBetweenUpdates` property of the `Accelerometer` class:

```
// Constructor
public MainPage()
{
  InitializeComponent();

  _theAccelerometer.CurrentValueChanged +=
    _theAccelerometer_CurrentValueChanged;

  _theAccelerometer.TimeBetweenUpdates =
    TimeSpan.FromSeconds(1);
}
```

The `Accelerometer` class supports two methods for starting and stopping the accelerometer (not coincidentally called `Start` and `Stop`). You should enable the accelerometer only when you actually need it. Deferring its use until the user needs it is fairly typical. For example, you might enable and disable it via buttons:

```
void startButton_Click(object sender, EventArgs e)
{
  _theAccelerometer.Start();
```

```
}

void stopButton_Click(object sender, EventArgs e)
{
  _theAccelerometer.Stop();
}
```

After you start the accelerometer, you will be notified as the readings change:

```
void _theAccelerometer_CurrentValueChanged(object sender,
                      SensorReadingEventArgs<AccelerometerReading> e)
{
  var position = e.SensorReading.Acceleration;

  // Update the User Interface
  Dispatcher.BeginInvoke(() =>
  {
    xValue.Text = position.X.ToString("0.00");
    yValue.Text = position.Y.ToString("0.00");
    zValue.Text = position.Z.ToString("0.00");
  });
}
```

The event argument (SensorReadingEventArgs<AccelerometerReading>) will pass you two pieces of information: a timestamp of when the reading changed and the sensor reading itself (in the form of an instance of the SensorReading class). Inside the SensorReading's Acceleration property will be the X, Y, and Z values of the reading. Because the accelerometer can call you very quickly, the calls to the event do not happen on the UI thread (so the readings don't overwhelm the user interface thread). If you want to update the UI (like this example shows), you must marshal those calls to the UI thread (which Dispatcher.BeginInvoke does nicely for you).

> ◼ **TIP**
>
> The accelerometer range is device-dependent. Don't depend on a single device to determine what the acceptable range is.

Emulating Motion

When developing an application that takes advantage of the accelerometer, you can debug directly on a real device if that makes the most sense. Otherwise, you can use the emulator to emulate motion for your development. The emulator has a button on the control bar to show a separate window with support for motion and location emulation. To show this additional window, you have to click the right-arrow icon on the control bar of the emulator, as shown in Figure 7.2.

FIGURE 7.2   Showing the Accelerometer window in the emulator

Clicking that button opens a window with an Accelerometer tab and a Location tab. To emulate motion, you will use the Accelerometer tab, as shown in Figure 7.3.

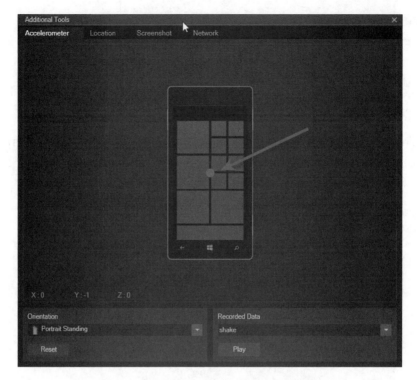

FIGURE 7.3 The Accelerometer window

You should notice the image of a phone floating in space on the Accelerometer tab. In the middle of the phone is a pink circle you can grab with your mouse to move it in 3D space. As you do that, the accelerometer values change (shown as X, Y, and Z in the lower left). This will enable you to see the relative axis values as you move the phone.

In the bottom-left area of the window is an Orientation drop-down where you can change your perspective to the phone. For example, if you change the orientation to Portrait Flat, you'll still see the phone, but it will be from the perspective of the phone lying flat on a table.

Finally, in the bottom-right area of the window is the Recorded Data drop-down that contains prerecorded sets of accelerometer data that you can run. By default, the only recorded data included is Shake, which emulates someone shaking the phone for a few seconds.

Creating Recorded Data

You can add your recorded data to the emulator by creating a simple XML file and dropping it into the emulator's accelerometer sensor data directory. The directory is as follows:

```
%PROGFILES%\Microsoft XDE\8.0\sensordata\acc
```

The XML files are labeled with the name you want to appear in the drop-down list (for instance, "Shimmy" with no extension for the Shake data file). The format of this XML file is shown here:

```xml
<?xml version="1.0" encoding="utf-8"?>
<WindowsPhoneEmulator
xmlns="http://schemas.microsoft.com/WindowsPhoneEmulator/2009/08/
SensorData">
  <SensorData>
    <Header version="1"/>
    <AccData offset="1000" x="1" y="0" z="0" />
    <AccData offset="2000" x="-1" y="0" z="0" />
    <AccData offset="3000" x="0" y="-1" z="0" />
  </SensorData>
</WindowsPhoneEmulator>
```

The important part of the format is the `SensorData` section. After the `Header` element is a list of `AccData` elements that contain the axis values as the number of milliseconds after the start of the recording to change the value to. This example moves the axis values after per second, but for something more complex you might need to change the values much more often than that. The Shake offsets change the values every few milliseconds to mimic the Shake action.

Using Sound

Like haptic feedback, using sound effectively can help you create a great application. As with any technique, though, some finesse is required to ensure optimal use. On Windows Phone, you have two options for playing sound: You can use the `MediaElement` or use XNA. In addition, the phone enables you to record sound. This section will cover all three of these aspects of using sound in your application.

Playing Sounds with MediaElement

Because sound is just another type of media, the easiest way for most people to play sound is to just use the MediaElement:

```
<Grid x:Name="ContentPanel">
  <MediaElement x:Name="soundElement"
                Source="/Assets/Foo.wav"
                AutoPlay="False" />
</Grid>
```

For playing sounds, the MediaElement is just an invisible part of the XAML and has no user interface. To use the MediaElement, you typically specify a source file (as a URL to the sound). By setting AutoPlay to false, you can play the sound with code:

```
private void playButton_Click(object sender, RoutedEventArgs e)
{
  soundElement.Play();
}
```

Although using a MediaElement is a straightforward way to play a sound, it has some drawbacks.

- You must tie the playing of the sound directly to the user interface (the MediaElement must exist in the XAML).
- Only one MediaElement can be playing a sound at a time. So playing different sounds means swapping the Source property as you use it.

When using the MediaElement you can use one of a number of formats, including the following:

- PCM WAV file (.wav)
- Microsoft Windows Media Audio (.wma)
- ISO MPEG-1 Layer III (.mp3)
- Unprotected ISO Advanced Audio Coding (.aac)

By using the MediaElement to play your audio files, you have full media control (for example, volume, stereo control, play/pause/stop, position). In most cases, if you want to play longer sounds like songs or albums, you should probably use the built-in media player functionality, discussed next.

Using XNA Libraries

At the center of a standard XNA library is a game loop that runs for the length of the program and handles the task of updating the UI and accepting input. It is not event-based, like XAML applications. The game loop's job is to give up control so that each frame of the game can be shown (that is, it updates the screen). This doesn't happen in XAML applications, so we must use the FrameworkDispatcher class's Update method to accomplish this for us. In some cases we can just call it after when we need to accomplish something with the XNA libraries (such as playing a sound effect); other times we need to mimic the updating. We can do this by using a DispatcherTimer to update the game loop periodically:

```
DispatcherTimer _updateTimer = new DispatcherTimer();

// Constructor
public MainPage()
{
  InitializeComponent();

  // Set up timer to call the XNA Dispatcher (for example, Game Loop)
  _updateTimer.Interval = TimeSpan.FromMilliseconds(50);
  _updateTimer.Tick += (s, e) =>
    {
      FrameworkDispatcher.Update();
    };
}
```

When we do this, we are periodically ceding to the XNA framework to do the work it normally does during the game loop.

Playing Sounds with XNA

Because you're using XAML to build your applications for the phone, you also can use some of the XNA libraries in your application. The key class is the SoundEffect class, which lets you play a short, fire-and-forget sound. This class supports only PCM WAV (.wav) files, but it will give you a high-performance sound effect when you need it (it is "high-performance" in that it does not require nearly the amount of system resources to play a sound as do formats that require decompression [for instance, .mp3 and .wma]). In addition, playing sounds with XNA will enable you to play multiple sounds at the same time.

To use the SoundEffect class you'll need a reference to the Microsoft. Xna.Framework.dll assembly and will have to import the Microsoft.Xna. Framework.Audio namespace. After you do that, you can create a sound effect by calling the SoundEffect.FromStream method, like so:

```
using Microsoft.Xna.Framework.Audio;

...

private void xnaPlayButton_Click(object sender, RoutedEventArgs e)
{
  // Get the sound from the XAP file
  var info = App.GetResourceStream(
    new Uri("assets/chord.wav", UriKind.Relative));

  // Load the SoundEffect
  SoundEffect effect = SoundEffect.FromStream(info.Stream);

  // Tell the XNA Libraries to continue to run
  FrameworkDispatcher.Update();

  // Play the Sound
  effect.Play();
}
```

After you load the file from the XAP (using the GetResourceStream method of the Application class), you can create the sound effect directly from the stream of the .wav file. Before you can play the effect, you must tell XNA to let updates happen to the rest of the application using the FrameworkDispatcher.Update method. Finally, you can play the effect. Playing the effect is not a blocking call (for example, Play returns immediately).

Adjusting Playback

You can also use the SoundEffect class to control the volume, pitch, and looping of a sound effect. To do this, you need to create an instance of the sound effect you've loaded, like so:

```
private void loopPitchButton_Click(object sender, RoutedEventArgs e)
{
  // Get the sound from the XAP file
```

```
var info =
    App.GetResourceStream(new Uri("alert.wav", UriKind.Relative));

// Load the SoundEffect
SoundEffect effect = SoundEffect.FromStream(info.Stream);

// Get an instance so we can affect the sound effect
SoundEffectInstance instance = effect.CreateInstance();

// Change the pitch and volume
instance.Pitch = -.35f; // Slow it down
instance.Volume = .95f; // Make it a little quiet

// Loop the sound
instance.IsLooped = true;

// Tell the XNA Libraries to continue to run
FrameworkDispatcher.Update();

// Play the Sound
instance.Play();
}
```

After you create the instance, you can specify the pitch (zero is normal speed) and volume (1.0 is normal volume). You can also specify whether the sound is to be looped. After you've made these changes, you can play the sound with the changes (using the Play method). Note that you're playing the instance and not the sound effect, which is different from earlier examples.

Recording Sounds

Using the XNA libraries, you can also record sound. To accomplish this, you can use the Microphone class (in the Microsoft.Xna.Framework.Audio namespace), which provides access to the phone's microphone. The Microphone class has a static property (called Default) that returns the default microphone. This should be the only microphone that a phone has, so you should be able to reliably use this microphone. You will also need to store the results of the recording. The easiest way to do this is to use a Stream to store the information. In this case, a MemoryStream is perfect for just storing the recording in memory:

```
public partial class MainPage : PhoneApplicationPage
{
    MemoryStream _recording = null;
```

```
    DispatcherTimer _updateTimer = new DispatcherTimer();

    // Constructor
    public MainPage()
    {
      InitializeComponent();

      // Set up timer to call the XNA Dispatcher
//(for example, Game Loop)
      _updateTimer.Interval = TimeSpan.FromMilliseconds(50);
      _updateTimer.Tick += (s, e) =>
        {
          FrameworkDispatcher.Update();
        };
    }
```

Note that I am using the DispatcherTimer to ensure we can use the XNA libraries (as detailed previously). Next, you need to turn the microphone on and off:

```
private void recordButton_Click(object sender, RoutedEventArgs e)
{
  // Create a new Memory Stream for the data
  _recording = new MemoryStream();

  // Start the timer to create the 'game loop'
  _updateTimer.Start();

  // Start Recording
  Microphone.Default.Start();
}

private void stopButton_Click(object sender, RoutedEventArgs e)
{
  // Stop Recording
  Microphone.Default.Stop();

  // Stop the 'game loop'
  _updateTimer.Stop();
}
```

You can see these event handlers are starting and stopping not only the microphone, but also the "game loop," which enables the recording APIs to work. When a new recording is started, a new MemoryStream is created to store the recording so that we get a new one for every recording.

The Microphone class has a BufferReady event that can accept the data from the microphone. As the buffer fills with the recording, the event will fire with a small amount of sound data you need to store:

```
public partial class MainPage : PhoneApplicationPage
{
  MemoryStream _recording = new MemoryStream();
  DispatcherTimer _updateTimer = new DispatcherTimer();

  // Constructor
  public MainPage()
  {
    InitializeComponent();

    // Set up timer to call the XNA Dispatcher
//(for example, Game Loop)
    _updateTimer.Interval = TimeSpan.FromMilliseconds(50);
    _updateTimer.Tick += (s, e) =>
      {
        FrameworkDispatcher.Update();
      };

    // Wire up an event to get the data from the Microphone
    Microphone.Default.BufferReady +=
      new EventHandler<EventArgs>(_mic_BufferReady);

  }

  void _mic_BufferReady(object sender, EventArgs e)
  {
    // Grab the Mic
    var mic = Microphone.Default;

    // Determine the #/bites needed for our sample
    var bufferSize = mic.GetSampleSizeInBytes(mic.BufferDuration);

    // Create the buffer
    byte[] buffer = new byte[bufferSize];

    // Get the Data (and return the number of bytes recorded)
    var size = Microphone.Default.GetData(buffer);

    // Write the data to our MemoryStream
    _recording.Write(buffer, 0, size);
  }
```

As you can see, the BufferReady event handler first retrieves the size of the buffer (by asking the Microphone class to get the sample size in bytes). Next, it creates a new buffer of bytes to store the data. Then it calls the

Microphone class to get the data (it takes the data, copies it into the buffer that is passed in, and returns the number of bytes that were used). Lastly, it uses the MemoryStream we created earlier and writes the new data into the stream. This event will be called enough times to store the data as it is being recorded.

After the recording is complete, you can do whatever you want with the stream of sound. The Microphone class returns the data as a .wav file, so you can store it in isolated storage and use it later or just play it back using the SoundEffect API mentioned earlier:

```
private void playBackButton_Click(object sender, RoutedEventArgs e)
{
  if (Microphone.Default.State == MicrophoneState.Stopped &&
      _recording != null)
  {
    // Load the SoundEffect
    SoundEffect effect = new SoundEffect(_recording.ToArray(),
      Microphone.Default.SampleRate,
      AudioChannels.Mono);

    // Tell the XNA Libraries to continue to run
    FrameworkDispatcher.Update();

    // Play the Sound
    effect.Play();
  }
}
```

You can see here that the Microphone class also has a State property you can use to ensure that you use the data only after the recording is over. Then, instead of loading the SoundEffect object from a stream (as shown earlier), this code creates a new SoundEffect passing in the contents of the stream, the sample rate (which the Microphone class contains), and the number of audio channels. Otherwise, this code is just like playing any other sound effect.

Working with the Camera

For the most basic usage of the camera on the phone, the CameraCaptureTask (covered in Chapter 8, "Phone Integration") will enable you to launch the camera and return an image. In many cases, it is more useful to have full control over the camera for real-time access to the camera hardware. For building your own camera applications, the `PhotoCamera` class represents access to the photo hardware. When you need real-time access to the hardware, Windows Phone also exposes raw hardware access APIs (including `CaptureSource`, `AudioSink`, and `VideoSink`).

Using the `PhotoCamera` Class

The `PhotoCamera` class represents the phone's camera and allows you to easily build photo-taking applications with it. To get started, you will need an instance of the `PhotoCamera` class. You can use that class as the source of a `VideoBrush` to paint the "viewfinder" in your application, like so:

```
public partial class MainPage : PhoneApplicationPage
{
  PhotoCamera theCamera = null;

  protected override void OnNavigatedTo(NavigationEventArgs e)
  {
    theCamera = new PhotoCamera();

    // Set the Camera as the source for the VideoBrush
    previewBrush.SetSource(theCamera);

    ...
```

Using the `PhotoCamera` as the source of the `VideoBrush` causes a real-time image to be painted wherever you're using a `VideoBrush`. After you have the camera created and showing up on the page, you need to wire up the camera's functionality to use it. The first thing to do in wiring the camera is to handle the `Initialized` event. This event is important to handle, as many of the camera settings (for example, setting the focus or the flash) are not available until this event is fired. For example, to set the flash for red-eye reduction, handle the `Initialized` event and then set the flash like so:

```
// Some settings require camera to be initialized first
theCamera.Initialized += (s, a) =>
  {
    if (a.Succeeded)
    {
      // Taking Portraits
      if (theCamera.IsFlashModeSupported(FlashMode.RedEyeReduction))
      {
```

```
        theCamera.FlashMode = FlashMode.RedEyeReduction;
    }
  }
};
```

The `Initialized` event argument includes a property to tell you whether it was successful (the `Succeeded` property). You should check this first to be certain that you can actually modify the `PhotoCamera`'s properties. In this case, we ask the camera if the red-eye reduction flash is supported on this phone, and if so, we can specify that is the flash mode we want.

To take a photo, you can use the `PhotoCamera`'s `CaptureImage` method. This tells the camera to take the photo and then fires events for both a full-size and a thumbnail version of the image. Typically, this is in response to some event such as a button click:

```
private void shutter_Click(object sender, RoutedEventArgs e)
{
  theCamera.CaptureImage();
}
```

After the image has been captured, the `PhotoCamera` class can raise the `CaptureImageAvailable` and `CaptureThumbnailAvailable` events. These events include the actual stream that contains the image, so you can handle these events and manipulate the resultant photo. For example, you can take the full image and save it to the media library (as shown earlier in this chapter):

```
// Photo was captured
theCamera.CaptureImageAvailable += (s,a) =>
  {
    // Save picture to the device media library.
    MediaLibrary library = new MediaLibrary();
    library.SavePictureToCameraRoll("SomeFile.jpg", a.ImageStream);
  };
```

The `CaptureImageAvailable` event argument includes an `ImageStream` property that contains the raw photo. You can manipulate this stream in any way you want, although saving it to the phone is more typical of what a user might expect.

Like you saw earlier, the `PhotoCamera` class offers several settings, including

- Flash mode
- Picture resolution

In addition, you can control the focus by using the Focus and Focus-AtPoint methods. These methods enable you to start the auto-focus functionality. You need to test to see whether these capabilities are available:

```
private void focus_Click(object sender, RoutedEventArgs e)
{
  // AutoFocus the Camera
  if (theCamera.IsFocusSupported)
  {
    theCamera.Focus();
  }
}
```

Focusing at a specified point works the same way, but you need to specify a place to center on. The values should be between 0.0 and 1.0, so focus at whatever is in the center of the viewfinder:

```
private void focusAtPoint_Click(object sender, RoutedEventArgs e)
{
  // Focus in the center of the image
  if (theCamera.IsFocusAtPointSupported)
  {
    theCamera.FocusAtPoint(.5, .5);
  }
}
```

Before taking a photo, you will need to be sure the focusing is complete. To do this, you can handle the AutoFocusComplete event:

```
bool _isFocusComplete = true;
...
theCamera.AutoFocusCompleted += (s, a) =>
  {
    _isFocusComplete = true;
  };
```

By keeping the state of whether your application is currently focusing, you can control when a picture is taken by flipping this flag during focus and shutter operations:

```
private void focus_Click(object sender, RoutedEventArgs e)
{
  // AutoFocus the Camera
  if (theCamera.IsFocusSupported)
  {
    _isFocusComplete = false;
    theCamera.Focus();
  }
}

private void shutter_Click(object sender, RoutedEventArgs e)
{
  if (_isFocusComplete) theCamera.CaptureImage();
}
```

You might want to use the hardware camera shutter to handle focus and shutter functions like the built-in camera application. The CameraButtons class gives you that capability. This class supports three events.

- **ShutterKeyPressed:** This occurs when the user fully presses the phone's dedicated camera button.
- **ShutterKeyHalfPressed:** This occurs when the user partially presses the phone's dedicated camera button. (It is usually used to start a focus operation.)
- **ShutterKeyReleased:** This occurs when the user releases the phone's dedicated camera button after fully pressing the button. (For example, it does not occur when the user half-presses the camera button.)

To allow the hardware button to control the camera app, you could handle these events as necessary:

```
// Wire up shutter button too (instead of UI control)
CameraButtons.ShutterKeyPressed += (s, a) => TakePicture();
CameraButtons.ShutterKeyHalfPressed += (s, a) => theCamera.Focus();
```

Finally, the PhotoCamera class gives you raw access to the preview buffer if you need to manipulate what the user sees in the virtual viewfinder. You would do this via the GetPreviewBufferXXX methods. You can get the buffer as 32-bit ARGB values, YCbCr, or just luminance data. You can see how this works here:

```
int[] buffer = new int[640 * 480];
theCamera.GetPreviewBufferArgb32(buffer);
// Manipulate the preview and show on the screen
```

The buffer you receive from these methods would have to be used to create a bitmap to show to the user. Often it is easier to just use the raw camera APIs (shown next) to accomplish this sort of real-time manipulation of the camera's feed.

> ## ■ Camera Capabilities
>
> To use the PhotoCamera class (and other associated classes), you will need to ensure that your application includes the ID_CAP_ISV_CAMERA capability in the WMAppManifest.xml file. You can see this capability in the WMAppManifest.xml editor, as shown in Figure 7.4.

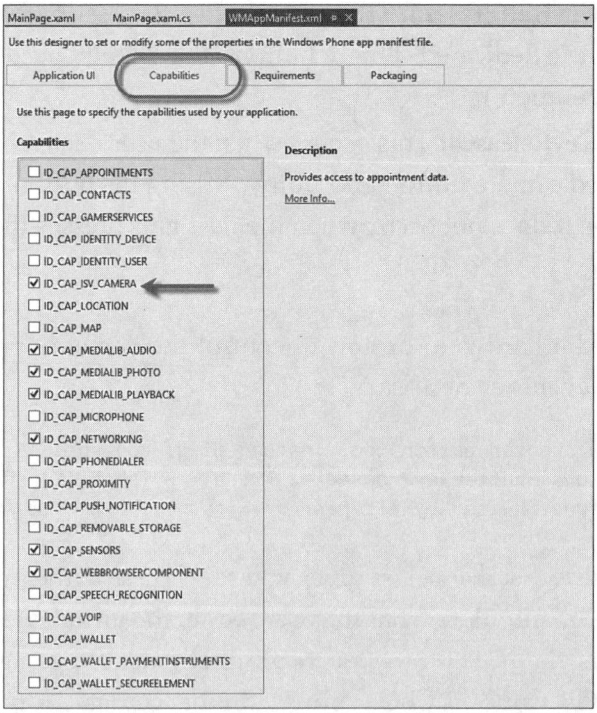

FIGURE 7.4 Setting the camera capability

Raw Hardware Access

The Windows Phone SDK includes a couple of key classes that support low-level access to the camera and microphone hardware. Although it is much easier to use the PhotoCamera class, if you need to capture video and/or audio and manipulate it in real time, these APIs are the best tool for the job.

The starting point to the raw camera API is the CaptureSource class. The CaptureSource class enables you to have access to video input on the phone. Like the PhotoCamera class, you can use the CaptureSource class as the source for a VideoBrush. This way, you can show the raw input from the camera in your application:

```
CaptureSource _src = new CaptureSource();

protected override void OnNavigatedTo(NavigationEventArgs e)
{
  // Show the preview
  previewBrush.SetSource(_src);
}
```

To enable the video, you need to enable the CaptureSource by using the Start method:

```
private void camButton_Click(object sender, RoutedEventArgs e)
{
  _src.Start();
}
```

> ## ⁃ Silverlight Developers
>
> Unlike desktop Silverlight, you can start the CaptureSource without asking for permission with the CaptureDeviceConfiguration class.

At this point, you have only the camera showing up in your own application. To deal with live input from the camera and microphone, you have to create special classes called **sinks**. To retrieve video you need a VideoSink class; for audio you need an AudioSink class. These are abstract classes from which you must derive in order to retrieve real-time data from the hardware. They have a small number of abstract methods (that you have to override). A skeleton VideoSink derived class would look like this:

```
public class MyVideoSink : VideoSink
{
  protected override void OnSample(long
sampleTimeInHundredNanoseconds,
    long frameDurationInHundredNanoseconds,
    byte[] sampleData)
  {
    // Encode or Save the stream
  }

  protected override void OnCaptureStarted()
  {
    // Handle Startup of Capture
  }

  protected override void OnCaptureStopped()
  {
    // Cleanup After Capture
  }

  VideoFormat _format = null;

  protected override void OnFormatChange(VideoFormat videoFormat)
  {
    // Store the Video Format
    _format = videoFormat;
  }
}
```

Here are the abstract methods you must override.

- **OnCaptureStarted:** This is where you can do any initialization necessary to prepare for data capture.
- **OnCaptureStopped:** This is where you can clean up or save after a capture is complete.
- **OnFormatChange:** This is where you would store the current format to determine how to consume the capture samples.

- **OnSample:** This is where most of the real work is accomplished in the sink. This is called periodically with a set of samples from the hardware.

After you have a sink, you can specify the `CaptureSource` of the sink before you start capturing:

```
protected override void OnNavigatedTo(NavigationEventArgs e)
{
  // Show the preview
  previewBrush.SetSource(_src);

  // Capture the video
  _sink.CaptureSource = _src;
}
```

When you specify the `CaptureSource`, your sink will be notified because the `CaptureSource` is manipulated by the user. In this way, you can have more than one audio and video sink per `CaptureSource`. Explaining how to manipulate raw video/audio samples is outside the scope of this book.

Because the raw camera API originated from Silverlight, it enables you to specify the camera on the device you want. The `CaptureDeviceConfiguration` class allows you to enumerate the different audio and video capture devices. In this way, you can specify the capture device for the `CaptureSource` to use, like so:

```
ICollection<VideoCaptureDevice> devices =
  CaptureDeviceConfiguration.GetAvailableVideoCaptureDevices();

// Pick the first device
_src.VideoCaptureDevice = devices.First();
```

The API supports multiple devices so that, in the future, if there are multiple video devices (for example, a front-facing camera), your code will be able to pick which device to use. By default, the `CaptureSource` uses the "primary device," which is usually the standard camera, so working with this API isn't necessary with the current crop of phones.

Camera Lens App

You can also create a specialized application called a Camera Lens application that enables the user to access your application as a "lens" in the camera of the phone directly. For a user, your application shows up in the lens in the camera application, as shown in Figure 7.5.

FIGURE 7.5   The Camera Lens button

After the user taps the Lens button, they are presented with all the applications that support the Lens functionality. You can see a sample app "MyLens" shown in Figure 7.6.

FIGURE 7.6   The camera lenses

When a user selects a lens, the specific app is launched and the app must implement a camera-like experience. If you are using the one of the previous methods to implement your camera (for example, `PhotoCamera` class), you can just show that page of your application. To be registered for this special type of application, you have to tell the `WMAppManifest.xml` file that your app supports an extension. Unfortunately, the editor in Visual Studio does not support setting these extensions directly. So you have to open the `WMAppManifest.xml` file as XML. You can accomplish this by right-clicking the `WMAppManifest.xml` file and selecting "View Code." As a child of the App element, you need to add a section called Extensions, like so:

```
<Deployment xmlns="..."
            AppPlatformVersion="8.0">
  <DefaultLanguage xmlns=""
                   code="en-US" />
  <App ...>
```

```
    . . .

    <Extensions>
      <Extension ExtensionName="Camera_Capture_App"
                 ConsumerID="{5B04B775-356B-4AA0-AAF8-6491FFEA5631}"
                 TaskID="_default" />
    </Extensions>

    . . .

  </App>
</Deployment>
```

The extension type and GUID for the ConsumerID are shown here. These are specific GUID values and not specific to your application. This value **must** be used. The TaskID should be "_default" that points to the default task in the list of Tasks in the XML file. After this is done, the lens will be registered with the camera on installation of the application.

The Clipboard API

Windows Phone supports a common clipboard much like Windows. Users can add items to the clipboard while working with TextBox controls, and the copied text will remain in the clipboard for other applications to use. You can also access the clipboard programmatically with the Clipboard class. The Clipboard class has three simple static methods: SetText, ContainsText, and GetText. You can set text to the clipboard programmatically by using the SetText method, like so:

```
Clipboard.SetText("Hello World");
```

You can test to see whether there is data in the clipboard by calling the ContainsText method as well:

```
if (Clipboard.ContainsText())
{
  // ...
}
```

The last method (GetText) exists on the Clipboard class but is not available to Windows Phone applications. Calling GetText will throw a security exception. This means your application cannot read the clipboard; it can only test to see whether it has text and then push text onto the clipboard. The reasoning behind this is to prevent accidental leaking of user data to unauthorized applications. For desktop Silverlight, user approval typically is required to access the clipboard, but currently the decision is to just disallow it instead of introducing another pop-up confirmation that needs to be explained to the user. This is a limitation of the phone SDK, and you will need to work around it if you need to copy text from the clipboard.

Location APIs

Your application can determine where in the world the phone is at any moment. This is the same technology your GPS device uses to determine how to give you driving directions. The phones are required to have Assisted Global Positioning System (A-GPS) hardware. This is different from simple GPS location technology as the "Assisted" part is very important. Typical GPS devices rely on being able to locate three orbiting satellites to triangulate your location. Sometimes these systems were hurt by the lag in "syncing" with the three satellites and often structures (such as buildings or bridges) made GPS unreliable. Assisted GPS improves this by using GPS to give you high-precision geolocation when possible but can also fall back to use other ways of determining your location, including cell-phone tower triangulation and the Wi-Fi Positioning System.[1]

Location Permission

To create a location-aware application, you will use the A-GPS on the phone. Because using location without the user's consent would likely be a violation of privacy, your application has to specify that it can use the location APIs in the SDK. To do this, you need to add a new capability via the WMAppManifest.xml file. If you open the manifest in the editor, you can check off the location capability in the Capabilities tab, as shown in Figure 7.7.

---

1   http://en.wikipedia.org/wiki/Wi-Fi_Positioning_System

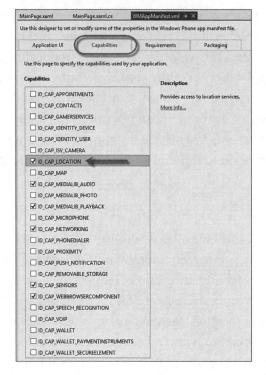

FIGURE 7.7   Requesting the location capability

When your application is installed, the Marketplace specifically asks the user whether he wants to allow your application to gather location information. Before your application can use location information, it must use the GeoLocationWatcher class (in the System.Device.Location namespace) to check whether the user has granted permission:

```
// using System.Device.Location;
// Create the Watcher (and clean it up when done)
using (var watcher = new GeoCoordinateWatcher())
{
  if (watcher.Permission == GeoPositionPermission.Granted)
  {
    // Find the location
  }
}
```

The Permission property of the GeoCoordinateWatcher class will tell your application whether it is allowed to use location information. If permission is denied and you attempt to use location information, the class will throw an exception. In addition to checking for permission, you must allow the user to disable this capability in your application. This is typically accomplished in a "Settings" page or other mechanism. In Chapter 12, "Making Money," we will discuss this requirement (and others) that your application must implement for certain phone features.

Accessing Location Information

The A-GPS on the phone enables you to retrieve location information without having to work with the sensor directly. You can use the `Geolocator` class to retrieve location information. This is the WinRT API for accessing geolocation information. When using the `Geolocator` class, you can specify the accuracy you're going to need for your application:

```
// Normal Accuracy
var locator = new Geolocator();
locator.DesiredAccuracy = PositionAccuracy.High;
```

The level of accuracy affects not only how accurate the information is, but also how fast you can get the information back. With the default level of accuracy, the `Geolocator` class will return after it can get a location instead of waiting for high-accuracy information.

When developing your application, you need to also determine how often you need the geolocation information. Retrieving geolocation information can be a drain on the battery, so deciding whether you need a one-time location or need to constantly monitor the change of location should be part of your application design. Let's look at ways to do both.

> ### ▪ What Happened to GeoCoordinateWatcher?
>
> The `GeoCoordinateWatcher` class was used prior to Windows Phone 8. By using the `Geolocator` class instead, you can have compatibility with Windows 8 applications. Both classes expose similar functionality, but the `Geolocator` class should be used in future development.

One-time Geolocation

The Geolocator class uses the asynchronous programming features new to Windows Phone 8. To perform a one-time retrieval of the location of the phone, you can call the Geolocator class's GetGeopositionAsync method. To use this method, you will need to decorate your method with the async modifier (as shown in the following code) and use the await keyword to tell the API to run the operation asynchonrously:

```
protected async override void OnNavigatedTo(NavigationEventArgs e)
{
  base.OnNavigatedTo(e);

  var locator = new Geolocator();

  Geoposition location = await _locator.GetGeopositionAsync();
}
```

By using await, the method will wrap the operation in an asynchronous handler so you can simply write the code as if it were asynchronous. If location information is not available, the method will return a null reference. After you have the Geoposition object, you can simply see the location information (or even the civic information like city, state, country, and postal code):

```
var locator = new Geolocator();


Geoposition location = await _locator.GetGeopositionAsync();


if (location != null)
{
  // Get coordinates
  double latitude = location.Coordinate.Latitude;
  double longitude = location.Coordinate.Longitude;
  double? altitude = location.Coordinate.Altitude;

  // Get civic location information
  string country = location.CivicAddress.Country;
  string city = location.CivicAddress.City;
}
```

You can also check the status of the location by using the Geolocator class's LocationStatus property:

```
var locator = new Geolocator();

Geoposition location = await _locator.GetGeopositionAsync();

if (location != null)
{
  // Get coordinates
  double latitude = location.Coordinate.Latitude;
  double longitude = location.Coordinate.Longitude;
  double? altitude = location.Coordinate.Altitude;

  // Get civic location information
  string country = location.CivicAddress.Country;
  string city = location.CivicAddress.City;
}
else
{
  if (locator.LocationStatus == PositionStatus.Disabled)
  {
    statusMessage.Text = "Location Information has been disabled";
  }
}
```

The LocationStatus property returns the status of the location information. This can be one of six statuses:

- **Ready:** Location information is available.
- **Initializing:** Location information should be available soon. The device is initializing.
- **NoData:** The device is working correctly, but no data is available. This could be because none of the different location information is available (no GPS, no cell towers, and no Wi-Fi).
- **NotInitialized:** The location services haven't been initialized. This usually happens before calling the GetPositionAsync method the first time.
- **NotAvailable:** The device doesn't support location services.
- **Disabled:** Location information was disabled for this application. This is usually if the user was asked and rejected the permission to let your application use location information or the user has disabled location services on the phone.

For this one-time use, the `Geoposition` result is all you need. The data available from the `Geoposition` class includes

- **Latitude:** This is the current latitude of the phone (location on the surface of the Earth).
- **Longitude:** This is the current longitude of the phone (location on the surface of the Earth).
- **IsUnknown:** This says whether the coordinate is invalid or unknown.
- **Speed:** This is an approximate speed of the user in meters per second.
- **Course:** This is an approximate heading as related to true north (0–360 degrees).
- **Altitude:** This is the approximate altitude above sea level.
- **HorizontalAccuracy:** This is the distance of uncertainty in this location information (in meters).
- **VerticalAccuracy:** This is the distance of uncertainty in this location information (in meters).

Tracking Geolocation Changes

For applications that require continuous monitoring of the user's movements, you can monitor the geolocation changes as they occur. Like many of the devices on the phone, using the geolocation functionality for long periods can adversely affect battery life. To combat this, you will want to be judicious in your use of this feature.

Continuously monitoring the geolocation of the phone is similar to a one-time retrieval of location information, but the method structuring the code is a little different. You should start by creating a `Geolocator` as a class-level variable (to maintain its lifetime) and register for both the `StatusChanged` and the `PositionChanged` events from the UI thread (for example, in response to an AppBar button click):

```
private void startButton_Click(object sender, EventArgs e)
{

    // Make sure we can only call it after
    ((ApplicationBarIconButton)sender).IsEnabled = false;
```

```
    // Wire up for events
    _locator.PositionChanged += _locator_PositionChanged;
    _locator.StatusChanged += _locator_StatusChanged;
}
```

Depending on your particular use-case, you also should specify when to update you with location information. You can set both time and movement thresholds that will dictate how often to update you on location changes:

```
// Set Thresholds
_locator.ReportInterval = 2000;    // 2 seconds
_locator.MovementThreshold = 100; // 100 meters

// Wire up for events
_locator.PositionChanged += _locator_PositionChanged;
_locator.StatusChanged += _locator_StatusChanged;
```

The ReportInterval property accepts time in milliseconds between calls. The MovementThreshold specifies how far the user needs to move before you are notified.

In both of the event handlers, you will have to marshal the data to the UI thread (using Dispatcher.BeginInvoke). For example, in the StatusChanged event you will need to tell the user what is happening based on the statuses that are returned, like so:

```
void _locator_StatusChanged(Geolocator sender,
                            StatusChangedEventArgs args)
{
  Dispatcher.BeginInvoke(() =>
    {
      switch (args.Status)
      {
        // Tell the user the location information is coming
        case PositionStatus.Initializing:
          statusMessage.Text = "Location Initializing";
          break;

        // Alert the user that data isn't available currently
        case PositionStatus.NoData:
          statusMessage.Text =
            "No location available...try again later";
          break;
```

```
        // If status is Ready, then PositionChanged fired correctly
        case PositionStatus.Ready:
          statusMessage.Text = "Receiving Location Information";
          break;

        // If Disabled, tell the user
        case PositionStatus.Disabled:
          statusMessage.Text = "Location Information is disabled";
          break;
      }
    });
  }
```

Because these statuses can change although your application is running, you should continue to monitor the PositionStatus values and keep the user apprised of the validity of this information. Note that, unlike the one-time retrieval, we do not get the status information from the watcher when the Ready status fires. This is because the other event (PositionChanged) will be fired as the location changes:

```
void _locator_PositionChanged(Geolocator sender,
                              PositionChangedEventArgs args)
{
  Dispatcher.BeginInvoke(() =>
    {
      // Just bind the position to the UI so we can data-bind to it
      DataContext = args.Position.Coordinate;
    });
}
```

Turning Coordinates into Addresses

Now that you have basic coordinates of where the phone is on the surface of the Earth, you will want to turn that into something the user can actually use. This requires use of certain services that we cover in Chapter 11, "Services."

Emulating Location Information

When using the emulator, you can emulate location (for example, A-GPS) information for your application for testing. To accomplish this, you need to open the Additional Tools sidebar of the emulator (like you did when you looked at the accelerometer emulation earlier in this chapter), as shown in Figure 7.8.

FIGURE 7.8   **Opening the emulator's Additional Tools sidebar**

The Additional Tools dialog box includes two tabs. For location information, you'll need to click the Location tab, as shown in Figure 7.9.

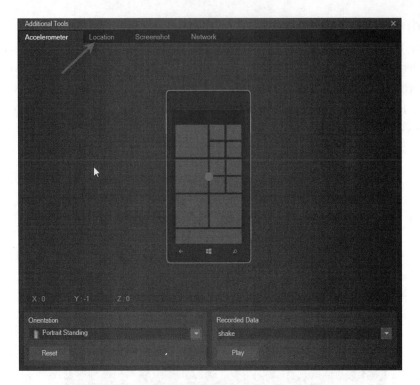

FIGURE 7.9   Selecting the Location tab

The Location section of the Additional Tools dialog box includes several pieces of key functionality. You can see the basic layout of the location user interface in Figure 7.10.

The main part of the window (labeled #1) is the map. You can scroll around and double-click/scroll-wheel to zoom on the map. In the upper-left corner of the window is a search box (#2) to enable you to find a location on the map. Typing in a name, ZIP Code, or other description will focus it on the map. Next to the search box are zoom tools to help you find the right level of detail. Next, the Live button (#3) is a toggle to enable live mode. In this mode, the emulator will use the center of the map as the current location for the phone.

FIGURE 7.10   Location tab of the Additional Tools dialog box

Finally, you can also specify map pins if the pin button (#4) is selected. This way, you can create routes (the pins are sequentially numbered as you click them) so that you can see what happens as you are simulating a set of locations. With the pin button pressed, every time you click the map it creates a waypoint, as shown in Figure 7.11.

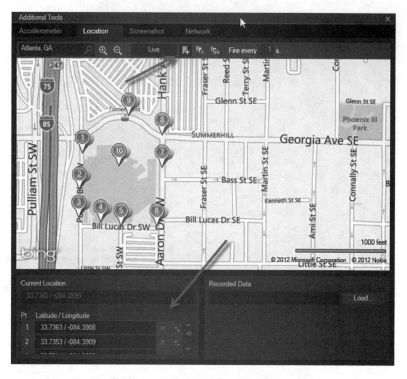

FIGURE 7.11   Using pins to create waypoints

If you unselect Live, you'll be able to press the play key in the upper-right corner to actually play through the set of waypoints. You should notice that the lower-left corner of the dialog box shows you all the waypoints and allows you to reorder and delete individual waypoints. You can also clear all the waypoints by clicking the "delete all points" button to the right of the pin button.

Finally, you can take your waypoints and timings and save them for replay. To do this, click the save button shown in Figure 7.12.

You can reload saved data by using the Load button in the lower-right part of the dialog box. This way you can create complex location information and use it to test your application. By using these features you can simulate location information in the emulator and enable testing scenarios that would be impossible in real life.

FIGURE 7.12   Saving recorded data

Voice Commands

When a user holds the home button for more than a couple of seconds, the speech recognition subsystem launches and enables a user to perform searches and other commands for the phone. She can say anything and the "Listening" screen (as shown in Figure 7.13) waits for the user to say something.

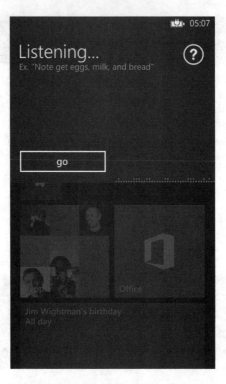

FIGURE 7.13   The "Listening" Screen

Although users can say anything they want to search, they can also use voice commands like "Call Mom" or "Open Twitter." By default the voice commands are based on the app name, but your app might want to have its own voice commands for specific functionality.

Before your application can add its own voice commands, it needs to first request certain capabilities for your app, including ID_CAP_MICROPHONE, ID_CAP_NETWORKING, and ID_CAP_SPEECH_RECOGNITION. You can see these capabilities added to the WMAppManifest.xml file in Figure 7.14.

Next, you will need to add a new file called a Voice Command Definition (VCD) file. This is just an XML file, but Visual Studio for the Windows Phone includes an item template for it (as shown in Figure 7.15).

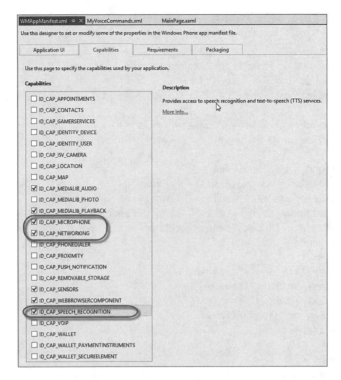

FIGURE 7.14 Adding the voice command capabilities

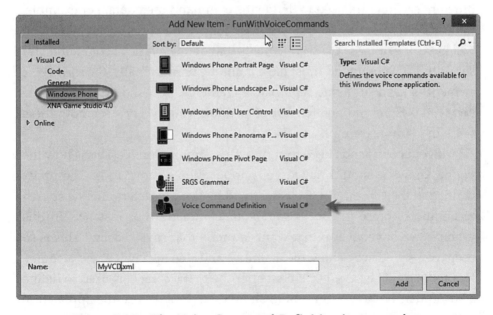

FIGURE 7.15 The Voice Command Definition item template

The XML file has a simple structure as shown here:

```
<?xml version="1.0" encoding="utf-8"?>
<VoiceCommands xmlns="http://schemas.microsoft.com/
voicecommands/1.0">
  <CommandSet xml:lang="en-US">

    <CommandPrefix>Facey</CommandPrefix>
    <Example> show me a smile </Example>

    <Command Name="ShowFace">
      <Example> show me a smile </Example>
      <ListenFor> show [me] [a] {facetype} </ListenFor>
      <Feedback> Your Face is Coming </Feedback>
      <Navigate Target="pages/facepage.xaml" />
    </Command>

    <PhraseList Label="facetype">
      <Item> smile </Item>
      <Item> frown </Item>
      <Item> grimace </Item>
    </PhraseList>

  </CommandSet>
</VoiceCommands>
```

The `CommandSet` element is used to define a set of commands. The different sections are used to define the command metadata. For example, the `CommandPrefix` and `Example` are used for all the commands. Next, you will have one or more `Command` elements that define a type of command you support. Each command must have a unique name. Finally, the `PhraseList` element is used to define replaceable elements. You should think of the `PhraseList` as an enumerated list of possible values. Let's see how these work in a simple example.

All your commands need to start with a common prefix. This is how the phone knows it should match your application's commands. The prefix defined in the `CommandPrefix` element will be used to determine the speech recognition phrase to use to start your command. For instance, in this example we have an app that wants a prefix that says "Facey." This is so users can say "Facey show me a smile," and this app will show a smiley face to them. The `Example` element after the `CommandPrefix` is used to define a string that is shown to users to show them how to use the app's voice commands.

Next we need to set up the command itself. The Command element in the example shows that we need a name to identify the Command. Then inside the element, you can specify the following:

- Example: Like the main example, this is a command-specific example.
- ListenFor: One or more patterns for the speech recognition engine to search for. The words in brackets (for example, [a]) are optional. The words in curly braces are words in a PhraseList element (for example, {facetype}).
- Navigate: This is an option URI for the part of your app to navigate to. If this is omitted, your first page (for example, MainPage.xaml) will be used.

The last element is the PhraseList. As the example shows, the PhraseList has a Label that identifies it as is used in the ListenFor elements to match the two. This list does not have to be hard-coded; we'll show you later how to programmatically specify the contents of a PhraseList.

After you have the VCD file created, you must register it with the VoiceCommandService class. This is done as an asynchronous call that can be handled during the first launch of your application. For example, to register the VCD file during the navigation to your main page:

```
protected async override void OnNavigatedTo(NavigationEventArgs e)
{
  base.OnNavigatedTo(e);

  await VoiceCommandService.InstallCommandSetsFromFileAsync(
    new Uri("ms-appx:///MyVoiceCommands.xml"));


}
```

The VoiceCommandService class has a static method called InstallCommandSetsFromFileAsync method. This method uses the new async support; therefore, you need to specify the async keyword in the containing method signature and use the await keyword to make the page wait until this method completes to continue.

You will specify the path to your VCD file using a new URI. You might notice that it uses a new URI moniker called "ms-appx." This specifies that the file path is in the installation directory for your phone application. The `ms-appx://` is the moniker and the `/MyVoiceCommands.xml` is the path to the VCD file. If you have placed this as a subdirectory of your project, make sure that the path is included here.

Now that you have created commands and registered them, the user will be able to launch your app using the commands you've defined. When your commands are executed, the Voice Command system launches your application and notifies the user that the voice command was accepted by showing your app name, icon, and voice command description, as shown in Figure 7.16.

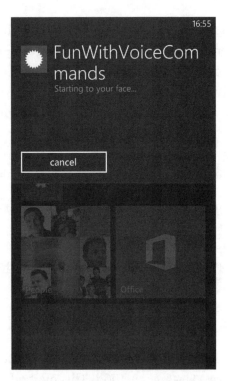

FIGURE 7.16   Voice Command launching your app

The next part of the puzzle is to react to the navigation to the page you want the voice command to execute. In the VCD, you can specify a path to a page in the option `Navigate` element (inside the `Command` element).

When the voice command is executed, your page will be shown and the navigation will include information in the query string for the command. So, on your page, just override the OnNavigatedTo method and first check to make sure the NavigationMode is New:

```
protected override void OnNavigatedTo(NavigationEventArgs e)
{
  base.OnNavigatedTo(e);

  // Only check for voice command on fresh navigation,
  // not tombstoning
  if (e.NavigationMode == NavigationMode.New)
  {
    // ...
  }
}
```

This will ensure that this is checked only when the page is launched from some external source (for example, the Voice Command). Next, you should check the NavigationContext.QueryString for the actual command name sent:

```
// Is there a voice command in the query string?
if (NavigationContext.QueryString.ContainsKey("voiceCommandName"))
{
  // If so, get the name of the Voice Command.
  var cmdName = NavigationContext.QueryString["voiceCommandName"];

  // If it's the command we expect,
  // then find the type of face to show
  if (cmdName == "ShowFace")
  {
    // ...
  }
}
```

The voiceCommandName query string parameter will be set to the Name of the Command element in the VCD that was matched. If so, you can retrieve the voiceCommandName and test it against the expected commands. This is useful if you need to have a specific page handle more than one type of command. After you've determined that it is the right command, then you can retrieve the query string parameter that matched the PhraseList item. In this case the facetype PhraseList supports three face types, as shown here:

```
var faceType = NavigationContext.QueryString["facetype"].ToLower();

// Show supported face types
switch (faceType)
{
  case "smile":
    VisualStateManager.GoToState(this, "Smile", false);
    break;
  case "grimace":
    VisualStateManager.GoToState(this, "Grimace", false);
    break;
  case "frown":
    VisualStateManager.GoToState(this, "Frown", false);
    break;
}
```

What you do with the data provided is completely up to you, but you can see an example here where we use the VisualStateManager to show the different smiles for us.

Using voice commands is simple, but sometimes you need to handle voice-based control within your app—and that's where speech recognition comes in.

Speech Recognition

Being able to let your users control your application with their voice can be really useful. That's where the Speech Recognition comes in. Before you can get started, you need the capabilities to include the network, speech recognition, and microphone support (for example, ID_CAP_NETWORKING, ID_CAP_SPEECH_RECOGNITION, and ID_CAP_MICROPHONE) in the WMAppManifest.xml file.

Now that you have the right capabilities, you can start to use the speech recognition system. There are two main ways to use speech recognition: with and without the system user interface. Using the system's user interface is the easiest method, but it might conflict with your branding or vision for your application.

The class responsible for speech recognition using the system UI is the SpeechRecognizerUI class. This class supports the IDisposable interface, which means you should take care to clean up its resources when you're done using it. Typically, you would create the object on the Loaded event of a page/control and dispose of it on the Unloaded event as shown:

```
public partial class MainPage : PhoneApplicationPage
{
  SpeechRecognizerUI _ui;

  // Constructor
  public MainPage()
  {
    InitializeComponent();

    Loaded += MainPage_Loaded;
    Unloaded += MainPage_Unloaded;
  }

  void MainPage_Loaded(object sender, RoutedEventArgs e)
  {
    _ui = new SpeechRecognizerUI();
  }

  void MainPage_Unloaded(object sender, RoutedEventArgs e)
  {
    _ui.Dispose();
  }
  ...
}
```

After you have the creation and tear-down specified, you can use the class. The method for listening for speech is called RecognizeWithUIAsync, and it uses the async pattern. So to use it, you should mark your method with async and use await to let the UI be shown and get the speech for recognition:

```
private async void speechUIButton_Click(object sender, EventArgs e)
{
  var result = await _ui.RecognizeWithUIAsync();

  if (result.ResultStatus == SpeechRecognitionUIStatus.Succeeded)
  {
    var recognized = result.RecognitionResult.Text;

    AddItem(recognized);
  }
}
```

When you call the `RecognizeWithUIAsync` method, it shows the UI and listens for any speech. You can see this in Figure 7.17.

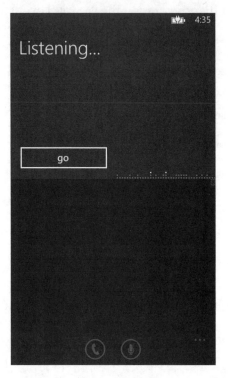

FIGURE 7.17 Using `SpeechRecognitionUI`

The result of the speech recognition is a structure that contains two properties. The first one is the `ResultStatus`, which is an enumeration of whether the operation succeeded. You can test for success (as shown previously). If the operation did not succeed, the result's `RecognitionResult` property (a `SpeechRecognitionResult` object) will not be valid. If it is, you can use the result to see the text that was recognized.

The speech recognition engine also calculates its confidence in the result. This is helpful to figure out whether the text it recognized could possibly be correct. You can use the `RecognitionResult`'s `TextConfidence` property to determine this:

```csharp
private async void speechUIButton_Click(object sender, EventArgs e)
{
  var result = await _ui.RecognizeWithUIAsync();

  if (result.ResultStatus == SpeechRecognitionUIStatus.Succeeded &&
      result.RecognitionResult.TextConfidence >=
      SpeechRecognitionConfidence.Medium)
  {
    var confidence = result.RecognitionResult.TextConfidence;
    var recognized = result.RecognitionResult.Text;

    AddItem(string.Concat(confidence, " - ", recognized));
  }
}
```

In this case we are using the result only if the confidence is at least medium. This will reduce the number of false positives.

The other method for using the speech recognition engine is to use it without the user interface. Unsurprisingly, the class involved is called SpeechRecognizer (note no "UI" suffix). The pattern for using it is very much the same as the UI class:

```csharp
public partial class MainPage : PhoneApplicationPage
{
  SpeechRecognizer _rec;

  // Constructor
  public MainPage()
  {
    InitializeComponent();

    Loaded += MainPage_Loaded;
    Unloaded += MainPage_Unloaded;
  }

  void MainPage_Loaded(object sender, RoutedEventArgs e)
  {
    _rec = new SpeechRecognizer();
  }

  void MainPage_Unloaded(object sender, RoutedEventArgs e)
  {
    _rec.Dispose();
  }
  ...
}
```

When actually using the speech recognition, you will again do it with the async pattern, but it is up to you to make your users aware that you are listening:

```
private async void speechButton_Click(object sender, EventArgs e)
{

  // Show User you are listening
  VisualStateManager.GoToState(this, "Listening", true);

  // Listen for speech
  var result = await _rec.RecognizeAsync();

  if (result.TextConfidence >= SpeechRecognitionConfidence.Medium)
  {
    var confidence = result.TextConfidence;
    var recognized = result.Text;

    AddItem(string.Concat(confidence, " - ", recognized));
  }
}
```

The only real difference in using the RecognizeAsync method is that it returns a SpeechRecognitionResult object directly. You can then just test the confidence as you did before. If the operation failed, the confidence will be the value of SpeechRecognitionConfidence.Rejected, which you can test for a failure with.

Speech Synthesis

Recognizing speech is interesting, but sometimes you need to communicate with users with voice, too. Luckily, the Windows Phone includes support to create speech from your application. Before you can get started, you will need to include the speech capability (called ID_CAP_SPEECH_RECOGNITION) to the WMAppManifest.xml file.

The class involved in generated speech is the SpeedSynthesizer class. This class supports IDisposable, so (like the speech recognition earlier in this chapter) you should create and dispose the class in your Loaded and Unloaded event handlers:

```
public partial class MainPage : PhoneApplicationPage
{
  SpeechSynthesizer _synth;

  // Constructor
  public MainPage()
  {
    InitializeComponent();

    Loaded += MainPage_Loaded;
    Unloaded += MainPage_Unloaded;
  }

  void MainPage_Loaded(object sender, RoutedEventArgs e)
  {
    _synth = new SpeechSynthesizer();
  }

  void MainPage_Unloaded(object sender, RoutedEventArgs e)
  {
    _synth.Dispose();
  }
  ...
}
```

To use the SpeechSynthesizer class, just call the SpeakTextAsync method and supply it with some text to speak:

```
private async void speakButton_Click(object sender,
                                     RoutedEventArgs e)
{
  await _synth.SpeakTextAsync(theText.Text);
}
```

The SpeakTextAsync method uses the async pattern, so it requires the method we marked as async and use the await for the speech to be synthesized. When you synthesize speech, it uses the default voice as specified by the user on the Speech settings, as shown in Figure 7.18.

FIGURE 7.18   Specifying the default language and voice

You can select other voices and languages by using the built-in voices on the phone. The `InstalledVoices` class contains a static property that contains all the voices on the phone. By using a simple LINQ query, you can find a voice that matches your required language and gender, like so:

```
var selectedVoices = from voice in InstalledVoices.All
                     where voice.Gender == VoiceGender.Male &&
                           voice.Language == "en-GB"
                     select voice;

_synth.SetVoice(selectedVoices.First());

await _synth.SpeakTextAsync(theText.Text);
```

In this example, the LINQ query would return a set of voices that were both male and from Great Britain (okay, I have a thing about British English). After you have the voice, you simply have to set it using the `SetVoice` method as shown.

The voices support a number of languages, such as German, Portuguese, French, Spanish, and Polish. The number of voices and languages might depend on the region in which the phone was sold. Be aware that the language of the voice also affects the pronunciation. These voices expect the text to be in the language that matches the voice. This means that supplying a language like English to a voice that matches another language will change the pronunciation. For example, if you supply "Jumping" to a Spanish voice, it will use the soft "J" sound from Spanish.

The Windows Phone also supports a system called Proximity. This system uses Near Field Communication (NFC) to allow two devices to communicate when they are 3–4 cm from each other. Usually this takes the form of tapping phones together.

Before you can use Proximity, you must add the capability. Proximity requires both networking and proximity capabilities (for instance, ID_CAP_ NETWORKING and ID_CAP_PROXIMITY). After you have them, there are several classes for dealing with proximity. For your applications, you'll be able to use the ProximityDevice class to get the default device to work with using the GetDefault method:

```
public partial class MainPage : PhoneApplicationPage
{
  ProximityDevice _device;

  // Constructor
  public MainPage()
  {
    InitializeComponent();

    Loaded += MainPage_Loaded;

  }

  void MainPage_Loaded(object sender, RoutedEventArgs e)
  {
    _device = ProximityDevice.GetDefault();
  }
  ...
}
```

By calling `GetDefault`, the main `ProximityDevice` is returned. Because this object is expensive to get, you should retrieve it at the page level and keep it around instead of creating it on every call.

In addition, the device might not be available due to the user not allowing NFC on the device. In that case, the returned object is a null reference. You should check for this before using:

```
if (_device != null)
{

  // ...

}
```

After you have the `ProximityDevice`, you can publish and subscribe to messages to be passed. You must first have a known message name. The NFC standard requires that this message name be a **protocol** and a **subtype** separated by a period. For the Windows Phone (and Windows 8), the **protocol** must be "Windows"; the **subtype** is up to you. After you have the message name, you can send a message using the `ProximityDevice`'s `PublishMessage` method:

```
const string MESSAGETYPE = "Windows.FunWithNFC";

long _pubId = -1;

private void publishButton_Click(object sender, EventArgs e)
{
  if (_device != null)
  {
    // Publish new message
    _pubId = _device.PublishMessage(MESSAGETYPE, "Hello World");
  }
}
```

The body of the message can be in multiple formats. There are methods for binary and text. In this case, we're just sending a simple text message. The call to `PublishMessage` returns a long integer that is used to unpublish a message. Only one message can be pending at a time. That means that if you want to republish a message, you must unpublish the first one, like so:

```
const string MESSAGETYPE = "Windows.FunWithNFC";

long _pubId = -1;

private void publishButton_Click(object sender, EventArgs e)
{
  if (_device != null)
  {
    // Remove old message if needed
    if (_pubId != -1) _device.StopPublishingMessage(_pubId);

    // Publish new message
    _pubId = _device.PublishMessage(MESSAGETYPE, "Hello World");
    status.Text = "Published Message";
  }
}
```

The other side of the call is to support subscribing to the message on
another phone. In this case you will want to call the ProximityDevice's
SubscribeForMessage:

```
long _subId = -1;

private void subscribeButton_Click(object sender, EventArgs e)
{
  if (_device != null)
  {
    // Unsubscribe if needed
    if (_subId != -1) _device.StopSubscribingForMessage(_subId);

    // Subscribe to message
    _subId = _device.SubscribeForMessage(MESSAGETYPE, OnMsgRecd);
    status.Text = "Subscribed for Message";
  }

}
```

The SubscribeForMessage method takes the message type to listen for
and a callback for when the message is received. Like the PublishMessage
method, SubscribeForMessage returns an ID so you can stop subscribing to
the message before subscribing to a new message.

One important caveat for using Proximity is that the emulator doesn't
support emulating the Proximity device so you have to use a physical
phone for your testing. In most cases, this will take two phones to do the
actual testing.

The publish and subscribe support in the API is only the tip of the iceberg. The API also supports socket connections between phones for more sophisticated proximity applications, but describing those types of uses are outside the scope of this book.

Bluetooth and VOIP

The Windows Phone also supports two other APIs that are outside the scope of the book, but I think they are worth mentioning here: Bluetooth and Voice over IP (VOIP).

The Bluetooth APIs support the capability to write socket apps to different Bluetooth devices so you can stream sound to wireless headsets or even communicate with special Bluetooth devices (such as printers and scanners). This enables a host of non-consumer scenarios that might be important for enterprise developers.

VOIP API support is another specialized set of features that will allow you to create applications that look and act like the phone app on the phone. This means you can interrupt the user with incoming voice and video calls and allow her to answer calls using your specialized service. This support is key for anyone building VOIP solutions but does not have much need for the larger developer community, so we've decided not to cover it in the book.

Where Are We?

This is where phone development is really different from almost every other type of application design: integration with the phone. In this chapter you saw how to access information from the device, store information on the device, and interact with the core phone functions such as the camera and the phone functions themselves. Making your application a real phone application will require use of these types of functionality; otherwise, it is just an app on a handheld device.

8

Phone Integration

INTEGRATING WITH THE PHONE HARDWARE is important for many applications, but integration takes other forms. The Windows Phone operating system has other key usage points for users. These include contacts, appointments, alarms, and the media hubs. In addition, working with the media library and lock screen can help you create great apps. This chapter shows you how.

Contacts and Appointments

Even though we can get caught up in the mystique of our phones as being little computers, most users actually use their phones to contact people and to keep their appointments. I know this must come as a big surprise to most developers, but it's true!

So, as a developer, you might want to access the user's contacts and appointments to more tightly integrate your applications into the phone experience. To do this, the Windows Phone SDK supports entry points into the user's contacts and appointments. These APIs provide a way to search by commonly used search semantics but also return results that can be further filtered using LINQ.

> **⬛ NOTE**
>
> All access to the contacts and appointments is read-only. You cannot change, add, or delete any information in the list of contacts or appointments.

Contacts

To access the contacts on a phone, you will start with the Contacts class (in the Microsoft.Phone.UserData namespace). This class provides the capability to perform an asynchronous search for the contacts on the phone:

```
var contactCtx = new Contacts();

contactCtx.SearchCompleted += (s, a) =>
  {
    IEnumerable<Contact> contacts = a.Results;
    contactList.ItemsSource = results;
  };

contactCtx.SearchAsync(null, FilterKind.None, null);
```

The SearchAsync call takes three parameters: a filter string, a type of filter, and an object that is passed to the completed event (a state object). The first two parameters typically allow you to do basic filtering in the underlying data store and are specified as the most common filtering semantics. The FilterKind enumeration tells the search API how to treat the filter string. For example, to find a specific person you can search by name, like so:

```
contactCtx.SearchAsync("Chris Sells", FilterKind.DisplayName, null);
```

The FilterKind enumeration includes the members shown in Table 8.1.

TABLE 8.1 FilterKind Enumeration

Value	Description
None	No filter is going to be used. The first parameter of SearchAsync is ignored.
DisplayName	Searches for contact based on the display name of the user. This type of filter supports substring matches (for example, "Sells" matches "Chris Sells").
EmailAddress	Searches for contact based on email address. Only supports full email address in the filter.
PhoneNumber	Searches for contact based on phone number. Must be complete phone number, but format is not important (for example, "2065550003" is the same as "(206) 555 0003").
PinnedToStart	Searches for contact that is pinned to the Start screen. The first parameter of SearchAsync is ignored.

To use the FilterKind enumeration, you can specify the filter and the FilterKind enumeration in the SearchAsync method:

```
contactCtx.SearchAsync("chris@example.com",
                       FilterKind.EmailAddress,
                       null);
```

The result of a search is an IEnumerable collection of Contact objects. The Contacts class supports all the information about a particular contact. Because the data structure can be verbose (for example, there can be multiple phone numbers, addresses, company names, and so on), the class supports many collections for the various items in the data store. For instance, you can get the simple display name as a property, but to get the phone number of a contact you have to use LINQ against the collection:

```
IEnumerable<Contact> contacts = a.Results;

var contact = contacts.First();

string displayName = contact.DisplayName;
string phoneNumber = contact.PhoneNumbers.First().PhoneNumber;
```

This means that to meaningfully bind to the Contact, you will likely need to create a class that represents the data you want to show:

```
public class ContactInfo
{
  public string Name { get; set; }
  public ContactPhoneNumber PhoneNumber { get; set; }
  public DateTime? Birthday { get; set; }
  public ContactCompanyInformation Company { get; set; }
  public ImageSource Picture { get; set; }
  public ContactEmailAddress EmailAddress { get; set; }
}
```

Although you can have the bindable class only include basic types, you can also use the built-in data structures (for example, ContactPhoneNumber) because they do support binding. Luckily, building a collection of these bindable objects is easy using LINQ projections:

```
IEnumerable<Contact> contacts = a.Results;

var qry = from c in contacts
          select new ContactInfo()
                 {
                   Name = c.DisplayName,
                   EmailAddress = c.EmailAddresses.FirstOrDefault(),
                   PhoneNumber = c.PhoneNumbers.FirstOrDefault(),
                   Company = c.Companies.FirstOrDefault(),
                 };

var results = qry.ToList();
```

By using this technique of projecting into a new list of the contact information, you can easily build a ListBox using data binding:

```
<ListBox x:Name="contactList">
  <ListBox.ItemTemplate>
    <DataTemplate>
      <StackPanel Width="470">
       <TextBlock Text="{Binding Name}" />
        <TextBlock Text="{Binding EmailAddress.EmailAddress}" />
        <TextBlock Text="{Binding Company.CompanyName}" />
        <TextBlock Text="{Binding PhoneNumber.PhoneNumber}" />
      </StackPanel>
    </DataTemplate>
  </ListBox.ItemTemplate>
</ListBox>
```

You can see in the data binding that you can navigate down the data structure to the object you want to bind to. And because they are data bindings, if the user does not have one of these objects, the binding silently fails (which is one of the advantages of doing this in a binding).

Of course, because you can use LINQ to query against the resultant collection, you can use it if the `FilterKind` enumeration does not give you the granularity you need to find contacts. Although this works well, be aware that loading all contacts in memory can consume a lot of memory. For example, if you want to find all the contacts who have a phone number in the 206 area code (as well as sort them by display name), you can just use LINQ:

```
var qry = from c in contacts
          where c.PhoneNumbers
                .Any(phone => phone.PhoneNumber.Contains("(206)"))
          orderby c.DisplayName
          select new ContactInfo()
              {
                  Name = c.DisplayName,
                  EmailAddress = c.EmailAddresses.FirstOrDefault(),
                  PhoneNumber = c.PhoneNumbers.FirstOrDefault(),
                  Company = c.Companies.FirstOrDefault(),
              };
```

In addition to the basic contact information, you can also ascertain which accounts the user contacts. The `Contacts` class exposes a list of the user's accounts. Each account will tell you the kind of account (for example, Facebook, Microsoft Account, Outlook, and so on) as well as the name of the account:

```
Account first = contactCtx.Accounts.FirstOrDefault();
if (first != null)
{
  string accountName = first.Name;
  if (first.Kind == StorageKind.Facebook)
  {
    MessageBox.Show("Your first account is Facebook");
  }
}
```

You cannot filter by account through the `SearchAsync` method, but you can filter any of the associated objects by account. For instance, to filter contacts by account, simply use the following:

```
Account first = contactCtx.Accounts.FirstOrDefault();

var qry = from c in contacts
          where c.Accounts.Contains(first)
          select new ContactInfo()
                 {
                     Name = c.DisplayName,
                     EmailAddress = c.EmailAddresses.FirstOrDefault(),
                     PhoneNumber = c.PhoneNumbers.FirstOrDefault(),
                     Company = c.Companies.FirstOrDefault(),
                 };
```

Most of the objects related to contacts also have an account associated with them. For example, if you have a contact, you can find out which email address is from Facebook, like so:

```
Contact theContact = contacts.First();

var addr = theContact.EmailAddresses
    .Where(email => email.Accounts
                         .Any(a => a.Kind == StorageKind.Facebook))
    .FirstOrDefault();
```

Lastly, each contact can have a picture associated with it. This picture is not immediately returned with the contact (because that could occupy a large chunk of memory). To access the picture, the Contacts class has a GetPicture method that returns a Stream object containing the image. Although this is useful, you'll probably need to wrap it with an ImageSource object to use it in data binding. One approach is to do this during the projection into the bindable class, like so:

```
var qry = from c in contacts
          select new ContactInfo()
                 {
                     Name = c.DisplayName,
                     EmailAddress = c.EmailAddresses.FirstOrDefault(),
                     PhoneNumber = c.PhoneNumbers.FirstOrDefault(),
                     Company = c.Companies.FirstOrDefault(),
                     Picture = CreateImageSource(c.GetPicture())
                 };
```

The implementation of the CreateImageSource method that does the wrapping looks like this:

```
ImageSource CreateImageSource(Stream stream)
{
  if (stream == null) return null;
  var src = new BitmapImage();
  src.SetSource(stream);
  return src;
}
```

Because data binding can't turn a Stream into an image automatically, either you need to do that when you create the object or perhaps you can do it with a value converter (refer to Chapter 3, "XAML Overview," for more information on value converters).

■ Looking Forward

Even though the contacts API is read-only, you can add new contacts via the SaveContactTask as detailed later in this chapter.

Appointments

Working with appointments follows the same pattern. It all starts with the Appointments class (like the Contacts class started with Contacts):

```
var appointmentCtx = new Appointments();

appointmentCtx.SearchCompleted += (s,a) =>
{
  IEnumerable<Appointment> appts = a.Results;

  // Bind to the UI
  apptList.ItemsSource = appts;
};

appointmentCtx.SearchAsync(DateTime.MinValue,
                           DateTime.Today,
                           null);
```

After creating the Appointments class, you can handle the SearchCompleted event and call the SearchAsync method to perform a search. The SearchAsync method enables you to specify a date range for the search (the last parameter is an optional piece of state to send to the completed event). The data returned by the search is an enumerable list of Appointment objects.

Unlike the `Contacts` class, the `Appointments` class supports binding because the nature of the data is fairly simple. For example, by using data binding, a `ListBox` to show appointments could look as simple as this:

```
<ListBox x:Name="apptList">
  <ListBox.ItemTemplate>
    <DataTemplate>
      <StackPanel Width="470">
        <TextBlock Text="{Binding StartTime, StringFormat=d}" />
        <TextBlock Text="{Binding IsPrivate}" />
        <TextBlock Text="{Binding Location}" />
        <TextBlock Text="{Binding Subject}" />
        <TextBlock Text="{Binding Status}" />
      </StackPanel>
    </DataTemplate>
  </ListBox.ItemTemplate>
</ListBox>
```

The `SearchAsync` method also enables you to specify an account to search as well as the maximum number of results. So, you can select an account and then search like so:

```
var outlookAccount = appointmentCtx.Accounts
                    .Where(a => a.Kind == StorageKind.Outlook)
                    .FirstOrDefault();

appointmentCtx.SearchAsync(DateTime.MinValue, // Start
                    DateTime.Today,    // End
                    25,                // Max Results
                    outlookAccount,    // Account
                    null);
```

By using these APIs, you can access the contacts and appointments for the phone's user.

Alarms and Reminders

When you're creating your application, you might need the ability to alert the user about specific notifications. Windows Phone supports this by enabling you to create two types of notifications: alarms and reminders.

Alarms are notifications that show a message and allow the user to tap the alarm to start your application. Additionally, the user can snooze the alarm or dismiss it. With an alarm, you can also specify a custom sound located in your application to use as the alarm sound. You can see an alarm in action in Figure 8.1.

FIGURE 8.1   An alarm

Reminders are similar to alarms, but they have additional functionality:

- You can specify the title of a reminder (which is always "Alarm" for alarms).
- The user can specify how long to snooze a reminder.
- You can decide to send contextual information when the user taps a reminder (whereas the alarm can simply launch the application).
- You cannot specify a specialized sound for reminders.

Figure 8.2 shows a reminder. If alarms or reminders are not closed when additional notifications appear, they will be stacked with an identifier that mentions how many notifications need to be handled, as shown in Figure 8.3.

FIGURE 8.2   A reminder

FIGURE 8.3   Stacked notifications

Alarms and reminders are both tied to your application. They are notifications for your application. If you want to allow users to disable/ enable these notifications, you must supply that functionality in your application. There is no operating system-level management UI for these notifications.

■ **TIP**

The precision of alarm and reminder times is to the minute. If you create notifications that need higher precision, the service that handles alarms and reminders will not show the notification more than after per minute. Be prepared for the alarms that are within a minute of a notification to be stacked.

Now that you've seen how notifications look, let's discuss how you actually create your own notifications.

Creating an Alarm

To create a new alarm, you can simply create a new `Alarm` object and instantiate all the relevant properties, like so:

```
// Create Alarm - name must be unique per app
var alarmName = Guid.NewGuid().ToString();

var alarm = new Alarm(alarmName)
{
  // When the Alarm should sound
  BeginTime = DateTime.Parse("2011-12-25T06:30"),

  // The Message in the Alarm
  Content = "Wake Up for Christmas!",

  // What sound to play for the alarm
  Sound = new Uri("santa.wav", UriKind.Relative)
};

// Add the Alarm to the Phone
ScheduledActionService.Add(alarm);
```

Each alarm must have a name that is unique to your application (that is, names do not need to be globally unique). So, it is common to just use a GUID to name your alarm. This name is not visible to the user. After you construct the alarm using the unique name, you would typically specify several key properties, including the following:

- **BeginTime:** This is the time the alarm will alert the user.
- **Content:** This is the text to be shown in the alarm beneath the "Alarm" title.
- **Sound:** This is a URI to the sound in your .xap file that should be used to play when the alarm occurs.

Finally, you will use the `ScheduledActionService` to add the alarm to the phone. This service is the starting point for both alarms and reminders (as they are both considered a `ScheduledAction`). You can simply add your alarm to the phone by using the service class as shown in the example.

You can also create alarms to have recurrence. To do this, you should set both the `RecurrenceType` and the `ExpirationTime`. The `RecurrenceType` is an enumeration that enables you to specify whether the alarm is hourly, daily, weekly, and so forth. The `ExpirationTime` specifies how long to repeat the recurrence:

```
// ...
// Set Recurrence
alarm.RecurrenceType = RecurrenceInterval.Yearly;
alarm.ExpirationTime = DateTime.Today.AddYears(10);

// ...
```

The `Alarm` class has a `Title` property that looks like you can set the title of your alarm, but this is not supported (that is, it throws a `NotSupported-Exception`). The title of all alarms is "Alarm."

Creating a Reminder

Because alarms and reminders both derive from `ScheduledAction`, you can correctly assume that creating a reminder is similar to creating an alarm:

```
// Create Reminder - name must be unique per app
var reminderName = Guid.NewGuid().ToString();

var reminder = new Reminder(reminderName)
{
  // Reminder Time
  BeginTime = DateTime.Today.AddHours(6),

  // Title for the Reminder
  Title = "Wake Up Reminder",

  // The description below the Title
  Content = "You should get up now...",

  // The page to navigate to (and any other context)
  // when the user taps the reminder
  NavigationUri =
    new Uri("/MainPage.xaml?wake=true", UriKind.Relative),
};

// Add the reminder
ScheduledActionService.Add(reminder);
```

However, creating a reminder is different from creating an alarm, in several ways. First, the Title property is supported, so you can specify what the title is on your reminder. Unfortunately, unlike the alarm, the Sound property is missing, so reminders can only have the sound that the system defines as the reminder sound (although the user can set that in the phone's Options section).

The biggest difference between an alarm and a reminder is that you can specify the NavigationUri to specify the deep linking of the reminder to a specific page (with context). The NavigationUri allows you to specify a relative URL of the page to show in your applications as well as an optional query string to include context to the reminder. If the user taps on the reminder, it will open your app and navigate to the URI you've specified.

Accessing Existing Notifications

After you've added notifications to the phone, you might want to support managing those notifications. The ScheduledActionService class has several members that can help you manage your notifications:

- **Add:** This adds a new notification to the phone.
- **Find:** This locates a notification by name.
- **GetActions<T>:** This returns a read-only collection of notifications based on the type (alarm or reminder).
- **Remove:** This removes a specifically named notification from the phone.
- **Replace:** This replaces a named notification with a new notification (of the same name).

For example, to get a list of reminders and bind them to a list box, you can simply use the GetActions method:

```
// Returns an IEnumerable<Reminder> object
var reminders = ScheduledActionService.GetActions<Reminder>();

// A ListBox named 'theBox'
theBox.ItemsSource = reminders;
```

The base class for the notifications (ScheduledAction) supports a read-only property called IsScheduled, which is used to tell you whether the alarm or reminder is still scheduled to show a notification in the future. Although the class supports the IsEnabled property, it is always true for alarms and reminders.

> ### ■ Looking Forward
>
> You can also use the ScheduledActionService and Scheduled-Action classes to create scheduled agents. We will discuss this in Chapter 10, "Multitasking."

Using Tasks

Windows Phone has several of the features of the operating system, including accessing the address book, launching the web browser, and using the camera. To give you access to these features, the Windows Phone SDK supports a list of tasks you can execute. These tasks are divided into two categories: launchers and choosers. A **launcher** simply takes the user to another part of the phone experience to accomplish some goal (for example, launch a web page, make a phone call, and so on). A **chooser** takes the user to a facility on the phone but returns to the app with some information (for instance, choose an email address, take a picture, and so on). Tables 8.2 and 8.3 show the launchers and choosers available for the phone.

TABLE 8.2   Launchers

Launcher	Description
EmailComposeTask	Launches a new email to be sent by the user
MapsDirectionsTask	Launches the map application to show you directions to a specific address
MapsTask	Launches the maps application on the phone
MapsDownloaderTask	Launches the map application so you can download specific maps for offline use
MarketplaceDetailTask	Launches the details page for a specific Marketplace item (app or music)
MarketplaceHubTask	Launches a specific hub of the Marketplace
MarketplaceReviewTask	Launches a specific apps review page (usually your application)
MarketplaceSearchTask	Launches the search page for the user to search through the Marketplace
MediaPlayerLauncher	Launches the media player (for example, Zune player)
PhoneCallTask	Launches the phone call user interface to make a phone call
SaveAppointmentTask	Launches the calendar to allow you to save specific appointment details
SearchTask	Launches the search UI on the phone
ShareLinkTask	Shares a link with a social media application
ShareStatusTask	Shares the user's current status with a social media application

Launcher	Description
SmsComposeTask	Launches a new SMS message to be sent by the user
WebBrowserTask	Launches the web browser

TABLE 8.3   Choosers

Chooser	Description
AddressChooserTask	Enables the user to pick a physical address from the user's address book
AddWalletItemTask	Enables the user to add a specific item to her phone wallet.
CameraCaptureTask	Launches the camera to enables the user to take a camera picture and return that taken picture to the app
EmailAddressChooserTask	Enables the user to select an existing contact's email to be returned to the app
GameInviteTask	Invites users to the current gaming session
PhoneNumberChooserTask	Enables the user to pick a phone number to be returned to the app
PhotoChooserTask	Enables the user to pick an existing photo from the photo collection on the phone and be returned to the app
SaveContactTask	Saves a new contact into an address book
SaveEmailAddressTask	Enables the user to save a new email address to the phone and return the new address to the app
SavePhoneNumberTask	Enables the user to save a new phone number to the phone and return the new number to the app
SaveRingtoneTask	Enables the user to save a sound file to the phone for use as a ring tone

All these tasks are in the same namespace: Microsoft.Phone.Tasks.

Launchers

Each launcher works in a consistent manner. They create an instance of the launcher, set optional properties that will help the launcher, and call a Show method to take the user to the phone's functionality. For example, the code for showing the Microsoft website in the web browser is as simple as this:

```
void webBrowserTask_Click(object sender, RoutedEventArgs e)
{
  var task = new WebBrowserTask();
  task.Uri = new Uri("http://microsoft.com");
  task.Show();
}
```

Although the launchers do not use a common interface, they do follow the same convention, so they should be easy to work with. Let's look at each one.

EmailComposeTask

The EmailComposeTask enables the user to compose and send an email without necessarily sharing those details with your app. For this task, you can set most of the information about an outgoing email, including information in the To, CC, Subject, and Body sections:

```
void composeEmailButton_Click(object sender, RoutedEventArgs e)
{
  var task = new EmailComposeTask();
  task.To = "shawn@hotmail.com";
  task.Cc = "youremail@hotmail.com";
  task.Subject = "Your Email";
  task.Body = "This is an email";
  task.Show();
}
```

All these properties are completely optional. If the user just wants to launch an email, you can create it and call Show. The Body property is always plain text. There is no support for creating a body with HTML in this release or adding attachments to emails.

MapsDirectionsTask

Inside the SDK are tasks for using the Bing maps, but because those are there for backward-compatibility with Windows Phone 7.5 and earlier, they've introduced new tasks for working with the built-in Nokia maps. To get at these new maps, there are three new tasks; the first of these is the MapsDirectionsTask. This task simply enables you to get directions in the Maps app (using the Nokia maps instead of the Bing maps).

This task is like the others in that you simply set default data and then call the Show method. In this case the task has a Start and Stop property. Each of these properties takes a structure called a LabeledMapLocation. The location, in turn, takes both a Label and a Location. The Label is a string that can contain a simple label or can contain a search term. The Location property takes a GeoCoordinate object that contains the latitude and longitude to use for the maps. For example

```
var start = new LabeledMapLocation()
{
  Label = "Home",
  Location = new GeoCoordinate(33.769138, -84.33596)
};

var end = new LabeledMapLocation()
{
  Label = "Turner Field",
  Location = new GeoCoordinate(33.735194, -84.389645)
};

var task = new MapsDirectionsTask()
{
  Start = start,
  End = end
};

task.Show();
```

When the Show method is executed, the Maps application is launched and attempts to calculate the directions. If your goal is to navigate from the user's current location, you can just omit the Start property on the MapsDirectionsTask altogether:

```
var end = new LabeledMapLocation()
{
  Label = "Turner Field",
```

```
    Location = new GeoCoordinate(33.735194, -84.389645)
};

var task = new MapsDirectionsTask()
{
  End = end
};

task.Show();
```

By leaving off the Start property, this simply assumes that you want to start from the user's current location. Calculating GeoCoordinates can be a pain so you can also omit the Location property to have the Label of the LabeledMapLocation act as a search phrase:

```
var end = new LabeledMapLocation()
{
  Label = "Turner Field"
};

var task = new MapsDirectionsTask()
{
  End = end
};

task.Show();
```

In this example, the ending location will be marked as "Turner Field" and the map application will attempt to find Turner Field from your location. You can also do this using any search information like an address as the Label:

```
var end = new LabeledMapLocation()
{
  Label = "755 Hank Aaron Drive Southeast  Atlanta, GA 30315"
};

var task = new MapsDirectionsTask()
{
  End = end
};

task.Show();
```

MapsTask

This task is specifically used to show and search in the maps app for the user. There are two ways to use the MapsTask. First, you can simply show a location and a zoom level. For this, you need a specific GeoCoordinate object. For instance:

```
var task = new MapsTask()
{
  Center = new GeoCoordinate(33.735194, -84.389645),
  ZoomLevel = 2
};

task.Show();
```

The Center property is the center of the map to show. The ZoomLevel is how far into the map to display. In this case, ZoomLevel of 2 is going to show most of the world. If you omit the Center property, it will simply center the map on the current location for the user.

The other way the MapsTask works is to enable you to search on the map. In this case you would just supply the SearchPhrase property with what you want to search for. If you simply want to show an address, just use the SearchPhrase with the address:

```
var task = new MapsTask()
{
  SearchTerm = "755 Hank Aaron Drive Southeast  Atlanta, GA 30315",
};

task.Show();
```

More commonly you would use the SearchTerm property to search the map. For instance, to find pizza restaurants, you would:

```
var task = new MapsTask()
{
  SearchTerm = "pizza",
};

task.Show();
```

Note that the ZoomLevel and Center properties are ignored if you use the SearchPhrase.

MapsDownloaderTask

The last of the maps tasks is the MapsDownloaderTask. This task simply launches the Maps app to allow the user to select which maps to download to the device for offline use. The task has no properties; you just call the Show method to launch that part of the Maps app, like so:

```
var task = new MapDownloaderTask();

task.Show();
```

MarketplaceDetailTask

This task's job is to launch the Marketplace app to show the details of a specific application. Although the task does allow you to show specific items using the ContentIdentifier and ContentType properties, it normally launches without specifying these properties and will launch the details page for your own application:

```
void marketplaceDetailButton_Click(object sender, RoutedEventArgs e)
{
  // Show our Detail Page
  var task = new MarketplaceDetailTask();
  task.Show();
}
```

If you have a specific application content identifier (the GUID that represents the application[1]), you can specify it:

```
void marketplaceDetailButton_Click(object sender, RoutedEventArgs e)
{
  // Show our Detail Page
  var task = new MarketplaceDetailTask();
  task.ContentIdentifier = "a518bd6c-280e-e011-9264-00237de2db9e";
  task.ContentType = MarketplaceContentType.Applications;
  task.Show();
}
```

---

1 The GUID for your application is supplied by the AppHub. This might be the same GUID from your WMAppManifest's ProductID, but it can be different in some cases.

MarketplaceHubTask

The purpose of the `MarketplaceHubTask` is to go to the Marketplace application on the phone to allow the user to browse different items in the Marketplace. When using this task, you need to specify whether the user needs to navigate to music or to applications:

```
void marketplaceHubButton_Click(object sender, RoutedEventArgs e)
{
  // Show the Marketplace Hub
  var task = new MarketplaceHubTask();
  task.ContentType = MarketplaceContentType.Applications; // Or Music
  task.Show();
}
```

Note that this task does not work in the emulator because the Marketplace isn't intended to work in emulation mode.

MarketplaceReviewTask

The `MarketplaceReviewTask` is used to take the user to the current application's review page to allow him to review the application. There are no properties to set for this particular task, as shown here:

```
void marketplaceReviewButton_Click(object sender, RoutedEventArgs e)
{
  // Show the Application Review Page for this application
  var task = new MarketplaceReviewTask();
  task.Show();
}
```

Because your application is not technically in the Marketplace during development, this task will take you to a review page; then it will complain that it cannot find the application. This is enough to test this task. After your application has been deployed, it will take the user to the correct review page.

MarketplaceSearchTask

The `MarketplaceSearchTask` enables you to send the user to the Search page of the Marketplace app specifying which types of search to perform as well as any keywords with which to prepopulate the search, as shown here:

```
void marketplaceSearchButton_Click(object sender, RoutedEventArgs e)
{
  // Show the Marketplace Search Page
  var task = new MarketplaceSearchTask();
  task.ContentType = MarketplaceContentType.Applications; // Or Music
  task.SearchTerms = "Shooting Games";
  task.Show();
}
```

MediaPlayerLauncher

The purpose of the MediaPlayerLauncher is to play media (audio and/
or video) that comes from your application (instead of media that is in
the media library). The media must be either in the application's install
directory (for example, in the .xap file) or in isolated storage. To specify the
location, you need to supply the task's Location property, which takes an
enumeration (MediaLocationType) with which you can specify either Install
(which indicates the file was in the .xap file) or Data (which indicates the
media file is in isolated storage). In addition, you have to specify the Media
property, which takes a relative Uri that points to the media either in the
.xap file or in isolated storage, like so:

```
void mediaPlayerButton_Click(object sender, RoutedEventArgs e)
{
  // Launch the Media Player
  var task = new MediaPlayerLauncher();
  task.Location = MediaLocationType.Install; // Or Data
  task.Media = new Uri("bear.wmv", UriKind.Relative);
  task.Controls = MediaPlaybackControls.All;
  task.Show();
}
```

In addition, you can specify which controls are shown in the media
player. When playing with the MediaPlayerTask, the media player can show
three different controls, as highlighted in Figure 8.4. The control on the left
is the Rewind control, the one on the right is the Fast-Forward control, and
the one in the center is for toggling between Pause and Play.

The MediaPlaybackControls includes a set of enumeration flags, so you can
select which controls are used. Table 8.4 shows the MediaPlaybackControls
enumeration.

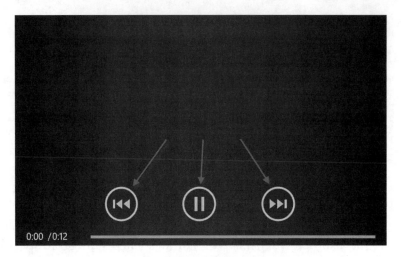

FIGURE 8.4   **Media player controls**

TABLE 8.4   `MediaPlaybackControls` Enumeration

Value	Description
All	Shows all the controls including Pause, Stop, Skip, Rewind, and Fast-Forward
None	Shows the media without any controls
Pause	Flag value for the Pause control
Stop	Flag value for the Stop control (not applicable to the `MediaPlayerTask`)
Skip	Flag value for the Skip control (not applicable to the `MediaPlayerTask`)
Rewind	Flag value for the Rewind control
FastForward	Flag value for the Fast-Forward control

Typically, you would show all controls. However, you can decide to use specific controls by mixing the flags, like so:

```
void mediaPlayerButton_Click(object sender, RoutedEventArgs e)
{
  // Launch the Media Player
```

```
    var task = new MediaPlayerLauncher();
    task.Location = MediaLocationType.Install; // Or Data
    task.Media = new Uri("bear.wmv", UriKind.Relative);
    task.Controls = MediaPlaybackControls.Pause |
                    MediaPlaybackControls.Rewind;
    task.Show();
}
```

PhoneCallTask

As its name suggests, the PhoneCallTask enables you to perform a phone call on the phone. All you need to do is specify the phone number and name to display to the user, like so:

```
void phoneCallButton_Click(object sender, RoutedEventArgs e)
{
  // Make a phone call
  var task = new PhoneCallTask();
  task.DisplayName = "Lottery Headquarters";
  task.PhoneNumber = "(404) 555 1212";
  task.Show();
}
```

When this task is launched, the user will be asked for permission to make the phone call, as shown in Figure 8.5.

SaveAppointmentTask

Like many of the other tasks, the SaveAppointmentTask is straightforward in its approach. The purpose, obviously, is to let users make a new appointment. Although not all fields of the appointment app are available, you can set quite a number of the fields with code, as shown here:

```
var task = new SaveAppointmentTask()
{
  Subject = "Dentist",
  StartTime = DateTime.Parse("11/11/2012 2:00pm"),
  EndTime = DateTime.Parse("11/11/2012 4:00pm"),
  AppointmentStatus = AppointmentStatus.Busy,
  IsAllDayEvent = false,
  Details = "Dr. Smith - 404-555-1212",
  Location = "123 Main Street, Atlanta, GA",
  Reminder = Reminder.FifteenMinutes
};

task.Show();
```

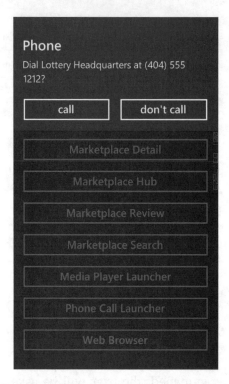

FIGURE 8.5 **PhoneCallTask confirmation**

None of these properties are actually required, but they can be used to fill in default details. The user will still be prompted by the Appointment app to confirm and possibly change the data you send in. The `Reminder` property is an enumeration of different `Reminder` values, not the `Reminder` class that is used to create reminders programmatically. These values specify how long before an appointment to create a reminder (if any).

SearchTask

The `SearchTask` class is used to direct the user to the phone's built-in search application (the one that launches when you press the Search button on the phone). You can specify a search query to be prefilled when the search is launched, as shown here:

```
void searchButton_Click(object sender, RoutedEventArgs e)
{
  // Launch the Search App
```

```
    var task = new SearchTask();
    task.SearchQuery = "XBox Games";
    task.Show();
}
```

ShareLinkTask

If you want your application to be capable of sharing a link on social networking sites for which the user has registered the phone (for instance, Facebook or Twitter), this is the task for you. It allows you to specify the link to share, the title of the link (that is, what to display in the hyperlink), and a message to include with the link:

```
private void ShareLink_Click(object sender, RoutedEventArgs e)
{
  // Share a link
  var task = new ShareLinkTask();
  task.LinkUri = new Uri("http://wildermuth.com");
  task.Title = "Shawn's Blog";
  task.Message = "I can't believe his head is turning!";

  task.Show();
}
```

The user must have a social networking account registered on the phone for this launcher to succeed. If she has more than one social networking account on the phone, it displays a list of which services to use (similar to when you create a new email with more than one account).

ShareStatusTask

Much like the ShareLinkTask, this launcher enables you to share your current status via social networking. This launcher has you specify the user's status to share:

```
private void ShareStatus_Click(object sender, RoutedEventArgs e)
{
  // Share a link
  var task = new ShareStatusTask();
  task.Status = "I'm writing a #wp7 book!";

  task.Show();
}
```

After shown, this will take you to the share status UI for the phone.

SmsComposeTask

The SmsComposeTask enables you to get the user to send a text message (for example, SMS message). You can specify both whom to send the text to and the body of the message. The To property specifies a semicolon-delimited list of recipients for the text message. The Body property enables you to specify the message to be sent via SMS:

```
void smsButton_Click(object sender, RoutedEventArgs e)
{
  // Send an SMS Message
  var task = new SmsComposeTask();
  task.To = "(404) 555-1212; (206) 555-1212";
  task.Body = "This is a text message!";
  task.Show();
}
```

> **▪ NOTE**
>
> This task does not allow you to send MMS messages (SMS messages with attachments).

WebBrowserTask

The WebBrowserTask launches the built-in browser (Internet Explorer) with a specified URI, as shown here:

```
void webBrowserTask_Click(object sender, RoutedEventArgs e)
{
  var task = new WebBrowserTask();
  task.Uri = new Uri("http://microsoft.com");
  task.Show();
}
```

Choosers

Now that you've seen the launchers, let's look at the choosers. The choosers present a similar development experience, but unlike the launchers, they expect to return to your application with some data. All the choosers support an event (usually called Completed) that is fired when the chooser is complete (whether it succeeds or not). Because your application can be tombstoned when a chooser is launched, you have to wire up this event in such a way that it will be rewired when the application is untombstoned. Typically, you would do this by having your task created at the page level and wired up during page initialization (for instance, in the constructor):

```
public partial class MainPage : PhoneApplicationPage
{
  CameraCaptureTask cameraCapture = new CameraCaptureTask();

  // Constructor
  public MainPage()
  {
    InitializeComponent();

    // Wire up completed event so it survives tombstoning
    cameraCapture.Completed +=
      new EventHandler<PhotoResult>(cameraTask_Completed);
  }
  ...
}
```

When you launch a chooser, you can simply call Show, like you did with the launchers in the earlier examples:

```
void cameraButton_Click(object sender, RoutedEventArgs e)
{
  cameraCapture.Show();
}
```

In the event handlers of all the choosers, you must check the Error property to ensure that an exception wasn't thrown during the chooser operation. In addition, you should check the TaskResult property on each chooser to ensure that the chooser was not canceled. You can check this by checking the TaskResult against the TaskResult enumeration:

```
void cameraTask_Completed(object sender, PhotoResult e)
{
  if (e.Error == null && e.TaskResult == TaskResult.OK)
  {
    // ...
  }
}
```

The following subsections provide examples showing how to use each chooser.

AddWalletItemTask

On the Windows Phone you can store payments and deals in something called the Wallet. This task enables you to add payment instruments (for example, accounts and/or credit cards) to the Wallet. To do this, you must create an instance of the PaymentInstrument class that contains the information about the payment type. Before you can use this task, you will need to add several capabilities, including ID_CAP_WALLET_SECUREELEMENT, ID_CAP_WALLET_PAYMENTINSTRUMENTS, and ID_CAP_WALLET.

First, you'll need to create the task itself directly at the class level because this task is a chooser. You should handle the Completed event so that you can know whether the payment was successfully added, like so:

```
public partial class MainPage : PhoneApplicationPage
{

  AddWalletItemTask addWalletTask = new AddWalletItemTask();

  // Constructor
  public MainPage()
  {
    InitializeComponent();

    addWalletButton.Click += addWalletButton_Click;

    addWalletTask.Completed += addWalletTask_Completed;
  }

  ...
}
```

After you have the task created, you need the data to send in with the task. First, create an instance of the PaymentInstrument class, like so:

```
var item = new PaymentInstrument()
{
  AccountNumber = "12345678",
  BillingPhone = "(404) 555-1212",
  DisplayName = "Wilder Minds Bank",
  CustomerName = "Shawn Wildermuth",
  ExpirationDate = new DateTime(2014, 12, 15),
  PaymentInstrumentKinds = PaymentInstrumentKinds.CreditAndDebit,
  Logo99x99 = logo99,
  Logo159x159 = logo159,
  Logo336x336 = logo336
};
```

In this case you can see the typical financial data such as account number, billing phone, and customer name. You can specify certain types of financial instruments using the PaymentInstrumentKinds enumeration. You can also see that the PaymentInstrument does require three size logos. These are simply images of the right size. You can create the logos directly from a remote or local resource, as shown here:

```
// Logos
var logo99 = new BitmapImage(new Uri("/assets/logo99.png",
                             UriKind.RelativeOrAbsolute));
logo99.CreateOptions = BitmapCreateOptions.None;

var logo159 = new BitmapImage(new Uri("/assets/logo159.png",
                              UriKind.RelativeOrAbsolute));
logo159.CreateOptions = BitmapCreateOptions.None;

var logo336 = new BitmapImage(new Uri("/assets/logo336.png",
                              UriKind.RelativeOrAbsolute));
logo336.CreateOptions = BitmapCreateOptions.None;
```

Note that the logos are being created using the BitmapCreateOptions value of "None." This indicates that the URL should be passed as the bitmap, but it's the responsibility of the AddWalletItemTask or the Wallet UI to actually create these bitmaps when necessary. Finally, you can create the task itself and set the new payment as the Item property:

```
addWalletTask.Item = item;

addWalletTask.Show();
```

This way, when the task is shown, if the user selects an item to add to their wallet, you can see whether the item is added successfully in the event handler for the Completed event.

```
void addWalletTask_Completed(object sender, AddWalletItemResult e)
{
  if (e.TaskResult == TaskResult.OK)
  {
    MessageBox.Show("Payment Type Added");
  }
}
```

Note that, even though the Wallet feature supports both deals and payments, this task only supports adding payments. You can use the Deal class to add deals to the Wallet.

AddressChooserTask

Sometimes you might need to allow the user to retrieve a physical address from the address book. That is what the AddressChooserTask is designed to do. You can wire up this task to let the user select an address:

```
AddressChooserTask addressChooser = new AddressChooserTask();

private void addressButton_Click(object sender, RoutedEventArgs e)
{
  addressChooser.Show();
}

void addressChooser_Completed(object sender, AddressResult e)
{
  if (e.Error == null)
  {
    string addressName = e.DisplayName;
    string address = e.Address;
  }
}
```

When the task completes, it returns both the name of the address (the display name of the person/company in the address book) and the address as a string. The address will have line breaks embedded if it is multilined (as most are) so that they can be displayed directly in a TextBlock without additional formatting.

CameraCaptureTask

The CameraCaptureTask is intended to   instruct your user to take a picture and return to you the raw results of the picture:

```
CameraCaptureTask cameraCapture = new CameraCaptureTask();

   void cameraButton_Click(object sender, RoutedEventArgs e)
{
  cameraCapture.Show();
}
```

```
void cameraTask_Completed(object sender, PhotoResult e)
{
  if (e.Error == null && e.TaskResult == TaskResult.OK)
  {
    // Create a BitmapImage from the photo
    BitmapImage bitmap = new BitmapImage();
    bitmap.SetSource(e.ChosenPhoto);

    // Paint the background with the bitmap
    ImageBrush brush = new ImageBrush();
    brush.ImageSource = bitmap;
    LayoutRoot.Background = brush;
  }
}
```

In the event handler that is called after the user takes a picture, you are handed the photo (as the PhotoResult's ChosenPhoto property) as a Stream object. You can then use the results of the photo in any way you want (for example, store it in isolated storage, upload it to a server, or show it in the UI).

> ### ■ Looking Back
>
> For access to the camera in real time (instead of requesting a photo from the photo-taking application), you can use the camera APIs detailed in Chapter 7, "Phone Hardware."

EmailAddressChooserTask

The purpose of this chooser is to enable the user to select an email address from his list of contacts on the phone. When you use this chooser, it shows only contacts with email addresses to pick from, and if a contact has more than one email address, it will let the user choose which one to use. To use the EmailAddressChooserTask, you simply handle the event and show the task:

```
void chooseEmailTask_Click(object sender, RoutedEventArgs e)
{
  // Pick an email address
  task.Show();
}
```

```
void task_Completed(object sender, EmailResult e)
{
  // Ensure no error and that an email was chosen
  if (e.Error == null && e.TaskResult == TaskResult.OK)
  {
    MessageBox.Show(e.Email);
  }
}
```

In the event handler that is called after a user picks an email, you can get at the email address via the Email property of the EmailResult object.

PhoneNumberChooserTask

Like the email chooser, this task is designed to get the user to give you a phone number from his contacts. It works in the same way as the email chooser:

```
void choosePhoneTask_Click(object sender, RoutedEventArgs e)
{
  // Get Phone Number from Contacts
  task.Show();
}

void task_Completed(object sender, PhoneNumberResult e)
{
  // Ensure no error and that a phone number was chosen
  if (e.Error == null && e.TaskResult == TaskResult.OK)
  {
    MessageBox.Show(e.PhoneNumber);
  }
}
```

After the user has selected a phone number, the event returns with the selected phone number.

PhotoChooserTask

This chooser is used to let the user get a photo and return it to your application. At first glance, it works just like the CameraCaptureTask, but instead it lets the user pick a picture from the ones stored on his phone:

```
void choosePhotoTask_Click(object sender, RoutedEventArgs e)
{
  // Get a Photo
  task.Show();
}
```

```
void photoChooser_Completed(object sender, PhotoResult e)
{
  if (e.Error == null && e.TaskResult == TaskResult.OK)
  {
    // Create a BitmapImage from the photo
    BitmapImage bitmap = new BitmapImage();
    bitmap.SetSource(e.ChosenPhoto);

    // Paint the background with the bitmap
    ImageBrush brush = new ImageBrush();
    brush.ImageSource = bitmap;
    brush.Stretch = Stretch.None;
    LayoutRoot.Background = brush;
  }
}
```

You can enable the user to take a photo instead of selecting a photo from the phone by setting the ShowCamera property on the task:

```
void choosePhotoTask_Click(object sender, RoutedEventArgs e)
{
  // Get a Photo
  task.ShowCamera = true;
  task.Show();
}
```

If you specify that the ShowCamera property is true, the ApplicationBar in the photo chooser will have a camera button to let the user take a photo instead.

The other option available to the chooser is to specify a photo size you need for your application:

```
void choosePhotoTask_Click(object sender, RoutedEventArgs e)
{
  // Get a Photo
  task.PixelHeight = 200;
  task.PixelWidth = 300;
  task.Show();
}
```

By specifying the PixelHeight and PixelWidth properties, you are telling the task to return the photo in that exact dimension. When the user selects a photo that does not match that size, he is presented with the ability to crop the photo to the selected size, as shown in Figure 8.6.

FIGURE 8.6   **Allowing photo cropping**

SaveContactTask

You can also allow the user to save new contacts to the phone, using the SaveContactTask. To do this, you specify the contact information in the SaveContactTask object, like so:

```
private void saveContact_Click(object sender, RoutedEventArgs e)
{
  saveContact.Company = "Tailspin Toys";
  saveContact.FirstName = "Walter";
  saveContact.LastName = "Harp";
  saveContact.MobilePhone = "(206) 555-0142";
  saveContact.PersonalEmail = "wharp@tailspintoys.com";

  saveContact.Show();
}
```

The SaveContactTask has properties to provide access to a large amount of a contact's information, including multiple phone numbers, multiple addresses, and a complete name. Any contact the user adds here will show up in the contacts API discussed earlier in this chapter. Note that you can add a contact and read contacts with the contacts API, but you can't currently edit a contact. The user has to do that.

SaveEmailAddressTask

The SaveEmailAddressTask is used to save an email into a new contact or attach it to an existing contact. To save an address, simply supply the email to save and call Show:

```
void saveEmailTask_Click(object sender, RoutedEventArgs e)
{
  // Save a new Email on the Phone
  saveEmailTask.Email = "shawn@aol.com";
  saveEmailTask.Show();
}

void saveEmailTask_Completed(object sender, TaskEventArgs e)
{
  if (e.Error != null)
  {
    MessageBox.Show("Error Occurred");
  }
  else if (e.TaskResult == TaskResult.Cancel)
  {
    MessageBox.Show("User Cancelled Task");
  }
  else
  {
    MessageBox.Show("E-mail Saved");
  }
}
```

Note that the task does not tell you to which contact the email was attached but simply tells you whether the task succeeded.

SavePhoneNumberTask

This chooser works just like SaveEmailAddressTask—you simply supply the phone number and then call the Show method to save the phone number to a user's contact:

```
void savePhoneTaskButton_Click(object sender, RoutedEventArgs e)
{
  // Save a new Email on the Phone
```

```
    savePhoneTask.PhoneNumber = "(404) 555-1212";
    savePhoneTask.Show();
  }

  void savePhoneTask_Completed(object sender, TaskEventArgs e)
  {
    if (e.Error != null)
    {
      MessageBox.Show("Error Occurred");
    }
    else if (e.TaskResult == TaskResult.Cancel)
    {
      MessageBox.Show("User Cancelled");
    }
    else
    {
      MessageBox.Show("Phone Number Saved");
    }
  }
}
```

Again, the TaskResult will indicate whether the task succeeded but does not share with your application the contact to which the phone number was attached.

SaveRingtoneTask

If you're in the business of selling ring tones, your application can add ring tones to the phone. For a ring tone to be added to the phone, you must use the SaveRingtoneTask. A ring tone must conform to certain requirements:

- It must not be more than 39 seconds in length.
- It must be no more than 1MB in size.
- It can be in MP3 or WMA format only.
- It must not include DRM copyright protection.

In addition to these requirements, you must save the ring tone to isolated storage. We discuss how to work with isolated storage in Chapter 9, "Databases and Storage." After you have the file saved in isolated storage, you can use the SaveRingtoneTask to add the ring tone to the phone. You need to specify a DisplayName (although the user can override it when the task launches), a URI to the ring tone in isolated storage, and whether the ring tone is shareable. Here is the relevant code:

```
void addRingtone_Click(object sender, EventArgs e)
{
  saveRingtoneTask.IsShareable = true;
  saveRingtoneTask.DisplayName = "Ahhh...";
  saveRingtoneTask.Source = new Uri("isostore:/ahhh.mp3");
  saveRingtoneTask.Show();
}

void task_Completed(object sender, TaskEventArgs e)
{
  if (e.Error == null && e.TaskResult == TaskResult.OK)
  {
    MessageBox.Show("RingTone Added!");
  }
}
```

The URI syntax used in this task specifies that it is an absolute URI that begins with "isostore:/" to specify that it is in your isolated storage. You can have structure to the location in isolated storage, so "isostore:/ringtones/sounds/ahhh.mp3" is perfectly acceptable. The return call to the Completed handler assures you that there wasn't an error and that the ring tone was successfully added.

Media and Picture Hubs

The phone can store music, pictures, and video. From the user's perspective, these are stored in the Music and Videos hub and the Pictures hub. You can work with these hubs in several ways. You can access the music in the Music and Videos hub, you can access the pictures in the Pictures hub, and you can register your application to be included in both of these hubs.

Accessing Music

You can access the music on the phone directly using the MediaLibrary class in the Microsoft.Xna.Framework assembly. This class belongs to the Microsoft.Xna.Framework.Media namespace. To use the MediaLibrary class, you have to create an instance of the class. The default (that is, empty) constructor creates an instance that contains a list of the media on the phone itself. This class supports IDisposable, so you must use care in calling Dispose when you're done with the class (usually via the using clause):

```
using (var library = new MediaLibrary())
{
  // use media library
}
```

> ### ■ Emulator Tip
>
> The emulator doesn't have any media. You should use an actual device to test the media library functionality.

The music library consists of the following types of objects:

- **Artist:** This is the name of the performer of a song or album.
- **Album:** This is a collection of songs from one or more artists.
- **Genre:** This is a named category for songs and albums.
- **Song:** This is a single piece of music that can belong to a genre, album, and artist.
- **Playlist:** This is a user-defined list of songs.

The MediaLibrary class exposes these types of objects into collections that can be navigated (as shown in Figure 8.7). Although these are discrete collections, they each contain all the music in the collection.

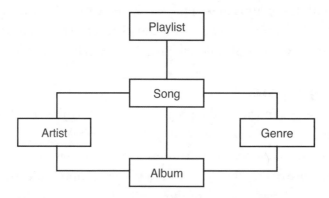

FIGURE 8.7   **Music library objects**

■ MediaSource

The `MediaLibrary` class has a constructor that takes a `MediaSource`, so you might think that there is more than one `MediaSource` for the phone; however, this API exists for other XNA platforms. The phone has one and only one source (the local media library). *You should always use the empty constructor.*

On the `MediaLibrary` class, each of these objects is exposed as collections (that support `IEnumerable`), so simple iteration is straightforward:

```
using (var library = new MediaLibrary())
{
  // use media library
  foreach (var artist in library.Artists)
  {
    theList.Items.Add(artist.Name);
  }
}
```

Because these collections support `IEnumerable`, we can use LINQ against these as well:

```
using (var library = new MediaLibrary())
{
  var qry = from artist in library.Artists
            where artist.Name == "Shawn Twain"
            select artist;

  var shawn = qry.FirstOrDefault();

  if (shawn != null)
  {
    // Retrieve the songs for that artist.
    var hisSongs = shawn.Songs;
  }
}
```

As this example shows, after you retrieve the artist you're looking for you can use the songs for a particular artist, album, or genre. You can also add and delete from the list of songs, but this functionality is implemented as extension methods so you have to add the right namespace to get the APIs for adding and deleting: `Microsoft.Xna.Framework.Media.PhoneExtensions`.

After you have those extension methods, you can call `SaveSong` to add a song:

```
using (var library = new MediaLibrary())
{
  var meta = new SongMetadata()
  {
    Name = "Anne",
    ArtistName = "Shawn Twain",
    AlbumReleaseDate = DateTime.Parse("04/24/2000"),
    AlbumArtistName = "Shawn Twain",
    Duration = TimeSpan.FromSeconds(254),
    TrackNumber = 4
  };

  library.SaveSong(new Uri("/Assets/02-anne.mp3", UriKind.Relative),
    meta,
    SaveSongOperation.CopyToLibrary);
}
```

Before you can add the song, you must first create a `SongMetadata` object that contains information about the song, as shown here. After you have that, you can call `SaveSong` to add the song to the library. The last parameter must specify whether you want to copy or move the song (when your source to the song is in the isolated storage). More about how URIs and application data are handled is covered in Chapter 9.

You can also remove a song from the library using the `Delete` method:

```
using (var library = new MediaLibrary())
{
  var song = library.Songs.First();

  library.Delete(song);
}
```

As you can see here, you must have a `Song` object from the library and then call the `Delete` method to remove it from the library.

Playing Music

Also built in to XNA's media functionality is access to the media player on the phone, via the MediaPlayer class. This is a static class that gives you access to what is playing currently and allows you to queue up songs to be played. Because the class throws events, you need to update the FrameworkDispatcher (as was discussed earlier in this chapter):

```
public partial class MainPage : PhoneApplicationPage
{
  DispatcherTimer _xnaTimer = new DispatcherTimer();

  // Constructor
  public MainPage()
  {
    InitializeComponent();

    // Because we're using XNA's MediaPlayer, we need to
    // Use the FrameworkDispatcher to allow events
    _xnaTimer.Interval = TimeSpan.FromMilliseconds(50);
    _xnaTimer.Tick += (s, a) => FrameworkDispatcher.Update();
    _xnaTimer.Start();
  }
  ...
}
```

After you do that, you can use the MediaPlayer class to play a song:

```
using (var library = new MediaLibrary())
{
  var qry = from artist in library.Artists
            where artist.Name == "Shawn Twain"
            select artist;

  var shawn = qry.FirstOrDefault();
  if (shawn != null)
  {
    // Retrieve the songs for that artist.
    var hisSongs = shawn.Songs;
    if (MediaPlayer.State != MediaState.Playing)
    {
      MediaPlayer.Play(hisSongs[0]);
    }
  }
}
```

You need to check the state of the MediaPlayer before you can play new songs, but as long as a song isn't currently playing, you can just play it by supplying the Song object to the media player. If you have songs you want to play that are not in the media library, you can create your own song objects using the FromUri static method:

```
var mySong = Song.FromUri("Bridges and Ghosts",
                        new Uri("song.mp3", UriKind.Relative));

if (MediaPlayer.State != MediaState.Playing)
{
  MediaPlayer.Play(mySong);
}
```

The FromUri method will take a relative URI that picks up songs in your .xap file or an absolute URI to add songs from anywhere on the Internet.

You can also supply a SongCollection to play the entire collection:

```
// Retrieve the songs for that artist.
var hisSongs = shawn.Songs;
if (MediaPlayer.State != MediaState.Playing)
{
  MediaPlayer.Play(hisSongs);
}
```

You are limited to playing only the SongCollections that already exist (for example, MediaLibrary.Songs, Artist.Songs, Playlist.Songs, and so on). There is no facility for creating your own list of songs to integrate with the MediaPlayer class.

▪ Playing Songs from Isolated Storage

If you want to play songs directly from isolated storage, you'll need to use the MediaElement because the MediaPlayer class does not support this capability.

Accessing Pictures

In addition to accessing the music on the phone, the MediaLibrary class also exposes the pictures that are stored on the phone. The MediaLibrary class has the following three properties that give you access to the pictures on the phone:

- **Pictures:** This is a collection of all the pictures on the phone.
- **SavedPictures:** This is the special folder for saved pictures on the phone.
- **RootPictureAlbum:** This is the starting point for a hierarchical collection of pictures on the phone.

The Pictures and SavedPictures properties are simple IEnumerable collections of Picture objects. For example, to access the name of each picture you could iterate through the list of Picture objects, like so:

```
using (var library = new MediaLibrary())
{
  foreach (Picture thePicture in library.Pictures)
  {
    theListBox.Items.Add(thePicture.Name);
  }
}
```

The Picture class exposes the name, date, height, and width of the picture as well as to which album the picture belongs. To get at the actual picture, you can call either GetThumbnailImage or GetImage to get a stream of the picture. GetThumbnailImage retrieves a much smaller version of the picture, whereas GetImage retrieves the full-size picture. You can wrap the image you retrieve with a BitmapImage object in the imaging system (in the System.Windows.Imaging namespace) to be able to show it as the source of an Image element, like so:

```
using (var library = new MediaLibrary())
{
  foreach (Picture thePicture in library.Pictures)
  {
    // Get the Picture Stream
    Stream imageStream = thePicture.GetImage();

    // Wrap it with a BitmapImage object
    var bitmap = new BitmapImage();
    bitmap.SetSource(imageStream);
```

```
        // Create an Image element and set the bitmap
        var image = new Image();
        image.Source = bitmap;

        // Add it to the ListBox to show it.
        theListBox.Items.Add(image);
    }
}
```

Although accessing individual pictures is useful, the MediaLibrary class also gives you access to the picture album structure. The PictureAlbum class contains a collection of that album's pictures (called Pictures) as well as a collection of the albums in that album (called Albums). The MediaLibrary. RootPictureAlbum is the top-level album and will contain a hierarchical collection of all albums and pictures. For instance, you could iterate through all the albums using a recursive function, like so:

```
void MainPage_Loaded(object sender, RoutedEventArgs e)
{
    using (var library = new MediaLibrary())
    {
        AddAlbum(library.RootPictureAlbum, "");
    }
}

void AddAlbum(PictureAlbum theAlbum, string indention)
{
    // Show Album Name
    theListBox.Items.Add(string.Concat(indention,
                                       "Album: ",
                                       theAlbum.Name));

    // List Albums in this Album
    foreach (PictureAlbum subAlbum in theAlbum.Albums)
    {
        AddAlbum(subAlbum, string.Concat(indention, "  "));
    }

    // List Pictures
    foreach (Picture thePicture in theAlbum.Pictures)
    {
        theListBox.Items.Add(string.Concat(indention,
                                           " - ",
                                           thePicture.Name));
    }
}
```

Walking through the list of albums results in a list of the albums and their resultant pictures, as shown in Figure 8.8.

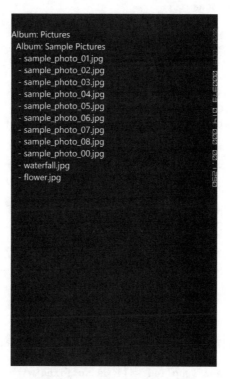

Album: Pictures
  Album: Sample Pictures
  - sample_photo_01.jpg
  - sample_photo_02.jpg
  - sample_photo_03.jpg
  - sample_photo_04.jpg
  - sample_photo_05.jpg
  - sample_photo_06.jpg
  - sample_photo_07.jpg
  - sample_photo_08.jpg
  - sample_photo_00.jpg
  - waterfall.jpg
  - flower.jpg

FIGURE 8.8 Displaying the albums and pictures

Storing Pictures

The `MediaLibrary` class also enables you to save pictures to the phone. The only limitation is that you can save images only directly to a special album called "Saved Pictures." You save the picture to this album using the `Media-Library.SavePicture` method. This method takes the name of the picture file as well as the contents of the picture (usually a stream or an array of bytes). For example, to capture a photo using the `CameraCaptureTask` (explained in more detail earlier in this chapter), you could take the stream from the `Completed` event, like so:

```
public partial class MainPage : PhoneApplicationPage
{
  CameraCaptureTask takePicture = new CameraCaptureTask();
```

```csharp
// Constructor
public MainPage()
{
  InitializeComponent();

  MouseLeftButtonUp += new
    MouseButtonEventHandler(MainPage_MouseLeftButtonUp);


  // Handle the picture after it's been taken
  takePicture.Completed += new
    EventHandler<PhotoResult>(takePicture_Completed);
}

void MainPage_MouseLeftButtonUp(object sender,
                               MouseButtonEventArgs e)
{
  // Take the picture
  takePicture.Show();
}

void takePicture_Completed(object sender, PhotoResult e)
{
  if (e.TaskResult == TaskResult.OK)
  {
    // Use the Media Library to save the picture
    using (MediaLibrary theLibrary = new MediaLibrary())
    {
      // The name supplied will be suffixed with .jpg
      theLibrary.SavePicture("My Camera Photo", e.ChosenPhoto);
    }
  }
}
}
```

The MediaLibrary class's SavePicture method takes a name (that it suffixes with ".jpg") and the photo itself, which can be in the form of a stream (like this example shows) or a byte array. After you save the picture, it shows up in a new album called "Saved Pictures" and is accessible from the MediaLibrary class's SavedPictures property.

Integrating into the Pictures Hub

Windows Phone allows you to make an application that can register itself as an app in three places: the Pictures hub, picture viewer, and share picker. You can see the apps menu in the Pictures hub (under "apps") in Figure 8.9.

FIGURE 8.9 **The apps in the Pictures hub**

To integrate your application into these parts of the picture experience, you need to include a new section in the WMAppManifest.xml file. This section is called "Extensions":

```
<Deployment ...>
  <App ...>
    ...
    <Extensions>
      <!-- Integrate into pictures hub -->
      <Extension ExtensionName="Photos_Extra_Hub"
             ConsumerID="{5B04B775-356B-4AA0-AAF8-6491FFEA5632}"
             TaskID="_default" />
    </Extensions>
  </App>
</Deployment> ·
```

The ExtensionName and ConsumerID are both used to determine the type of integration your application will use (for example, Pictures hub, picture viewer, and picture sharing). The TaskID is used to determine how to launch your application. Using the _default indicates that your application should be launched normally and is typical.

As stated earlier, you can integrate into any or all of the three picture extensions. Each extension has its own entry in the Extensions section of the WMAppManifest.xml file:

```xml
<Deployment ...>
  <App ...>
    ...
    <Extensions>

      <!-- Integrate into pictures hub -->
      <Extension ExtensionName="Photos_Extra_Hub"
              ConsumerID="{5B04B775-356B-4AA0-AAF8-6491FFEA5632}"
              TaskID="_default" />

      <!-- Integrate into picture viewer -->
      <Extension ExtensionName="Photos_Extra_Viewer"
              ConsumerID="{5B04B775-356B-4AA0-AAF8-6491FFEA5632}"
              TaskID="_default" />

      <!-- Integrate into picture sharing -->
      <Extension ExtensionName="Photos_Extra_Share"
              ConsumerID="{5B04B775-356B-4AA0-AAF8-6491FFEA5632}"
              TaskID="_default" />

    </Extensions>
  </App>
</Deployment>
```

A picture extension application will be launched either from one of the picture integration locations (for example, from the Pictures hub) or in the normal way (for example, from the Start menu or app list). You will need to determine which way your application is being launched and show the chosen photo if launched via the Extras menu. This is typically handled by overriding the OnNavigatedTo method of your application's first page (for instance, MainPage.xaml) and using the NavigationContext property to test for the existence of a token that was passed to your application from the Pictures hub:

```csharp
public partial class MainPage : PhoneApplicationPage
{
    // ...
```

```
protected override void OnNavigatedTo(NavigationEventArgs e)
{
  base.OnNavigatedTo(e);

  // If token is in the query string,
  // we launched here from Extras menu
  if (NavigationContext.QueryString.ContainsKey("token"))
  {
    var token = NavigationContext.QueryString["token"];

    // Use Media Library to open the image
    using (MediaLibrary library = new MediaLibrary())
    {
      Picture selectedPicture = library.GetPictureFromToken(token);

      // Use the Picture
      Stream picture = selectedPicture.GetImage();

      // Use the picture. Typically should show it on launch page
    }
  }
}
// ...
}
```

After you see the "token" in the query string, you can use that token to retrieve the picture from the MediaLibrary class by calling the GetPictureFromToken method, as shown earlier.

Integrating into the Music and Videos Hub

If you are building an application that will be playing music or showing videos, you can integrate it into the Music and Videos hub. The main hub contains several areas into which you can integrate your application. The hub consists of five sections:

- **Collection:** This is the starting point for users to play music/videos/podcasts that are synced onto their phones.
- **History:** This is a list of recently played items.
- **New:** This is a list of music and video items newly added to the phone.
- **Apps:** These are the applications that are integrated into the Music and Videos hub.

- **Xbox:** This is Xbox-specific integration for SmartGlass and other Xbox apps.

After you specify you are integrating with the phone, you should integrate with the History and New sections of this hub. By using the Media and Videos APIs, your application will automatically be listed in the Marquee section of the hub.

Debugging Music and Videos Hub Integration

Hub integration is enabled as your application is passed through the Marketplace certification process. To debug your application's integration, you can add HubType="1" to the App element of the WMAppManifest.xml file, as shown here:

```
<?xml version="1.0" encoding="utf-8"?>
<Deployment
    xmlns="http://schemas.microsoft.com/windowsphone/2009/deployment"
    AppPlatformVersion="7.0">
  <App xmlns=""
        ProductID="{1f6ccd50-764b-4247-ba61-253a287ab640}"
        Title="FunWithMediaLibrary"
        RuntimeType="Silverlight"
        Version="1.0.0.0"
        Genre="apps.normal"
        Author="FunWithMediaLibrary author"
        Description="Sample description"
        Publisher="FunWithMediaLibrary"
        HubType="1">
```

Note that there is no way to run and test this behavior with the emulator. You must debug this on a physical device. It is recommended that you use the WPConnect.exe tool to connect the phone to the development computer, as connecting with Zune will not allow you to have access to the Media and Videos hub (showing the "Syncing" message instead).

Integrating with the Now Playing Section

Whenever a user plays music or a video in your application, it is customary for you to tell the hub that a recently used piece of music or video was played. You accomplish that with the MediaHistoryItem class. This class contains information that will be used to show what media is now playing as well as information that is passed back to your application when it is launched through the hub. To use this class, you create an instance of this class with the information required and add it to the hub via the `MediaHistory` class:

```
// You will need an image for the Now Playing section of
// the Hub.
Stream songImage = GetImageForSong();

// Create an object that contains the history information
MediaHistoryItem item = new MediaHistoryItem();
item.Source = ""; // Must Be an empty String
item.ImageStream = songImage;
item.Title = "NowPlaying";
item.PlayerContext.Add("keyString", "mysong.mp3");
MediaHistory.Instance.NowPlaying = item;
```

When you create the `MediaHistoryItem`, the `Source` property must be an empty string. The `ImageStream` must be a JPEG image that is 358 pixels by 358 pixels in size. It should include your application's name and logo if any. For the Now Playing section of the Media and Videos hub, the `Title` must be `"NowPlaying"`. The `PlayerContext` property is a name/value list of information that you will have access to when an item launches your application.

Integrating with the History Section

When any media is played, you should create a new `MediaHistoryItem` for each media item. When you add them to the History section, they will show up in the History part of the Media and Videos hub. To do this, create a `MediaHistoryItem` like we did for the Now Playing section:

```
// Create an object that contains the history information
MediaHistoryItem item = new MediaHistoryItem();
item.Source = "";
item.ImageStream = songImage;
item.Title = "RecentPlay";
item.PlayerContext.Add("keyString", "mysong.mp3");
MediaHistory.Instance.WriteRecentPlay(item);
```

The differences between this and the Now Playing section are that the `Title` property must be `RecentPlay` and you must add it to the `MediaHistory` via the `WriteRecentPlay` method. Lastly, images for the History tab are different and must be 173 pixels by 173 pixels instead of the larger Now Playing size. You should not just resize the larger image because the text on that image would likely be unreadable at the smaller size.

Integrating with the New Section

When new media is added via your application, you will need to add `MediaHistoryItems` as you did for the other sections:

```
// Create an object that contains the new information
MediaHistoryItem item = new MediaHistoryItem();
item.Source = "";
item.ImageStream = songImage;
item.Title = "MediaHistoryNew";
item.PlayerContext.Add("keyString", "mysong.mp3");
MediaHistory.Instance.WriteAcquiredItem(item);
```

This works identically to adding history items except that the `Title` must be "MediaHistoryNew" and adding the item to the New section requires that you call the `WriteAcquiredItem` method. The size of the image is 173 pixels by 173 pixels, just like the History section example.

Handling Launching from the Hub

When an item is launched from the hub, your main page is launched with a query string parameter that matches the `PlayerContext` item you added previously. What is in the `keyString` is entirely application-specific. What you put in the `PlayerContext`'s `keyString` value will be passed back to your application. Usually you would handle this in the `OnNavigatedTo` overrideable method of your main page, like so:

```
protected override void OnNavigatedTo(NavigationEventArgs e)
{
  base.OnNavigatedTo(e);

  // If "keyString" is in the query string, we were launched
  // from the hub
  if (NavigationContext.QueryString.ContainsKey("keyString"))
  {
    var key = NavigationContext.QueryString["keyString"];

    // Find the media by your special key
    Song song = FindSongByKey(key);
```

```
    // Play the song normally

  }
}
```

By retrieving the key from the `NavigationContext`'s `QueryString`, you can retrieve the `keyString` you added with the `MediaHistoryItem`. After you have it, you can use the contents of the `keyString` to find the appropriate piece of media to play.

Live Tiles

In the Windows Phone operating system, applications can pin themselves to the start screen and be live views into what is happening in your application. For example, a Twitter application might put the number and content of new tweets on the Live Tile to tell the user that it's time to revisit the application. For example, you can see different-sized Live Tiles in Figure 8.10.

FIGURE 8.10   Different-sized Live Tiles

It's not just different-sized live tiles that are supported, but also different types of live tiles. These live tile types are called Flip, Cycle, and Icon live tiles.[2] Each of these has its own way of working.

The Flip style live tiles have a back and front. They usually show the front of the tile but occasionally show information on the back of the live tile. You can see this shown in Figure 8.11.

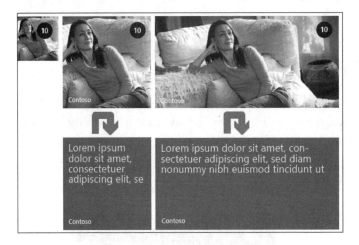

FIGURE 8.11   Flip style live tiles

The Iconic style live tiles show an icon plus other text. They do not flip but will show more information on a wide-tile or just the icon (and optional count) when changed to be the small- or medium-sized live tiles, as shown in Figure 8.12.

FIGURE 8.12   Iconic style live tiles

---

2   These tile types were introduced in Windows Phone 8 and are also supported in Windows Phone 7.8.

Finally, the Cycle style live tiles have a simple icon representation when small, but in the medium and large sizes, they cycle through up to nine images with just the name of the app on them. You can see how the Cycle style live tiles look in Figure 8.13.

FIGURE 8.13   Cycle style live tiles

You can specify the settings for the live tiles in the WMAppManifest.xml editor, as shown in Figure 8.14.

As shown in Figure 8.14, you can change the default type of tile and set the images directly in the WMAppManifest.xml file. You can also opt into the large-size tiles (small and medium are supported for all apps). For each type of live tile, there are required images. These images are marked as required when you change the type of live tile, as shown in Figure 8.15.

For live tiles, all the images must be .png files. There are also size requirements for the various styles of live tiles. These size requirements are shown in Table 8.5.

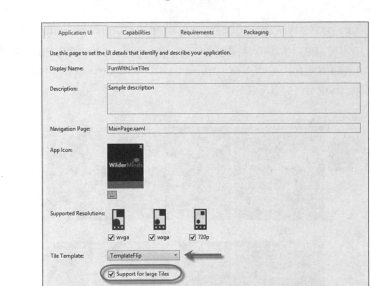

FIGURE 8.14   Editing the live tile settings

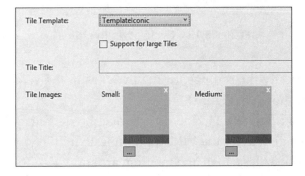

FIGURE 8.15   Required images for live type styles

TABLE 8.5   Live Tile Size Requirements

	Flip and Cycle	Iconic
Small	159x159	101x101
Medium	336x336	202x202
Large	691x336	Not Applicable

▪▪ Live Tile Sizes and Screen Resolution

The sizes specified in Table 8.5 are applicable to the WXGA screen size (768×1280). The Windows Phone also supports WVGA (480×800) and 720p (720×1280). These image sizes are scaled for the other screen sizes automatically.

The Iconic style live tile is special in that the images used are not just different sizes but are expected to be a single color with transparency. You can see this in Figure 8.12. Whatever is non-transparent is created as a single monochrome block so the transparency becomes critical to making the icon appear.

You can change your live tile when your application (or its background task) is running. This is useful for updating the live tile with important information. In addition to updating the pinned tiles, you can create secondary live tiles for different uses (such as deep linking into your app). Let's start with the main live tile so you can change your standard pinned live tile.

Main Live Tile

Your application has a single main Live Tile that is added to the home screen when a user manually pins your application. You can get at this Live Tile (whether it has been pinned or not) by accessing the `ShellTile.ActiveTiles` property. This property returns an enumerable list of the tiles in your application:

```
IEnumerable<ShellTile> tiles = ShellTile.ActiveTiles;

// Get the default tile
var tile = tiles.First();
```

The ShellTile class represents a tile for the home screen. The Active-Tiles property is a collection of these ShellTile objects. The first one is always the default tile. This class allows you to update the default tile. To update the default tile, you can create a data structure that matches the style of live tile you want. For instance, to create a Flip style, you would use a class called FlipTileData that contains the data with which to update the tile:

```
IEnumerable<ShellTile> tiles = ShellTile.ActiveTiles;

// Get the default tile
var tile = tiles.First();

// The new tile information to use to update the tile
var tileData = new FlipTileData()
{
  Title = "Live Tile Updated!",
  Count = 54,
  BackgroundImage =
    new Uri("/Assets/Tiles/icon-336.png", UriKind.Relative),
  SmallBackgroundImage =
    new Uri("/Assets/Tiles/icon-159.png", UriKind.Relative),
  WideBackgroundImage =
    new Uri("/Assets/Tiles/icon-wide.png", UriKind.Relative),
};

// Update the Tile
tile.Update(tileData);
```

Calling the Update method will update the tile with the new information. If the default tile (in this case) has not been pinned yet, when the application is pinned it will include this new set of information instead of the information contained in the WMAppManifest.xml file.

The Flip style of icon supports both the front (which we set previously) and a set of properties for the back of the live tile. To set these, just set the rest of the properties like so:

```
var tileData = new FlipTileData()
{
  Title = "Live Tile Updated!",
```

```
    Count = 54,
    BackgroundImage =
        new Uri("/Assets/Tiles/icon-336.png", UriKind.Relative),
    SmallBackgroundImage =
        new Uri("/Assets/Tiles/icon-159.png", UriKind.Relative),
    WideBackgroundImage =
        new Uri("/Assets/Tiles/icon-wide.png", UriKind.Relative),
    BackTitle = "Live Tiles",
    BackContent = "This is standard content",
    WideBackContent = "This is even more content!"
};
```

These properties are used to specify what is on the back of the tile. You can also specify a background image if you don't want to simply use the theme color as a background.

Be careful selecting the style of live tile in your WMAppManifest.xml file because you can't change the style of your main live tile. This means when you update the main live tile, you have to use the correct `StandardData` derived class to update it (for example, `FlipTileData`, `CycleTileData`, and `IconicTileData`).

Secondary Tiles

You can also create all-new tiles that are pinned to the home screen for the user. The purpose of these secondary tiles is to open deeper parts of your application. For example, imagine you have an application that shows the user RSS feeds. You might create a Live Tile that goes to a specific RSS feed instead of the default view that a new launching of the application would go to. This enables you to deep-link into your application. To do this, you use the same `StandardTileData` derived classes that were used to update the main live tile, but in this case you can create a new tile using the `ShellTile.Create` method:

```
var tileData = new IconicTileData()
{
    IconImage =
        new Uri("/Assets/Tiles/icon-202.png", UriKind.Relative),
    SmallIconImage =
        new Uri("/Assets/Tiles/icon-101.png", UriKind.Relative),
    Count = 5,
    WideContent1 = "This is line 1",
    WideContent2 = "This is line 2",
```

```
    WideContent3 = "This is line 3"
};

var deepUri = new Uri("/DeepLinkPage.xaml?id=Hello World",
                      UriKind.Relative);

ShellTile.Create(deepUri, tileData, true);
```

You should notice that the `ShellTile.Create` method requires a URI to be specified. This URI is used as the location from which to launch the navigation in your application. This is how deep-linking works. You can see in this example the URI is going to a view we have called `DeepLinkPage.xaml` and I am passing in a query string to help that view know how to show the data the Live Tile is specifying. This URI must be unique for all secondary tiles, so if you try to create a new secondary tile with the same URI, it will throw an exception. In addition, the last parameter is required (there is an overload without the third parameter, but it's there only for backward-compatibility). This last parameter specifies whether the tile supports a wide tile.

When `ShellTile.Create` is called, it takes the user to the home screen and scrolls to the new tile (to allow the user to move it on the home screen if she desires). This behavior is not overrideable. The purpose of going to the home screen is to prevent applications from hiding from the user the fact that they are adding new tiles. Because it deactivates the application, if the user did not want the Live Tile added, he could just delete it and not launch the nefarious application again.

You can find your own Live Tiles by interrogating the `NavigationUri` property of the `ShellTile` class (in the `ActiveTile` collection), like so:

```
var myTile = ShellTile.ActiveTiles
                    .Where(t => t.NavigationUri
                              .OriginalString
                              .Contains("DeepLinkPage.xaml"))
                    .FirstOrDefault();

// If it was found
if (myTile != null)
{
  // ...
}
```

After you find the appropriate tile, you can update it like you did the default tile:

```
  // If it was found
if (myTile != null)
{
  var tileData = new IconicTileData()
  {
    IconImage =
      new Uri("/Assets/Tiles/icon-202.png", UriKind.Relative),
    SmallIconImage =
      new Uri("/Assets/Tiles/icon-101.png", UriKind.Relative),
    Count = 15,
    WideContent1 = "It was updated!",
    WideContent2 = "This is line 2",
    WideContent3 = "This is line 3"
  };

  myTile.Update(tileData);
}
```

Typically you should change the tile with some information for the user to see that she should revisit your application (like updating the Count property).

If you need to change something else (like the NavigationUri), you need to delete the tile and re-create it. The ShellTile class allows you to delete a Live Tile (as long as it is not the default tile):

```
myTile.Delete();
```

On the whole, secondary tiles can be a very powerful feature, but the user will not necessarily tolerate a lot of tiles from a single application, so using this functionality judiciously is encouraged!

▪ Looking Forward

You can also update tiles using push notifications or with background agents. In Chapter 10, we discuss how to use agents to update tiles. In Chapter 11, "Services," you will learn how to use push notifications to update tiles.

Other Ways of Launching Your App

Although having the user run your app directly from the start screen or the list of apps is interesting, it would be useful if there were other ways to invoke your application. In fact, you might want other apps to be able to launch your app. For example, if you've created a Twitter application, you might want to be able to have other apps launch your app (instead of just being able to share with the "official" Twitter integration). Luckily, that is supported.

There are two ways of automatically launching your app:

- Launching from a custom protocol
- Launching from a file association

Launching from a custom protocol involves allowing other apps to launch using a special method and a shared protocol name. Launching from a file association involves registering a custom file extension with the phone to enable your users to launch your application when they tap on a file from an email, SkyDrive, or documents. Let's see how each of these works.

Using a Custom Protocol

A custom protocol is simply a specially formatted URI that contains a special moniker (that is, `myapp:someotherdata?and=querystring`). The special moniker is used to allow other apps to launch your application using the `LaunchUriAsync` on the `Launcher` class:

```
async void secondQuery_Click(object sender, RoutedEventArgs e)
{
  await Launcher.LaunchUriAsync(
    new Uri("funwithassociations:showsecond?id=foo"));
}
```

This allows one application to launch another with data included so that the other app knows what action to perform. The moniker is what is before the colon (:); what is after is completely up to you. Monikers have to follow these simple rules:

- Must be a name of 2–39 characters

- Can contain numbers, lowercase letters, periods (.), and hyphens (-)

- Cannot be one of the reserved URIs (as documented at http:// shawnw.me/WPReservedFiles)

To register a protocol, you must open the WMAppManifest.xml in the text editor (right-clicking and selecting "View Code" works well). The built-in application manifest editor cannot be used to add protocols. Just after the Tokens element, create a new element called Extensions. Inside the new element, add an element called Protocol, like so:

```
<Deployment xmlns="..."
            AppPlatformVersion="8.0">
  <App ...>
  ...
    <Tokens>
      ...
    </Tokens>
    <Extensions>
      <Protocol Name="funwithassociations"
                NavUriFragment="encodedLaunchUri=%s"
                TaskID="_default" />

    </Extensions>
    ...
  </App>
</Deployment>
```

The Protocol element's Name attribute is the name of the moniker (adhering to the rules listed previously). The NavUriFragment and TaskID must be the same as this example. Now that you have that, you will need to listen for launching with the new URI.

To facilitate listening for the launching URI, you will need a class that derives from the UriMapperBase class. This class will get called as the navigation framework gets notified of the navigation using the protocol URI, like so:

```
public class AssociationMapper : UriMapperBase
{

}
```

In this new class, you need to override the MapUri method. This is the method that will be called as the navigation framework attempts to navigate. In this case, you'll look for your URI and return a URI that maps it to the resulting page in your application, like so:

```
public override Uri MapUri(Uri uri)
{
  var decodedUri = HttpUtility.UrlDecode(uri.ToString()).ToLower();

  if (decodedUri.Contains("funwithassociations:showfirst"))
  {
    return new Uri("/ShowFirst.xaml", UriKind.Relative);
  }
  else
  {
    // Let normal navigation happen
    return uri;
  }
}
```

The first thing to do is to decode the URI as it comes to the navigation framework URI encoded. After you have done that, you can search to see whether the URI contains your moniker. Remember that anything after your protocol (and the colon) is data specific to your application. In this example, we are specifying that if the characters after the protocol moniker say "showfirst," then we can change the navigation to go to the FirstPage.xaml file. If it doesn't match what we expect, we simply let the original URI pass through to the navigation framework. In this way, you can handle multiple types of uses for the protocol and data:

```
public override Uri MapUri(Uri uri)
{
  var decodedUri = HttpUtility.UrlDecode(uri.ToString()).ToLower();

  if (decodedUri.Contains("funwithassociations:showfirst"))
  {
    return new Uri("/ShowFirst.xaml", UriKind.Relative);
  }
  else if (decodedUri.Contains("funwithassociations:showsecond"))
  {
    var split = decodedUri.Split(new char[] { '?' },
      StringSplitOptions.RemoveEmptyEntries);
```

```
      if (split.Count() > 2) // There is a questionmark after protocol
      {
        // Add query string
        return new Uri(string.Concat("/ShowSecond.xaml?", split[2]),
                       UriKind.Relative);
      }
      else
      {
        return new Uri("/ShowSecond.xaml?", UriKind.Relative);
      }
    }
    else
    {
      // Let normal navigation happen
      return uri;
    }
  }
}
```

In this example, the code is looking for the showsecond command after the moniker to do something different. In this case, the user could have passed in a query string with useful data for us to start the application with. Notice that the code uses split to separate the URI at the question mark. This is common if you're using a query string, but be careful because the decoded URI that is actually launched looks like this (the second question mark and colon were URI-encoded to protect the URI):

```
/protocol?encodedlaunchuri=funwithassociations:showsecond?id=foo
```

This means that if you want to split off the query string, you will need to manipulate the entire string correctly. The example does this by splitting on the question mark and just taking the entire third part of the split to post-pend to the page URI.

Now that we have the handler, we need to register it with the phone. You should open the standard App class file (usually App.xaml.cs). Near the bottom of the file is a private method called InitializePhoneApplication. Just before the handling of the NavigationFailed method, add a new line that assigns the UriMapper to a new instance of your UriMapperBase derived class (AssociationMapper in this case):

```
private void InitializePhoneApplication()
{
  if (phoneApplicationInitialized)
    return;
```

```
// ...
RootFrame = new PhoneApplicationFrame();
RootFrame.Navigated += CompleteInitializePhoneApplication;

// Add my mapper
RootFrame.UriMapper = new AssociationMapper();

// Handle navigation failures
RootFrame.NavigationFailed += RootFrame_NavigationFailed;

// Handle reset requests for clearing the backstack
RootFrame.Navigated += CheckForResetNavigation;

// Ensure we don't initialize again
phoneApplicationInitialized = true;
}
```

The non-bold version of the code should already exist—you're just adding your new URI mapper to the RootFrame object so you can intercept the navigation calls. At this point, you should be able to call your app from another app by calling the following:

```
await Launcher.LaunchUriAsync(
    new Uri("funwithassociations:showsecond?id=foo"));
```

Using a File Association

Like the custom protocol, the file association enables you to launch your app from other parts of the phone. The difference is that you are really launching a file, not just the app. You can specify a file extension for your application to handle. You can choose any file extension except for the reserved file extensions (see http://shawnw.me/WPReservedFiles for a complete list of reserved file extensions).

To get started, you must modify the WMAppManifest.xml file as text. File associations use the application manifest file to specify the different file extensions. You can open the WMAppManifest.xml file as text by right-clicking the file and selecting View Code.

Just after the Tokens element, you must add a new element called Extensions (as you might have done in the protocol example earlier in this chapter). Inside the Extensions element, you will create a FileTypeAssociation element, as shown here:

```
<Deployment xmlns="..."
            AppPlatformVersion="8.0">
  <App ...>
    ...
    <Tokens>
      ...
    </Tokens>
    <Extensions>
      <FileTypeAssociation TaskID="_default"
                           Name="SAMPLE"
                           NavUriFragment="fileToken=%s">
        <Logos>
          <Logo Size="small"
                IsRelative="true">Assets/Logo33x33.png</Logo>
          <Logo Size="medium"
                IsRelative="true">Assets/Logo69x69.png</Logo>
          <Logo Size="large"
                IsRelative="true">Assets/Logo176x176.png</Logo>
        </Logos>
        <SupportedFileTypes>
          <FileType
            ContentType="application/sample">.sample</FileType>
        </SupportedFileTypes>
      </FileTypeAssociation>
    </Extensions>
    ...
  </App>
</Deployment>
```

The FileTypeAssociation element has several parts. First is a set of logos that are used in various parts of the operating system. You must specify all three logo sizes and supply them. The SupportedFileTypes element contains an extension name and the related ContentType. If you do not have a standard content type, you can use application/YOURAPPNAME. This means that you can now deal with the files that end in .foo. The FileTypeAssociation element's NavigationUriFragment and TaskID attributes must both have the same values as is shown in the example.

When your application is launched, it will be executed with a special URI that contains information about the file that was launched. Like the protocol handler example earlier in this chapter, you'll need to create a UriMapperBase derived class. Unlike the earlier example, though, the URI you're looking for is /FileTypeAssociation:

```
public class AssociationMapper : UriMapperBase
{
  public override Uri MapUri(Uri uri)
  {
    var fileUri = uri.ToString();

    if (fileUri.Contains("/FileTypeAssociation"))
    {
      // Get the File Token
      var index = fileUri.IndexOf("fileToken=") + 10;
      var token = fileUri.Substring(index);

      // Create path to the XAML to Show File
      var path = string.Concat("/ShowFile.xaml?token=", token);

      return new Uri(path, UriKind.Relative);
    }
    else
    {
      // Let normal navigation happen
      return uri;
    }
  }
}
```

As you can see here, the operating system is passing in a query string value called `fileToken` that contains a token to the file that was launched. In this case we're just post-pending it to the URI for the page we want to launch when a file is shown.

After you have created this new `UriMapperBase` derived class, you can register it with the application class as shown earlier in the protocol association example.

Back on the page that will handle the file, you can get that token from the query string and use it to interact with the file:

```
protected async override void OnNavigatedTo(NavigationEventArgs e)
{
  base.OnNavigatedTo(e);

  var token = NavigationContext.QueryString["token"];

  if (!string.IsNullOrWhiteSpace(token))
  {
    var fileName =
      SharedStorageAccessManager.GetSharedFileName(token);
```

```
IStorageFile file = await
  SharedStorageAccessManager.
    CopySharedFileAsync(ApplicationData.Current.LocalFolder,
      fileName,
      NameCollisionOption.GenerateUniqueName,
      token);

// ...

    }
}
```

After you're in the OnNavigatedTo method of the page that is handling the file association, you can use the SharedStorageAccessManager class to get the name of the file by passing in the token. If you need the contents of the file, you can also use the CopySharedFileAsync to copy the file into a local folder (shown here as the ApplicationData.Current.LocalFolder). The CopyShareFileAsync copies the file into a location from which your application can access it and then returns an IStorageFile object that contains the file. You can see more about how to deal with the StorageFile and other data classes in Chapter 10. But at this point, you have an object you can use to read the contents of the file (not shown).

Where Are We?

This is where phone development is really different from almost every other type of application design: integration with the phone. In this chapter you saw how to access information from the device, store information on the device, and interact with the core phone functions such as the camera and the phone functions themselves. Making your application a real phone application will require the use of these types of functionality; otherwise, it is just an app on a handheld device.

▗9▖

Databases and Storage

A S YOU'RE WRITING YOUR NEW, WORLD-CHANGING APPLICATION you will sometimes need to store information directly on the phone. This information can be simple files, or caches to serialized versions of data, or even a full-fledged database. Because the storage is on the phone, it is important to understand all your options so that you can make the right decision about where to store information as well as take the fewest system resources necessary to do the job. In this chapter you will learn how to make those decisions as well as implement them.

Storing Data

Apps need data. Data needs to be persistent. That's the big picture. You need to be able to store data on a phone for use by your application. That data needs to remain on the phone between invocations of your application as well as through reboots. Although Windows Phone supports this in several ways, you will need to understand the various facilities to best decide how to accomplish this.

The two main ways to store data are through storage and a local database. **Storage** enables you to store data as files in a virtualized file system that only your application has access to as well as read data from your installation directory and on external storage (for example, SD cards). In addition to storage, you can also store information in a **local database** that provides you with a way to store data and query the data for retrieval. From those broad strokes, it might seem that storing data in a database is the way to go. This is often the most common approach for developers transitioning to the phone. The problem is that you need to determine whether you need a database.

Using the phone's database requires more resources than simply storing files. It might seem easier, but that simplicity comes at a cost. The reality is that many applications do not need the query and update facilities of a full-blown database system. Often what they really need is to simply store data for the next time the application is started.

Storage

As stated earlier, one of the options is to use the file system on the phone. Each application has access to three types of storage: local folder, application folder, and external storage. You can write only to the local folder, but you can read from both your app's installation directory and any external storage such as SD cards.

The local folder is allocated a separate private part of the internal file system for its use. This means any files you store in the local folder is for your application's use only. It is not accessible by any other application (although the operating system has access to these files). When your application is installed, this area of the file system is allocated. Likewise, when your application is uninstalled, any files that are in the local folder are lost.

Accessing the local folder on the phone can be accomplished by using the isolated storage classes from .NET or using the Storage API from WinRT. Although System.IO and the related APIs work and are useful if you are sharing code with .NET libraries, the preference is to use the WinRT storage classes because they are friendlier to the asynchronous access supported on the phone.

> ## ■ Windows Phone 7.0/7.5 Developers
>
> Although Windows Phone 8 (and later) supports using the storage APIs from Windows 8, the older System.IO.IsolatedStorage namespace classes still work. They are there for backward compatibility, and you can still use it if you need to share code with .NET or older Windows Phone applications. But you should migrate to the WinRT Storage API because it supports the most mature way of dealing with asynchronous file storage available.

To work with the data in the local folder, you start with the ApplicationData class in the Windows.Storage namespace. This class enables you to get the Current starting point for your application data. This lets you access the LocalFolder object that represents the place to store data for your application. The ApplicationData class includes the properties and methods for the other endpoints that are supported on Windows 8, but they are not implemented on the phone (for example, LocalSettings or RoamingFolder):

```
var folder = ApplicationData.Current.LocalFolder;
```

From this folder object, you can create a new file using the CreateFileAsync method. As you might expect, the Async suffix indicates that this is an asynchronous method. Because the Windows Phone is based on .NET 4.5, it supports the async and await keywords. By specifying the async keyword on the method that contains this code, you can use the await keyword to let you write the asynchronous code easier:[1]

```
async void saveButton_Click(object sender, RoutedEventArgs e)
{
  var folder = ApplicationData.Current.LocalFolder;

  var file = await folder.CreateFileAsync("foo.txt",
    CreationCollisionOption.ReplaceExisting);
}
```

The CreateCollisionOption enumeration supports several options when the file creation finds an existing file. This includes replacing the file, open

---

1 For more information on how async and await keywords work, see the MSDN documentation: http://shawnw.me/Z42UlP

an existing file, throwing an error, or even generating a unique name. After the file is created, the file object is returned.

Typically, the WinRT APIs use different types of objects to work with the data inside a file, but using the System.IO classes can make your code easy to use. Therefore, you should work directly with the Stream class. The System.IO namespace has extension methods on the Windows.Storage classes to retrieve actual Stream objects. For example, on the OpenStreamForWriteAsync is an extension method on the StorageFile class to get a Stream object so you can use the standard System.IO classes:

```
using System.IO;
...
async void saveButton_Click(object sender, RoutedEventArgs e)
{
  var folder = ApplicationData.Current.LocalFolder;
  var file = await folder.CreateFileAsync("foo.txt",
    CreationCollisionOption.ReplaceExisting);

  using (var stream = await file.OpenStreamForWriteAsync())
  {
    var writer = new StreamWriter(stream);
    await writer.WriteLineAsync("color=blue;");
    await writer.FlushAsync();
    writer.Close();
  }
}
```

Notice the multiple uses of the await keyword. Each of these operations is asynchronous, but with the async and await keywords, you can write the code as if it were synchronous without worrying about locking up the user interface thread (and leaving your app hanging during this operation).

Opening a file is similar in that you would use the OpenStreamForReadAsync to retrieve a stream of the file. Again, this is returning a stream, and you can use the System.IO classes to do the work of reading the file for you:

```
async void loadButton_Click(object sender, RoutedEventArgs e)
{
  var folder = ApplicationData.Current.LocalFolder;

  using (var stream = await folder.OpenStreamForReadAsync("foo.txt"))
  {
    var reader = new StreamReader(stream);
    var result = await reader.ReadToEndAsync();
```

```
    MessageBox.Show(result);
  }
}
```

Although you can get the folder and then read a file, you can actually skip the folder step by using a URI with a moniker instead:

```
var fileUri = new Uri("ms-appdata:///local/foo.txt");

var file = await StorageFile.GetFileFromApplicationUriAsync(fileUri);

using (var stream = await file.OpenStreamForReadAsync())
{
  var reader = new StreamReader(stream);
  var result = await reader.ReadToEndAsync();
  MessageBox.Show(result);
}
```

In this example, you can just use a full URI to specify that you want to get from the local folder. The ms-appdata:///local/ start of the URI tells the storage API to find the file in the local folder. You can also load a file from the installation directory using the ms-appx:///[2] moniker, like so:

```
var fileUri = new Uri("ms-appx:///someconfig.xml");
var file = await StorageFile.GetFileFromApplicationUriAsync(fileUri);

using (var stream = await file.OpenStreamForReadAsync())
{
  var reader = new StreamReader(stream);
  var result = await reader.ReadToEndAsync();
  MessageBox.Show(result);
}
```

The ms-appx:/// moniker tells the storage API to look in the directory of the installation of your application. Specifically, this means that if you mark any file as "Content" in your project, it will be packaged with the code and delivered to the installation directory. This is an easy way to access files delivered with your application. The installation directly can be accessed only for reading. Writing to the installation directory is not allowed; if you need to write new files, you should always use the local folder instead.

---

2   Note the moniker must have three slashes!

> ■■ **What About** isostore **and** appdata **Monikers?**
>
> These monikers (ms-appx:/// and ms-appdata:///) are used by the WinRT components that are exposed in Windows Phone. Some older APIs such as the Isolated Storage APIs from earlier versions of Windows Phone support other monikers for these same paths. For these, you must use appdata:/ to access the installation directory and isostore:/ for the local folder. Note that both of these require only a single slash, whereas the WinRT monikers require three slashes.

> ■■ **Reading from Memory Cards**
>
> The Windows Phone also supports the capability to read external storage in the form of memory cards that can be used in some phones. The limitation is that your application can read only file types that are registered for your application. These file types are the same types registered during File Type Association as explained in Chapter 8, "Phone Integration." The purpose of this functionality is to allow specific files to be read from the memory card, not allow generalized file manager-like support for memory cards.

Before you can access this functionality, you have to specify several things. First, your application must specify the ID_CAP_REMOVABLE_STORAGE capability in the WMAppManifest.xml file.

To access files on the memory card, you'll need to retrieve all the external storage files. You can do this by calling the ExternalStorage's GetExternalStorageDevicesAsync method, as shown here:

```
async void sdButton_Click(object sender, RoutedEventArgs e)
{
  var devices = await
    ExternalStorage.GetExternalStorageDevicesAsync();

  var sdCard = devices.FirstOrDefault();
```

```
    if (sdCard != null)
    {
      // ...
    }
  }
```

In this case you can just get the first device found (there is only one support on the Windows Phone). If the device is null, no card is installed.

After you have a valid card, you can simply open a file based on the path using `GetFileAsync`:

```
var file = await sdCard.GetFileAsync("some.foo");

using (var stream = await file.OpenForReadAsync())
{
  var reader = new StreamReader(stream);
  var result = await reader.ReadToEndAsync();
  MessageBox.Show(result);
}
```

Calling the file object's `OpenForReadAsync` is similar to the operations you saw earlier in this chapter because it returns a `Stream` object that can be manipulated directly using the `System.IO` classes in .NET. This API does support iterating through supported files and directories as well. For instance, to iterate through all the files in the root folder of the memory card, you can do the following:

```
foreach (var file in await sdCard.RootFolder.GetFilesAsync())
{
  MessageBox.Show(file.Name);
}
```

Serialization

In general, creating your own files and directories will help you store the information you need, but inventing your file formats is usually unnecessary. There are three common methods for storing information in a structured way using serialization: XML serialization, JavaScript Object Notation (JSON) serialization, and isolated storage settings.

XML Serialization

XML is a common approach to formatting data on the phone. .NET provides built-in support for XML serialization using the `XmlSerializer` class. This class enables you to take a graph of managed objects and create an XML version. Additionally (and crucially), you can read that XML back into memory to re-create the object graph.

To get started writing an object graph as XML, you need to know about the class you want to serialize. For the examples here, assume you have something like a class that holds user preferences, like so:

```
public class UserPreferences
{
  public DateTime LastAccessed { get; set; }
  public string FirstName { get; set; }
  public string LastName { get; set; }
  public bool UsePushNotifications { get; set; }
}
```

Standard XML serialization requires certain constructors (empty constructors) to work. If you don't create a constructor explicitly, the compiler will create an empty constructor implicitly. Because XML serialization requires an empty constructor, you can rely on the one the compiler created (as in the previous example), but if you add an explicit constructor you need to make sure you also include a constructor without any parameters (that is, an empty constructor). Now that we have something to serialize, let's go ahead and store the data.

First, you must add the System.Xml.Serialization assembly to your project. Then you can use the XmlSerialization class (located in the System.Xml.Serialization namespace) by creating an instance of it (passing in the type you want to serialize):

```
using (var store = IsolatedStorageFile.GetUserStoreForApplication())
using (var file = store.CreateFile("myfile.xml"))
{
  XmlSerializer ser = new XmlSerializer(typeof(UserPreferences));
}
```

This creates a serializer for this type. The instance of the class can serialize or deserialize your type (and associated types) to XML. To serialize into XML, simply call the Serialize method:

```
async void saveXmlButton_Click(object sender, RoutedEventArgs e)
{
  var prefs = new UserPreferences()
  {
```

```
        FirstName = "Shawn"
    };

    var folder = ApplicationData.Current.LocalFolder;
    var file = await folder.CreateFileAsync("prefs.xml",
      CreationCollisionOption.ReplaceExisting);

    using (var stream = await file.OpenStreamForWriteAsync())
    {
        XmlSerializer ser = new XmlSerializer(typeof(UserPreferences));

        // Serializes the instance into the newly created file
        ser.Serialize(stream, prefs);

        // Clean up Stream
        await stream.FlushAsync();
        stream.Close();

    }
}
```

This stores the instance of the UserPreferences class into the file created in the local folder. To read that file back, you can reverse the process by using the Deserialize method, like so:

```
async void loadXmlButton_Click(object sender, RoutedEventArgs e)
{
    UserPreferences prefs = null;

    var folder = ApplicationData.Current.LocalFolder;

    using (var stream =
                await folder.OpenStreamForReadAsync("prefs.xml"))
    {
        XmlSerializer ser = new XmlSerializer(typeof(UserPreferences));

        // Re-creates an instance of the UserPreferences
        // from the Serialized data
        prefs = (UserPreferences)ser.Deserialize(stream);

    }
}
```

By using the Deserialize method, you can re-create the saved data and instantiate a new instance of the data with the serialized data. The serialization class also supports a CanDeserialize method, so you can test to see whether the stream contains serializable data that is compatible with the type:

```
async void loadXmlButton_Click(object sender, RoutedEventArgs e)
{
  UserPreferences prefs = null;

  var folder = ApplicationData.Current.LocalFolder;

  using (var stream =
                  await folder.OpenStreamForReadAsync("prefs.xml"))
  {
  {
    XmlSerializer ser = new XmlSerializer(typeof(UserPreferences));

    // Use an XmlReader to allow us to test for serializability
    var reader = XmlReader.Create(file);

    // Test to see if the reader contains serializable data
    if (ser.CanDeserialize(reader))
    {
      // Re-creates an instance of the UserPreferences
      // from the Serialized data
      prefs = (UserPreferences)ser.Deserialize(reader);
    }
  }
 }
}
```

To test whether the data contains serializable data, you need to create an XmlReader object that contains the file contents (as a stream) using the XmlReader.Create method. After you have an XmlReader, you can use the serializer's CanDeserialize method. If you are going to wrap the file in an XmlReader, you should also send the reader object into the Deserialize method (because this is more efficient than the XmlSerializer creating a new reader internally).

▪ XML Serialization Choices

Although you can serialize your objects using the built-in XML serialization classes, you can also use third-party classes or even the DataContractXmlSerialization class from WCF to perform the serialization. The concepts are the same.

JSON Serialization

XML is the first choice of a lot of developers, but it probably should not be today. The proliferation of JSON means that using the same format for local serialization and any web- or REST-based interaction is commonplace. In addition, JSON tends to be smaller when serialized than XML. Although size alone isn't a reason to choose JSON, smaller generally means faster— and that is a good reason to pick it.

In place of the XmlSerializer class, you can use the DataContract-JsonSerializer class. This class is part of the WCF (or Service Model) classes that are part of the Windows Phone SDK. This class lives in the System.Runtime.Serialization namespace but is implemented in the System.ServiceModel.Web assembly. This assembly is not included by default, so you need to add it manually.

To use the DataContractJsonSerializer class, you can create it by specifying the data type to store, like so:

```
var prefs = new UserPreferences()
{
  FirstName = "Shawn"
};

var folder = ApplicationData.Current.LocalFolder;
var file = await folder.CreateFileAsync("prefs.xml",
  CreationCollisionOption.ReplaceExisting);

using (var stream = await file.OpenStreamForWriteAsync())
{
  // Create the Serializer for our preferences class
  var serializer = new
    DataContractJsonSerializer(typeof(UserPreferences));

  // Save the object as JSON
  serializer.WriteObject(file, someInstance);
}
```

You can see here that the DataContractJsonSerializer class's WriteObject method is used to serialize the instance of the UserPreferences class as JSON. For deserializing the data back into an instance of the UserPreferences class, you would use the ReadObject method instead:

```
UserPreferences someInstance = null;

var folder = ApplicationData.Current.LocalFolder;

using (var stream = await folder.OpenStreamForReadAsync())
{
  // Create the Serializer for our preferences class
  var serializer = new
    DataContractJsonSerializer(typeof(UserPreferences));

  // Load the object from JSON
  someInstance = (UserPreferences)serializer.ReadObject(file);
}
```

In this case, the serialization code simply used the DataContract-
JsonSerializer class's ReadObject method to load a new instance of the
options class by reading the JSON file that was earlier saved to storage.

Isolated Storage Settings

Sometimes it is just easier to let the system handle serialization for you. That's
the concept behind isolated storage settings. The IsolatedStorageSettings
class represents access to a simple dictionary of things to store for the phone.
This type of storage is useful for small pieces of information (for example,
application settings) that you need to store without the work of building a
complete serialization scheme.

To get started, you must get the settings object for your application
through a static accessor on IsolatedStorageSettings (in the System.
IO.IsolatedStorage namespace) called ApplicationSettings, like so:

```
IsolatedStorageSettings settings =
  IsolatedStorageSettings.ApplicationSettings;
```

This class exposes a dictionary of properties that are automatically
serialized to the local folder for you. For example, if you want to store a
setting when closing the application and read it back when launching the
application, you can do this with the IsolatedStorageSettings class, like so:

```
Color _favoriteColor = Colors.Blue;
const string COLORKEY = "FavoriteColor";

void Application_Launching(object sender, LaunchingEventArgs e)
{
  if (IsolatedStorageSettings.ApplicationSettings.Contains(COLORKEY))
```

```
    {
      _favoriteColor =
      (Color)IsolatedStorageSettings.ApplicationSettings[COLORKEY];
    }
}

void Application_Closing(object sender, ClosingEventArgs e)
{
    IsolatedStorageSettings.ApplicationSettings[COLORKEY] =
      _favoriteColor;
}
```

By using the `IsolatedStorageSettings` class's `ApplicationSettings` property, you can set and get simple values. You can see that during the launch of the application, the code first checks whether the key is in the `ApplicationSettings` (to ensure that it has been saved at least once); if so, it loads the value from the local folder.

The `IsolatedStorageSettings` class does work well with simple types, but as long as the data you want to store is compatible with XML serialization (like our earlier example), the settings file will support saving it as well:

```
UserPreferences _preferences = new UserPreferences();
const string PREFKEY = "USERPREFS";

void Application_Launching(object sender, LaunchingEventArgs e)
{
    if (IsolatedStorageSettings.ApplicationSettings.Contains(PREFKEY))
    {
      _preferences = (UserPreferences)
        IsolatedStorageSettings.ApplicationSettings[PREFKEY];
    }
}

void Application_Closing(object sender, ClosingEventArgs e)
{
    IsolatedStorageSettings.ApplicationSettings[PREFKEY] =
      _preferences;
}
```

Local Databases

When you are building an application that needs data that must be queried and support smart updating, a local database is the best way to accomplish that. Windows Phone supports databases that exist directly on the phone.

When building a Windows Phone application, you won't have access to the database directly; instead you can use a variant of LINQ to SQL married to a code-first approach to build a database to accomplish your database access. Let's walk through the meat of the functionality.

Getting Started

To get started, you need a database file. Under the covers the database is SQL Server Compact Edition (SQL CE), so you could just create an .sdf file for your project, but usually you start by telling the database APIs to create the database for you.

> ### ■ Looking Forward
>
> You can include local database files (SQL Server Compact Edition or .sdf files) with your application. We cover this later in this chapter in the "Using an Existing Database" section.

The first step is to have a class (or several) that represents the data you want to store. You can start with a simple class:

```
public class Game
{
  public string Name { get; set; }
  public DateTime? ReleaseDate { get; set; }
  public double? Price { get; set; }
}
```

This class holds some piece of data you want to be able to store in a database. Before you can store it in the database, you have to add attributes to tell LINQ to SQL that this describes a table:

```
[Table]
public class Game
{
  [Column]
  public string Name { get; set; }

  [Column]
  public DateTime? ReleaseDate { get; set; }
```

```
    [Column]
    public double? Price { get; set; }
}
```

By using these attributes, you are creating a class that represents the storage for a table in the database. Some of the column information is inferred (such as nullability in the `ReleaseDate` column). With this definition, you can read from the database, but before you can add or change data, you need to define a primary key:

```
[Table]
public class Game
{
    [Column(IsPrimaryKey = true, IsDbGenerated = true)]
    public int Id { get; set; }

    [Column]
    public string Name { get; set; }

    [Column]
    public DateTime? ReleaseDate { get; set; }

    [Column]
    public double? Price { get; set; }
}
```

As you can see, the `Column` attribute has several properties that can be set to specify information about each column. In this case, the `Column` attribute specifies that the `Id` column is the primary key and that the key should be generated by the database. To support change tracking and writing to the database, you must have a primary key.

Like any other database engine, SQL CE enables you to improve query performance by adding your own indexes. You can do this by adding the `Index` attribute to the table classes:

```
[Table]
[Index(Name = "NameIndex", Columns = "Name", IsUnique = true)]
public class Game
{
    // ...
}
```

The Index attribute enables you to specify a name, a string containing the column names to be indexed, and optionally whether the index should also be a unique constraint. This attribute is used when you create or update the database. You can also specify an index on multiple columns by separating the column names with a comma:

```
[Table]
[Index(Name = "NameIndex", Columns = "Name", IsUnique = true)]
[Index(Columns = "ReleaseDate,IsPublished")]
public class Game : INotifyPropertyChanging, INotifyPropertyChanged
{
  // ...
}
```

At this point, you have defined a simple table with two indexes and can move on to creating a data context class. This class will be your entry point to the database itself. It is a class that derives from the DataContext class, as shown here:

```
public class AppContext : DataContext
{
}
```

This class is responsible for exposing access to the database as well as handling change management. You will expose your "tables" as a public field:

```
public class AppContext : DataContext
{
  public Table<Game> Games;
}
```

The generic class wraps your table class to represent a queryable set of those objects. This way, your context class will not only give you access to the objects stored in the database, but also track them for you. The base class (DataContext) is where most of the magic happens. Because the DataContext class does not have an empty constructor, you'll also need to implement a constructor:

```
public class AppContext : DataContext
{
  public AppContext()
```

```
    : base("DataSource=isostore:/myapp.sdf;")
{
}

public Table<Game> Games;
}
```

The typical call to the base class's constructor requires that you send it a connection string. For the phone, all this connection string requires is a description of where the database exists or where it will be created. You specify this by specifying a URI to where the database file belongs. The URI is a path to the file from either the local folder or the application folder. To specify a file to exist (or be created) in the local folder, you use the isostore moniker[3] like so:

isostore:/myapp.sdf

For a database that ships with your application (and will be delivered in the .xap file), you can use the appdata moniker as well. If you want to access data that resides in the application folder, you will be able to only read the database, not write to it. Later in this chapter, you will learn how to copy the database to the isostore folder if you need to write to an app-delivered database. To specify the location of the database in the application folder, you can use the appdata moniker just like the isostore moniker:

appdata:/myapp.sdf

The end of the URI should be a path and a file name to the actual file. The underlying database is SQL CE, so the file is an .sdf file. If you want your database file to be within a subfolder, you can specify it in the URI with the folder name, like so:

isostore:**/data/myapp.sdf**

After you have created your data context class, you can create the database by calling the CreateDatabase method (as well as checking whether it exists by calling DatabaseExists):

---

3   The Database API uses the older isostore and appdata monikers. The newer WinRT monikers mentioned earlier in the chapter do not work with the database APIs.

```
// Create the Context
var ctx = new AppContext();

// Create the Database if it doesn't exist
if (!ctx.DatabaseExists())
{
  ctx.CreateDatabase();
}
```

The context's table members allow you to perform CRUD[4] on the underlying data. For example, to create a new Game object in the database, you would just create an instance and add it to the Games member:

```
// Create a new game object
var game = new Game()
{
  Name = "Gears of War",
  Price = 39.99,
};

// Queue it as a change
ctx.Games.InsertOnSubmit(game);

// Submit all changes (inserts, updates and deletes)
ctx.SubmitChanges();
```

The new Game object can be passed to the Games member of the context through the InsertOnSubmit method to tell the context to save this the next time changes are submitted to the database. The SubmitChanges method will take any changes that have occurred since the creation of the context object (or since the last call to SubmitChanges) and batch them to the underlying database. Note that the new instance of Game didn't set the Id property. This is unnecessary because the Id property is marked not only as the primary key (which is required to support writing to the database), but also as database-generated. This means that when SubmitChanges is called, it will let the database generate the Id and update your object's ID to the database-generated one.

Querying the Games stored in the database takes the form of LINQ queries. So, if you have created some data in the database, you can query it like this:

---

4 Create, Read, Update, and Delete

```
var qry = from g in ctx.Games
          where g.Price >= 49.99
          order by g.Name
          select g;

var results = qry.ToList();
```

This query will return a set of Game objects with the data directly from the database. This LINQ query is translated into a parameterized SQL query and executed against the local database for you when this code calls the ToList method.

What might not be obvious is that if you change these objects, the context class tracks those changes for you. So if you change some data, calling the context's SubmitChanges method updates the database as well:

```
var qry = from g in ctx.Games
          where g.Name == "Gears of War"
          select g;

var game = qry.First();

game.Price = 34.99;

// Saves any changes to the game
ctx.SubmitChanges();
```

In addition, you can delete individual items using the table members on the context class by calling DeleteOnSubmit like so:

```
var qry = from g in ctx.Games
          where g.Name == "Gears of War"
          select g;

var game = qry.FirstOrDefault();

ctx.Games.DeleteOnSubmit(game);

// Saves any chances to the game
ctx.SubmitChanges();
```

You do need to retrieve the entities to delete them (unlike the full version of LINQ to SQL where you could execute arbitrary SQL). You can submit a deletion by calling DeleteAllOnSubmit and supplying a query:

```
var qry = from g in ctx.Games
          where g.Price > 100
          select g;

ctx.Games.DeleteAllOnSubmit(qry);

ctx.SubmitChanges();
```

The query in this example defines the items to be deleted in the database. It does not retrieve them in this place; it uses the query to define which items are to be deleted. After all the items are marked for deletion, the call to SubmitChanges causes the deletion to happen (as well as any other changes detected).

By creating your table classes and a context class, you can access the database and perform all the necessary queries and changes to the database. Next let's look at additional database features you will probably want to consider as part of your phone application.

Optimizing the Context Class

Although the context class will track your objects, you can help the context class by ensuring that your table classes support the INotifyPropertyChanging and INotifyPropertyChanged interfaces. Implementing these interfaces has the additional benefit of assisting with data binding in XAML. Therefore, it is recommended that all your table classes support this interface, like so:

```
[Table]
public class Game : INotifyPropertyChanging, INotifyPropertyChanged
{
  // ...

  public event PropertyChangingEventHandler PropertyChanging;

  public event PropertyChangedEventHandler PropertyChanged;

  void RaisePropertyChanged(string propName)
  {
    if (PropertyChanged != null)
    {
      PropertyChanged(this, new PropertyChangedEventArgs(propName));
    }
  }

  void RaisePropertyChanging(string propName)
```

```
    {
      if (PropertyChanging != null)
      {
        PropertyChanging(this,
                         new PropertyChangingEventArgs(propName));
      }
    }
  }
}
```

Implementing both interfaces will add the PropertyChanging and PropertyChanged events to your class. As seen here, creating a simple helper method to raise these events is a common practice. Now that the interfaces are implemented, you have to use them. This involves calling the helper methods in each property setter. The original Game class used automatic properties to expose the columns, but because you need to call the helper method, you need standard properties:

```
[Table]
public class Game : INotifyPropertyChanged
{
  int _id;

  [Column(IsPrimaryKey = true, IsDbGenerated = true)]
  public int Id
  {
    get { return _id; }
    set
    {
      RaisePropertyChanging("Id");
      _id = value;
      RaisePropertyChanged("Id");
    }
  }

  string _name;

  [Column]
  public string Name
  {
    get { return _name; }
    set
    {
      RaisePropertyChanging("Name");
      _name = value;
      RaisePropertyChanged("Name");
    }
```

```
    }

    DateTime? _releaseDate;

    [Column]
    public DateTime? ReleaseDate
    {
      get { return _releaseDate; }
      set
      {
        RaisePropertyChanging("ReleaseDate");
        _releaseDate = value;
        RaisePropertyChanged("ReleaseDate");
      }
    }

    double? _price;

    [Column]
    public double? Price
    {
      get { return _price; }
      set
      {
        RaisePropertyChanging("Price");
        _price = value;
        RaisePropertyChanged("Price");
      }
    }

    // ...
}
```

You should notice that each property now has a backing field member (for example, _id for the Id property) and calls the RaisePropertyChanging and RaisePropertyChanged methods with the name of the property when the setter is called. By using these interfaces, the memory footprint of the context object is much smaller because it uses these interfaces to monitor changes.

In addition to these interfaces, you can improve the size of your update and delete queries by including a version member of your class:

```
[Table]
public class Game : INotifyPropertyChanging, INotifyPropertyChanged
{
    // ...
```

```
    [Column(IsVersion = true)]
    private Binary _version;
}
```

The version column (`IsVersion = true`) is optional but will improve the performance of change tracking when using database data. The version must be of type `Binary` from the `System.Data.Linq` namespace. It can be a private field (so it's not visible to users) but does need to be marked as `IsVersion = true` for LINQ to SQL to consider it the version column.

■ Performance Recommendation

Your table classes should support a primary key column and a version column and should implement the `INotifyProperty-Changing` and `INotifyPropertyChanged` interfaces to be as efficient as possible in your database access code.

Finally, if your database is only performing queries, you can tell the context class that you do not want to monitor any change management. You would accomplish this by setting the context class's `ObjectTrackingEnabled` property to `false`, like so:

```
using (var ctx = new AppContext())
{
  ctx.ObjectTrackingEnabled = false;

  var qry = from g in ctx.Games
            where g.Price < 19.99
            orderby g.ReleaseDate descending
            select g;

  var results = qry.ToList();
}
```

By disabling change management, the context object will be much more lightweight. Also, because the context is not necessary for tracking the change, you can create it locally and dispose of it when the query is complete. You usually would keep the context around for the lifetime of the page or application so that it can monitor and batch those changes back to the database, but because you are only reading from the database, the lifetime can be shortened if needed.

Associations

The data types for each property in the table classes you have seen have been simple types. The types have been simple because they need to be stored in the local database. To be stored in the local database, they need to be convertible to database types (for example, strings are stored as NVARCHARs). Even though you're going to be dealing with classes, you will still have to remember that it is a relational database underneath the covers. So when you need more structure, you will need associated tables (or associations).

For instance, let's assume we have a second table class that holds information about the publisher of a game:

```
[Table]
public class Publisher :
  INotifyPropertyChanging, INotifyPropertyChanged
{
  int _id;

  [Column(IsPrimaryKey = true, IsDbGenerated = true)]
  public int Id
  {
    get { return _id; }
    set
    {
      RaisePropertyChanging("Id");
      _id = value;
      RaisePropertyChanged("Id");
    }
  }

  string _name;

  [Column]
  public string Name
  {
    get { return _name; }
    set
    {
      RaisePropertyChanging("Name");
      _name = value;
      RaisePropertyChanged("Name");
    }
  }

  string _website;
```

```
[Column]
public string Website
{
  get { return _website; }
  set
  {
    RaisePropertyChanging("Website");
    _website = value;
    RaisePropertyChanged("Website");
  }
}

[Column(IsVersion = true)]
private Binary _version;

public event PropertyChangingEventHandler PropertyChanging;

public event PropertyChangedEventHandler PropertyChanged;

void RaisePropertyChanged(string propName)
{
  if (PropertyChanged != null)
  {
    PropertyChanged(this, new PropertyChangedEventArgs(propName));
  }
}

void RaisePropertyChanging(string propName)
{
  if (PropertyChanging != null)
  {
    PropertyChanging(this,
      new PropertyChangingEventArgs(propName));
  }
}
}
}
```

This new class is implemented just like the Game class (because we want it to allow change management). To be able to save it in the database, we need to expose it on our context class as well as on a public field:

```
public class AppContext : DataContext
{
  public AppContext()
    : base("DataSource=isostore:/myapp.sdf;")
  {
  }
```

```
public Table<Game> Games;

public Table<Publisher> Publishers;
}
```

At this point you could create, edit, query, and delete both the Game and Publisher objects. But what you really want is to be able to relate the two objects to each other. That's where associations come in.

To add an association, you need to start by having a column on the Game class that represents the publisher's primary key:

```
[Table]
public class Game : INotifyPropertyChanging, INotifyPropertyChanged
{
  // ...

  [Column]
  internal int _publisherId;

}
```

This new column is used to hold the ID of the related publisher for this particular game. The data is not public (it is internal in this case) because users of this class won't set this value explicitly. Instead, you will create a nonpublic member that will store an object called an EntityRef. The EntityRef class is a generic class that wraps a related entity:

```
[Table]
public class Game : INotifyPropertyChanging, INotifyPropertyChanged
{
  // ...

  [Column]
  internal int _publisherId;

  private EntityRef<Publisher> _publisher;
}
```

The EntityRef class is important here because it will also support lazy loading of the related entity so that large object graphs aren't loaded accidentally. But the real magic of linking the column and the EntityRef happens in the public property for the related entity:

```
[Table]
public class Game : INotifyPropertyChanging, INotifyPropertyChanged
{
  // ...

  [Column]
  internal int _publisherId;

  private EntityRef<Publisher> _publisher;

  [Association(IsForeignKey = true,
    Storage = "_publisher",
    ThisKey = "_publisherId",
    OtherKey = "Id")]
  public Publisher Publisher
  {
    get { return _publisher.Entity; }
    set
    {
      // Handle Change Management
      RaisePropertyChanging("Publisher");

      // Set the entity of the EntityRef
      _publisher.Entity = value;

      if (value != null)
      {
        // Set the foreign key too
        _publisherId = value.Id;
      }

      // Handle Change Management
      RaisePropertyChanged("Publisher");
    }
  }

}
```

There is a lot going on in this property, so let's take it one piece at a time. First, let's look at the Association attribute. This attribute has a number of parameters, but these are the basic ones to set. The IsForeignKey parameter tells the association that this is a foreign key relationship. The Storage parameter describes the name of the class's member that holds the EntityRef for this association. The ThisKey and OtherKey are the columns of the keys on each side of the association. ThisKey refers to the name of the column on this class (Game); OtherKey refers to the column name on the other side of the association (Publisher).

When someone accesses this property, you will return the entity from within the EntityRef object as shown previously in the property getter.

Finally, the setter has a number of operations. The first and last operations in the setter handle the change management notification just like any column property on your table class. Then it takes the value of the property and sets it to the Entity inside the EntityRef object. Finally, if the value being set is not null, it sets the foreign key ID on the table class so that the column that represents the foreign key is set.

By doing all of this, you can have a one-to-many relationship between two table classes. But so far that association is only one-way. To complete the association, you might want to have a collection on the Publisher table class that represents all the games by that publisher.

Adding the other side of the relationship is similar, but in this case you need an instance of a generic class called EntitySet:

```
[Table]
public class Publisher :
  INotifyPropertyChanging, INotifyPropertyChanged
{
  // ...

  EntitySet<Game> _gameSet;

  [Association(Storage = "_gameSet",
    ThisKey = "Id",
    OtherKey = "_publisherId")]
  public EntitySet<Game> Games
  {
    get { return _gameSet; }
    set
    {
      // Attach any assigned game collection to the collection
      _gameSet.Assign(value);
    }
  }
}
```

The EntitySet class wraps around a collection of elements associated with a table class. In this case, the EntitySet wraps around a collection of games that belong to a publisher. As in the other side of the association, specifying the Storage, ThisKey, and OtherKey helps the context object figure out how the association is created. The only surprising thing is that when the setter on the Games property is called, it attaches whatever games are assigned to it to the set of Games. This is typically called by the context class only when executing a query.

Although not obvious, the construction of the _gameSet field isn't shown. This needs to be done in the constructor:

```
[Table]
public class Publisher :
  INotifyPropertyChanging, INotifyPropertyChanged
{
  // ...

  public Publisher()
  {
    _gameSet = new EntitySet<Game>(
      new Action<Game>(this.AttachToGame),
      new Action<Game>(this.DetachFromGame));
  }

  void AttachToGame(Game game)
  {
    RaisePropertyChanging("Game");
    game.Publisher = this;
  }

  void DetachFromGame(Game game)
  {
    RaisePropertyChanging("Game");
    game.Publisher = null;
  }
}
```

In the constructor you must create the EntitySet. Note that in the constructor, you will also pass in two actions that handle attaching and detaching a game to and from the collection. The purpose of these two actions is to ensure that the individual games that are attached/detached also set or clear their association property. In addition, raising the PropertyChanging event helps the context object to be very efficient when the association is changing.

Using an Existing Database

Because the underlying database is SQL CE, you might want to use an existing database (.sdf file). To do this, you can simply add it to your phone project (as Content), as shown in Figure 9.1.

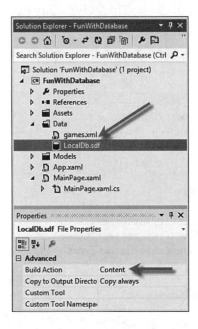

FIGURE 9.1   SQL Server CE database as content

By marking the database as Content, it will be deployed to the application data folder when your application is installed. Using an existing database means you will have to build your context and class files to match the existing database. Currently, there are no tools to build these classes for you.[5]

When you have a database as part of your project, you can refer to it using the appdata moniker when setting up a context object, like so:

```
public class AppContext : DataContext
{
    public AppContext()
        : base("DataSource=appdata:/DB/LocalDB.sdf;File Mode=read only;")
```

---

5   There are online walkthroughs for using the desktop tools to build the classes and then refactoring them for use on the phone, but it is not a trivial effort.

```
  {
  }

  // ...
}
```

When you use a database directly in the application directory, the database can be accessed only for reading. That means you must include the "file mode" directive in the connection string as well to indicate that the database is read-only.

It is often preferable to use the database in the application directory as a template for your database. To do this, you must first copy the database to the local folder:

```
// Get a Stream of the database from the Application Directory
var dbUri = new Uri("/DB/LocalDB.sdf", UriKind.Relative);
using (var dbStream = Application.GetResourceStream(dbUri).Stream)
{
  // Open a file in the local folder for writing
  var folder = ApplicationData.Current.LocalFolder;
  var file = await folder.CreateFileAsync("LocalDB.sdf",
    CreationCollisionOption.ReplaceExisting);

  using (var stream = await file.OpenStreamForWriteAsync())
  {
    byte[] buffer = new byte[4096];
    int sizeRead;

    // Write the database out
    while ((sizeRead = dbStream.Read(buffer, 0, buffer.Length)) > 0)
    {
      file.Write(buffer, 0, sizeRead);
    }
  }
}
```

You can do this by simply copying the database from the application directory using Windows Phone's Application class to get a stream that contains the database. Then just create a new file in isolated storage (as shown earlier in this chapter) to save the database as a new file. If you copy the database, you can use your context class with the simple isostore moniker to read and write to the newly copied database.

Schema Updates

So, you've created your database-driven application, and now you're ready to update it to a new version. But your users have been dutifully adding data to your database, and you have to change the database. What do you do?

The local database stack for the Windows Phone SDK can help you accomplish this. In the SDK is a DatabaseSchemaUpdater class that can take an existing database and make additive changes that are safe for the database. These include adding nullable columns, adding tables, adding associations, and adding indexes.

To get started, you must get an instance of the DatabaseSchemaUpdater class. You retrieve this using the DataContext class's CreateDatabaseSchemaUpdater method:

```
using (AppContext ctx = new AppContext())
{
  // Grab the DatabaseSchemaUpdater
  var updater = ctx.CreateDatabaseSchemaUpdater();
}
```

This updater class enables you to not only make additive changes, but also handle a database version. This gives you a simple way to determine the update level of any database. The updater class supports a simple property called DatabaseSchemaVersion:

```
var version = updater.DatabaseSchemaVersion;
```

With the database version, you can make incremental updates:

```
// If specific version, then update
if (version == 0)
{
  // Some simple updates (Add stuff, no remove or migrate)
  updater.AddColumn<Game>("IsPublished");
  updater.DatabaseSchemaVersion = 1;
  updater.Execute();
}
```

The database version always starts at zero and can be changed to a specific database version using the updater. As is typical for a schema change, you would add any of the new columns, tables, indexes, or associations. You would then update the database schema version to ensure that this update can't be executed a second time. Then, over time, you can test for more version blocks. For example, as your application receives more updates, the code might look like this:

```
// If specific version, then update
if (version == 0)
{
  // So simple updates (Add stuff, no remove or migrate)
  updater.AddColumn<Game>("IsPublished");
  updater.DatabaseSchemaVersion = 1;
  updater.Execute();
}
else if (version == 1)
{
  // So simple updates (Add stuff, no remove or migrate)
  updater.AddIndex<Game>("NameIndex");
  updater.DatabaseSchemaVersion = 2;
  updater.Execute();
}
```

You can see that, for the first update, the version was incremented. Then when the application matured, it added a new update. This is the central use for the database version.

The four updates that are supported are as follows:

```
updater.AddTable<Genre>();
updater.AddColumn<Game>("IsPublished");
updater.AddIndex<Game>("NameIndex");
updater.AddAssociation<Game>("Genre");
```

When adding a table, the entire table is added (including all columns, associations, and indexes). This means that when you add a table, you do not need to enumerate all the columns, indexes, and associations specifically. Adding a column adds a specific new column. Any new columns must be nullable because there is no way to specify migration to non-nullable columns. Adding an index is based on the name of the index. Finally, an association is added and is based on the property that contains the Association attribute.

> ### ■ Complex Schema Changes
>
> If you need to make schema changes that are too complex for the DatabaseSchemaUpdater class to accomplish, you will need to do the hard work of creating a new database as well as transferring and migrating the data manually. There is no shortcut for this work.

Database Security

Although you are the only person who will have access to the database contained in the application directory or in isolated storage, at times you might want to increase the security of the database by adding levels of security to the database itself.

The two main ways to secure your database are to add a password for access to the database and to enable encryption. When creating a Windows Phone application, you can do both of these at the same time. You can specify a password for the database directly in the connection string to the database. This is typically specified in the DataContext class:

```
public class AppContext : DataContext
{
  public AppContext()
    : base("DataSource=isostore:/Games.sdf;Password=P@ssw0rd!;")
  {
  }

  public Table<Game> Games;

  public Table<Publisher> Publishers;
}
```

When you specify a password before you create the database, the database is password-protected as well as encrypted. You cannot add a password or encryption after the database has been created. If you decide after your application has been deployed to add a password (and encryption), you must create a new database and migrate all your data manually.

Where Are We?

Dealing with data in a smart way when you build a Windows Phone application is important to the success of your application. By understanding the basics of both isolated storage and local database support, you can store the kinds of data you want in the most efficient way possible.

To reiterate, the main benefit of using the database engine is to support querying of the underlying data in an efficient way. If you do not need the query support, you will find that it is generally more efficient to just use isolated storage and serialization to save your data. Making the right decision here can be the difference between a fast, slick application and a slow, groggy mess.

10
Multitasking

PHONES ARE DIFFERENT. That's the essential point of this chapter. On these small devices, which we like to think of as small computers, doing too much at one time can hurt the end-user experience. This is why running multiple applications simultaneously is discouraged—in fact, it's disallowed. As you've seen in previous chapters, your application must be able to switch between activated, deactivated, and dormant phases. But what if you need to run tasks in the background? What if you are checking the server for data, downloading files, or performing other tasks that should be done periodically? How can you do that? This chapter will help you figure out how you can accomplish these tasks.

Multitasking

Back in Windows Mobile 6.5 (and before), you had a lot of power as a developer. You could run multiple applications at the same time and, while in the background, actively do work. Although this gave developers a lot of power, it had the side effect of slowing down the phone. Because there was no good monitor of who wrote good or bad code, a single bad application could cause a lot of pain for the phone's user. In fact, most users became familiar with a task management application (or app-killing application) to help minimize this pain.

When Windows Phone was designed, Microsoft decided that this pain was not acceptable, although iPhone using the same strategy certainly enforced the company's reasoning. The first version of Windows Phone did not allow developers to do anything when their applications were not "in the foreground." As you saw in earlier chapters, using tombstoning to mimic the running of multiple applications is a main tenet of the design philosophy around the phone.

Windows Phone introduced additional functionality to enable background code to run, but your application still cannot run in the background. This functionality includes

- Background agents
- Background Transfer Service
- File and URI app launching

Background agents enable you to run a small piece of code that runs without the benefit of a user interface. Background agents are expected to run in the background and come in several flavors: periodic agents, resource-intensive agents, location-aware agents, and audio agents. These agent types enable you to determine whether you want to run a regularly scheduled task, a task that is long-running but can run in only a limited number of scenarios, and a specific type of agent for playing background audio.

The **Background Transfer Service (BTS)** is a set of APIs for asking the phone to download or upload data for your application. Although the BTS doesn't let you run arbitrary code, it does handle the common case of sending or receiving data across a network connection.

Background Agents

If you are a desktop or web developer, you are used to being able to decide when and where your code runs. On the phone you do not have that luxury, so you have to let the operating system dictate exactly when you run your application or some background operations. But how does the operating system handle background operations?

Normally when you build a typical phone application, you submit a .xap file with all the code your application requires to launch the application's user interface. Your application can be launched, but when it is not in the foreground, none of your code will execute.

Background agents enable you to supply some code that is executed periodically by the operating system. This code does not have any user interface but shares information with the main application. The information it can share includes isolated storage and application storage (for example, where the .xap file contents are located), as shown in Figure 10.1.

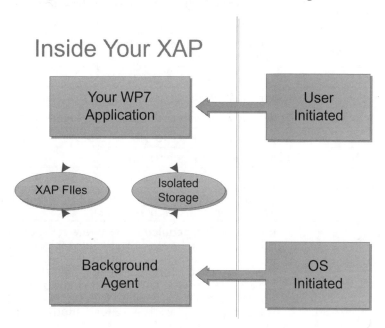

FIGURE 10.1   Relationship between application and scheduled task

Although the main application is an assembly that contains the startup code, a background agent works similarly. The background agent consists of an additional assembly that is included in the main application's .xap file and contains the code to execute in the background. The main goal of the operating system is to protect the phone from you, the developer. All agents have some specific limitations, as shown in Table 10.1.

TABLE 10.1   Scheduled Task Limitations

Limitation	Description
Forbidden APIs	Scheduled tasks are forbidden from using certain APIs for the phone, including (but not limited to):
	`Microsoft.Devices.Camera` class
	`Microsoft.Devices.VibrateController` class
	`Microsoft.Devices.Radio` namespace
	`Microsoft.Devices.Sensors` namespace
	Background Transfer Service
	`Microsoft.Windows.Controls.WebBrowser` class
	`Microsoft.Phone.Tasks` namespace
	Scheduled tasks (can't schedule tasks in a scheduled task)
	`System.Windows.MessageBox` class
	`System.Windows.Clipboard` class
	`System.Windows.Controls.MediaElement` class
	`System.Windows.Controls.MultiScaleImage` class
	`Microsoft.Xna` namespaces
	`System.Windows.Navigation` namespace
Memory	It can only use 6MB of memory total (though audio agents can go as high as 15MB).
Scheduling	It must be rescheduled every two weeks. Usually this means you have to reschedule tasks on every launch of your main application. If your application is not launched every two weeks, the scheduled task will stop being launched. If your application updates the tile (via a call to `Update(ShellTileData)`), the background task is extended another two weeks automatically.

Now that you understand the basic reasons and limitations of using background agents, let's look at each agent type.

Periodic Agent

The **periodic background agent** is a background agent that is meant to execute some code every 30 minutes. To optimize the battery life of the phone, this can wander as much as 10 minutes earlier or later to align with operating system processes. These processes can run for only a maximum of 25 seconds (along with the limitations mentioned in Table 10.1). To get started, you will need a Schedule Task Agent project in your solution. To add a Scheduled Task Agent project, right-click the solution in the Solution Explorer and select Add | New Project.

After you are in the Add New Project dialog, select the Windows Phone Scheduled Task Agent project type under the Windows Phone section of your language, as shown in Figure 10.2.

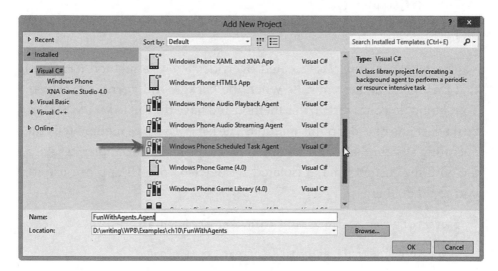

FIGURE 10.2   Selecting the Windows Phone Scheduled Task Agent

This creates a new project in your solution that contains a single class file:

```csharp
using Microsoft.Phone.Scheduler;

public class ScheduledAgent : ScheduledTaskAgent
{
  static ScheduledAgent()
  {
    // Subscribe to the managed exception handler
    Deployment.Current.Dispatcher.BeginInvoke(delegate
    {
      Application.Current.UnhandledException += UnhandledException;
    });
  }

  static void UnhandledException(object sender,
    ApplicationUnhandledExceptionEventArgs e)
  {
    if (Debugger.IsAttached)
    {
      Debugger.Break();
```

```
    }
  }

  protected override void OnInvoke(ScheduledTask task)
  {
    //TODO: Add code to perform your task in background

    NotifyComplete();
  }
}
```

The ScheduledAgent class created overrides a single method (OnInvoke) that the operating system calls when the background agent is executed. You should do your work in this method and have the call to NotifyComplete be the last line of code in this method. The NotifyComplete method tells the operating system that your operation is complete. For example, to save a file with the current time in isolated storage (so your UI app can use it), you could do this:

```
protected async override void OnInvoke(ScheduledTask task)
{
  var folder = ApplicationData.Current.LocalFolder;

  using (var stream =
    await folder.OpenStreamForWriteAsync("time.txt",
          CreationCollisionOption.ReplaceExisting))
  {
    var writer = new StreamWriter(file);
    writer.WriteLine(DateTime.Now);
  }

  NotifyComplete();
}
```

Because this code writes directly to isolated storage for the application, that means the main application can read the file you created here. As shown here, you can call the NotifyComplete method when you have completed your operation. You also might want to know whether the operation fails. You can accomplish this by calling the Abort method:

```
try
{
  var folder = ApplicationData.Current.LocalFolder;

  using (var stream =
```

```
        await folder.OpenStreamForWriteAsync("time.txt",
                CreationCollisionOption.ReplaceExisting))
    {
      var writer = new StreamWriter(stream);
      writer.WriteLine(DateTime.Now);
    }

    NotifyComplete();
}
catch
{
  Abort();
}
```

You should call either `NotifyComplete` or `Abort` in your agent, to let the runtime (and potentially your application) know whether the task was successfully completed.

When you added the new scheduled agent, the project also reached into the main application and added a new section to the `WMAppManifest.xml` file:

```
<Deployment ...>
  <App ...>
  ...
    <Tasks>
      <DefaultTask Name="_default"
                   NavigationPage="MainPage.xaml" />
      <ExtendedTask Name="BackgroundTask">
        <BackgroundServiceAgent Specifier="ScheduledTaskAgent"
                                Name="BackgroundAgent"
                                Source="BackgroundAgent"
                                Type="BackgroundAgent.ScheduledAgent"
        />
      </ExtendedTask>
    </Tasks>
    ...
  </App>
</Deployment>
```

Inside the `Tasks` element, the project item added a section called `ExtendedTask`, which is responsible for indicating the project and code for any background tasks. The `ExtendedTask` element is where all agents are registered, including periodic, resource-intensive, and audio agents. Although the `ExtendedTask` is named, the name is not significant. Inside the `ExtendedTask` element is a set of elements that reference the different background agent or agents in your application. Each attribute in the `BackgroundServiceAgent` element has a specific meaning:

- **Name:** This is the name of the element, not referenced in code.
- **Specifier:** This is the type of agent. The types of specifiers are as follows:
  - *ScheduledTaskAgent:* This is a periodic or resource-intensive task.
  - *AudioPlayerAgent:* This task plays specific songs from a list of audio files.
  - *AudioStreamingAgent*: This task streams audio directly to the phone.
- **Source:** This is the assembly name that contains the background agent.
- **Type:** This is the type of the class that represents the background agent.

This part of the WMAppManifest.xml file is what links your application to the assembly that contains your background task. This means your background agent must be in a separate assembly (as the separate project would indicate). You still have to do a little more work to make your agent actually run in the background.

Before your application can register the background task, you need to make a reference to the new background project. This just requires you to select Add Service Reference and pick the assembly in the Solution tab, as shown in Figure 10.3.

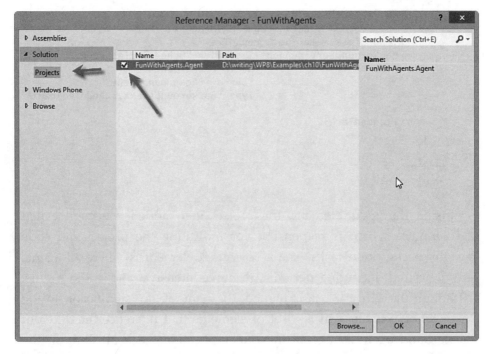

FIGURE 10.3 **Adding a reference to the Scheduled Task Agent project**

After your main project has a reference to the background task, you can register it to be executed periodically. To do this, you need to create a new instance of your task using the `PeriodicTask` class:

```
// A unique name for your task. It is used to
// locate it in from the service.
var taskName = "MyTask";

// Create the Task
PeriodicTask task = new PeriodicTask(taskName);

// Description is required
task.Description = "This saves some data to Isolated Storage";

// Add it to the service to execute
ScheduledActionService.Add(task);
```

The unique name here is used to locate the service if you need to stop or renew the service, but it is not related to the task name in the `WMAppManifest.xml` file. After your task is created, you must set the `Description` property as well (at a minimum). After your `PeriodicTask` object is constructed, you can add it to the phone by using the `ScheduledActionService`'s `Add` method as shown. This will cause your background task to be periodically executed (every 30 minutes).

> ### ■ Periodic Agent Timing
>
> Although the phone attempts to execute your code every 30 minutes, it can be executed as much as 10 minutes early or late depending on the state of the system (for instance, memory, battery, and so on).

You should set the `Description` property of the `PeriodicTask` class to something significant. The description is a string that is visible to the end user and that is shown in the background task management UI (see Figure 10.4).

FIGURE 10.4   The `PeriodicTask`'s description in the management
user interface

Each periodic task will execute for up to two weeks before it has to be
reregistered. The only exception to this is if you are updating your live
tile. When you update the live tile (either through the app or through a
background agent), this will extend the length of the registration another
two weeks. When you launch your app, you should remove and re-create
it on every execution of your application:

```
// A unique name for your task. It is used to
// locate it in from the service.
var taskName = "MyTask";

// If the task exists
var oldTask = ScheduledActionService.Find(taskName);
if (oldTask != null)
{
  ScheduledActionService.Remove(taskName);
}
```

```
// Create the Task
PeriodicTask task = new PeriodicTask(taskName);

// Description is required
task.Description = "This saves some data to Isolated Storage";

// Add it to the service to execute
ScheduledActionService.Add(task);
```

■ Best Practice

You should not enable any background task by default, and you should always allow your users to disable background tasks in your application.

Now that you have your agent registered, you will need to be able to debug it. The problem on the face of it is that you might not want to wait the 30 minutes for your agent to execute. The ScheduledActionService has a way to run the agent immediately so that you can debug it more easily:

```
var taskName = "MyTask";

ScheduledActionService.LaunchForTest(taskName,
  TimeSpan.FromMilliseconds(250));
```

The LaunchForTest method takes the name of the task (which you specified earlier when you created the PeriodicTask) and a delay before the task is launched. Lastly, because the background task (in this example) was able to write to isolated storage, you can access that data in your main application anytime you want. The background task and your application simply need to communicate by storing information in these shared locations (local folder, the Internet, or reading from the installation folder).

In addition, you might want to alert the user about new information the background task detected (for example, a new message is available). You can use the ShellToast class to open a toast (or update Live Tiles):

```
protected override void OnInvoke(ScheduledTask task)
{
  // If the Main App is Running, Toast will not show
  ShellToast popupMessage = new ShellToast()
```

```
{
  Title = "My First Agent",
  Content = "Background Task Launched",
  NavigationUri = new Uri("/Views/DeepLink.xaml", UriKind.Relative)
};
popupMessage.Show();

NotifyComplete();
}
```

By using the ShellToast class, you can alert the user that the background task detected something and give her a chance to launch the application. If the main application is currently running, the ShellToast class will not show the pop-up and will be reserved to show when your application is not currently being executed.

Creating your own periodic tasks is an easy way to do simple background processing, be able to alert the user to ongoing events, and allow her to interact with your application. But sometimes you will need a periodic task that consumes more resources. That is where resource-intensive agents come in.

Resource-Intensive Agent

Like a periodic agent, a resource-intensive agent is a repeatable task that performs some discrete process in the background. Unlike the periodic agent, though, the resource-intensive agent is not meant to be executed very often. In fact, there are a strict set of rules as to when resource-intensive agents are executed. These agents are meant to be able to run for a longer period (up to 10 minutes) and consume more resources (for instance, network, and memory). But to allow your agent to be executed, the operating system must only allow it when doing so is not detrimental to the phone itself. To that end, the criteria for executing a resource-intensive agent include

- On external power
- When using a noncellular network (for example, Wi-Fi or plugged into a PC)
- When the minimum battery level is 90%

- When the device must be screen-locked
- When no phone call is active

These rules should imply the fact that resource-intensive agents are meant for syncing large amounts of data or processing that will be accomplished occasionally. These agents are often executed only once a day, at most. Deciding whether to use an agent (or deciding to use a periodic agent or resource-intensive agent) can increase the overall usefulness of your application.

If the criteria for executing a resource-intensive agent change while the agent is being executed (for instance, a phone call comes in or the phone is removed from external power), the resource-intensive agent will immediately be aborted to allow the user full access to the phone.

■ **WARNING**

Resource-intensive agents have so many requirements to enable them to be executed that some users will never be able to execute these agents. For example, users who don't dock their phone with a PC or use Wi-Fi will never execute a resource-intensive agent.

Both resource-intensive and periodic agents are scheduled agents. So whether you're adding a periodic or a resource-intensive agent (or even if you need both), you will have a single Scheduled Task Agent project (similar to the one shown previously in the "Periodic Agent" section).

Registering a resource-intensive agent is virtually identical to registering a periodic agent:

```
// A unique name for your task. It is used to
// locate it in from the service.
var taskName = "IntensiveTask";

// If the task exists
var oldTask = ScheduledActionService.Find(taskName);
if (oldTask != null)
{
  ScheduledActionService.Remove(taskName);
}

// Create the Task
```

```
ResourceIntensiveTask task = new ResourceIntensiveTask(taskName);

// Description is required
task.Description = "This does a lot of work.";

// Add it to the service to execute
ScheduledActionService.Add(task);
```

The only real difference is that the class you create is an instance of ResourceIntensiveTask (instead of PeriodicTask). By specifying that the new task is a resource-intensive task, the operating system will know to execute the agent only when the phone is ready for a resource-intensive operation (for example, it is in a state as defined by the previously mentioned limitations).

You can test resource-intensive agents in the same way as well, by calling the ScheduledActionService's LaunchForTest method:

```
var taskName = "IntensiveTask";

ScheduledActionService.LaunchForTest(taskName,
  TimeSpan.FromMilliseconds(10));
```

You might want to have both a periodic and a resource-intensive task registered for the phone. The problem is that an application can have only a single background agent (the Scheduled Task Agent project) associated with an application. You can register one (and only one) of each type of scheduled task. This means you can have a periodic task and a resource-intensive task for your application, but because there is only one agent, you must discriminate which type of task is being called in your agent by checking the task type, like so:

```
public class ScheduledAgent : ScheduledTaskAgent
{
  protected override void OnInvoke(ScheduledTask task)
  {
    if (task is ResourceIntensiveTask)
    {
      DoHeavyResources();
    }
    else
    {
      DoPeriodic();
    }
```

```
    NotifyComplete();
  }

  // ...
}
```

In this way, you can determine the type of task the OnInvoke is meant to execute. You could discriminate by name as well, but because you can have only one of each type, testing by object type is just as effective.

Audio Agent

Although you can write applications that play audio (as you've seen in prior chapters), you also might want that audio to continue regardless of whether your application is running. In addition to continuing to play the audio, you might want to integrate with the Universal Volume Control (which enables the user to move to pause audio as well as move to the previous and next tracks). You can see the Universal Volume Control (UVC) in Figure 10.5.

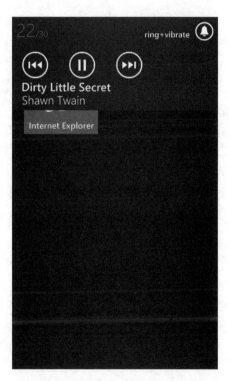

FIGURE 10.5 The Universal Volume Control in action

To be able to have audio play in the background, you need to have an audio agent. There are two types of audio agents: audio playback agents and audio streaming agents. For this example, we'll focus on adding an audio playback agent because that is a much more common case.

Background audio works by your application having an audio agent associated with it. This audio agent is solely responsible for handing requests to change the audio in any way (for example, move tracks, pause, and so on). Your application can have controls that request those changes, but it is ultimately the agent that does the work so that the same agent code is used when the user changes the audio (again, moving tracks, pausing, and so on) through the phone's built-in controls (like the UVC).

To get started, you need to add a new Audio Playback Agent project to your project (like you did for scheduled task agents earlier in this chapter), as shown in Figure 10.6.

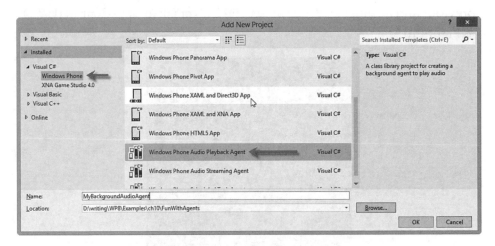

FIGURE 10.6 **Adding an audio agent to your project**

This new project not only creates a project for the audio agent, but also modifies your WMAppManifest.xml file (similar to what the Scheduled Task Agent project did earlier):

```
<Deployment ...>
  <App ...>
    ...
    <Tasks>
```

```
        <DefaultTask Name="_default"
                     NavigationPage="MainPage.xaml" />
        <ExtendedTask Name="BackgroundTask">
          <BackgroundServiceAgent Specifier="AudioPlayerAgent"
                                  Name="MyAudioAgent"
                                  Source="MyAudioAgent"
                                  Type="MyAudioAgent.AudioPlayer" />
        </ExtendedTask>
      </Tasks>
      ...
    </App>
</Deployment>
```

The `BackgroundServiceAgent` element added here specifies that the specifier of the agent is an `AudioPlayerAgent`, which tells the operating system that the `AudioPlayer` class is responsible for playing audio if the application decides to play background audio. Before you can use the new audio agent, you will need to add a reference to the audio agent project from your main phone application project.

Unlike the prior agent types, you do not need to register this type of agent with the `ScheduledActionService`. Instead, you will simply use the `BackgroundAudioPlayer` class. This class has a static property called `Instance` that returns the singleton background player object. You can use this class to tell the background audio to start, skip, or stop (or even seek). For instance, to implement a button in your application that can play or pause the current audio, you could do the following:

```
private void playButton_Click(object sender, RoutedEventArgs e)
{
  // Tell the agent to play or pause
  if (BackgroundAudioPlayer.Instance.PlayerState !=
      PlayState.Playing)
  {
    BackgroundAudioPlayer.Instance.Play();
  }
  else
  {
    BackgroundAudioPlayer.Instance.Pause();
  }
}
```

What is important to see here is that all your application's code should do is send commands to the background audio player (which is controlled by the agent). When you tell the BackgroundAudioPlayer class to "play," it then routes that command to the agent where all the hard work is done. So, let's look at the skeleton of the audio agent the new project created for you:

```csharp
public class AudioPlayer : AudioPlayerAgent
{
  protected override void OnPlayStateChanged(
    BackgroundAudioPlayer player,
    AudioTrack track,
    PlayState playState)
  {
    //TODO: Add code to handle play state changes

    NotifyComplete();
  }

  protected override void OnUserAction(
    BackgroundAudioPlayer player,
    AudioTrack track,
    UserAction action,
    object param)
  {
    //TODO: Add code to handle user actions
    // through the application and system-provided UI

    NotifyComplete();
  }

  protected override void OnError(
    BackgroundAudioPlayer player,
    AudioTrack track,
    Exception error,
    bool isFatal)
  {
    //TODO: Add code to handle error conditions

    NotifyComplete();
  }

  protected override void OnCancel()
  {
  }
}
```

The agent class contains four different methods that are called in different cases while background audio is playing. Let's start with OnUserAction:

```
protected override void OnUserAction(
  BackgroundAudioPlayer player,
  AudioTrack track,
  UserAction action,
  object param)
{
  // May be initiated from the app or the UVC
  switch (action)
  {
    case UserAction.Play:
      {
        PlayCurrentTrack();
        break;
      }
    case UserAction.Pause:
      {
        player.Pause();
        break;
      }
    case UserAction.SkipNext:
      {
        MoveToNextSong();
        break;
      }
    case UserAction.SkipPrevious:
      {
        MoveToPreviousSong();
        break;
      }
  }

  NotifyComplete();
}
```

This method is called whenever the user makes a request to manipulate the currently playing music (including the first request to "play" a song). It passes in the current instance of the BackgroundAudioPlayer so you can manipulate the song to be played directly (as is shown when the UserAction is Pause). For playing and moving tracks, the list of tracks is owned by the audio agent (not the background audio player). This means you will typically need your audio agent to keep track of the list of tracks and the current position in that list. Any state you need to keep around needs to be static as the specific instance of the audio agent should be stateless (because it can be destroyed or garbage-collected if necessary). So, for this example you need to store both the list of tracks and the track counter as static data:

```
public class AudioPlayer : AudioPlayerAgent
{
  // Song Counter
  static int _currentSong = 0;

  // Songs
  static SongList _songList = new SongList();

  // ...
}
```

This enables you to keep the list of songs the user has requested (it can be stored in isolated storage or another mechanism for sharing between the audio agent and the application). Then the audio agent can implement the PlayCurrentTrack (which this example calls when a user requests to begin playing), like so:

```
void PlayCurrentTrack()
{
  // Retrieve a Song object that contains the song to play
  var song = _songList.Songs.ElementAt(_currentSong);

  // Build Audio Track
  var track = new AudioTrack(song.Path,
    song.Name,
    song.Artist,
    song.Album,
    song.Art);

  // Instruct the player that this is the current track to play
  BackgroundAudioPlayer.Instance.Track = track;
}
```

This simply returns the current song in the list as a custom type (called Song in this example) and builds a new AudioTrack object from the Song object (by setting a URI to the path to the song as well as descriptive properties for the song name, artist name, album name, and URI to an image for the album art).

> **⬛ Audio Paths**
>
> The first parameter to the `AudioTrack` class's constructor is a `Uri` that points at the song. This could be a song in isolated storage (as a relative URI):
>
> ```
> var path = new Uri("/audio/SomeTrack.mp3", UriKind.Relative);
> ```
>
> Or the first parameter could be a URI for a song out across a network connection:
>
> ```
> var path = new Uri("http://shawntwain.com/01-anne.mp3");
> ```
>
> Only network and isolated storage URIs are supported. If you want to include audio in your .xap file, you'll need to copy it to isolated storage manually.

After a track has been set, the audio will not automatically start playing. Setting the track simply tells the background audio to attempt to find the audio to play. When it finds the audio, it will change its play state. Luckily, one of the audio agent's generated methods is called when the play state changes:

```
protected override void OnPlayStateChanged(
  BackgroundAudioPlayer player,
  AudioTrack track,
  PlayState playState)
{
  switch (playState)
  {
    // Track has been selected and is ready to be played
    // (includes starting to download if audio is remote)
    case PlayState.TrackReady:
      {
        player.Play();
        break;
      }
    case PlayState.TrackEnded:
      {
        MoveToNextSong();
        break;
      }
  }
}
```

```
    NotifyComplete();
}
```

The `PlayState` enumeration has a number of values, but in your case you most want to pay attention to two states:

- **TrackReady:** This indicates that the `BackgroundAudioPlayer` has located and loaded the audio and is ready to actually play.
- **TrackEnded:** This indicates that a track just ended.

When this method is called with `TrackReady`, that's your cue to go ahead and play the audio that has been readied. This is what actually causes the audio to start. You can also handle other states (for instance, `TrackEnded`) to determine what to do next. In this example the code simply moves the track to the next item, eventually calling `PlayCurrentTrack` to load the next track. No matter what happens at this point, you should call `NotifyComplete` or `Abort` (like the earlier scheduled task agent example explained).

So far, you've seen how to play the first track, but what about changing tracks? Earlier in this section, when the user requested to go to the next or previous track, you called methods that would do that work, but what do those methods actually do? They do the simple work of changing the current track number and telling the audio agent to play the current track after the counter has changed:

```
private void MoveToPreviousSong()
{
  if (--_currentSong < 0)
  {
    _currentSong = _songList.Songs.Count() - 1;
  }

  PlayCurrentTrack();
}

private void MoveToNextSong()
{
  if (++_currentSong >= _songList.Songs.Count())
  {
    _currentSong = 0;
  }

  PlayCurrentTrack();
}
```

The work of determining what to set the _currentSong value to is trivial code after that track number has changed. It calls PlayCurrentTrack, which you saw earlier as simply setting the BackgroundAudioPlayer's Track property to the new track.

Back in the main application, you can use the BackgroundAudioPlayer class to retrieve the current state of background audio. For example, to show the currently playing song, you might check the current Track:

```
public partial class MainPage : PhoneApplicationPage
{

  protected override void OnNavigatedTo(NavigationEventArgs e)
  {
    base.OnNavigatedTo(e);

    if (BackgroundAudioPlayer.Instance.Track != null)
    {
      currentSong.Text = BackgroundAudioPlayer.Instance.Track.Title;
    }
  }

  // ...
}
```

When the page is launched, it simply tests whether there is a current track, and if so, it sets the title in the user interface to indicate to the user what the current song is. But because the audio agent is controlling the state of the background audio, you might need to know about the change to the PlayState as well. This enables your application to show the current track and enable/disable buttons as necessary:

```
public partial class MainPage : PhoneApplicationPage
{
  // Constructor
  public MainPage()
  {
    InitializeComponent();

    BackgroundAudioPlayer.Instance.PlayStateChanged +=
      Instance_PlayStateChanged;
  }

  void Instance_PlayStateChanged(object sender, EventArgs e)
  {
```

```
    if (BackgroundAudioPlayer.Instance.Track != null)
    {
      currentSong.Text = BackgroundAudioPlayer.Instance.Track.Title;
    }
  }

  // ...
}
```

When the event is fired, the play state has changed and (as this example shows) you can change the current audio track if it is valid.

This should give you a general feel for the nature of how audio agents work. The specifics of sharing data between the agent and the application will greatly vary depending on how you want to use background audio, but this way you can allow the user to control the audio without it necessarily being part of the phone's media library.

Location-Aware Apps

Another type of agent you should be aware of is the location-aware applications. Unlike the background agents, this type of app continues to run in the background when a user navigates away from it. In this mode, the number of APIs you can use is minimal and a special geolocation class can be used to be notified when a user changes location. This type of app is specifically for apps that want to track the user (for instance, jogging and bike applications are common).

To create a location-aware app, you must also set up the WMAppManifest. xml file to tell the phone that you want to be able to run in the background. To do this, you have to add the ID_CAP_LOCATION capability. In addition, you have to manually edit the WMAppManifest.xml file to include a special option to run as a location-aware application. If you open the WMAppManifest.xml file as text, you'll find the DefaultTask element inside the Task element. Inside that element you will need to add a new element called BackgroundExecution:

```
<Deployment ...>
  <App ...>
    ...
    <Tasks>
      <DefaultTask Name="_default" NavigationPage="MainPage.xaml">
```

```
      <BackgroundExecution>
        <ExecutionType Name="LocationTracking" />
      </BackgroundExecution>
    </DefaultTask>
  </Tasks>
  ...
</App>
</Deployment>
```

The ExecutionElement's name must be LocationTracking for this to work. With both of those changes made, you can now create a location-aware application. But how do you know when your app is running in the background?

If you open the App.xaml file, you'll find the PhoneApplicationService element that contains event handlers for the four main application events (for instance, Launching, Activated, and so on). In a location-aware app, you can also handle the RunningInBackground event as shown here:

```
<shell:PhoneApplicationService Launching="Application_Launching"
  Closing="Application_Closing"
  Activated="Application_Activated"
  Deactivated="Application_Deactivated"
  RunningInBackground="Application_RunningInBackground" />
```

Because this is another state the application can go into, you should communicate to the rest of your application that you are in background mode. In this mode you can't update the UI but can do other work (such as updating a Live Tile or showing notifications). A common approach is to have an App class-level flag for when the application is running in background mode, like so:

```
// In app.xaml.cs
public static bool IsRunningInBackground { get; set; }

private void Application_Launching(object sender,
                                    LaunchingEventArgs e)
{
}

private void Application_Activated(object sender,
                                    ActivatedEventArgs e)
{
  IsRunningInBackground = false;
```

```
    }

    private void Application_Deactivated(object sender,
                                        DeactivatedEventArgs e)
    {
    }

    private void Application_Closing(object sender, ClosingEventArgs e)
    {
    }

    private void Application_RunningInBackground(object sender,
                                        RunningInBackgroundEventArgs e)
    {
      IsRunningInBackground = true;
    }
```

By changing the flag, you can then decide how to handle location events in your application. But how do you get notified of a change in location?

That is where the Geolocator class comes in (as we discussed in Chapter 9, "Databases and Storage"). This class enables you to be notified via an event about a change in location as well as being able to tell the class how far a user has to move before you're notified. This enables you to specify how much granularity you need. A jogging app might require much more granularity than a driving app, for example.

Typically, the App class exposes a property that will hold an instance of the Geolocator class:

```
// In App.xaml.cs
public static Geolocator Locator { get; set; }
```

This way, in the page responsible for starting the geolocation, you can simply create an instance. For example, when a user clicks a start button, you could simply do the following:

```
    private void startButton_Click(object sender, EventArgs e)
    {
      if (App.Locator == null)
      {
        App.Locator = new Geolocator()
        {
          DesiredAccuracy = PositionAccuracy.High,
          MovementThreshold = 100 // Meters
        };
```

```
    App.Locator.PositionChanged += Locator_PositionChanged;
  }
}
```

When you create an instance to the `Geolocator` class, you specify how accurate the locator should be (same as the Normal and High accuracy from the `GeoCoordinateWatcher` class). You can also specify how far (in meters) to use as a movement threshold. In this instance, you'll be notified only if the user has moved a minimum of 100 yards.

Creating this instance and registering for the event tells the class to notify you as the user moves. There are no start and stop methods—just creating it is enough. To stop geolocation, simply unregister the event and set the reference to null (to allow the garbage collector to destroy it):

```
private void stopButton_Click(object sender, EventArgs e)
{
  App.Locator.PositionChanged -= Locator_PositionChanged;
  App.Locator = null;
}
```

Finally, you can handle the `PositionChanged` event:

```
void Locator_PositionChanged(Geolocator sender,
                             PositionChangedEventArgs args)
{
  var coordinate = args.Position.Coordinate;

  if (App.IsRunningInBackground)
  {
    var title = string.Format("{0:F2} x {1:F2}",
                              coordinate.Longitude,
                              coordinate.Latitude);

    var tileData = new FlipTileData()
    {
      Title = title
    };
    var tile = ShellTile.ActiveTiles.First();
    tile.Update(tileData);
  }
  else
  {
    // Not happening on the UI thread
    Dispatcher.BeginInvoke(() =>
    {
```

```
    DataContext = new
    {
      Long = coordinate.Longitude,
      Lat = coordinate.Latitude,
      Alt = coordinate.Altitude
    };
  });
  }
}
```

Because this class will fire regardless of whether the application is running in the background, you can simply check the `App.IsRunningInBackground` property you created earlier. This is where you will decide what to do with the event. You should avoid updating the user interface when running in the background. In this example, you update the Live Tile with the coordinates instead of showing them in the UI.

Consequently, when you are running in the foreground, you can update the user interface. This event won't fire on the UI thread, so you should use the Dispatcher to marshal the call back to the UI thread, as shown in the call to BeginInvoke above.

Background Transfer Service

One of the most common reasons developers want to use background processes for Windows Phone is so that they can download or upload data from the Internet. Having to create an entire agent (and have the user manage that agent) just to accomplish that sort of work seems unnecessary—because it is.

The Windows Phone includes a special service called the Background Transfer Service (BTS). This service's job is to allow you to queue up downloads and uploads to be performed by the system. These transfers do not require that your application stay running to be performed. Essentially, the service enables you to send it a small number of requests that it will perform on your behalf. But to be able to use the service, you need to be aware of a number of requirements and limitations.

Requirements and Limitations

An overarching goal of the BTS is to enable you to perform the work you need to do without affecting the performance of the phone, or affecting the user of the phone, in a negative way. To meet these goals, the BTS works in the following specific ways:

- Transfer protocol:
  - All transfers are made via HTTP or HTTPS.
  - Supported verbs include GET and POST for downloads and POST for uploads.
- Transfer location:
  - All transfers must take place to or from isolated storage in a special subdirectory called /shared/transfers.
  - This directory is created during installation, but if your application deletes it, you must re-create it before any transfers.
  - You can create any files or directories under this subdirectory.
- Forbidden headers:
  - If-Modified-Since
  - If-None-Match
  - If-Range
  - Range
  - Unless-Modified-Since
- Size policies:
  - Maximum upload: 5MB
  - Maximum download via cellular connection: 20MB[1]
  - Maximum download via Wi-Fi on battery: 100MB
  - Maximum download via Wi-Fi on external power: unlimited
- Request limits:
  - Maximum outstanding requests per application: 5
  - Maximum concurrent requests: 2
  - Maximum number of headers per request: 15
  - Maximum size of each HTTP header: 16KB

---

1 If a download exceeds 20MB, the remaining data will require download via Wi-Fi or PC connection and external power.

- Supported networks:
  - 2G, EDGE, Standard GPRS: not supported
  - 3G or higher: supported but must have minimum 50Kbps throughput
  - Wi-Fi/PC connection: supported but must have minimum 100Kbps throughput

Requesting Transfers

To get the BTS to perform a transfer, you must first create a new request. A request takes the form of a `BackgroundTransferRequest` object. At a minimum, you must specify the source and destination of your request like so:

```
// Determine the source and destination
var serverUri = new Uri("http://shawntwain.com/01-Anne.mp3");
var isoStoreUri = new Uri("/shared/transfers/01-Anne.mp3",
                          UriKind.Relative);

// Create the Request
var request = new BackgroundTransferRequest(isoStoreUri, serverUri);
```

The constructor for the request can accept two URIs that specify where to copy from and where to copy to. Typically this takes the form of an Internet URI for the source (for downloading) and a relative URI to the special /shared/transfers directory in isolated storage. To make the request, you can simply add this to the requests on the service (for instance, the `BackgroundTransferService` class):

```
BackgroundTransferService.Add(request);
```

This will queue up the request and have the service perform the transfer for you. To request an upload the method is similar, but the source and destination are reversed as well as specifying the method:

```
// Determine the source and destination
var serverUri = new Uri("http://shawntwain.com/01-Anne.mp3");
var isoStoreUri = new Uri("/shared/transfers/01-Anne.mp3",
                          UriKind.Relative);

// Create the Request
```

```
var request = new BackgroundTransferRequest(serverUri);

// Set options
request.UploadLocation = isoStoreUri;
request.Method = "POST";

// Queue the Request
BackgroundTransferService.Add(request);
```

The constructor for the BackgroundTransferRequest that takes two arguments is specifically for downloading files from the server. When you want to request an upload, you need to create the request by specifying the server URI that represents where the upload is going. Then you need to specify the UploadLocation as a URI that represents the path to files in the special transfer directory from which to upload.

In addition to simply specifying the source and destination for your request, you can also specify other optional properties on the BackgroundTransferRequest class, including the following.

- **Headers:** This enables you to set specific headers for the HTTP transfer.
- **Tag:** This enables you to set an arbitrary string that contains additional information you can use when retrieving the request.
- **TransferPreferences:** This is an enumeration that specifies which circumstances are allowed, including
    - *None:* Only allow transfers while on external power and using a high-speed network (for example, Wi-Fi or PC connection). This is the default.
    - *AllowCellular:* Allows the request while on a cellular network but must be on external power.
    - *AllowBattery:* Allows the request on Wi-Fi but does not require an external power source.
    - *AllowCellularAndBattery:* Allows the transfer on cellular and while on battery. You should use this only for small and immediately needed requests. Use judiciously!

Requesting the transfers is adequate, but it is also up to your application to monitor the transfers (and possibly let the user know the status of the transfer). That is where monitoring of your own transfers becomes necessary.

Monitoring Requests

The `BackgroundTransferService` class supports a static property called `Requests` that represents an enumerable list of all the current requests (including those that have completed and those that have failed). Because access to the requests is through a property, you might be lured into expecting that the collection represents the overall status of requests, but that is not how it works. When you access the property, it returns a copy of the current state of the requests, but these are not updated as the requests are processed. So even though you can use data binding to show the user the list of requests and their current status, they will not update until you retrieve the list of results again.

> ### ■ Retrieving the Requests
>
> Every time you access the `Requests` property on the `Background-TransferService`, it makes a copy of the current state of each request. This process is not cheap, so it is recommended that you do not access this property in a tight loop or based on a subsecond timer.

Let's look at a strategy for keeping the user apprised of the status of requests. To start, you should keep a local cache of the last requests you retrieved from the `BackgroundTransferService` class, like so:

```
public partial class MainPage : PhoneApplicationPage
{
  // Constructor
  public MainPage()
  {
    InitializeComponent();
  }
```

```
IEnumerable<BackgroundTransferRequest> _requestCache = null;

// ...
}
```

You should retrieve the requests when someone navigates to the page,
so you can show the status to the user:

```
protected override void OnNavigatedTo(NavigationEventArgs e)
{
  base.OnNavigatedTo(e);

  // Update the Page
  RefreshBindings();
}
```

In this example, the RefreshBindings method is used to retrieve the
requests again, as well as bind them to the user interface:

```
void RefreshBindings()
{
  // Dispose of the old cache to stop memory leaks
  if (_requestCache != null)
  {
    foreach (var request in _requestCache)
    {
      // Clean up the cache to prevent leaks
      request.TransferProgressChanged -=
        request_TransferProgressChanged;
      request.TransferStatusChanged -= request_TransferStatusChanged;
      request.Dispose();
    }
  }

  // Get the Updated Requests
  _requestCache = BackgroundTransferService.Requests;

  // Wire up the events
  foreach (var request in _requestCache)
  {
    request.TransferProgressChanged +=
      request_TransferProgressChanged;
    request.TransferStatusChanged += request_TransferStatusChanged;
  }

  // Rebind
  filesListBox.ItemsSource = _requestCache;
}
```

The first part of this method takes any existing cache (as this will be called in a number of cases as the transfers change in status) and cleans them so that they don't leak resources. The returned requests support the IDisposable interface, so you must call Dispose on each of them. In addition, this example is unwiring two events you are wiring up every time you retrieve the requests. After the cleanup is complete, the code retrieves the current state of the requests. When it has the new requests, it wires up two events—one that indicates that the request's progress has changed (for instance, the transfer is proceeding) and one that is fired when the status of the transfer changes (succeeded or failed). Lastly, the new cache is rebound to the user interface (a ListBox in this case).

On the face of it, this is a lot of work where you might be used to just binding to a collection that simply changes the underlying data using binding interfaces (for instance, INotifyPropertyChanged and INotifyCollectionChanged). This is not how the BackgroundTransferService's requests work. You must rebind them on every update.

To ensure that the page is updated as the progress is changed, the handler for each request's TransferProgressChanged event simply calls the RefreshBinding method:

```
void request_TransferProgressChanged(object sender,
                                     BackgroundTransferEventArgs e)
{
  // Update the Page
  RefreshBindings();
}
```

This does mean that the underlying data is being refreshed quite a lot, but that's necessary to update the user with the latest progress information. You can decide to update it only as transfers complete (which happens less often). This example handles that event as well:

```
void request_TransferStatusChanged(object sender,
                                   BackgroundTransferEventArgs e)
{
  // Limited to 5 requests
  // So remove it when it's done
  if (e.Request.TransferStatus == TransferStatus.Completed)
  {
    if (BackgroundTransferService.Find(e.Request.RequestId) != null)
    {
      BackgroundTransferService.Remove(e.Request);
```

```
  }
    e.Request.Dispose();
  }

  // Update the Page
  RefreshBindings();
}
```

The difference here is that not only is the code calling `RefreshBindings`, but if a request is complete, it is being removed from the service. Although removing the completed items is suggested, you can decide exactly when to do this. The reason completed requests are removed automatically is so that when the user relaunches your application, you can see which requests succeeded; therefore as this example shows, you will need to remove those requests. This becomes important because (as stated earlier) you can have only five requests at a time. If you have five requests in the service—even if they are all complete—the sixth request will throw an exception. It is up to you to manage the list of transfers.

When displaying the status of the requests, the `BackgroundTransfer-Request` objects that are returned include several pieces of read-only data:

- **RequestId:** This is a generated GUID that can be used to track the request.

- **TotalBytesToReceive:** This is the total number of bytes to be downloaded in the request. This value is 0 until the request has started.

- **BytesReceived:** This is the number of bytes downloaded so far.

- **TotalBytesToSend:** This is the total number of bytes to be uploaded in the request.

- **BytesSent:** This is the number of bytes sent so far.

- **TransferStatus:** This is an enumeration that indicates the current state of the transfer. The state can be one of the following:
  - *None:* The system has not queued the request yet.
  - *Transferring:* The request is being performed.
  - *Waiting:* Typically this means it is waiting for other pending transfers to be completed.

- *WaitingForWiFi:* The request is queued, but it cannot start until a Wi-Fi connection is available.
- *WaitingForExternalPower:* The request is queued, but it is waiting for external power to be available (for instance, the phone is on battery).
- *WaitingForExternalPowerDueToBatterySaverMode:* The battery is low and all requests have been suspended.
- *WaitingForNonVoiceBlockingNetwork:* The request is queued, but it is waiting for a higher-speed cellular network or Wi-Fi to be available to complete the request.
- *Paused:* The BTS has stopped the request temporarily.
- *Completed:* The request is complete. You should check the `Transfer-Error` to ensure that the request was successful.
- *Unknown:* The system is unable to determine the state of the transfer.

- **StatusCode:** This is the HTTP status code (a number) that indicates what was returned by the server.
- **TransferError:** This is the exception (if any) that was encountered during the transfer. You should check to see that the `TransferError` is null when a transfer is complete to ensure that the transfer completed successfully.

The way your application manages requests is crucial if you are going to use the BTS because your application is the only place to manage your requests. The user does not have an operating system management screen for the BTS.

Although keeping the user apprised of the status of the transfers is important (no matter how you let him know about the status), the work is worth the effort because building an efficient and robust download and upload system expressly for your application is not an easy task. By relying on the BTS to accomplish these types of transfers, it should be easier to write your application.

Where Are We?

Windows Phone generally wants to dissuade you from affecting the performance of the overall phone experience. The multitasking support on the phone gives you a number of performance- and resource-friendly ways to accomplish much of what you might need to accomplish by running background processes. If you're coming from desktop or server development, at first the challenges posed by these limitations can be daunting. But you should be able to achieve most of the types of applications you want to build without hurting the overall experience on the phone. By using background agents and the BTS, most of your needs should be met.

┏ 11 ▪
Services

WINDOWS PHONE IS A SMALL, MOSTLY CONNECTED DEVICE, meaning that most of the time you can expect to be able to access the Internet from the phone. In many ways, Internet access is what has really changed smartphones over the past few years. When you are building your Windows Phone application, you can use the Internet to get information, assets, or whatever your application requires. In this chapter we review the ways in which you can use services, from the generic use of REST or web services, to specific examples of using push notifications and Windows Live services.

> **▪ NOTE**
>
> The free tools included in the Windows Phone SDK are adequate for most of the development story on the phone. But if you need to write your own services to be consumed by the phone, there is no way to get Visual Studio Express to create those web projects for you. There are several approaches to make this work, but in this chapter we will use Visual Studio Professional to create the services to simplify the code.

The Network Stack

The network stack on the phone enables you to access network (for example, Internet) resources. The phone dictates that all network calls must be performed asynchronously. This is to ensure that an errant network call does not tie up the user interface (or more importantly, make the phone think your application has locked up or crashed). If you are new to asynchronous programming, this will be a good place to start learning.

The WebClient **Class**[1]

In most cases the framework helps with classes that follow a common pattern which includes a method that ends with the word *Async* and starts an asynchronous execution, as well as an event that is called when the execution is complete.

One class that follows this pattern is the WebClient class. It is a simple way to make a basic web request on the phone, as shown here:

```
public partial class MainPage : PhoneApplicationPage
{
  // Constructor
  public MainPage()
  {
    InitializeComponent();

    // Create the client
    WebClient client = new WebClient();

    // Handle the event
    client.DownloadStringCompleted += client_DownloadStringCompleted;

    // Start the execution
    client.DownloadStringAsync(new Uri("http://wildermuth.com/rss"));
  }
}
```

In this example the WebClient class is created, the DownloadStringCompleted event is wired up, and the DownloadStringAsync method is called to start the download. When the download is complete, the event is fired like so:

---

1   WebClient represents the main way you'll communicate with websites and services, but WinRT supports a new class called HttpClient. You should keep an eye on this class because it's clear that Windows Phone 8 is headed toward more WinRT compatibility.

```
void client_DownloadStringCompleted(object sender,
                                    DownloadStringCompletedEventArgs
e)
{
  // Make sure the process completed successfully
  if (e.Error == null)
  {
    // Use the result
    string rssFeed = e.Result;
  }
}
```

In the event argument, you are passed any exception that is thrown when the download is being attempted. This is returned to you as the Error property. In the preceding code, the error is null, which means no error occurred and the Result property will be filled with the result of the network call. Because of this pattern, you have to get used to the process of performing these types of operations asynchronously. Although still asynchronous, you can simplify the pattern a little by using a lambda for the event handler:

```
// Create the client
WebClient client = new WebClient();

// Handle the event
client.DownloadStringCompleted += (s, e) =>
  {
    // Make sure the process completed successfully
    if (e.Error == null)
    {
      // Use the result
      string rssFeed = e.Result;
    }
  };

// Start the execution
client.DownloadStringAsync(new Uri("http://wildermuth.com/rss"));
```

In this case, you're writing the handling of the completed event as an inline block of code, which makes the process feel more linear. If you're not familiar with lambda expressions, please see the Microsoft documentation[2] for more details.

---

2 http://msdn.microsoft.com/en-us/library/bb397687.aspx

> ### ▪ **What about** async **and** await**?**
>
> Although the .NET code running on the phone supports the async and await keywords, the WebClient client wasn't updated with support for these keywords. You will continue to need to do the asynchronous work via event handlers. You could write wrappers to support this. You can see an example of these handlers at http://shawnw.me/UnoSLR.

The WebClient class is the starting point for most simple network calls. The class matches up an "Async" method and a "Completed" event for several types of operations, including the following:

- **DownloadString:** This downloads a text result and returns a string.
- **OpenRead:** This downloads a binary stream and returns a Stream object.
- **UploadString:** This writes text to a server.
- **OpenWrite:** This writes a binary stream to a server.

The code for using these other types of calls looks surprisingly similar. To download a binary stream (for example, any nontext object, such as an image), use this code:

```
// Create the client
WebClient client = new WebClient();

// Handle the event
client.OpenReadCompleted += (s, e) =>
  {
    // Make sure the process completed successfully
    if (e.Error == null)
    {
      // Use the result
      Stream image = e.Result;
    }
  };

// Start the execution
client.OpenReadAsync(new
Uri("http://wildermuth.com/images/headshot.jpg"));
```

Although the pattern is the same, the event and method names have changed and the result is now a stream instead of a string.

> ■ HttpWebRequest/HttpWebResponse
>
> If you've written .NET networking code before, you might be used to working with the HttpWebRequest and HttpWebResponse classes. Because these are on the phone, though, these classes support only asynchronous execution. These classes are supported, but the WebClient class is more commonly used because it always fires its events on the same thread as they were originally called (usually the UI thread).

Accessing Network Information

Before you can execute network calls, you must have access to the network. On the phone you can test for whether connectivity is supported as well as the type of connectivity (which might help you decide how much data you can reliably download onto the phone). Although the .NET Framework contains several APIs for accessing network information, a specialized class in the Windows Phone SDK supplies much of this information all in one place. The DeviceNetworkInformation class enables you to access this network information.

The DeviceNetworkInformation class supports a number of static properties that will give you information about the phone's network, including

- **IsNetworkAvailable:** This is a Boolean value that indicates whether any network is currently available.

- **IsCellularDataEnabled:** This is a Boolean value that indicates whether the phone has enabled cellular data (as opposed to Wi-Fi data).

- **IsCellularDataRoamingEnabled:** This is a Boolean value that indicates whether the phone has enabled data roaming.

- **IsWifiEnabled:** This is a Boolean value that indicates whether the phone has enabled Wi-Fi on the device.

- **CellularMobileOperator:** This returns a string that contains the name of the mobile operator.

You can use this class to determine whether an active network connection is available:

```
if (DeviceNetworkInformation.IsNetworkAvailable)
{
  status.Text = "Network Found";
}
else
{
  status.Text = "Network not Found";
}
```

You can also access an event that indicates that the network information has changed:

```
public partial class MainPage : PhoneApplicationPage
{
  // Constructor
  public MainPage()
  {
    InitializeComponent();

    DeviceNetworkInformation.NetworkAvailabilityChanged +=
      DeviceNetworkInformation_NetworkAvailabilityChanged;
  }

  void DeviceNetworkInformation_NetworkAvailabilityChanged(
    object sender, NetworkNotificationEventArgs e)
  {
    switch (e.NotificationType)
    {
      case NetworkNotificationType.InterfaceConnected:
        status.Text = "Network Available";
        break;
      case NetworkNotificationType.InterfaceDisconnected:
        status.Text = "Network Not Available";
        break;
      case NetworkNotificationType.CharacteristicUpdate:
        status.Text = "Network Configuration Changed";
        break;
    }
  }
  // ...
}
```

The DeviceNetworkInformation class's NetworkAvailabilityChanged event fires whenever the network changes. This example shows that you can access the NotificationType from the NetworkNotificationEventArgs class to see whether a network connection was just connected, disconnected, or just changed its configuration. In addition, this event passes in the network type:

```csharp
public partial class MainPage : PhoneApplicationPage
{
  // Constructor
  public MainPage()
  {
    InitializeComponent();

    DeviceNetworkInformation.NetworkAvailabilityChanged +=
      DeviceNetworkInformation_NetworkAvailabilityChanged;
  }

  void DeviceNetworkInformation_NetworkAvailabilityChanged(
    object sender, NetworkNotificationEventArgs e)
  {
    switch (e.NetworkInterface.InterfaceSubtype)
    {
      case NetworkInterfaceSubType.Cellular_1XRTT:
      case NetworkInterfaceSubType.Cellular_EDGE:
      case NetworkInterfaceSubType.Cellular_GPRS:
        status.Text = "Cellular (2.5G)";
        break;
      case NetworkInterfaceSubType.Cellular_3G:
      case NetworkInterfaceSubType.Cellular_EVDO:
      case NetworkInterfaceSubType.Cellular_EVDV:
        status.Text = "Cellular (3G)";
        break;
      case NetworkInterfaceSubType.Cellular_HSPA:
        status.Text = "Cellular (3.5G)";
        break;
      case NetworkInterfaceSubType.WiFi:
        status.Text = "WiFi";
        break;
      case NetworkInterfaceSubType.LTE:
        status.Text = "LTE";
        break;
      case NetworkInterfaceSubType.Desktop_PassThru:
        status.Text = "Desktop Connection";
        break;
    }
  }
  // ...
}
```

By using the `NetworkInterfaceInfo` class's `NetworkInterfaceSubType` enumeration, you can determine the exact type of network connection on the phone. The `NetworkInterfaceInfo` class also gives you access to several other useful properties, including the following:

- **Bandwidth:** This is an integer that specifies the speed of the network interface.
- **Characteristics:** This is an enumeration that specifies whether the phone is currently roaming.
- **Description:** This is a description of the network interface.
- **InterfaceName:** This is the name of the network interface.
- **InterfaceState:** This states whether the network interface is connected or disconnected.

▪ Ethernet Network Connections

Ethernet connections are available only if the phone is hooked up to a computer via a USB cable. This is a common way to tell whether the user is plugged into a computer.

By using this `DeviceNetworkInformation` class, you can have access to much of the network information you will need for your application.

Consuming JavaScript Object Notation

Many types of services on the Internet are easy to consume with JavaScript on web pages and use a special type of data called JavaScript Object Notation (JSON). This format is useful because it is easy to consume from JavaScript and tends to be smaller than XML for certain types of data. As you work with different Internet services, you will find a number of APIs that support JSON. For more information on how JSON is structured, visit http://json.org.

Consuming JSON on the phone is fairly straightforward. You have two approaches:

- Serialize JSON to and from managed objects (for example, classes).
- Parse JSON much like you would XML.

Before you can handle the JSON, you have to retrieve it. The network stack can do this for you. For instance, if you wanted to retrieve statuses from Twitter's live feed, you could make a call using the `WebClient` class to retrieve the information:

```
// Create the client
WebClient client = new WebClient();

// Handle the event
client.DownloadStringCompleted += (s, e) =>
  {
    // Make sure the process completed successfully
    if (e.Error == null)
    {
      // Retrieve the JSON
      string jsonString = e.Result;

    }
  };

// Start the execution
string api =
"http://api.twitter.com/1/statuses/public_timeline.json";
client.DownloadStringAsync(new Uri(api));
```

Retrieving data from services that expose their data via JSON is like any other type of network request; therefore, you can use the `WebClient` class to accomplish this. As this example shows, you can use the `DownloadString` API to retrieve JSON data.

Although the phone does have built-in support for serializing objects to and from JSON[3], the current version is not very forgiving. In both of these cases, I suggest you look at using an open-source library that has existed for .NET for quite a while and supports Windows Phone: Json.NET. You can start by downloading the Json.NET libraries from http://json.codeplex. com. The following sections show you how to serialize objects to and from JSON as well as parse JSON using the Json.NET library.

---

3 See MSDN for the built-in support: http://shawnw.me/wp8jsonser

Using JSON Serialization

The Json.NET libraries support serialization through a class called JsonConvert, which enables you to serialize and deserialize objects to and from JSON. Passing in an object to JsonConvert's SerializeObject method will return a string made up of JSON:

```
var guy = new Person()
{
  FirstName = "Shawn",
  LastName = "Wildermuth",
  BirthDate = new DateTime(1969, 4, 24)
};

string json = JsonConvert.SerializeObject(guy);

// Returns:
// {
//    "FirstName":"Shawn",
//    "LastName":"Wildermuth",
//    "BirthDate":"\/Date(-21758400000-0400)\/"
// }
```

The SerializeObject method takes a single object but will serialize an entire object tree or collection. The passed-in object is the start of the serialization. To reverse the process, you would use the generic Deserialize-Object method:

```
string theJson = @"{
  ""FirstName"":""Shawn"",
  ""LastName"":""Wildermuth"",
  ""BirthDate"":""\/Date(-21758400000-0400)\/""
}";

Person recreated = JsonCon
vert.DeserializeObject<Person>(theJson);
```

Put this together with the WebClient class and you can interact with JSON-powered services (usually REST services). For example, to call Twitter to get the latest tweets in the public feed, you can call a REST interface like so:

```
// Create the client
WebClient client = new WebClient();

// Handle the event
client.DownloadStringCompleted += (s, e) =>
{
```

```
  // Make sure the process completed successfully
  if (e.Error == null)
  {
    // Use the result
    string jsonString = e.Result;

    Tweet[] tweets =
      JsonConvert.DeserializeObject<Tweet[]>(jsonString);

    tweetList.ItemsSource = tweets;

  }
};

// Start the execution
string req =
"http://api.twitter.com/1/statuses/public_timeline.json";
client.DownloadStringAsync(new Uri(req));
```

By using the `WebClient` class's networking to request data from Twitter, the JSON returned can be turned into objects directly. When you use Json. NET's `DeserializeObject` method, it is smart enough to try to match the fields of the managed object to the JSON properties. It does not require that the entire object graph in JSON be modeled as classes. This means that when it maps the JSON object to your class, it will include only properties that both your class and the JSON object have in common.

Parsing JSON

Another option with dealing with JSON is to parse it and consume it without having to create classes to hold the data. The Json.NET library includes a couple of classes that simplify this: `JObject` and `JArray`. For instance, to read a simple object, just call the `JObject` class's `Parse` method:

```
string theJson = @"{
  ""FirstName"":""Shawn"",
  ""LastName"":""Wildermuth"",
  ""BirthDate"":""\/Date(-21758400000-0400)\/""
}";

JObject jsonObject = JObject.Parse(theJson);

string firstName = jsonObject["FirstName"].Value<string>();
string lastName = jsonObject["LastName"].Value<string>();
DateTime birthDate = jsonObject["BirthDate"].Value<DateTime>();
```

Parsing the JSON into an instance of JObject gives you first-class access to the properties of the JSON. You can retrieve the specific values in the JSON by using the Value method. The generic version of the Value method lets you specify the type of data you expect to retrieve, as shown previously.

Although this example shows you a simple object, you can retrieve collections in JSON as well. The JArray class is how you parse and consume JSON collections:

```
string jsonCollection = @"[
{
  ""FirstName"":""Shawn"",
  ""LastName"":""Wildermuth"",
  ""BirthDate"":""\/Date(-21758400000-0400)\/""
},
{
  ""FirstName"":""Pennie"",
  ""LastName"":""Wildermuth"",
  ""BirthDate"":""\/Date(-21758400000-0400)\/""
},
]";

JArray jsonArray = JArray.Parse(jsonCollection);

foreach (JObject item in jsonArray)
{
  string firstName = item["FirstName"].Value<string>();
  string lastName = item["LastName"].Value<string>();
  DateTime birthDate = item["BirthDate"].Value<DateTime>();
}
```

Because the JSON being parsed here is an array of items (note the square bracket that starts the JSON), the JArray class will parse this into an array of JObject items, as shown here. This also means that JSON objects that contain collections will enable you to iterate through them as JArray objects, like so:

```
string json = @"{
  ""FirstName"":""Shawn"",
  ""LastName"":""Wildermuth"",
  ""BirthDate"":""\/Date(-21758400000-0400)\/"",
  ""FavoriteGames"" :
  [
    {
      ""Name"" : ""Halo 3"",
      ""Genre"" : ""Shooter""
```

```
      },
      {
        ""Name"" : ""Forza 2"",
        ""Genre"" : ""Racing""
      },
    ]
}";

JObject guy = JObject.Parse(json);

string firstName = guy["FirstName"].Value<string>();
string lastName = guy["LastName"].Value<string>();
DateTime birthDate = guy["BirthDate"].Value<DateTime>();

foreach (JObject item in guy["FavoriteGames"])
{
  string name = item["Name"].Value<string>();
  string genre = item["Genre"].Value<string>();
}
```

Although the object being parsed is a JObject, the collection in the JSON (accessed via the indexer, like any other field) would yield a JArray object (that can be iterated through). In this way, you can go through a complex object graph in JSON as needed.

The Json.NET library even lets you execute LINQ queries against parsed JSON. You can do this by writing LINQ queries over JArray objects, like so:

```
string json = @"[
{
  ""FirstName"":""Shawn"",
  ""LastName"":""Wildermuth"",
  ""BirthDate"":""\/Date(-21758400000-0400)\/"",
  ""FavoriteGames"" :
    [
      {
        ""Name"" : ""Halo 3"",
        ""Genre"" : ""Shooter""
      },
      {
        ""Name"" : ""Forza 2"",
        ""Genre"" : ""Racing""
      },
    ]
},
{
  ""FirstName"":""Pennie"",
  ""LastName"":""Wildermuth"",
```

```
    ""BirthDate"":""\/Date(-21758400000-0400)\/"",
    ""FavoriteGames"" : []
  },
  ]";

  JArray people = JArray.Parse(json);

  var qry = from p in people
            where p["FavoriteGames"].Count() > 0
            select p;

  var peopleWithGames = qry.ToArray();
```

In this example the query is searching for people who have at least one item in their FavoriteGames field in the JSON. This returns the raw Json.NET objects so that you can continue to pull out the data manually as shown in earlier examples, though you can use LINQ to project into classes as well. This technique is commonly used when you want to query the JSON result but end up with a subset of the JSON results as managed objects.

The major reason you want to end up with managed objects (such as instances of classes) is to use data binding. Although data binding can work with JObject objects, there is no way to have the name in a binding element do a lookup into the field of a JSON object. In most cases, you will need to project these into managed objects like so:

```
// Create the client
WebClient client = new WebClient();

// Handle the event
client.DownloadStringCompleted += (s, e) =>
{
  // Make sure the process completed successfully
  if (e.Error == null)
  {
    JArray tweets = JArray.Parse(jsonString);

    var qry = from t in tweets
              where t["source"].Value<string>() == "web"
              let username = t["user"]["screen_name"].Value<string>()
              orderby username
              select new Tweet()
              {
                Text = t["text"].Value<string>(),
                User = new User()
                {
```

```
                    Screen_Name = username,
                }
            };

    tweetList.ItemsSource = qry.ToList();

  }
};

// Start the execution
string req =
"http://api.twitter.com/1/statuses/public_timeline.json";
client.DownloadStringAsync(new Uri(req));
```

By projecting into a class structure, you can end up with classes that easily handle data binding directly to XAML objects. This approach is often better than using serialization because you might need only a subset of the result of the data you retrieved from a REST-based interface. This way, you can use LINQ to filter, sort, and shape your data into objects that better represent what you want to use on the phone.

Web Services

When writing applications for Windows Phone, you can use existing or new web services to communicate with the server. Visual Studio enables you to make references to existing web services, although the free version of Visual Studio for the phone (Visual Studio Express for Windows Phone) does not support a method of creating new web projects to host services. If you need to create your own services to be hosted on your own servers, you will need Visual Studio Professional or better.

You can consume a web service by adding a service reference to your project. In Visual Studio, you can right-click the phone project and select Add Service Reference, as shown in Figure 11.1.

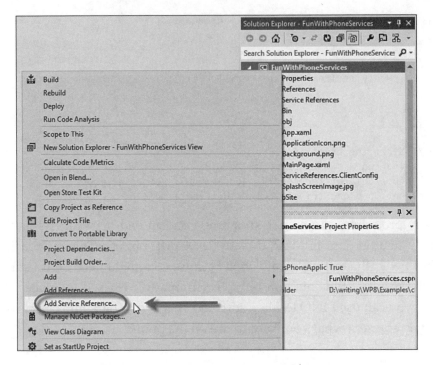

FIGURE 11.1   **Adding a service reference**

This will open a dialog box in which you can enter a service's address or just discover your own web services. The dialog box has an address bar in which you can simply enter the address of the web service; when you click the Go button, Visual Studio will find your service, as shown in Figure 11.2. After your service is discovered, you can specify the namespace and click OK to generate a set of classes that will let you call the web service. The address in this example is a service that returns the weather based upon ZIP Code.[2]

---

2   www.webservicex.net/WeatherForecast.asmx

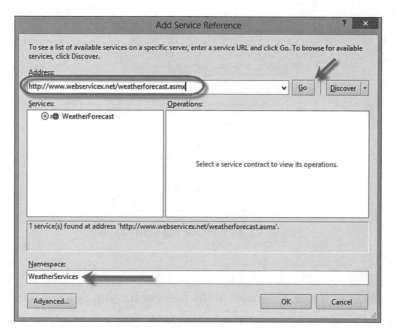

FIGURE 11.2   The Add Service Reference dialog box

This will add the code that is required to interact with the web service.

Source Code for Service References

In the project tree, a new node called Service References will show every service you've added a reference to. Normally these are single nodes for each service, but if you want to look at the code that is generated, you can click the Show All Files button in the Solution Explorer to show all the generated files. The file with the code in it is called Reference.cs, as shown in Figure 11.3.

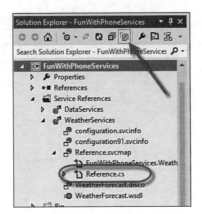

FIGURE 11.3 **Service files displayed**

After the service reference is added, you will have a number of new classes and interfaces generated in the namespace that you specified in the dialog box. The most important of these interfaces is a WebClient-like class that exposes all the methods of the web service as asynchronous methods. The name of this class depends on how the service was written, but it always ends in "Client." In this example the class is called WeatherForecastSoapClient. The service contains an operation called GetWeatherByZipCode, which the service reference splits into a Completed event and an Asynchronous call, as shown here:

```
// Open with default address/binding information
var client = new WeatherForecastSoapClient();

// Handle the Completed Event
client.GetWeatherByZipCodeCompleted += (s, a) =>
  {
    if (a.Error == null)
    {
      theList.ItemsSource = a.Result.Details;
    }
    else
    {
      MessageBox.Show("Failed to get weather data.");
    }
  };

// Get Weather Asynchronously
client.GetWeatherByZipCodeAsync("30307");
```

Calling a web service follows the same pattern as the WebClient class shown earlier in this chapter. The results of the web service are passed into the Completed event as the Result property of the second argument in the event handler. In this case the result the web service returns contains a list of details for each day. By assigning this to the ItemsSource of a control in the XAML, data binding will show the list of details.

In the previous example, you might have noticed that you did not have to specify the server address. When the service reference was added, a new file was added to your project, called ServiceReferences.ClientConfig. This file is the configuration for your service:

```
<configuration>
  <system.serviceModel>
    <bindings>
      <basicHttpBinding>
        <binding name="WeatherForecastSoap"
                 maxBufferSize="2147483647"
                 maxReceivedMessageSize="2147483647">
          <security mode="None" />
        </binding>
      </basicHttpBinding>
    </bindings>
    <client>
      <endpoint
        address="http://www.webservicex.net/WeatherForecast.asmx"
        binding="basicHttpBinding"
        bindingConfiguration="WeatherForecastSoap"
        contract="WeatherServices.WeatherForecastSoap"
        name="WeatherForecastSoap" />
    </client>
  </system.serviceModel>
</configuration>
```

The key part of this configuration for the phone is the address of the endpoint (shown in bold). For a public web service such as the one in the example, you don't need to change this. But for services that you are going to host yourself, you will likely have a test address (probably on your own machine) and need to change this when you deploy your application to specify a production machine. The best solution is to create a duplicate endpoint section and name the endpoints something significant:

```
<client>
  <endpoint address="http://www.webservicex.net/WeatherForecast.asmx"
```

```
           binding="basicHttpBinding"
           bindingConfiguration="WeatherForecastSoap"
           contract="WeatherServices.WeatherForecastSoap"
           name="Production" />
 <endpoint address="http://localhost:8888/WeatherForecast.asmx"
           binding="basicHttpBinding"
           bindingConfiguration="WeatherForecastSoap"
           contract="WeatherServices.WeatherForecastSoap"
           name="Debugging" />
</client>
```

When you create the client object, you can specify the name of the endpoint. For instance, if you wanted to use the production web server in release builds, you could do the following:

```
        // Open with default address/binding information
#if DEBUG
        var client = new WeatherForecastSoapClient("Debugging");
#else
        var client = new WeatherForecastSoapClient("Production");
#endif
```

■ Creating Your Own Services

Although you might find that using web services across the Internet is a common approach, at some point you will need to write your own way of communicating with the phone. Unfortunately, you can't do this with the Visual Studio 2012 Express for Windows Phone that comes free with the phone tools. You could use Visual Web Developer 2012, but that would require that you run and coordinate two developer tools to get it to work. This is awkward and difficult. In general, it is better to get Visual Studio 2012 Professional (or better) so that you can create your own web projects that can host your own web services in the same solution as your phone applications.

Consuming OData

The Open Data Protocol[4] (OData) is a standard way of exposing relational data across a service layer. OData is built on top of other standards including HTTP, JSON, and Atom Publishing Protocol (AtomPub, which is an XML format). OData represents a standard way to query and update data that is web-friendly. It uses REST-based URI syntax for querying, shaping, filtering, ordering, paging, and updating data across the Internet.

How OData Works

OData is meant to make handling typical data operations over HTTP simple. Although it is common in web services to expose different methods for data operations such as Create, Read, Update, and Delete (CRUD), OData takes a different approach. Instead of creating different operations, it leans on the HTTP stack to allow for different HTTP verbs to mean different operations. OData maps HTTP verbs to these CRUD operations, as shown in Table 11.1.

TABLE 11.1 OData HTTP Verb Mappings

HTTP Verb	Data Operation
GET	Read
POST	Update
PUT	Insert
DELETE	Delete

OData supports two data formats: JSON and AtomPub. These formats are used to communicate in both directions. So if you wanted to insert a record into an OData feed, you would use an HTTP PUT to push a JSON or AtomPub version of a new entity. Each type of entity you can manipulate using OData is called an **endpoint.** An endpoint is a type of entity that can be queried, inserted, updated, and/or deleted (although not all operations might be permitted). When you navigate to an OData feed, it returns a document that tells you about the endpoints it exposes. For example, if you navigate to http://www.nerddinner.com/Services/OData.svc, it returns an AtomPub document, like so:

```
<?xml version="1.0" encoding="iso-8859-1" standalone="yes"?>
<service xml:base="http://www.nerddinner.com/Services/OData.svc/"
        xmlns:atom="http://www.w3.org/2005/Atom"
        xmlns:app="http://www.w3.org/2007/app"
```

---

4 http://odata.org

```
          xmlns="http://www.w3.org/2007/app">
  <workspace>
    <atom:title>Default</atom:title>
    <collection href="Dinners">
      <atom:title>Dinners</atom:title>
    </collection>
    <collection href="RSVPs">
      <atom:title>RSVPs</atom:title>
    </collection>
  </workspace>
</service>
```

The collection elements in the AtomPub document tell us that the service supports two endpoints (Dinners and RSVPs). These endpoints have an href attribute that points to their name. This link to the endpoint indicates the path to the data. For example, to show the dinners in the feed, you would resolve the Dinners href attribute to create a URI such as http://www.nerddinners.com/Services/OData.svc/Dinners.

By navigating to that URI, it returns an AtomPub document that contains all the dinners.

The URI

You might be wondering why OData returns an AtomPub document. After all, if OData supports both AtomPub and JSON as data formats, why is the browser returning AtomPub data? OData determines the correct type of data to return based on HTTP Accept headers. When an HTTP call is made, a header usually exists to say which kinds of data the recipient can receive. Browsers make their requests with HTML and XML as accepted types; OData detects this and returns XML (AtomPub). If you were to call this in a context such as from JavaScript on an HTML page, the Accept headers would have JSON as an Accept header and OData would then return JSON instead.

The URI syntax says that the service URI can be post-pended with the path to a named endpoint. So both URIs are the path to the NerdDinner OData endpoints:

- http://www.nerddinner.com/Services/OData.svc/Dinners
- http://www.nerddinner.com/Services/OData.svc/RSVPs

When you look at the AtomPub data returned by the endpoints, each result is in an element called `entry`:

```
<entry>
  <id>http://www.nerddinner.com/Services/OData.svc/Dinners(1)</id>
  <title type="text" />
  <updated>2011-02-13T00:02:47Z</updated>
  <author>
    <name />
  </author>
  <link rel="edit"
        title="Dinner"
        href="Dinners(1)" />
  <link rel="..."
        type="application/atom+xml;type=feed"
        title="RSVPs"
        href="Dinners(1)/RSVPs" />
  <category term="NerdDinnerModel.Dinner"
            scheme="..." />
  <content type="application/xml">
    <m:properties>
      <d:DinnerID m:type="Edm.Int32">1</d:DinnerID>
      <d:Title>ALT.NERD Dinner</d:Title>
      <d:EventDate m:type="Edm.DateTime">
        2009-02-27T20:00:00
      </d:EventDate>
      <d:Description>
Are you in town for the ALT.NET Conference? Are you a .NET person?
Join us at this free, fun, nerd dinner. Well, you pay for your food!
But, still! Come by Red Robin in Redmond Town Center at 8pm Friday.
      </d:Description>
      <d:HostedBy>shanselman</d:HostedBy>
      <d:ContactPhone>503-766-2048</d:ContactPhone>
      <d:Address>7597 170th Ave NE, Redmond, WA</d:Address>
      <d:Country>USA</d:Country>
      <d:Latitude m:type="Edm.Double">47.670172</d:Latitude>
      <d:Longitude m:type="Edm.Double">-122.1143</d:Longitude>
      <d:HostedById>shanselman</d:HostedById>
    </m:properties>
  </content>
</entry>
```

Although this format is usually hidden from you on the phone, there are a couple of pieces of information in an entry that are of interest. In the entry is a list of links. The first is an "edit" link, which shows the address of the entry on its own. The format takes the form of parentheses with the primary key of the entry. So to retrieve just this entry, you could use this link via the relative URI:

```
http://www.nerddinner.com/Services/OData.svc/Dinners(1)
```

The other link listed in this example is a related entity link. To retrieve the list of RSVPs for this particular dinner, you could also use the relative URI:

```
http://www.nerddinner.com/Services/OData.svc/Dinners(1)/RSVPs
```

This is at the heart of the relational nature of the OData feed. You can navigate using simple REST-style URIs to get at related entities.

As mentioned earlier, it depends on the HTTP verb during the request as to what the endpoint does with the request. In the browser, all the requests are GET requests, which means they read the data. OData supports a number of query options that enable you to decide how you want to retrieve the data. These query options enable you to specify a query against the endpoint including filtering, sorting, shaping, and paging. For instance, to sort the dinners by date, you can use the $orderby query option:

```
http://www.nerddinner.com/Services/OData.svc/
Dinners?$orderby=EventDate
```

Table 11.2 shows the supported query options.

TABLE 11.2   OData Query Options

Query Option	Meaning
$orderby	Sorts the results (ascending or descending)
$skip	Seeks into the results before returning results
$top	Limits the results to a set number of results
$filter	Limits the results based on a predicate
$expand	Embeds related entities instead of providing links
$select	Limits the fields returned on an entity

Each of these can be combined to change the result from the OData feed. Let's look at each in the sections that follow.

`$orderby`

This query option enables you to specify one or more field names (separated by a comma) to use when sorting the results. Each field name can have the suffix "desc" added to mark that the sorting should be done in descending order. Some examples include the following:

```
http://.../Dinners?$orderby=Title
http://.../Dinners?$orderby=Title desc
http://.../Dinners?$orderby=Title,EventDate
http://.../Dinners?$orderby=Title desc,EventDate
http://.../Dinners?$orderby=Title desc,EventDate desc
```

`$skip` **and** `$top`

These query options are used to limit and span the number of results in the entire result. The `$top` query option specifies the maximum number of results to return and the `$skip` query option is used to specify how many of the results to not return before starting to return results. Although using the `$top` query option to return only a set number of results is typical on its own, `$skip` is used almost exclusively with the `$top` option to provide a paging mechanism. When using `$top` and `$skip` for paging, `$skip` should be preceded by the `$top` query option so that the records are skipped first and then limited by the number. Otherwise, you will not get the paging you expect. Here are some samples:

```
http://.../Dinners?$top=10
http://.../Dinners?$skip=10&$top=10
```

`$filter`

The purpose of the `$filter` query option is to provide a predicate with which to return only results that match the predicate. The language definition for predicates is a robust set of operators and functions. Typically, you will need to specify the name of a field to use in the predicate along with an operator and/or functions. The `$filter` query can specify the name of a simple field such as

```
http://.../Dinners?$filter=Country eq 'China'
```

In this example, Country is the field name followed by an operator (eq means equals) and a value to compare it to. Strings should be delimited by single quotes. Instead of the simple field name, you can use navigation to a related entity as well (as long as it is a 1-to-1 relationship). For example:

```
http://.../Suppliers?$filter=Address/City eq 'Atlanta'
```

In this example, the Supplier has a property called Address that contains a City field. So you can filter the Suppliers by the city name in this way. Table 11.3 lists the operators, and Table 11.4 lists the functions you can use in a $filter query option.

TABLE 11.3 $filter **Operators**

Operator	Description	Example
Logical Operators		
Eq	Equal	/Suppliers?$filter=Address/City eq 'Redmond'
Ne	Not equal	/Suppliers?$filter=Address/City ne 'London'
Gt	Greater than	/Products?$filter=Price gt 20
Ge	Greater than or equal	/Products?$filter=Price ge 10
Lt	Less than	/Products?$filter=Price lt 20
Le	Less than or equal	/Products?$filter=Price le 100
And	Logical and	.../Products?$filter=Price le 200 and Price gt 3.5
Or	Logical or	.../Products?$filter=Price le 3.5 or Price gt 200
Not	Logical negation	.../Products?$filter=not endswith (Description,'milk')
Arithmetic Operators		
Add	Addition	.../Products?$filter=Price add 5 gt 10
Sub	Subtraction	.../Products?$filter=Price sub 5 gt 10
Mul	Multiplication	.../Products?$filter=Price mul 2 gt 2000
Div	Division	.../Products?$filter=Price div 2 gt 4
Mod	Modulo	.../Products?$filter=Price mod 2 eq 0
Grouping Operator		
( )	Precedence grouping	.../Products?$filter=(Price sub 5) gt 10

TABLE 11.4 $filter **Functions**[5]

Function	Example
String Functions	
bool substringof(string po, string p1)	.../Customers?$filter=substringof ('Alfreds',CompanyName) eq true
bool endswith(string p0, string p1)	.../Customers?$filter=endswith (CompanyName,'Futterkiste') eq true
bool startswith(string p0, string p1)	.../Customers?$filter=startswith (CompanyName,'Alfr') eq true
int length(string p0)	.../Customers?$filter=length(Company Name)eq 19
int indexof(string p0, string p1)	.../Customers?$filter=indexof(Company Name,'lfreds') eq 1
string replace(string p0, string find, stringreplace)	.../Customers?$filter=replace(Company Name,' ', '') eq 'AlfredsFutterkiste'
string substring(string p0, int pos)	.../Customers?$filter=substring (CompanyName,1) eq 'lfreds Futterkiste'
string substring(string p0, int pos, intlength)	.../Customers?$filter=substring (CompanyName,1, 2) eq 'lf'
string tolower(string p0)	.../Customers?$filter=tolower(Company Name)eq 'alfreds futterkiste'
string toupper(string p0)	.../Customers?$filter=toupper(Company Name)eq 'ALFREDS FUTTERKISTE'
string trim(string p0)	.../Customers?$filter=trim(Company Name)eq 'Alfreds Futterkiste'
string concat(string p0, string p1)	.../Customers?$filter=concat (concat(City,', '), Country) eq 'Berlin, Germany'
Date Functions	
int day(DateTime p0)	.../Employees?$filter=day(BirthDate) eq 8
int hour(DateTime p0)	.../Employees?$filter=hour(Birth Date)eq 0
int minute(DateTime p0)	.../Employees?$filter=minute(Birth Date)eq 0
int month(DateTime p0)	.../Employees?$filter=month(Birth Date)eq 12

---

5 Function table from the OData spec: www.odata.org/developers/protocols/uri-conventions# FilterSystemQueryOption

int second(DateTime p0)	.../Employees?$filter=second(Birth Date)eq 0
int year(DateTime p0)	.../Employees?$filter=year(Birth Date)eq 1948
Math Functions	
double round(double p0)	.../Orders?$filter=round(Freight)eq 32
decimal round(decimal p0)	.../Orders?$filter=round(Freight)eq 32
double floor(double p0)	.../Orders?$filter=filter=round (Freight)eq 32
decimal floor(decimal p0)	.../Orders?$filter=floor(Freight)eq 32
double ceiling(double p0)	.../Orders?$filter=ceiling(Freight) eq 33
decimal ceiling(decimal p0)	.../Orders?$filter=floor(Freight)eq 33
Type Functions	
bool IsOf(type p0)	.../Orders?$filter=isof('Northwind Model.Order')
bool IsOf(expression p0, type p1)	.../Orders?$filter=isof(ShipCountry,' Edm.String')

$expand

The purpose of this query option is to enable you to embed specific related data in the results of a request. As you saw earlier, you can access a related entity by following the path to the related entries, like so:

```
http://.../Dinners(1)/RSVPs
```

The $expand query option lets you return not only the main endpoint you are making a quest from, but also the related entries in a single call. For instance, you can include the RSVPs in the request for dinners, like so:

```
http://.../Dinners?$expand=RSVPs
```

This will return the dinners plus any RSVPs for those dinners. If you have a complex chain of related entities such as Customer→Order→ OrderDetails→Products, a single $expand query option can include the entire chain by including the path to the deepest part of the object tree:

```
http://.../Customers?$expand=Orders/OrderDetails/Products
```

Finally, you can include multiple expansions by separating individual expansion query options with a comma:

```
http://.../Customers?$expand=Orders/OrderDetails,SalesPeople
```

This request would return the customers and include the orders and the details for each order, as well as any salespeople for each customer.

$select

This query option is used to limit the fields the endpoint returns in the request. The `$select` query option lets you specify a comma-delimited list of fields to return:

```
http://.../Dinners?$select=DinnerID,Title,EventDate
```

Use of this query option tells the OData feed to return only the specified fields:

```
<entry>
  <id>http://www.nerddinner.com/Services/OData.svc/Dinners(1)</id>
  <title type="text"></title>
  <updated>2011-02-13T02:36:44Z</updated>
  <author>
    <name />
  </author>
  <link rel="edit" title="Dinner" href="Dinners(1)" />
  <category term="NerdDinnerModel.Dinner" scheme="..." />
  <content type="application/xml">
    <m:properties>
      <d:DinnerID m:type="Edm.Int32">1</d:DinnerID>
      <d:Title>ALT.NERD Dinner</d:Title>
      <d:EventDate m:type="Edm.DateTime">
        2009-02-27T20:00:00
      </d:EventDate>
    </m:properties>
  </content>
</entry>
```

Note that when you use the `$select` query option, you are specifying the fields to return for every entity. This affects when you use it in conjunction with the `$expand` query option in that you must include the fields you want from the related entities as well. For example, you could use `$select` to limit the fields from the main endpoint as well as the related entries:

```
/Dinners?$expand=RSVPs&$select=Title,EventDate,RSVPs/AttendeeName
```

This query would result in filtering the main endpoint (Dinners) but would include only the AttendeeName in the related entry (RSVPs).

Using OData on the Phone

One of the unique challenges of the phone is to create efficient access to data supported by services. Public services such as Twitter, eBay, and others have already defined the types of services they are supporting. OData is one of those formats you might find yourself supporting if you want to consume data from a provider that supports it. You also might decide to expose your own data via OData when you want to expose it to the phone. The main reason OData is a compelling option on the phone is that it enables you to be very specific with how you want to query the data. Being able to tune an application and return only the data (for instance, fields) required using the $select query option means you can be very efficient when accessing data via the phone.

Another reason using OData with the phone is compelling is that it is supported by a rich client-side model to the data you are dealing with. This is especially helpful if you need to be able to support data modification. The OData client for the phone supports a client-side context object that tracks changed objects for you automatically and enables you to batch those changes back to the server.

OData supports a variety of platforms (PHP, iOS, .NET, and Java), and support for OData is included natively in the Windows Phone SDK.

Generating a Service Reference for OData

In the Web Services section, you used Visual Studio to add a service reference, which built an object model for the service. Creating a service reference to an OData feed is accomplished in the same way. You simply use the Add Service Reference option on your project (refer to Figure 11.1 earlier in this chapter). When the Add Service Reference dialog box appears, you insert an OData feed (or click Discover for data services in your own project), as shown in Figure 11.4.

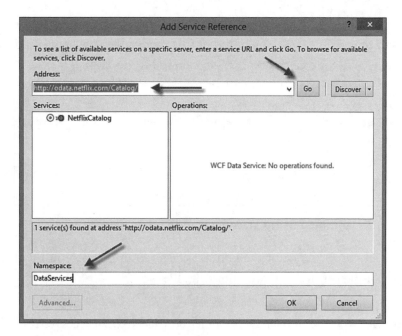

FIGURE 11.4   **Adding a service reference to an OData feed**

Much like adding a service reference to a web service, adding a service reference to an OData feed requires a feed location (for instance, http://www.nerddinner.com/Services/OData.svc). When you press the Go button, it retrieves the metadata about the feed to enable you to create the reference classes to the OData feed. Adding this service reference not only creates classes for the different entities on the OData feed, but also creates a context class that is used when interacting with the OData feed. By using this context class, you can retrieve and update data in the OData feed (assuming it supports updating). Let's see how that is accomplished.

Retrieving Data

To start accessing data with OData, you must create an instance of the context class. This class gives you access to the different endpoints in the service. Depending on the service, this class name could end in "Entities" or "Context." For example, in the NerdDinner OData service, it is called `NerdDinnerEntities`. This context class (and the other classes generated by the service reference) are contained in a namespace specified by the OData service. Figure 11.5 shows adding the `DataServices` namespace to have access to the entity class. The name of this namespace was specified in the Add Service Reference dialog box (shown in Figure 11.4).

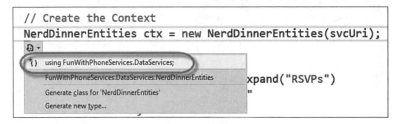

```
// Create the Context
NerdDinnerEntities ctx = new NerdDinnerEntities(svcUri);
```

FIGURE 11.5 **Adding a using statement to the data service**

Creating an instance of the context class requires that you include the address of the service you are querying, like so:

```
// The Service Address
var svcUri = new Uri("http://www.nerddinner.com/Services/OData.svc");

// Create the Context
NerdDinnerEntities ctx = new NerdDinnerEntities(svcUri);
```

This context class enables you to track the date you get back from the server, but the `DataServiceCollection` class is at the center of how you will query data. The `DataServiceCollection` class is a generic collection that supports the `INotifyCollectionChanged` interface so it easily supports data binding. You effectively can ask the collection to load itself with a query, as shown here:

```
// Craft the Query
var query = from d in ctx.Dinners
            where d.HostedBy == "Shawn Wildermuth"
            orderby d.Title
            select d;

// Create a collection to hold the results
DataServiceCollection<Dinner> results = new
  DataServiceCollection<Dinner>();

// Handle the completed event to do error handling
results.LoadCompleted += (s, e) =>
  {
```

```
    if (e.Error != null)
    {
      MessageBox.Show("An error occurred");
    }
  };

// Load the Collection using the Query
results.LoadAsync(query);

// Bind it to the UI
theList.ItemsSource = results;
```

Although you could craft the query directly via the URI syntax, the OData libraries for the phone enable you to use LINQ to describe your query, which it automatically converts to the URI query syntax for you. Next, the code creates a new instance of the DataServiceCollection that expects it to be filled with Dinner objects. Then it handles the collection's LoadCompleted event to handle any errors. And finally it calls LoadAsync to actually start the operation asynchronously. At that point, you can bind the collection to the user interface, and the query will execute and fill in the DataServiceCollection in the background. After the collection is filled, the data binding will take over and display the results.

If you are using projections in your queries, the results will continue to be the full objects but only the requested fields will be filled in. For example, if you request only some of an entity's properties, it will return just those properties as shown here:

```
// Craft the Query
var query = from d in ctx.Dinners
            where d.Country == "USA"
            orderby d.Title
            select new Dinner()
            {
              DinnerID = d.DinnerID,
              Title = d.Title,
              HostedBy = d.HostedBy
            };
```

If you are using expansion in your queries, the results will continue to be the main objects you've requested, but the navigated objects will be serialized as part of your query. For instance, adding an expansion (via the Expand method) will eager-load any related entities:

```
// Craft the Query
var query = from d in ctx.Dinners.Expand("RSVPs")
            where d.Country == "USA"
            orderby d.Title
            select d;
```

Updating Data

Querying the OData feed via the DataServiceCollection and context classes enables you to track any changes to the collection so that as objects are changed that exist in the DataServiceCollection, those objects are marked as changed. In addition, if you want to delete an item, you can simply remove it from the DataServiceCollection. Removing the item from the collection marks it as a deleted element. And finally, you can add items to the collection to mark them as new (or inserted) objects. You can see examples of this here:

```
// Changing items from the collection marks them as changed
Dinner dinner = _dinnerCollection[0];
dinner.EventDate = DateTime.Today;

// Adding Items marks them as New (Inserted)
Dinner newDinner = new Dinner()
{
  EventDate = DateTime.Today,
    HostedBy = "ShawnWildermuth"
};
_dinnerCollection.Add(newDinner);

// Removing Items marks them as Deleted
Dinner oldDinner = _dinnerCollection[1];
_dinnerCollection.Remove(oldDinner);
```

As changes are tracked, you can update those changes with the server (assuming you have permission to update the server) by calling BeginSaveChanges on the context object. Remember, even though the DataServiceCollection is the holder of the objects, ultimately it's the context object that actually tracks them so that when you call BeginSaveChanges it will batch these changes back to the server, like so:

```
// Save the changes
_theContext.BeginSaveChanges(new AsyncCallback(r =>
  {
```

```
    // Response is a collection of errors
    DataServiceResponse response = _theContext.EndSaveChanges(r);

    // If there are any errors, show message
    if (response.Any(op => op.Error != null))
    {
      MessageBox.Show("Sorry, update failed.");
    }
  }), null);
```

Unlike reading data using OData, the saving of changes uses an older asynchronous style using an AsyncCallback object. The code can be simplified (as shown here) by using a lambda to handle the changes inline, but it still requires the BeginSaveChanges and EndSaveChanges methods to be called. The DataServiceResponse object returned at the end of the save operation is a collection of OperationResponse objects. These OperationResponse objects contain the exception that was encountered on the server. In this instance, the LINQ Any operator checks whether any of the responses have an error, which is the Exception. If the collection is empty or responses do not contain errors, you can assume that the operation completed successfully.

▪ OData and Transactions

Updates to an OData service are handled in a transactional way so that if any errors were found, you can assume the complete update failed.

Using Push Notifications

At times you will want to keep the user apprised of some change that happen on the server. Although you could write a background agent (as shown in Chapter 9 "Databases and Storage"), making network requests every 30 minutes might not be often enough. You might also decide that you want to determine when to update a phone remotely (as close to the data as possible). So instead, you should use the phone's ability to receive messages from the cloud. These messages are called **push notifications**.

Push notifications enable your application to register a particular phone to receive these notifications. After the phone is registered, you can send messages from an Internet-connected server to Microsoft's Push Notification Service (MPNS). This service is hosted by Microsoft and enables your messages to reach users' phones (and deals with the hard problems of out-of-range and powered-off phones). Using push notifications does require that you have a way to communicate with a service you are responsible for; typically this is a web service hosted on a public Internet server. You can see the general flow of push notifications in Figure 11.6.

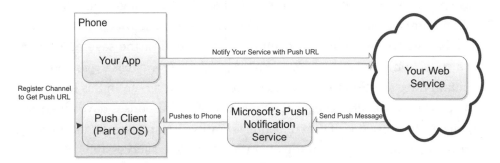

FIGURE 11.6　Push notification message flow

Using push notifications requires several steps, but they are all fairly straightforward:

- Your app opens a push notification channel.
- Your app receives a special URL that can be used to send messages to this specific phone.
- Your app sends that URL to a service that wishes to send you notifications.
- Sometime later, the service can post a new message to MPNS using the special URL from the phone.
- The MPNS finds your phone and sends the message to the phone.

Push notifications can be used to do three tasks on the phone: alert the user with a toast notification, update a Live Tile, and send your application raw messages. You will see how to do all three, but let's start with the basics so that you can learn how all the moving parts work together.

Push Notification Requirements

Using push notifications comes with several requirements. To use push notifications, you must do the following:

- Add the push notification requirement to your WMAppManifest. xml file:

  ```
  ...
  <Capabilities>
    <Capability Name="ID_CAP_PUSH_NOTIFICATION"/>
  </Capabilities>
  ...
  ```

- Alert the user in the user interface of the application (usually during the first launch of your application) that you are using push notifications.
- Allow the user to disable push notifications.

You can have only one push notification channel per application. In addition, a limited number of applications on a phone can use push notifications. When you first open your HTTP notification channel, you might receive an error message stating that the channel could not be opened. This is typically thrown when there are too many push notification applications on the phone.

Preparing the Application for Push Notifications

To get started, you will need an instance of a class that will register your application for push notifications as well as listen for certain events (for example, notifications, errors, and so on). This class is called HttpNotificationChannel. When you launch your application the first time, you will register this instance of the application (specifically the application on this particular phone) with the MPNS by creating a new instance of the class and passing in a channel name that is specific to the application (for instance, the app name):

```
HttpNotificationChannel  myChannel =
  new HttpNotificationChannel("MYAPP");
```

The name of the channel is usually the name of the application, but because you can have only one channel, it is not important that this name be unique to the phone or user. On subsequent launches of your application, you can get the channel by calling the static Find method using the name like so:

```
HttpNotificationChannel  myChannel =
  HttpNotificationChannel.Find("MYAPP");
```

In practice, determining whether this is the first invocation can be tedious, so you should just try to find the channel, and if it is not found just create it like so:

```
public class PushSignup
{
  const string CHANNELNAME = "FunWithToast";
  private HttpNotificationChannel _myChannel = null;

  public void CreateChannel()
  {
    try
    {
      if (_myChannel == null)
      {
        // Attempt to get the channel
        _myChannel = HttpNotificationChannel.Find(CHANNELNAME);

        // Can't Find the Channel, so create it
        if (_myChannel == null)
        {
          _myChannel = new HttpNotificationChannel(CHANNELNAME);
...
```

This way, you won't need to worry about keeping state on the first invocation of your application.

After you have a valid channel, that channel will give your server access to a special URI that is used to send push notifications. Again, the channel is a little different, depending on whether it was newly created or located with the Find method. You would think that you should be able to take the newly created channel and retrieve the URI, but that only works on existing channels (that is, channels located with Find):

```
...

// If the channel uri is valid now, then send it to the server
// Otherwise it'll be registered when the URI is updated
if (_myChannel.ChannelUri != null)
{
  // Use the ChannelUri to tell your server about the phone
}

...
```

Newly created channels will get the URI asynchronously. To know when the URI is available, you need to register the ChannelUriUpdated event on the channel object. When this event is fired, you can use the ChannelUri. In practice you should handle this in both cases to ensure that any changes to the URI are caught and reported:

```
_myChannel.ChannelUriUpdated += myChannel_ChannelUriUpdated;

...

void myChannel_ChannelUriUpdated(object sender,
                                 NotificationChannelUriEventArgs e)
{
  // Use the ChannelUri to tell your server about the phone
}
```

After you have the channel open and a way to get the ChannelUri, you're ready to set up the server side of the equation.

Setting Up the Server for Push Notifications

Because push notifications come from the server (and are not necessarily triggered by a running application on the phone), you need some code somewhere on a server that is reachable by the phone. The reasoning for this is that the server uses the channel URI to send any push notifications to the phone. How you choose to send that information to the server is up to you, but a common approach is to use a simple web service.

■ Server-Side Code

There is nothing special about the server-side code that requires the server technology and operating system to be Microsoft servers or ASP.NET, but this example will use WCF and ASP.NET because that is a common approach. You can use whatever server technology and operating systems you choose. This chapter does not go into detail about how WCF or ASP.NET works. If you are not proficient in .NET server-side technologies, you will need an additional reference for those technologies.

For example, we can have an ASP.NET web project that hosts a WCF service that accepts the channel URI from the phone. In this example, I've set up a simple database to hold the channel URIs as well as a WCF service that can accept the channel URIs. The WCF service interface looks simple enough:

```
[ServiceContract]
public interface IMyPhoneService
{
  [OperationContract]
  void RegisterPhoneApp(string channelUrl);
}
```

The expectation is that the phone will call a service method with the channel URI when it receives it so that the server has a list of people to notify. It would be common to include additional information, but for this example let's keep it simple. The implementation of the service would look like this:

```
public void RegisterPhoneApp(string channelUrl)
{
  // Add to list of URIs to notify
  using (var ctx = new PhoneEntities())
  {
    if (ctx.Phones.Where(p => p.PhoneUrl == channelUrl).Count() == 0)
    {
      var phone = Phone.CreatePhone(0, channelUrl, DateTime.Now);
      ctx.Phones.AddObject(phone);
      ctx.SaveChanges();
    }
  }
}
```

In this case the code just uses the Entity Framework to store the channel URI in the database for use later. This means the phone code has to change to actually use this web service. To do this, you can just create a small helper method that calls the service:

```
void SendChannelUriToService(string uri)
{
  var client = new MyPhoneServiceClient();

  // Handle the completed event
  client.RegisterPhoneAppCompleted += (s, e) =>
    {
      if (e.Error != null)
      {
        // Log Error (User Can't Fix this error)
      }
    };

  // Send the channel URI to the server
  client.RegisterPhoneAppAsync(uri);
}
```

This code should look familiar because it is just a web service call similar to what we discussed earlier in the chapter. Now that you have the helper method, you can call this when you have the channel URI:

```
public void CreateChannel()
{
  try
  {
    if (_myChannel == null)
    {
      // Attempt to get the channel
      _myChannel = HttpNotificationChannel.Find(CHANNELNAME);

      // Can't Find the Channel, so create it
      if (_myChannel == null)
      {
        _myChannel = new HttpNotificationChannel(CHANNELNAME);

        // Add Event Handlers
        _myChannel.ChannelUriUpdated += myChannel_ChannelUriUpdated;

        // Open the channel since it's a new channel
        _myChannel.Open();
      }
      else
```

```
      {
        // Add Event Handlers
        _myChannel.ChannelUriUpdated += myChannel_ChannelUriUpdated;
      }

      // If the channel uri is valid now, then send it to the server
      // Otherwise it'll be registered when the URI is updated
      if (_myChannel.ChannelUri != null)
      {
        // Use the ChannelUri to tell your server about the phone
        SendChannelUriToService(_myChannel.ChannelUri.ToString());
      }
    }

    return;
  }
  catch (Exception)
  {
    MessageBox.Show("Failed to create Push Notification Channel");
  }
}

...

void myChannel_ChannelUriUpdated(object sender,
                           NotificationChannelUriEventArgs e)
{
  // Use the ChannelUri to tell your server about the phone
  SendChannelUriToService(e.ChannelUri.ToString());
}
```

With the channel URI in hand, you are ready to push notification messages to the phone!

> ## ▪ Authenticating Push Notifications
>
> The MPNS can use a custom certificate you send to Microsoft during the submission process for authenticating your phone. Push notifications are specifically from your own server(s). The documentation covers this in detail and is beyond the scope of this book.

Raw Notifications

The first type of push notification you can send is a raw notification. This type of message is sent directly to a running application. If your application isn't running when you send a raw notification, it is just dropped. Raw notifications enable you to send any sort of message to your application.

To send a raw notification, you have to use an HTTP call to POST a message to MPNS. The messages you send to this service are simple HTTP calls and are not using web services. So you can write your server code to send a message using the HttpWebRequest and HttpWebResponse classes. First, you would set up your request like so:

```
HttpWebRequest request =
  (HttpWebRequest)WebRequest.Create(pushUri);

// For Raw Update use type of body
// (text/plain or text/xml are typical)
request.ContentType = "text/plain";

// Specify the HTTP verb (must be POST)
request.Method = "POST";
```

This creates the web request, sets the content type of the message (usually a string or XML fragment), and specifies that the request is posting data. Next, you need to add some headers to make the push notification message make sense to the MPNS:

```
// Use a generated unique ID to prevent duplicate push messages
request.Headers.Add("X-MessageID", Guid.NewGuid().ToString());

// Send Raw Immediate requires class == 3
request.Headers.Add("X-NotificationClass", "3");
```

To ensure that the message doesn't get duplicated, you should add a message ID header with a unique ID. The X-NotificationClass header is required for the MPNS to know how to handle the request. This header needs to be 3 for a raw request. The X-NotificationClass header specifies the type of message (3 is a raw notification). This tells the MPNS to send the message immediately. It also enables you to add 10 to the value if you want to post it to be sent in 450 seconds (7.5 minutes), or you can add 20 to send it in 900 seconds (15 minutes). So, for a raw notification, the valid values are 3, 13, and 23, respectively. Next, you will need to push the message into the request stream to have it become part of the message:

```
// Send it
byte[] notificationMessage = Encoding.UTF8.GetBytes(message);
request.ContentLength = notificationMessage.Length;
using (Stream requestStream = request.GetRequestStream())
{
  requestStream.Write(notificationMessage,
                      0,
                      notificationMessage.Length);
}
```

First, the message is encoded into UTF-8 and converted to a byte array
so that you can stuff it into the request stream. After the size of the message
is known, you can specify the length of the message (ContentLength). Then
you can use the stream to push the message into the request. Finally, you
are ready to send the message:

```
// Sends the notification and gets the response.
try
{
  HttpWebResponse response = (HttpWebResponse)request.GetResponse();

  return HandleResponse(response);
}
catch (Exception ex)
{
  return string.
  Concat("Exception during sending message", ex.Message);
}
```

By calling the GetResponse method, you will retrieve an HttpWebResponse,
which will tell you about the status of the message you just posted to the
server. Here is the entire example for pushing a raw notification to a phone:

```
string SendRawMessage(string pushUri, string message)
{
  HttpWebRequest request =
    (HttpWebRequest)WebRequest.Create(pushUri);

  // For Raw Update use type of body
  // (text/plain or text/xml are typical)
  request.ContentType = "text/plain";

  // Specify the HTTP verb (must be POST)
  request.Method = "POST";

  // Use a generated unique ID to prevent duplicate push messages
  request.Headers.Add("X-MessageID", Guid.NewGuid().ToString());
```

```
    // Send Raw Immediate requires class == 3
    request.Headers.Add("X-NotificationClass", "3");

    // Send it
    byte[] notificationMessage = Encoding.UTF8.GetBytes(message);
    request.ContentLength = notificationMessage.Length;
    using (Stream requestStream = request.GetRequestStream())
    {
      requestStream.Write(notificationMessage,
                          0,
                          notificationMessage.Length);
    }

    // Sends the notification and gets the response.
    try
    {
      HttpWebResponse response = (HttpWebResponse)request.
GetResponse();

      return HandleResponse(response);
    }
    catch (Exception ex)
    {
      return string.Concat("Exception during sending message",
                           ex.Message);
    }
  }
}
```

The response from the server takes the form of two pieces of information that are handled in the HandleResponse method:

```
string HandleResponse(HttpWebResponse response)
{
  // Pull status from headers if they exist
  string notificationStatus =
    response.Headers["X-NotificationStatus"];
  string deviceStatus = response.Headers["X-DeviceConnectionStatus"];
  string subscriptionStatus =
    response.Headers["X-SubscriptionStatus"];

  switch (response.StatusCode)
  {
    case HttpStatusCode.OK: // 200
      {
        //
        return "Success";
      }
    case HttpStatusCode.BadRequest: // 400
      {
```

```
        return
"Failed, bad request";
      }
    case HttpStatusCode.Unauthorized: // 401
      {
        return
"Not authorized";
      }
    case HttpStatusCode.NotFound: // 404
      {
        return
"Not Found";        }
    case HttpStatusCode.MethodNotAllowed: // 405
      {
        return "Only POST Allowed";
      }
    case HttpStatusCode.NotAcceptable: // 406
      {
        return "Request Not Acceptable";
      }
    case HttpStatusCode.PreconditionFailed: // 412
      {
        return "Failed to Meet Preconditions";
      }
    case HttpStatusCode.ServiceUnavailable: // 503
      {
        return "Service down";
      }

  }

  return "Success";
}
```

First, the service returns three headers with the response to indicate certain status information to help you determine what the service actually did. Table 11.5 details these headers.

These header response values will mean different things depending on the HTTP status code that was returned. Table 11.6 shows the mix of HTTP status codes and these header values (from the Windows Phone OS documentation).

Using the information, you can glean from the HTTP status and the headers, you can determine what to do with the message. This example does not show any retry mechanism and simply loses the notification if the message fails. Depending on the value of the message, you may choose which retry level you need to accomplish on the server.

TABLE 11.5 Push Notification Response Headers

Value	Description
X-NotificationStatus	The status of the notification that was attempted. Valid values include Received, Dropped, and QueueFull.
X-DeviceConnectionStatus	The status of the device the notification attempted to push your message to. Valid values include Connected, InActive, Disconnected, and TempDisconnected.
X-SubscriptionStatus	The status of the channel that the phone created. Valid values include Active and Expired.

TABLE 11.6 Response Codes and Header Status Codes

Response Code	Notification Status	Device Connection Status	Subscription Status	Comments
200 OK	Received	Connected	Active	The notification request was accepted and queued for delivery.
200 OK	Received	Temporarily Disconnected	Active	The notification request was accepted and queued for delivery. However, the device is temporarily disconnected.
200 OK	QueueFull	Connected	Active	Queue overflow. The web service should resend the notification later. A best practice is to use an exponential backoff algorithm in minute increments.

200 OK	QueueFull	Temporarily Disconnected	Active	Queue overflow. The web service should resend the notification later. A best practice is to use an exponential backoff algorithm in minute increments.
200 OK	Suppressed	Connected	Active	The push notification was received and dropped by the Push Notification Service. The Suppressed status can occur if the notification channel was configured to suppress push notifications for a particular push notification class.
200 OK	Suppressed	Temp Disconnected	Active	The push notification was received and dropped by the Push Notification Service. The Suppressed status can occur if the notification channel was configured to suppress push notifications for a particular push notification class.
400 BadRequest	N/A	N/A	N/A	This error occurs when the web service sends a notification request with a bad XML document or malformed notification URI.

401 Unauthorzed	N/A	N/A	N/A	Sending this notification is unauthorized. This error can occur for one of the following reasons.
				There is a mismatch between the subject name of the certificate on the web service and the subject name of the certificate on the Push Notification Service.
				The token has been modified.
				The token is not valid for its subscription.
404 Not Found	Dropped	Connected	Expired	The subscription is invalid and is not present on the Push Notification Service. The web service should stop sending new notifications to this subscription, and drop the subscription state for its corresponding application session.

404 Not Found	Dropped	Temporarily Disconnected	Expired	The subscription is invalid and is not present on the Push Notification Service. The web service should stop sending new notifications to this subscription, and drop the subscription state for its client.
404 Not Found	Dropped	Disconnected	Expired	The subscription is invalid and is not present on the Push Notification Service. The web service should stop sending new notifications to this subscription, and drop the subscription state for its client.
405 Method Not Allowed	N/A	N/A	N/A	Invalid method (PUT, DELETE, CREATE). Only POST is allowed when sending a notification request.

406 Not Acceptable	Dropped	Connected	Active	This error occurs when an unauthenticated web service has reached the per-day throttling limit for a subscription. The web service can try to resend the push notification every hour after receiving this error. The web service might need to wait up to 24 hours before normal notification flow will resume.
406 Not Acceptable	Dropped	Temp Disconnected	Active	This error occurs when an unauthenticated web service has reached the per-day throttling limit for a subscription. The web service can try to resend the push notification every hour after receiving this error. The web service might need to wait up to 24 hours before normal notification flow will resume.

| 412 Precondition Failed | Dropped | Inactive | N/A | The device is in an inactive state. The web service might reattempt sending the request one time per hour at maximum after receiving this error. If the web service violates the maximum of one reattempt per hour, the Push Notification Service will deregister or permanently block the web service. |
| 503 Service Unavailable | N/A | N/A | N/A | The Push Notification Service is unable to process the request. The web service should resend the notification later. A best practice is to use an exponential backoff algorithm in minute increments. |

■ SOCKS Proxies

If your phone attaches to a network (for instance, Wi-Fi) that requires a SOCKS proxy to get out to the Internet, push messages will not work.

Now that you know how to send the message to the phone, it's time to discuss how the phone reacts to the message. The only change in the phone code to receive raw notifications is to handle the HttpNotification-Received event to receive the specific type of message:

```
_myChannel.HttpNotificationReceived +=
  channel_HttpNotificationReceived;
```

This event is fired when the application receives a raw notification:

```
void channel_HttpNotificationReceived(object sender,
                                      HttpNotificationEventArgs e)
{
  StreamReader rdr = new StreamReader(e.Notification.Body);
  string msg = rdr.ReadToEnd();

  Deployment.Current.Dispatcher.BeginInvoke(() =>
  {
    MessageBox.Show(string.Concat("Raw received while app running:",
                                  msg));
  });
}
```

The event sends an object in the `HttpNotificationEventArgs` object that contains information about the notification, including the body of the message as well as the headers. Depending on how you intend to use the raw message, you might add your information as the body of the message or as headers. The event here gives you access to either. It is entirely application-specific how you use raw notifications.

> ## ■ Debugging Push Notifications
>
> Debugging both the phone and the ASP.NET server-side code requires that you set up your solution to start both projects. You can do this via the Solution Properties as shown in Figure 11.7. Alternative, you could log this information for later analysis or error handling.

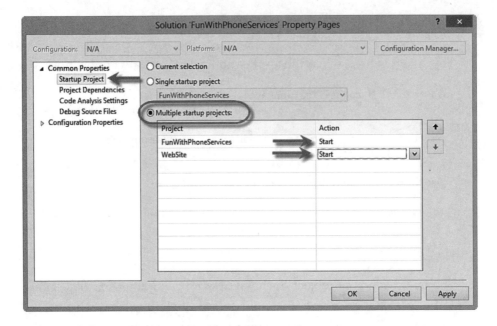

FIGURE 11.7   **Debugging push notifications**

Sending Toast Notifications

Toast notifications are simple messages that appear on the top of the phone to alert the user with a specific message from the application. If the user taps the toast message, the application that notified the user will launch. Toast messages are shown only when your application is not currently running. They provide a convenient way to get the user to go to your application and see new or updated information.

For your application to accept toast messages, you must tell the phone's shell service that you want to accept toast notifications. You do this by adding this code to the phone's channel registration:

```
// Make sure that you can accept toast notifications
if (!_myChannel.IsShellToastBound) _myChannel.BindToShellToast();
```

Because toast messages are typically received while the application is not running, they are usually used to alert users of certain information or to alert them to start the application. You might also want to be notified when a toast message is sent while your application is running. You can do this by handling the ShellToastNotificationReceived event on the channel:

```
_myChannel.ShellToastNotificationReceived +=
    channel_ShellToastNotificationReceived;
```

This event enables you to be alerted if a toast message comes in while the application is running:

```
void channel_ShellToastNotificationReceived(object sender,
                                            NotificationEventArgs e)
{
    Deployment.Current.Dispatcher.BeginInvoke(() =>
        {
            MessageBox.Show("Toast received while app running");
        });
}
```

■ Toast Notifications

If a toast message comes in while the application is running, the toast notification will not appear. Toast notifications appear only when your application is not currently in the foreground.

Back on the server, creating these types of messages is similar to creating a raw notification, but the format of the toast message is specific. The message you send must be a small XML document that contains information about what to show in the toast message:

```
<?xml version="1.0" encoding="utf-8"?>
<wp:Notification xmlns:wp="WPNotification">
  <wp:Toast>
    <wp:Text1>Title</wp:Text1>
    <wp:Text2>Message</wp:Text2>
  </wp:Toast>
</wp:Notification>
```

The message must look exactly like this, except the first (bolded) part of the message will be in the Text1 section and the second part (unbolded) will be in the Text2 section. The code to send this message is the same as a raw message, but with some minor changes:

```csharp
string SendToastMessage(string pushUri, string message)
{
  HttpWebRequest request =
    (HttpWebRequest)WebRequest.Create(pushUri);

  // For Raw Update use type of body
  // (text/plain or text/xml are typical)
  request.ContentType = "text/xml";

  // Specify the HTTP verb (must be POST)
  request.Method = "POST";

  // Use a generated unique ID to prevent duplicate push messages
  request.Headers.Add("X-MessageID", Guid.NewGuid().ToString());

  // Send Toast Immediate requires class == 2
  request.Headers.Add("X-NotificationClass", "2");

  // Specify that the message is a Toast message
  request.Headers.Add("X-WindowsPhone-Target", "toast");

  // Create the XML of the Toast Message
  string toastMessage = @"<?xml version=""1.0"" encoding=""utf-8""?>
                        <wp:Notification
                            xmlns:wp=""WPNotification"">
                            <wp:Toast>
                              <wp:Text1>{0}</wp:Text1>
                              <wp:Text2>{1}</wp:Text2>
                            </wp:Toast>
                        </wp:Notification>";
  string toastXml = string.Format(toastMessage,
                            "This is Toast",
                            message);

  // Send it
  byte[] notificationMessage = Encoding.UTF8.GetBytes(toastXml);
  request.ContentLength = notificationMessage.Length;
  using (Stream requestStream = request.GetRequestStream())
  {
    requestStream.Write(notificationMessage,
                      0,
                      notificationMessage.Length);
  }
```

```
// Sends the notification and gets the response.
try
{
  HttpWebResponse response =
   (HttpWebResponse)request.GetResponse();

  return HandleResponse(response);
}
catch (Exception ex)
{
  return string.Concat("Exception during sending message",
                       ex.Message);
}
}
```

Because the toast message is XML, you must change the content type to text/xml. The X-NotificationClass value for toast messages is 2 (instead of 3 for raw messages). Like raw messages, you can add 10 and 20 to increase the time before the message is sent (making 2, 12, and 22 the three values for the X-NotificationClass header). As it is a toast message, you must add a new header called X-WindowsPhone-Target and set it to toast to indicate it's a toast message. Finally, the format of the message is different, so you need to create the XML message; you can upload it like any other string.

Creating Live Tiles

In Chapter 8, "Phone Integration," you learned that you could create and update live tiles via code. You can also do this via push notifications.

Sending a Live Tile notification is similar to sending a raw notification, but first you must bind your channel to the shell via the BindToShellTime (after first checking to ensure that the channel hasn't already been bound):

```
// Bind to the Shell Tile
if (!_myChannel.IsShellTileBound)
{
  _myChannel.BindToShellTile();
}
```

Binding it to the shell in this way tells the phone to expect Live Tile notifications. Over on the server side, the code is similar to raw push notifications, but a couple of small changes need to occur. The body of the Live Tile update must be in the format of a specific XML document:

```
<?xml version=""1.0"" encoding=""utf-8""?>
<wp:Notification xmlns:wp=""WPNotification"">
  <wp:Tile>
    <wp:BackgroundImage>URL</wp:BackgroundImage>
    <wp:Count>0</wp:Count>
    <wp:Title>Title</wp:Title>
    <wp:BackBackgroundImage>URL</wp:BackBackgroundImage>
    <wp:BackTitle>Title</wp:BackTitle>
    <wp:BackContent>Content</wp:BackContent>
  </wp:Tile>
</wp:Notification>
```

The format of this file is similar to the different tile types indicated in WMApplication.xml file. The .xml file represents the data for the specific type of tile (as explained in Chapter 8).

After you create this XML document, you are ready to push the change to the phone. So when you push this update from the server, you need to make a couple of small changes from the raw push notifications:

```
string SendTileMessage(string pushUri, string imageUrl)
{
  HttpWebRequest request =
    (HttpWebRequest)WebRequest.Create(pushUri);

  // For Raw Update use type of body
  // (text/plain or text/xml are typical)
  request.ContentType = "text/xml";

  // Specify the HTTP verb (must be POST)
  request.Method = "POST";

  // Use a generated unique ID to prevent duplicate push messages
  request.Headers.Add("X-MessageID", Guid.NewGuid().ToString());

  // Send Tile Immediate requires class == 1
  request.Headers.Add("X-NotificationClass", "1");

  // Specify that the message is a Toast message
  request.Headers.Add("X-WindowsPhone-Target", "token");

  // Create the XML of the Tile Message
  string tileMessage = @"<?xml version=""1.0"" encoding=""utf-8""?>
  <wp:Notification xmlns:wp=""WPNotification"">
```

```
  <wp:Tile>
    <wp:BackgroundImage>{0}</wp:BackgroundImage>
    <wp:Count>0</wp:Count>
    <wp:Title>Fun With Push</wp:Title>
    <wp:BackTitle>Back of Tile</wp:BackTitle>
    <wp:BackContent>More Content</wp:BackContent>
  </wp:Tile>
</wp:Notification>";

string tileXml = string.Format(tileMessage, imageUrl);

// Send it
byte[] notificationMessage = Encoding.UTF8.GetBytes(tileXml);
request.ContentLength = notificationMessage.Length;
using (Stream requestStream = request.GetRequestStream())
{
  requestStream.Write(notificationMessage,
                    0,
                    notificationMessage.Length);
}

// Sends the notification and gets the response.
try
{
  HttpWebResponse response =
    (HttpWebResponse)request.GetResponse();

  return HandleResponse(response);
}
catch (Exception ex)
{
  return string.Concat("Exception during sending message",
                    ex.Message);
}
}
```

The first change is to ensure that the `ContentType` is set to `text/xml` because the body will be the XML document you're going to create. Next the `X-NotificationClass` header needs to be set to 1 for tile updates. Like the raw and toast notifications, you can delay the delivery of the notification by adding 10 or 20, making the valid `X-NotificationClass` values 1, 11, and 21 for Live Tile updates. Next, you need to add a new header for the `X-WindowsPhone-Target` header and specify its value as `token` to tell the MPNS that this is a tile update. Lastly, you simply need to format the XML message as described earlier. Pushing this to the phone will enable you to update the tile on the phone (if it's pinned to the home screen).

It's a common practice to send an Internet-accessible URI for the BackgroundImage value. The image must be exactly 173×173 pixels in size and be a 24-bit .png file.

If you need to update a secondary tile, you must include a property of the tile called Id that has the URI used for the secondary tile:

```
// Create the XML of the Tile Message
string tileMessage = @"<?xml version=""1.0"" encoding=""utf-8""?>
<wp:Notification xmlns:wp=""WPNotification"">
  <wp:Tile Id="/views/AnotherView.xaml?flightNo=465">
    <wp:BackgroundImage>{0}</wp:BackgroundImage>
    <wp:Count>0</wp:Count>
    <wp:Title>Fun With Push</wp:Title>
    <wp:BackTitle>Back of Tile</wp:BackTitle>
    <wp:BackContent>More Content</wp:BackContent>
  </wp:Tile>
</wp:Notification>";
```

This Id attribute must match the URI of the secondary tile exactly; otherwise, it will not update the tile and just ignore the request.

Handling Push Notification Errors

When working with push notifications, you should also handle the Error-Occurred event to deal with any exceptional conditions. You should always handle this event because it will help you locate badly formatted messages and low-battery issues that will stop push messages from working. You can handle this event like any other event:

```
_myChannel.ErrorOccurred += channel_ErrorOccurred;
```

The event passes in an error argument that has an ErrorType property that can be used to determine the type of error. You should change the way you alert the user to this based on the type of error. In addition, the handler should use the Dispatcher to ensure that any reporting of these errors occurs on the UI thread (as the ErrorOccurred event could be thrown on any thread):

```
void channel_ErrorOccurred(object sender,
                           NotificationChannelErrorEventArgs e)
{
  Deployment.Current.Dispatcher.BeginInvoke(() =>
  {
```

```
switch (e.ErrorType)
{
  case ChannelErrorType.ChannelOpenFailed:
    MessageBox.Show("Failed to open channel");
    break;
  case ChannelErrorType.NotificationRateTooHigh:
    MessageBox.Show("Push Notifications are too frequent.");
    break;
  case ChannelErrorType.PayloadFormatError:
    MessageBox.Show(@"XML or Headers were incorrect
                      for the Push Message");
    break;
  case ChannelErrorType.MessageBadContent:
    MessageBox.Show("Live Tile Data is invalid.");
    break;
  case ChannelErrorType.PowerLevelChanged:
    {
      MessageBox.Show(@"Push Notifications are
                        affected by the current power level");

      // Can get the power level from the event info
      ChannelPowerLevel level =
        (ChannelPowerLevel)e.ErrorAdditionalData;

      switch (level)
      {
        case ChannelPowerLevel.NormalPowerLevel:
          // All Push Messages are processed
          break;
        case ChannelPowerLevel.LowPowerLevel:
          // Only Raw Push Messages are processed
          break;
        case ChannelPowerLevel.CriticalLowPowerLevel:
          // No Push Messages are processed
          break;
      }
      break;
    }
  }
});
}
```

The ChannelErrorType is returned in the event arguments and can be used to determine the error types. These error types are detailed in Table 11.7.

TABLE 11.7   `ChannelErrorType` **Enumeration**

Value	Description
`ChannelOpenFailed`	The channel failed to open.
`NotificationRateTooHigh`	Too many messages are being sent to the phone in a fixed period of time.
`PayloadFormatError`	The format of the headers or XML format of the message is incorrect.
`MessageBadContent`	This is used specifically for bad information in live tile image URLs.
`PowerLevelChanged`	The power level of the phone has changed, which will affect the push messages that are processed. The `NotificationChannelErrorEventArgs` class passed into the event includes an `ErrorAdditionalData` property, which can be cast into a `ChannelPowerLevel` enumeration that indicates the level of the power.

The `PowerLevelChanged` enumeration's values are detailed in Table 11.8.

TABLE 11.8   `ChannelPowerLevel` **Enumeration**

Value	Description
`NormalPowerLevel`	All push notification messages are being processed.
`LowPowerLevel`	Only raw push notification messages are being processed.
`CriticalLowPowerLevel`	No push messages are processed.

Where Are We?

Now that you've made it through this chapter, you should be ready to interact with services across the Internet. Windows Phone is a mostly connected device, which means you should be able to reach into the cloud and not only retrieve data with different services, but also push information to your application from your own services. By doing this, you can create great, connected experiences for your users.

▪ 12 ▪
Making Money

S O YOU'VE PUT YOUR SWEAT AND TEARS into an amazing idea that will revolutionize the way people use their phones; or you just created a cool app that outputs sounds of human flatulence. Either way, you want to share your creation with the world. How do you go about it?

What Is the Store?

The Store (or the Windows Phone Store) is where phone users can download and/or buy applications. On the phone, an app called "Store" lets users browse, download, and optionally buy applications that developers have written. The Store is one of the main hubs on the phone, so it encourages users to look around and find applications (as shown in Figure 12.1).

The Store is segregated into several categories of applications. The hub also shows highlighted apps that the Store team decides to promote on the hub. You do not have control over whether your application shows up here or not. In addition to the Store on the phone, the Store is available on the Internet. This site enables users to look in the Store and browse/buy applications. Items purchased from the online Store are wirelessly delivered to the phone. You can find the Store on the Windows Phone[1] website by choosing "Apps and Games" as shown in Figure 12.2.

FIGURE 12.1   **The Store hub**

FIGURE 12.2   **The Windows Phone Store**

---

1 http://windowsphone.com

This is where you want your Windows Phone application to be showcased. Although developers can install .xap files manually for up to 10 applications and enterprises can add applications directly to phones (as we will show you in Chapter 13, "Enterprise Phone Apps"), for mass appeal you need to be in the Store.

How It Works

The purpose of the Store is to provide a place for your application to get the exposure it needs to be successful. For any application sales, Microsoft splits the profits for direct purchases from the Store. Microsoft keeps 30% and pays you the remaining 70% of any sales you make on the Store.

You will develop your application using the Windows Phone SDK and get it ready for submission. Submitting your app involves uploading the .xap file as well as metadata about your application. Microsoft takes this information and performs a series of tests against your .xap file, including testing it on several devices (although the devices it uses are random per application). If your application passes, it is signed by the Store (which is what makes the .xap file executable on the phone) and deployed so that it can be downloaded/sold. Before you plan to submit an application to the Store, you will need a membership to the Store's Dev Center.[2] The Dev Center is the gateway to your applications in the Store. Figure 12.3 shows the join button on the Dev Center's home page (http://dev.windowsphone. com).

The cost for joining the Dev Center is $99 in the United States (and should be similar in other markets) per year for individuals or companies (students can join for free by being in the DreamSpark[3] program). If you have an active MSDN subscription, you can use a code to get a free membership as well. By joining you get several important benefits:

- You can submit an unlimited number of paid applications to the Store.

---

2 You might already have an App Hub membership, as it's required to unlock a device to test your application on a phone.

3 A Microsoft student program that helps students get Microsoft development resources: https://www.dreamspark.com/.

- You can submit up to 100 free applications to the Store. (Additional submissions cost $19.99 per application.)
- You can update your applications on the Store for free (regardless of whether the application is a paid app or a free app).
- You can unlock up to 10 phones for development purposes. Unlocking a phone enables you to debug on the phone and manually install up to 10 applications.

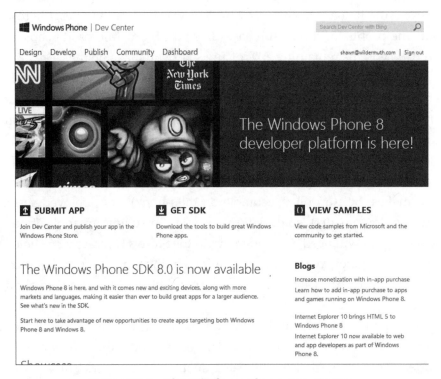

FIGURE 12.3   **The Windows Phone Dev Center**

When you join the Dev Center, the membership is not instantaneous; before you can submit your own applications, you must follow these steps:

1. You apply for membership to the Dev Center.
2. You supply identity information during signup.
3. You supply a credit card number (or PayPal) to pay the $99 fee.

4. An identity company (probably GeoTrust[4]) contacts you to confirm you or your company's identity. This information is used to ensure that people publishing apps on the Store are who they say they are.

After you have completed the signup and identity check, you'll be able to use the Dev Center to unlock phones and submit applications.

Charging for Apps

If your goal is to make money on the Store, you will need to understand how Store sales work. You can price your app anywhere from $0.99 to $499.99 in U.S. dollars. There are fixed price points between those two amounts, so you can't choose any random price for your application. These price points are picked purposely so that they can be converted into local currency in all the countries the Store serves. Currently, the Store is supported in many countries (although new countries might be added at any time). In these countries, the amount you charge is converted from U.S. dollars to a standard price in those countries. For instance, if you charge $2.99 for an application in U.S. dollars, this would be converted into a standard price in the other markets (this is not a straight currency conversion, so the pricing will be attractively described), as shown in Table 12.1.

TABLE 12.1   **International Pricing Example**

Country	Price
Australia	AUD $4.00
Austria	EUR € 2,99
Belgium	EUR € 2,99
Canada	CAN $3.49
France	EUR € 2,99
Germany	EUR € 2,99

---

4 www.geotrust.com

Country	Price
Hong Kong	HKD $25.00
India	INR Rs. 160.00
Ireland	EUR € 2,99
Italy	EUR € 2,99
Mexico	MXN $45.00
New Zealand	NZD $4.99
Singapore	SGD $4.99
Spain	EUR € 2,99
Switzerland	CHF Fr. 4.00
United Kingdom	GBP £2.49
United States	USD $2.99

You can set up special pricing per market on the website, but using the standard price matching is easy and appropriate. Fixed pricing is the only model available (for instance, subscription pricing is not available through the Store). You cannot charge for updates to an existing application. And there are no refunds from the Store.

When you are determining what you want to charge for an application, you also should consider the fact that users will want to try your application before they buy it. Allowing users to try your application will improve its overall sales and downloads.

Your two options in this regard are to offer a "Lite" version (a free version) of your app or to support a trial mode for your app. There are benefits to both approaches. A free version will help to attract users who might be looking only for free applications (and your great app might get them to decide to purchase the app). Free apps also can get higher visibility because the top 100 apps on Windows Phone are separated into "Free" and "Paid" categories. A free version would be a separate version of the application (although probably sharing 99% of the same source code) that is limited by ads, nag screens, or limited functionality.

Supporting a trial mode for your app will enable users to download it before they buy it. Unlike the Lite version approach, the trial mode allows users to upgrade quickly (instead of having to install the full version as a separate application). See the sidebar "Using Trial Mode" for more information on how to implement a trial mode version.

◾ Using Trial Mode

Some applications in the Store are available in trial versions, enabling users to try the applications before they buy them. You as the developer have programmatic access to whether a user is using the trial mode or the full version of your application through a class called LicenseInformation. This class has a property on it called IsTrial that returns a Boolean value that states whether the app is a trial mode or full version. You can create an instance of the class and test the property like so:

```
LicenseInformation lic = new LicenseInformation();

if (lic.IsTrial)
{
  // Buy Me Nag Screen
}
```

Using this class, you can test whether trial mode is enabled to prompt the user to purchase the application. You should cache this value in your application after it starts up because testing this property can be resource-intensive. In fact, the Application Certification Requirements require that you cache this value, or at least not call it frequently.

Getting Paid

As stated earlier, when you sell applications on the Store you receive 70% of the total sales you make. Currently, Microsoft is paying members of the

Dev Center after they break the minimum $200 threshold in a particular quarter. All payments are made via bank transfer, so you need to be able to give Microsoft banking information in your local market. The Store currently allows for payments to developers living in a number of markets. In fact, Microsoft is supporting payments to developers in more markets than the number of countries the Store supports, so you can be a Windows Phone developer in quite a number of countries.

During registration you will need to give Microsoft your banking information so the company knows how to pay you, as well as your tax information. This tax information is different for U.S.-based developers than developers outside the United States.

Tax Information for Developers in the United States

Developers residing in the United States must provide a tax identification number for Microsoft to report any earnings to. This would be a Social Security number (SSN); an Individual Taxpayer Identification Number (ITIN) for individual developers; or an Employee Identification Number (EIN) for corporations, partnerships, or associations (including nonforeign estates and domestic trusts). These tax identifiers are used to report any revenue you receive from the sale of your applications.

Tax Information for Developers Outside the United States

For non-U.S. developers, the process is a little more complex. Because you are likely not considered a "U.S. person" by the U.S. Internal Revenue Service (IRS), you must provide a U.S. tax identification number; otherwise, Microsoft is required (by law) to hold back 30% of all revenue for tax reporting. Your country might have a tax treaty with the United States, so that income earned in the United States will be paid without the withholding tax. Most developers will want to apply to avoid the 30% holdback, a process that requires you to send a copy of the IRS's W-8 form to Microsoft. However, this form requires an identification number. As a non-U.S. entity (person or company), you can register for an ITIN by filing a W-7 form with the IRS. Microsoft provides on its website a form letter that you can submit to the IRS with the W-7 form. You can see a complete walkthrough of the process for non-U.S. developers on the Dev Center at http://create. msdn.com/en-US/home/faq/windows_phone_7#wp7faq50.

You can also optionally submit to Microsoft a Valued Added Tax (VAT) identification number if you want to avoid being charged VAT in your country. This relates to VAT, GST, and QST (depending on which country you're in). When you supply the VAT identification number, Microsoft will send you a hard-copy tax invoice (HCTI) if that is applicable in your particular country.

When pricing your application, understand that the pricing might or might not include these taxes depending on your country. Depending on the specific country, you may be responsible for paying the taxes directly or Microsoft might remit them for you. You will want to see the current tax and payout implications for your country of origin. You can find this by going to the MSDN documentation on pricing (available via this short URL: http://shawnw.me/wp7pricing). Users can decide to pay by credit card through Microsoft billing or mobile operator billing. How quickly you are paid depends on how the user pays for your application (still dependent on reaching the $200 plateau before payments are processed). Here are the options:

- If the user pays by credit card (currently the majority of payments), you will get paid 15–30 days after billing the user.
- If the user uses mobile operator billing, you will get paid 90–120 days after billing.

Submitting Your App

So you have registered for the Dev Center and completed the first version of your application. You are ready to get that app in the Store and start sharing your creation with users. You might think you're ready to submit your creation, but before you get started, some preparation is required.

Preparing Your Application

After your application code is ready, you should perform some simple steps to ensure that the submission process goes smoothly. Here is a checklist of tasks you should complete before you submit your application.

To simplify this experience, the Windows Phone SDK provides an option called the Store Test Kit to package your application and run tests to ensure it's going to be approved the first time. To get started, open the Project menu and select Open Store Test Kit, as shown in Figure 12.4.

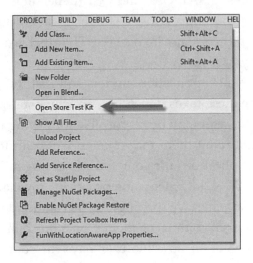

FIGURE 12.4   **Opening the Store Test Kit**

When the kit is opened, you'll see three tabs on the left that indicate the various parts of the application testing. The first tab contains the Store images you should supply when submitting your application. This can ensure that your images are the correct size for submitting to the Store. You can see the first tab in Figure 12.5.

To create the Store Tile, I just use any image editor for my logo. But for the screenshots, I usually use the emulator and take screenshots. When running your application in the emulator, you can press the small right-arrow icon to open the emulator tools. One of the tabs is called Screenshots. Clicking the Capture button will take the screenshot; clicking the Save button lets you save the image. You can see the screenshot emulator tool in Figure 12.6.

When including screenshots, you must supply screenshots for every screen resolution you support. In your WMAppManifest.xml file, you can specify which resolutions you support. By default, all three resolutions are enabled, as shown in Figure 12.7.

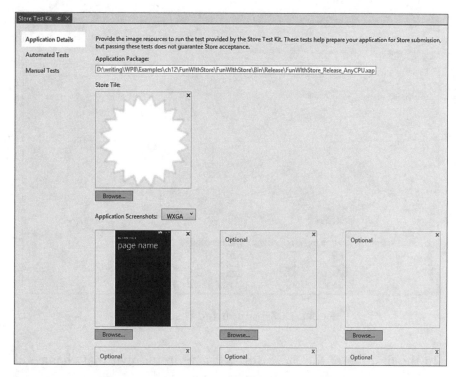

FIGURE 12.5   Store Test Kit image validation

FIGURE 12.6   Screenshot tool in the emulator

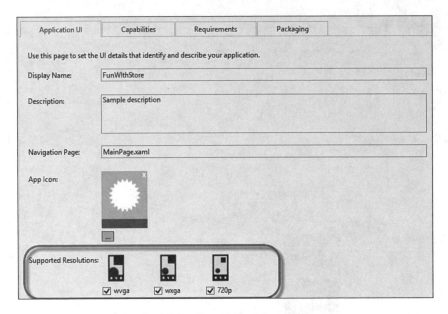

FIGURE 12.7   **Supported resolutions**

In the first tab of the Store Test Kit is a drop-down that changes the screenshots for each of these resolutions. You should supply screenshots in all three resolutions. The easiest way is to rerun your application in each of the emulator sizes.

Normally you can include these images in your project to have a common place to put them. If you do include them directly in your project, be sure to change the Build Action to "None" to prevent them from being included in the .xap file. Including them will unnecessarily bloat your application package. You can change the Build Action in the Properties panel as shown in Figure 12.8.

The next tab in the Store Test Kit are the automated tests. These tests do static analysis on the .xap package itself looking for errors. You must change the build type to "Release" before these tests can be performed. You can select the "Run Tests" button to execute the automated tests. The results will be shown in the window (see Figure 12.9).

From this window, you can also profile your application using the built-in profiler. The Start Windows Phone Application Analysis button launches this tool. This tool enables you to see how your application performs and tweak memory, CPU, and animation performance to make your application the best it can be.

FIGURE 12.8 Changing the Build Action of images in your project

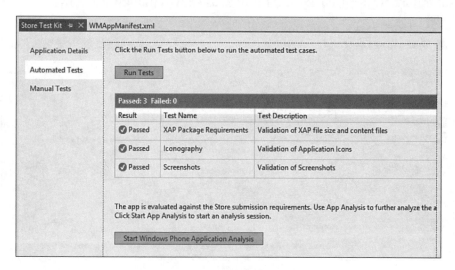

FIGURE 12.9 Automated tests

The last tab in the Store Test Kit is a set of manual tests. The number of these tests varies (61 at the time of the writing of this book) and encourages you to perform this series of manual tests on your applications. Many of the tests are not necessarily applicable to every application (for example, VoIP tests). After you've prepared your application, you're ready to submit it!

The Submission Process

To begin submitting your application, go to the Dev Center and log in to your account. In the Dev Center is a Dashboard on the top menu, as shown in Figure 12.10.

FIGURE 12.10   Accessing your Dashboard

Once on the Dashboard, you'll see some summary information about how much money you've earned and other data. To get to your apps (or submit a new app), click the App link, as shown in Figure 12.11.

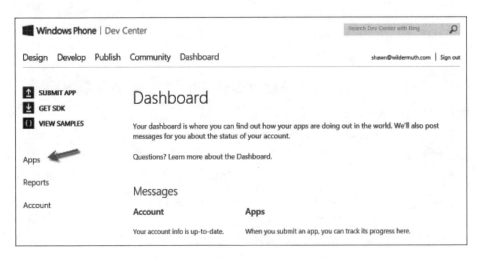

FIGURE 12.11   Accessing your apps

On the apps page is a list of all your submitted applications (although for your first application, this list will be empty). To begin submitting your application, click the Submit App link, as shown in Figure 12.12.

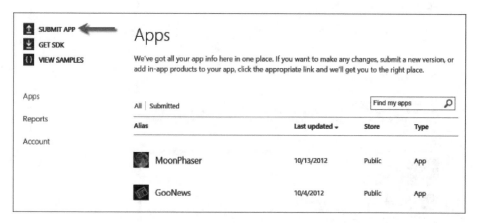

FIGURE 12.12 Starting the submission process

This will start you through the steps of submitting your application. This first page (as shown in Figure 12.13) displays the five steps that can be involved in submitting your application. The first two steps are required; the last three are optional. But for this first app, let's just go through the two required steps. Click the first step (the big #1) to get started.

This launches the App Information Page. This page (shown in Figure 12.14) requires you to give your application a name, description, and categorization. In addition, you'll need to specify a base price. For free apps, just leave the price at zero. The term "base price" indicates the price in your local currency (U.S. dollars in the screenshot). This base price is adjusted to the local currency of the buyer for her local market. For example, a price of $0.99 USD will be 0.79 British pounds in the United Kingdom. The Windows Phone store attempts to convert the price but has specific levels in other markets to achieve a pleasing price (for instance, 0.99, 0.79, 1.99) to improve the sales in those markets. This will not be a strict conversion to the local currency and won't fluctuate as the daily currency valuations change. As mentioned earlier, you can override these prices per market if you want to, but the price levels is usually easier and appropriate. Just below the price, you can click the check box to allow a trial of your application as shown earlier in this chapter.

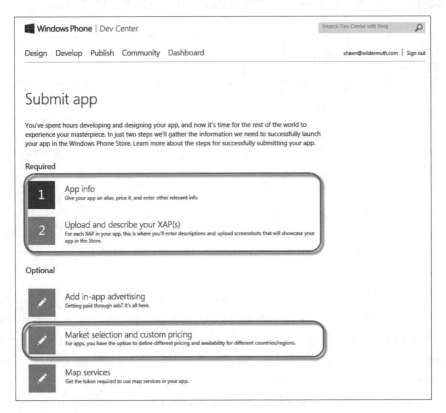

FIGURE 12.13   The steps of submitting your app

The last part of this page involves selecting the markets in which to distribute your application. You can decide to distribute it to all markets or to only markets that do not have strict content policies (for instance, China). Unless your application is distributing information that might cause it to be rejected for content policies (for example, news applications), you should distribute your app to all available markets. If you need to tweak the markets and the prices, you can do that later in the submission process.

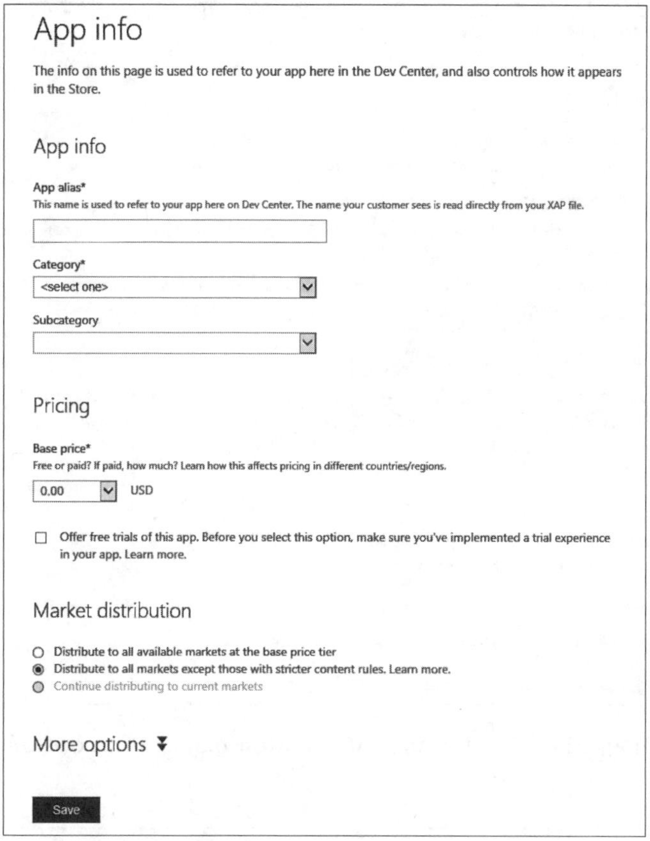

FIGURE 12.14   App Information page

If you open the More options at the bottom of the information page, you can also specify whether to make your app publicly available or to provide the app to specific beta users, as shown in Figure 12.15. If you select to publish this to beta testers (which can be a good way to test the app before you publish it widely), you can select up to 10,000 users to distribute the application without publishing directly to the store.

The App Information page is used to set data that is common to all versions of your application. The next step ("Upload and describe your xap(s)") lets you upload the app itself and specify other information about this version of the app. To get started, you should use the browse link (as shown in Figure 12.16) to point to the release version of your application. The .xap file is generated in the "bin/release" folder of your application directory.

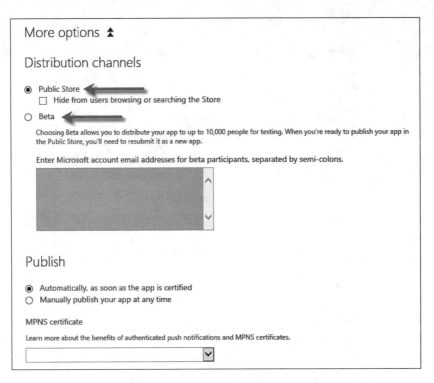

FIGURE 12.15   The App Information pages More options

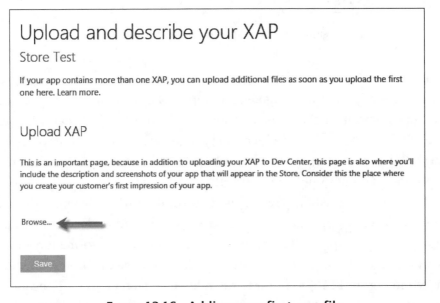

FIGURE 12.16   Adding your first .xap file

After you upload the first .xap file, the screen changes to allow you to specify new .xap-specific information including screenshots, icons, and other images, as shown in Figure 12.17.

FIGURE 12.17   Adding the .xap specific information

After you add all the required images and metadata (for example, name and description), you will be returned to the Submit App page with check marks on the first two steps, as shown in Figure 12.18. Pressing Submit will start the submission process.

FIGURE 12.18   Ready to submit your app

This final page shows you that your application has been submitted (see Figure 12.19). You can click the Go to the Lifecycle Page link to see a page that shows the current status of the application (in the testing cycle), as shown in Figure 12.20.

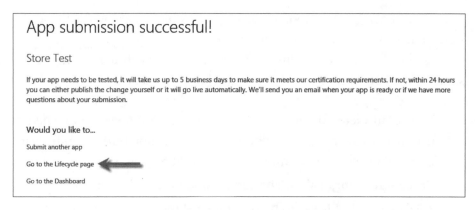

FIGURE 12.19 The submitted page

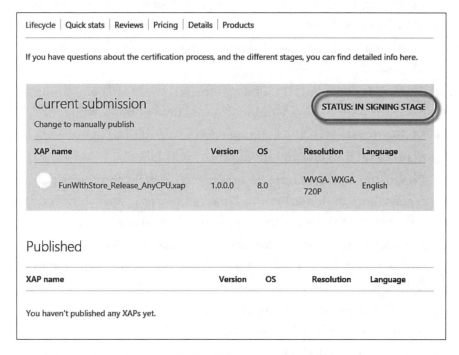

FIGURE 12.20 The app status page

After the Submission

After you submit your application, the Dashboard will become a pretty regular page to visit as you check the status of your application(s). Clicking the My Apps link on the Dashboard takes you to the application status page. You can see the current status of your submission by looking at the status page (as indicated in Figure 12.20).

The status messages on this page mean different things. Here are the statuses your application can be in and what they mean:

- **Not completed:** You've started a submission but have not finished it (for instance, clicking the Submit for Certification button on the last page). This means you can continue to edit the submission.
- **Processing submission:** The submission process has begun.
- **XAP processing failed:** The .xap failed static validation and the .xap must be fixed and submission restarted.
- **In signing stage:** The .xap is being signed so that it can be trusted by the Windows Phone.
- **Signing passed:** Your application is queued to be certified by Microsoft.
- **Signing failed:** Signing failed and the .xap needs to be resubmitted. Not clear why signing would fail at the time of this writing.
- **Malware detected:** The validation of the .xap found illegal code or malware in the code and the submission is failed.
- **Processing certification:** The signing is complete and the actual certification (both machine and manual testing) has begun. Your app will remain in this state the longest of all the states.
- **Certification passed:** Certification succeeded and Microsoft is creating a signing certificate for your application to prepare it to go to the Store.
- **Certification failed:** The certification process failed and you can retrieve a report of why your application failed.
- **Ready to be published:** Your application can be pushed to the Store now. You can choose to publish the application whenever you are ready.
- **Published:** The application has been published to the Store and is available for purchase. This status is indicated before the application shows up in the Store. The process flow to get in the Store usually takes less than six hours.

After your application has been submitted, you can't make any changes or cancel the certification. The wheels are in motion, and until the application is certified or fails to certify, there is nothing you can do with your application.

When viewing your app page, links near the top allow you to see information about your application (including Reviews, Pricing, Details, and so on). If you click the Details link, you will see a summary of the information you submitted with the application (see Figure 12.21). Near the top are links to Update the App and to Hide App in Store. These enable you to upload new application updates to the app that are delivered to the users. The Hide App in Store link takes the application out of the store but does not remove it from phones that have the app installed.

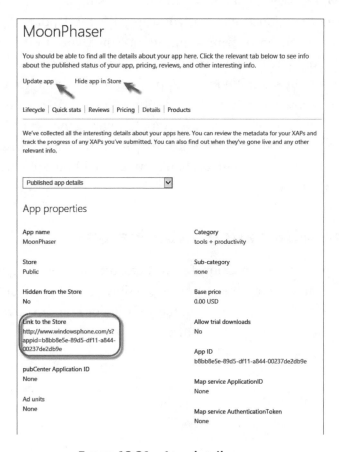

FIGURE 12.21 App details page

When you view the details of your application, you can also find the Link to the Store, which is a URL that enables you to publicize a way to navigate to your app directly in the Store. If this URL is launched on the phone itself, it will open the Store application and allow them to install the app. This URL is how you promote your app. Put it in your Twitter feed, on your blog, or in your marketing information. Then the money will start rolling in!

Modifying Your Application

When you finally get your application out to the Store, you might find a bug, decide on a brand-new feature, or just want to change the price of your application. The Dev Center makes this process simple. On the application details page (mentioned earlier), you can click the Update App link to upload a new version of your application. When you do this, you'll get the Update App page, shown in Figure 12.22. This process is the same as when you initially submitted your app, although the certification process is somewhat abbreviated from the full submission process of a new app.

Although you can update the .xap to send a new version of the application to users, you can also edit the App info to simply change pricing, distribution, and other metadata about your app without submitting a new .xap file to the store.

Dealing with Failed Submissions

If your application submission fails, Microsoft attempts to give you as much information about the failure as possible so that you can fix it. You can retrieve the failure report from the website, or you can have it sent to the email of record for the Dev Center account.

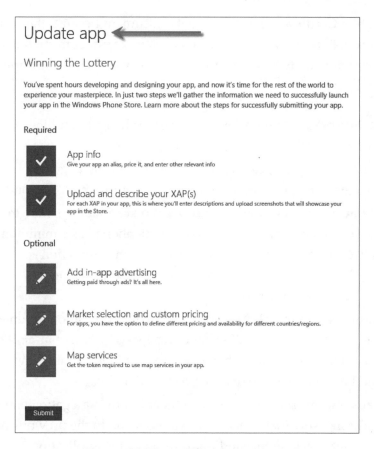

FIGURE 12.22 Application actions

The process of certifying your application consists of testing the way the application functions (for example, does it run or lock up) and testing it against the Windows Phone Application Certification Requirements.[5] These include stability, performance, resource consumption, and content requirements. An application could be rejected for a variety of reasons based on the requirements. If your application is rejected, Microsoft gives you a detailed report of why it failed and to which section of the certification requirements the failure is related. It's important to read the

---

5 http://shawnw.me/wp7certreq

Application Certification Requirements document because there are a lot of reasons failures occur. It is an actively changing document, but some of the major pain points that seem to bite developers submitting applications include the following:

- **Stability:** Your application can't crash or hang. (Handling `Application.UnhandledException` is important.)

- **Launch:** Your application must show its landing page within five seconds. It must be responsive to user input within 20 seconds.

- **Memory consumption:** Your application cannot take more than 90MB of memory at any time (when the phone has a minimum of 256MB of memory). It's not clear what this limitation is for phones with more memory. You can test this using the `DeviceExtendedProperties` class.

- **Running under lock:** You can enable your application to run while the phone is locked (if the phone was locked when your application was running). You must have the user opt in to running under lock and have an option to disable this functionality.

- **Back button:** You need to be careful about the navigation pattern and make sure that "Back" always takes you to the previous page and that "Back on the landing page" exits the application.

- **Using push notifications:** If you're going to use any push notifications, you must tell the user when you first enable this capability and allow the user to disable it in the UI (usually via a Settings or Options page).

- **Size:** The maximum size of a .xap file is 225MB.

- **Age requirements:** If your application enables person-to-person communication (for instance, chat, IM, SMS), you must have a way to verify that the user is more than 13 years old.

- **Location service:** You must allow the user to enable or disable use of location information. You also must have a privacy policy to let the user know how you're using the location information.

- **Personal information:** If you publish or share any personal information (for instance, photos, phone numbers, contacts, SMS, or browsing history), you must make the user opt in to use the functionality.

- **Content:** You cannot use nudity, sexual content, violence, or hate speech in your applications.

Using Ads in Your Apps

Although you've read that you can charge for your applications and that this can help you make money, it's also fairly common to create free applications that contain advertising instead. Several options exist and all have their pros and cons, as shown in Table 12.2.

TABLE 12.2 **Advertising Vendors for the Phone**

Vendor	URL	Model	Markets	Notes
pubCenter	http://pubcenter.microsoft.com	Per impression	U.S. only, international in future	Supports a phone SDK.
AdMob	www.admob.com	Per click	International	No SDK, but simple API.
Millennial	http://developer.millennialmedia.com	Per click	International	Looks like they only accept U.S. developers.
Smaato	www.smaato.com/	Per click	International	Supports SDK; aggregates 50+ ad networks for high fill rate.

The big players in in-app advertising are shown in the table, but there are some details you'll need to determine before you decide which platform to use. By far, Microsoft's pubCenter is the most attractive because it pays per impression with bonuses for click-throughs. Also, the SDK is fairly drop-in usable (although there have been reports of crashing problems). Although this is the most profitable of the advertising choices, it only works for U.S. users, so non-U.S. users applications won't have advertising.

The other vendors all use a per-click model (which means you get paid only if the user clicks on the ad). This generally means less money, but these vendors do offer ads internationally, and most support paying developers who are outside the United States. So, there is no magical best offering for advertising inside your application.

Where Are We?

At this point you should be ready to get your application on the millions of phones out there. In this chapter you saw how to register with the Dev Center, submit your application, and get it certified. Hopefully you've carefully read the checklist to ensure that your application meets all the requirements to get it approved to the Store. The only hard part now is coming up with that great application idea that takes the world by storm!

▉ 13 ▪
Enterprise Phone Apps

Much of this book has focused on building apps for the general consumer. Prior to Windows Phone 8, you could build enterprise or internal applications, but you had to certify and deliver them through the public phone store. This was less than preferable for most organizations that didn't want to have to go through the store to install applications onto phones. There were some odd workarounds to make apps for just the employees of an organization, but they are not required any longer.

Enterprise Apps?

But what is an *enterprise app*? Generally, enterprise apps are pieces of software that are made by and used by employees within a specific company. They could be anything your company needs, like a time billing system, a sales-reporting app, or anything in between.

When building enterprise apps, you will typically need to control the whole breadth of the application ecosystem including development, deployment, and services. This involves several pieces all working together.

There are a number of steps in the process:

1. **Register for a Developer Account**: For the owning company.
2. **Buy a Symantec Code Signing Certificate**: To sign your apps so that they are secure on your phone.
3. **Create an Application Enrollment Token (AET)**: Used to allow a phone to have access to your company's apps.
4. **Build a Company Hub App**: An app that will be used to deliver your apps (and other information) to an employee's phone.
5. **Build Your Apps**: Build and compile your apps including converting to native code and signing them.
6. **Deploy Your Apps:** Your apps are deployed from your servers and are never submitted to Microsoft for certification.

Although the prep work for getting company applications on phones working is somewhat involved, most of the steps are a one-time process. After the signup and certificates are created, it is relatively simple to develop and add new apps to the phones. Let's walk you through each of these processes.

Registering Your Company

To get started, you'll first need to join the Windows Phone Dev Center. To deploy your own enterprise apps, your Dev Center account must be a Company account (see Figure 13.1).

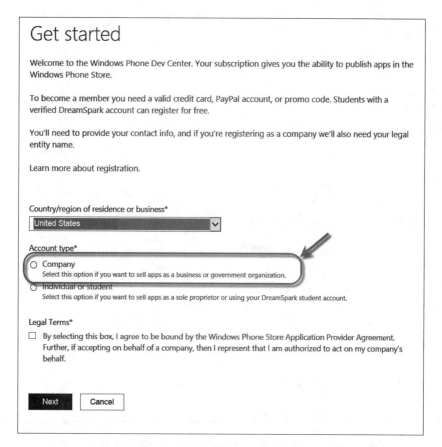

FIGURE 13.1   Registering a Company account

The process for registering a company is the same as creating an individual account, but marking your account as a company is critical to being able to create your own Company Hub. It needs to be a company account because you need to be able to request a code-signing certificate. After your company account is approved, the account page will show a special ID that is called the Symantec ID (as shown in Figure 13.2).

After you have this ID, you can proceed to requesting the certificate from Symantec.

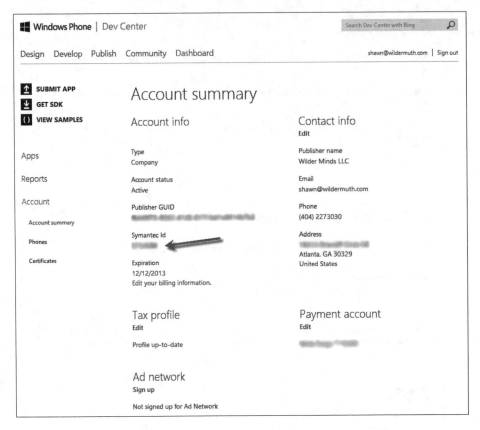

FIGURE 13.2 The Symantec ID for code-signing certificate

Buying a Symantec Code-Signing Certificate

To sign your own apps (including the Company Hub) as well as enable your employee's phones for your apps, you first need a certificate that certifies that your company is who it says it is. To this end, Microsoft has partnered with Symantec to supply the code-signing certificates for the Windows Phone.

The exact type of certificate required is called an *Enterprise Mobile Code Signing Certificate*. To get this certificate, you must visit Symantec's site (http://shawnw.me/wp8companycert) and request one. The cost is $299 USD. When you reach the site, you must enter the Symantec ID that you got from the account screen, as shown in Figure 13.2, and the primary email address from your account. You can see the first registration page in Figure 13.3.[1]

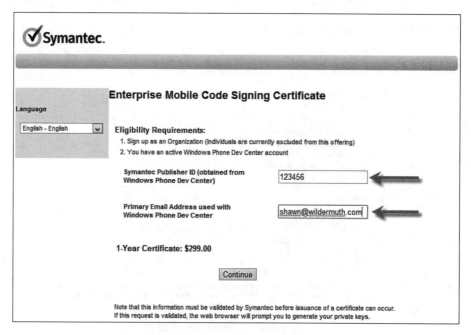

FIGURE 13.3   Ordering your enterprise mobile code-signing certificate

After you enter the Symantec ID and email, you are prompted to give your company and payment information (a credit card is required). After the order is made, you'll receive two emails. The first of these is an email that contains a link to enable you to approve the request. You must approve this request before the creation of the certificate can proceed. This first email will take you to a Symantec page (as shown in Figure 13.4) where you will need to approve the request.

After you pay for and approve the request, Symantec will send you yet another email that contains the certificate. You'll need to get this installed on your machine before you can get a form that is necessary for signing your own applications.

---

1   If this initial page fails to validate your Symantec ID and email combination, make sure the email you used is the main Approver email, not the main email of the account, if they are different.

FIGURE 13.4   **Approving the certificate request**

Installing the Certificate

Before you can install your new certificate locally, you need to get the Symantec intermediate certificates added to your machine. To do this, you should follow the instructions from the Symantec site[2] that are also linked in the email with your certificate.

The intermediate certificates are Symantec's own that ensure that the chain of certificates are trusted on your machine. After you have followed those directions to install the intermediate certificates, you can simply use the pickup link, as shown in Figure 13.5.

---

2   http://shawnw.me/wp8intermediatecerts

```
--------------------------------
ORDER NUMBER: [redacted]

Congratulations! Symantec has approved your request for an Enterprise Code Signing Certificate.

ORDER NUMBER: [redacted]
COMMON NAME:  Wilder Minds LLC

Note: Please see the instructions at the bottom of this email for adding the Root and Intermediate certificates prior to
installing your code signing certificate.

Please use the pickup link below to install your certificate.

https://products.websecurity.symantec.com/orders/enrollment/CertPickup.do?
[redacted]
```

FIGURE 13.5   **The pickup link in the Symantec email**

The last step here is to export the newly installed certificate as a .pfx file. This file will be used in the next step to create the Application Enrollment Token (AET) that is used to enable the phones and sign your code.

To export the certificate, you should start the Microsoft Management Console (MMC) by running "mmc.exe" from a console window. This is the same tool you used to install the intermediate certificates as explained in the Symantec email. After MMC is started, you might need to add the certificate plug-in. You can do this by selecting the File, Add/Remove Snap-in option in the menu. Simply select Certificate Snap-in to add it to the console. You can see the certificate snap-in installed in Figure 13.6.

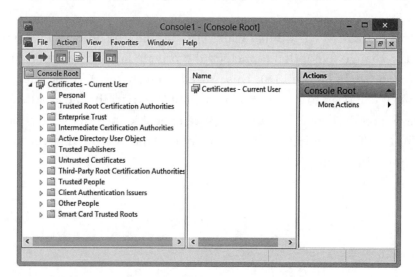

FIGURE 13.6   **The MMC with the certificate snap-in installed**

You'll need to open the Personal node of the Certificate folder and and find the Certificates node under that. If you click that node, you'll see a list of your personal certificates including the new Symantec Mobile Code Signing Certificate (it will have the company name displayed, as shown in Figure 13.7). Right-click the certificate and select All Tasks, Export to export the file to a .pfx file (also shown in Figure 13.7).

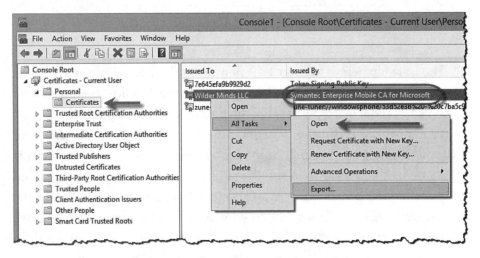

FIGURE 13.7 **Exporting the new certificate**

This will start a wizard that walks you through the process. First, you'll need to change the option to include the private key in the exported .pfx file (as shown in Figure 13.8). This is used to create the AET file later.

Next, you need to specify that you want to export the file as a Personal Information Exchange file (.pfx). Be sure to enable Include All Certificates In The Certificate Path If Possible to include all the intermediate certificates (as shown in Figure 13.9).

FIGURE 13.8   Including the private key in the .pfx file

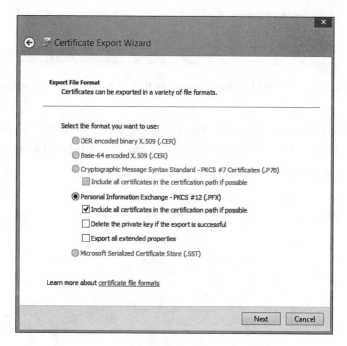

FIGURE 13.9   Specifying the .pfx file type

Because including the private key was required, specifying a password is also required. Be sure to remember this password because there is no way to recover it except by re-exporting the .pfx file. This is shown in Figure 13.10.

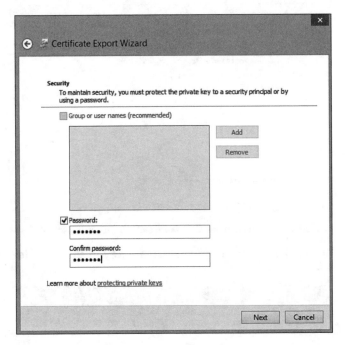

FIGURE 13.10   **Including a password in the .pfx file (required)**

Lastly, you'll need to name the file (and location) for the .pfx file (as shown in Figure 13.11). After this is exported, you'll be able to create the AET file and start deploying apps!

FIGURE 13.11   Naming the .pfx file

Application Enrollment Token

Now that you have your shiny new certificate exported as a .pfx file, you can now create the magic token that is used to enable deployment of your enterprise applications onto phones. The trick here is that the token created contains the same certificate that the applications will be signed with. The AET is then registered with each phone so that applications that match the signing certificate will be allowed.

First, we need to produce the token. To do this, you'll need to start a command prompt as an administrator.[3] Then you should navigate to the same directory as your .pfx file. In this directory you'll need to execute the AETGenerator, which is located in a subdirectory of the Program Files directory called Microsoft SDKs/Windows Phone/v8.0/Tools/ AETGenerator. The AETGenerator.exe tool takes the .pfx file as a parameter (and the password). For example:

---

3   In Windows 8, the easy way is to Windows+X to open the tools pop-up and select Command Prompt (Admin).

```
C:\>"%ProgramFiles(x86)%\Microsoft SDKs\Windows Phone\v8.0\To
ols\AETGenerator\AETGenerator.exe" YourCert.pfx YourPassword
```

This will generate three files:

- **AET.xml**: The raw AET in XML format
- **AET.aet**: A Base64-encoded version of the AET for use with Mobile Device Management systems that need to deploy the AET
- **AET.aetx**: Special version of the AET in XML format that can be launched on the phone from Internet Explorer, or from within an email as an attachment

Now you've done the hard work of getting the AET. This work is required once (or at least once a year as the certificates expire). Now let's get your phone(s) ready for your enterprise apps!

Registering Phones

Before your applications can run on the phone, you will need to get the AET onto the phones. There are a couple of ways to do this: use a Mobile Device Management service, or manually install the AET.

The Windows Phone supports Mobile Device Management (MDM) systems. MDMs will enable you to deploy the .aet file directly onto the phones en masse. This is the most effective way to get the AET onto the phones. Please see the manufacturer of your MDM as to how this is accomplished.

If you are not using a MDM, the other way is to manually add the .aetx file to the phones. The most effective way to do this is to either email the .aetx file to each of the employees to add to the phone, or to supply a URL to a secured server that delivers the .aetx file to each user. When you send the .aetx file in an email,[4] the user will see it as an attachment (as shown in Figure 13.12). Selecting and downloading the .aetx file will result in the phone asking your permission to add the company account to the phone (as shown in Figure 13.13).

---

4   If you send .aetx or .xaps files via email, Microsoft suggests you use IRM protection to ensure these assets are secured.

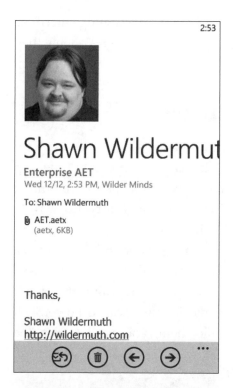

FIGURE 13.12   Receiving an AET via email

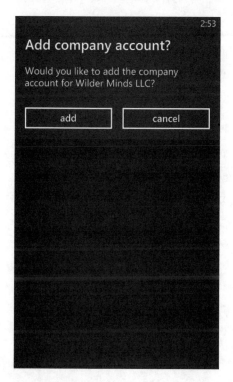

FIGURE 13.13   Approving the AET to the phone

After they've done that, the phone is ready to start executing enterprise applications. But before your enterprise apps can run on the phone, they need to be prepared for distribution.

Preparing Apps for Distribution

If you simply take a .xap file (whether downloaded via Internet Explorer or attached to an email), the phone won't install the app without the .xap being in a special form that involves two separate steps: precompiling for the phone and signing the code. The most straightforward way to accomplish this is with an included Powershell Script.

You will need to run PowerShell as an administrator and navigate to a subdirectory of the Program Files (x86) directory called Microsoft SDKs\ Windows Phone\v8.0\Tools\MDILXAPCompile. Although the script exists in that directory, you can't run it by default because PowerShell scripts are disabled by default. To enable them, you need to run the following command:

```
set-executionpolicy RemoteSigned
```

Calling this command will ask you whether you want to allow remotely signed scripts (like the one shipped with the SDK) to be able to be executed. You simply need to press Enter to allow it. After scripts are allowed, you can then call the script that will precompile and sign your application.

To call the script, you must supply three parameters:

- **-xapfilename**: The path to the xap (this must be a full path, not just the filename, even if you're in the same directory)
- **-pfxfilename**: The path to the .pfx file that you created your AET from earlier
- **-password**: The password to access the .pfx file

For example, to precompile and sign a xap file, do the following:

```
./BuildMDILXap.ps1 -xapfilename c:\yourproject\your.xap -pfxfilename
D:\wmcerts\yourcert.pfx -password yourpwd
```

When the command completes, you will have a new .xap file in the same directory with the name of the xap appended with "_new" (that is, "your_new.xap"). This is the .xap that you need to deploy to the phones. You can send them to the phones via an email message or URL like the .aetx file. If you give the phone access to a precompiled/signed xap, your users will be prompted as to whether they want to install the app, as shown in Figure 13.14.

FIGURE 13.14 Confirming a company app's installation

Although you can deploy your applications in this way, a better way is by using a Company Hub, as you'll see in the next section.

Building a Company Hub

What is a *Company Hub*? This is an application you write (and precompile/sign) that works as the starting point for your company. This is typically a place where you can enable users to install any enterprise applications you are creating, as well as get other information from the company (for example, news, alerts, and so on). The Company Hub is usually deployed via email or URL as shown in the earlier section, but this should be required only for this first application. The Company Hub should be the application responsible for installing the rest of the applications for users. The Company Hub ends up just becoming a bootstrap application installed to enable installation (and uninstallation) of your company's apps on the phones.

When you create your own Company Hub, it's important that you know that this application will be responsible for installing and updating your own enterprise applications. This typically means you will need to be able to let the Company Hub request the list of applications (and versions) from a central location (for example, a web service). After you have a list of the applications, you can show the application list and enable your users to install an application directly from your Hub. This is accomplished by using the `InstallationManager` class's `AddPackageAsync` method. This method takes the name of the app and an URI to the prepared .xap file, usually on your server. For example:

```
InstallationManager.AddPackageAsync("Your App",
    new Uri(installationUrl));
```

When you call this method, it prompts the user with an approval to install the app like the example earlier in this chapter (refer to Figure 13.14). But other than the approval, there is no UI for telling the user the app is being installed. Instead, you should handle the return value from the `AddPackageAsync` method. This method returns an `IAsyncOperatoinWithProgress<PackageInstallResult, uint>` object. This interface is used to enable you to handle both completion and progress callbacks from the asynchronous operations. For example:

```
IAsyncOperationWithProgress<PackageInstallResult, uint> result;

result = InstallationManager.AddPackageAsync("YourApp",
    new Uri(installationUrl));

// Use the result to handle progress and completion
result.Completed = (info, status) =>
    {
```

```
    if (status == AsyncStatus.Completed)
    {
      // ...
    }
    else if (status == AsyncStatus.Error)
    {
      // ...
    }

  };

result.Progress = (info, progress) =>
  {
    // ...
  };
```

The return value of the AddPackageAsync method can be used to handle the Completed and Progress delegates. In the case of the Completed delegate, you can test whether the installation succeeded or failed. The Progress can be used to show the user the ongoing status of the installation. In both of these cases, these delegates aren't guaranteed to be called on the UI thread, so you should protect any data change that could affect the user interface with the Dispatcher. For example, showing the progress percentage by changing a view model should be protected by wrapping it in a call to the Dispatcher, like so:

```
result.Progress = (info, progress) =>
  {
    Dispatcher.BeginInvoke(() =>
      {
        app.Status = string.Format("Installing: {0}% done",
                                    progress);
      });
  };
```

Before you install an application, though, you might be interested in whether it is already installed. The same InstallationManager class comes to the rescue. You can use the InstallationManager's FindPackagesForCurrentPublisher method to get all the apps that are installed for your company (you're considered a "publisher"):

```
var packages = InstallationManager.FindPackagesForCurrentPublisher();
```

This method returns an enumerable list of Package objects. The Package class contains information about each installed application. Information about the installed app (or Package) is contained in the Id property of the Package class. This property contains a structure called PackageId. The PackageId class contains information such as the Name, Version, and ProductId. With these three pieces of information, you can make decisions about whether a particular application is installed. The ProductId is the identifier (for example, Guid) that is contained in the WMAppManifest.xml file of each Windows Phone applications. You should use this to uniquely identify each application your enterprise produces. This way, when you compare the list of applications that your company makes available, you can simply use a LINQ query to find out whether the app is installed, like so:

```
var packages = InstallationManager.FindPackagesForCurrentPublisher();

foreach (var app in yourApps)
{
  // Determine if installed
  var package = packages.FirstOrDefault(p =>
                   p.Id.ProductId == app.ProductId);

  if (package != null)
  {
    app.IsInstalled = true;
  }
}
```

You can see in this example that you can search through the packages returned by the InstallationManager to match up the ProductId's to see whether it is already installed. The Package object itself can be used to launch the application directly from your Company Hub. This is accomplished using the Package.Launch method:

```
var package = packages.FirstOrDefault(p =>
                 p.Id.ProductId == app.ProductId);

if (package != null)
{
  // Launch without initialization parameters
  package.Launch("");
}
```

The Launch method enables you to specify start-p parameters (usually the starting page of an app). Calling it with an empty string launches it as if the user tapped the icon on the phone itself.

Lastly, you can use the PackageId's Version property to determine whether the latest version is installed. To update an enterprise application, you simply install a newer version of the .xap file using the same InstallationManager.AddPackageAsync method:

```
var packages = InstallationManager.FindPackagesForCurrentPublisher();

var package = packages.FirstOrDefault(p => p.Id.ProductId == app.
ProductId);

if (package != null)
{
  if (app.Version != package.Id.Version.ToString())
  {
    InstallationManager.AddPackageAsync("YourApp",
      new Uri(installationUrl));
  }
}
```

By calling AddPackageAsync with a new version of the app, the system will update the currently installed app (although the user will still get a confirmation dialog box).

By using the built-in support for iterating, installation, and upgrading your enterprise applications from your own servers, you can create a Company Hub that will manage all the applications you need on the phone for your own users.

Where Are We?

The need to build applications just for your internal customers (for example, within the enterprise) is a common requirement in most businesses. The Windows Phone supports this by allowing you to build and deploy your own applications without involving Microsoft or the Store. This enables you to avoid the pitfalls of waiting for Microsoft to certify your own applications or sharing your own intellectual property with the Store. The only caveat here is that you are then responsible for securing access to those apps.

Index

D

Safari
Books Online

FREE
Online Edition

Your purchase of **Essential Windows® Phone 8** includes access to a free online edition for 45 days through the **Safari Books Online** subscription service. Nearly every Addison-Wesley Professional book is available online through **Safari Books Online**, along with thousands of books and videos from publishers such as Cisco Press, Exam Cram, IBM Press, O'Reilly Media, Prentice Hall, Que, Sams, and VMware Press.

Safari Books Online is a digital library providing searchable, on-demand access to thousands of technology, digital media, and professional development books and videos from leading publishers. With one monthly or yearly subscription price, you get unlimited access to learning tools and information on topics including mobile app and software development, tips and tricks on using your favorite gadgets, networking, project management, graphic design, and much more.

Activate your FREE Online Edition at
informit.com/safarifree

STEP 1:   Enter the coupon code: QAXXDDB.

STEP 2:   New Safari users, complete the brief registration form.
Safari subscribers, just log in.

If you have difficulty registering on Safari or accessing the online edition,
please e-mail customer-service@safaribooksonline.com

JUL 22 2013